CHRIS PEDERSEN

2 Funds for Life

A quest for simple & effective investing strategies

The Merriman Financial Education Foundation

2 Funds for Life

First published by The Merriman Financial Education Foundation 2021

Copyright © 2021 by Chris Pedersen

All rights reserved. No part of this publication may be reproduced, stored or transmitted in any form or by any means, electronic, mechanical, photocopying, recording, scanning, or otherwise without written permission from the publisher. It is illegal to copy this book, post it to a website, or distribute it by any other means without permission. Chris Pedersen has no responsibility for the persistence or accuracy of URLs for external or third-party Internet Websites referred to in this publication and does not guarantee that any content on such Websites is, or will remain, accurate or appropriate.

ISBN: 978-1-7361196-9-3

Illustration by Maren Pedersen
Editing by Sandra Hickman
Proofreading by Daryl Bahls
Editorial Consulting by Aysha Griffin
Formatting by Margie Baxley
Cover Design by Reneé Ashley

Disclaimer: The content of this book is provided for informational and entertainment purposes only and is not intended to substitute for obtaining professional financial, legal or tax advice. Nothing contained here or by other means of communication by Chris Pedersen or those associated with The Merriman Financial Education Foundation implies a consulting or coaching relationship. Please consult a licensed professional for advice on your own situation.

For Kent and Jean, who asked only that I pay it forward.

Investing is not nearly as difficult as it looks. Successful investing involves doing a few things right and avoiding serious mistakes.

John C. Bogle

Contents

Praise For 2 Funds for Life	ix
Foreword	xi
Preface	xv
Acknowledgement	xvii
Chapter 1 Introduction — The Quest for Simplicity	1
Chapter 2 Backtesting — Our HMS Beagle	9
Chapter 3 Setting Off — How Much to Save?	25
Chapter 4 Elements — Stocks & Bonds	31
Chapter 5 Discerning Differences — Subclasses & Styles	39
Chapter 6 Geography — How Far to Go?	47
Chapter 7 Ecosystems — Diversification & Combinations	59
Chapter 8 Individual Variation — Risk, Age & Temperament	69
Chapter 9 Elegant Simplicity — Target-Date Funds	77
Chapter 10 Symbiosis — 2 Funds Combinations	83
Chapter 11 Intermediates — 3-Fund Combinations	97
Chapter 12 Complexity — 4- to 13-Fund Combinations	109
Chapter 13 Resilience — Surviving the Unexpected	135
Chapter 14 Contrarian Views — A Dose of Humility	145
Chapter 15 Bringing it Home — Conclusions	151
Appendix Detours & Details	157
Appendix 1 Alternative 2 Fund Recipes	159
Appendix 2 Alternative Second Funds	185
Appendix 3 Early Retirement, or FIRE, with 2 Funds for Life	203
Appendix 4 Recommended Funds	207
Appendix 5 Target-Date Funds Other Than Vanguard	211
Appendix 6 Target-Date Funds with Early or Late Dates	213
Appendix 7 Backtesting to 1928	223

Appendix 8 Backtesting Return Sources & Methods	237
Appendix 9 Contribution Frequency & Drawdowns	241
Appendix 10 Nudge Withdrawals vs. Rebalancing	243
Appendix 11 Changing an Existing Portfolio	253
Appendix 12 2 Funds for Life Yearly Allocation Tables	255
List of Figures	261
List of Tables	269
Glossary	271
Disclaimers	277

Praise For 2 Funds for Life

A masterpiece for people who want to dig into the details of two funds for life whether it's before or in retirement.

Paul Merriman, founder of The Merriman Financial Education Foundation, Co-author of *We're Talking Millions*

Good investing is simple, but not always easy. 2 Funds for Life takes readers on a fascinating journey to build simple & effective portfolios. I learned a lot from this book. Read it.

Wesley. R. Gray Ph.D., CEO of Alpha Architect, Co-author of *Quantitative Value and Quantitative Momentum*

Mastery of a topic often leads to an odd conclusion - simple is usually better. Chris brings the heavy-duty research to make the point. You don't need dozens of funds -- what we call in industry-speak "mutual fund salad." In fact, you may only need a few. Read this book and simplify your portfolio and your life!

Meb Faber, Founder and Chief Investment Officer, Cambria Investment Management

"2 Funds for Life" is a tour de force on how to think about investing for a lifetime. If you want to understand how to personalize your investment approach and increase the chance of reaching your long-term financial goals, this book is for you.

**Daryl Bahls, Director of Analytics
The Merriman Financial Education Foundation**

If you're ready for a deep dive into the analytics of performance, Chris is your guy! Plus, he outlines a straightforward portfolio model that makes sense.

Craig Israelsen, Ph.D., Founder of the 7Twelve® Portfolio

Recognizing that the investor matters more than the investment, Chris Pedersen has combined just two funds into a sophisticated but simple investing strategy that incorporates lessons learned from both financial theorists and behavioral economists. Wonderful!

James M. Dahle, MD, Founder of The White Coat Investor

With just two mutual funds or ETFs, Chris shows investors how they can take advantage of well-known investing concepts. The beauty of the strategy is in its simplicity. Investors get a high level of diversification and the potential for building lifetime wealth with very little effort.

Charles Rotblut, CFA, Vice President & AAII Journal Editor
American Association of Individual Investors

2 Funds for Life applies the KISS Principle to Investing. Investing Made Understandable!

Ed Fulbright, CPA, PFS   Host of Mastering Your Money Radio

"The investment industry goes out of its way to convince you investing is far too complex for any regular person to even try, much less succeed. Luckily for us, Chis Pedersen has done the research to find the perfect balance between simplicity and performance in investing, and his extraordinary book *2 Funds for Life* presents the succinct and elegant case for how you can invest confidently for the long-term and your ultimate financial independence."

Brad Barrett,
Co-host and co-founder of the ChooseFI Podcast

Foreword

I first met Chris Pedersen in a phone conversation after he had sent me an email offering to help me in my work of educating investors.

I was immediately impressed with his generosity, his thoughtful intelligence, and his openness to new ideas: all hallmarks of a great teacher.

As I described my 50-plus years as a financial educator, author, and founder of an investment advisory firm, we started talking about the very best long-term equity portfolio I have ever discovered: something I call the "Ultimate Buy and Hold Strategy."

Over the long term, this combination of 10 equity asset classes has significantly outperformed the Standard & Poor's 500 Index while adding only minimal additional risk.

However, Chris and I both knew this portfolio was too complex for many do-it-yourself investors.

Though Chris started doing work for The Merriman Financial Education Foundation right away, it wasn't until many months later that I threw out a challenge: Could he figure out a way to capture the long-term benefits of this strategy using only two funds?

Chris immediately accepted my challenge, and his solution turned out to be brilliant.

I told him something I've been hearing from investors for a long time: "I wish I had known about this 40 years ago."

Chris's solution led to a book that Richard Buck and I wrote in 2020, *We're Talking Millions! 12 Simple Ways to Supercharge Your Retirement.*

While we were writing this book, Chris's help was invaluable as he repeatedly applied his data-crunching skills to make sure we identified the best ways to use the plan he had figured out.

In our book, Rich and I summarized the research behind this two-fund strategy, but we didn't dig deeply into the underlying data. Our focus was to outline a plan that can be quickly understood and implemented.

However, even the best possible investment plan will work only to the extent that an investor trusts it. To my mind, trust is strongest when it's backed up by research.

That's where Chris's book comes in.

I've been delighted to see how well, in the following pages, Chris describes this two-fund strategy and the data behind it.

I regard this book as an "owner's manual" for any investor who's embarking on this two-fund strategy.

2 Funds for Life should help create the trust that can lead to the lifetime discipline that will extract the maximum value from this two-fund strategy.

The heart of this strategy is the target-date retirement fund, and Chris does a fine job of explaining it – along with its most important shortcoming, the lack of a way for investors to achieve above-average returns.

2 Funds for Life is based on the best academic research available – and more than 90 years of stock-market data.

In my view, this book is a home run for patient long-term investors – especially those in their 20s and 30s. It combines the undeniable benefits of small-cap value stocks with a defensive strategy built on massive diversification, low expenses, and a glide path to gradually decrease risk.

In addition, Chris shows more conservative investors how to turn down the heat – and more aggressive investors how to turn it up.

If you want to retire with more money, this book shows you how.

If you want to retire earlier, this book shows you how.

If you want to have more money to spend in retirement, this book shows you how.

If – in addition to all that — at the end of your life you want to have money to leave to individuals and/or organizations, this book shows you how.

Investors often ask me if this is the right time to put a plan like this to work.

For at least 40 years I've been telling them: "The best time to plant a tree is 20 years ago. The second-best time is right now!"

Paul Merriman

Preface

I am a financial wizard.

At least, that's what my grandfather taught me to say when I was learning to talk.

Sadly, my deep dive into personal finance didn't begin until I was on the verge of retirement. Fortunately, the lessons I'd learned from my parents' and grandparents' examples were enough to set us on the right course. Still, as I stood at the precipice that marks the end of a career and the beginning of retirement, I was scared. Had we saved enough? Should we change how we were invested? Where would the money come from when paychecks stopped? And how much would we be able to spend every year without running out? It was time to realize my grandfather's dream. Maybe I couldn't become a financial wizard, but I could certainly learn about investing. I've always learned best by doing and trying to teach others. It was time to apply another lesson I'd learned from my mother: When in doubt, volunteer.

I can still remember getting the call. I'd been listening to Paul Merriman's podcasts for several months when I emailed him and offered my help. Paul did what he often does—he picked up the phone and called me. I paced around in our garage as we discussed ways I could help. For whatever reason, things clicked. The first thing I did was create a set of Best-in-Class ETF recommendations. Then we made it easy for Paul's listeners to use The Merriman Financial Education Foundation's recommended portfolios at Motif and later M1 Finance. After that, we began researching ways to study dynamic allocations like the ones in target-date funds. It was fun, and I was learning.

Somewhere in all of this, Paul mentioned that he had an open invitation to visit John Bogle but hadn't done it yet. Given Bogle's age, I encouraged Paul to prioritize the visit before the opportunity was gone. Paul did. When he came back from the visit, he shared a gem: "Simplify." To this point, the foundation's focus had been on the Ultimate Buy-and-Hold portfolio, which was made of 10 equity funds and three bond funds. Mr. Bogle thought we could do better, and we agreed.

By the fall of 2017, we were ready to share 2 Funds for Life with the world. Target-date funds are good, but many investors could do better, and we showed them how. I knew the topic deserved a book, but I also knew it would take some time to do it well. Four years later, this book is the result. There are new variations of the 2 Funds for Life strategy and new research to answer some of the many user questions that have come up over the years.

I've been "retired" for four years now. The fears that gripped me in the transition to retirement have given way to appreciating the investor's paycheck. Since I'm a shareholder, the CEO who used to get me so worked up now works for me. My former colleagues do as well. If you've invested in the broader stock market, they work for you too. Our invested capital is fueling innovation for the future. The companies that need it reward us for taking the risk by growing their businesses' value and sharing their profits.

I may never be a financial wizard, but I've developed some skills that might seem magical. In the pages ahead, we'll travel back in time to see how various simple investing approaches we use now would have worked in the past. And we'll estimate how choices we make now will likely impact our future. Whether it's wizardry or not, I think my grandfather would be pleased.

Acknowledgement

The true financial legacy we get from our parents is measured more in knowledge, attitudes, and behaviors than in dollars and cents. I was lucky to be born to parents who instilled in me a desire to work hard and invest in myself, my future, and others. They weren't the first links in this long chain, and I'm striving not to be the last.

I thank my best friend and eternal companion, Suzanna, for supporting and celebrating my efforts. She may never read or appreciate this book, but she's the best and only financial advisor I'm likely to need. Her common sense and cool head have helped us avoid many mistakes and resiliently bounce back from others.

For the illustrations in this book, I'm deeply indebted to my daughter Maren. Her love of nature shows in everything she does. Her art also inspired me to write a better book. If savings and wealth don't help us live better lives, what's the point?

To my daughter Katrina, thanks for the many discussions on imputing data and modeling. I know my puzzles are simpler than yours, but your insights got me unstuck more than once on this quest.

Of course, Paul Merriman gets a big shout-out. Working with his Foundation has given me the chance to learn by teaching. It's exposed me to hundreds of listener questions, mounds of data, and frequent opportunities to stretch myself. Perhaps more important than all of that, it's given me an added sense of purpose in retirement. The friendship and collaboration I've enjoyed working with Paul have been one of life's great gifts.

Our colleague, Daryl Bahls, has also been instrumental in the creation of this book. He was my main sounding board and collaborator for the rhyme and regress asset class return histories that power the backtests. He also provided the method for calculating the safe withdrawal rates and the heatmaps for Appendix 1. He is by far the most detail-focused reviewer we have. His tireless and patient reviews, edits, and suggestions have greatly improved this book. I'm delighted to be able to work with and learn from him at the Merriman Foundation. Paul puts up with us patiently when we head down rabbit holes chasing technical topics. What fun!

Several of our Merriman Foundation listeners and followers have also contributed. Many of their questions helped develop the story. Jeff Mattice deserves special thanks for his early review of the manuscript and detailed feedback.

I've also received generous help from many experts. Larry Swedroe has answered several questions about his book *Your Complete Guide to Factor-Based Investing*. Tuomo Lampinen also patiently answered numerous questions regarding his wonderful website, Portfolio Visualizer. Wes Gray at Alpha Architect provided interesting insights regarding momentum and factor-based investing. Craig Israelsen stands out for introducing me to the importance of calming investors down and finding good Thai food in Utah. Meb Faber provided a wealth of information through his podcasts and financial education service, The Idea Farm. I especially appreciate his observation that diversifying into almost anything other than a cap-weighted portfolio is likely to help.

The last shout-out goes to you. Thank you for reading this book. Many of you have provided questions, corrections, and observations that have helped shape the story. This voyage may be over, but the Beagle Backtester is safely docked and ready to sail again.

Chapter 1
Introduction — The Quest for Simplicity

HMS Beagle — The ship that enabled Charles Darwin's voyage of discovery

We're on a quest to find simple, effective, long-lived investing strategies — the kind we can adopt with confidence and live with for a lifetime.

Most of us know we need to invest for the future, but it's hard to know where to start.

Investment choices are as old as life itself. For billions of years, all living things have made conscious or unconscious choices about how much risk to take and energy to expend foraging, hunting, reproducing, and nurturing. So why does figuring out how to invest for our future feel like an unnatural and befuddling challenge?

Investing feels unnatural because our cultural innovations have outpaced our biological evolution. Our brains evolved over millions of years to find food, shelter, safety from predators, and to nurture family and tribal connections — not to understand the ups and downs of financial markets, choose between thousands of investment options, and make sense of the waves of information that bombard us daily. The good news is that investing doesn't have to be complex to be effective, and we don't have to follow the markets to succeed.

Academic researchers have shown that even the most expert investors struggle to predict when markets will go up or down. They also find stock-picking skills among professionals to be rare, and expensive. According to them, the success of many famous stock pickers can be explained by the riskiness of the companies they invested in, and similar results could have come from investing broadly in comparable stocks through funds. And those with genuine skill often keep the benefits of higher returns for themselves through the higher fees they charge. If neither market timing nor stock picking is the solution, what is?

I'm sure many of you have already heard today's conventional wisdom that we should simply buy and hold low-cost index funds. It's sound but incomplete advice. With literally thousands of indexes and possible combinations, what sounds simple is actually complex.

We're also told that we should combine stock funds with bond funds to manage our risk. This raises more questions: What is meant by "risk"? How much risk can we tolerate? What percentage of bonds should we hold? Does it change over time? If so, how should we adjust the mix over time?

CHAPTER 1: INTRODUCTION — THE QUEST FOR SIMPLICITY

It's easy to see why many people become quickly confused and throw up their hands.

It's also easy to see why many of those same people just accept it when their employer auto-enrolls them in a retirement savings plan that invests 100% of their retirement savings in a target-date fund.

Target-date funds are one of the greatest financial innovations of our time. They are today's default retirement savings vehicle for good reason: They are simple, low-cost, broadly diversified, age-appropriate, automatic, and ubiquitous. Most of them are essentially a collection of index funds, but there's a clever twist: Target-date funds are customized to fit a particular retirement year. The Vanguard Target Retirement 2060 Fund (VTTSX), for example, is built to lower risk for investors as they near retirement around the year 2060. Beyond selecting the date, target-date funds are one-size-fits-all. They must be. There is no way for those who manage them to know whether the investors using them have higher or lower risk tolerances. Consequently, they build them conservatively, preferring to err on the side of lower volatility and lower returns to avoid exceeding the risk tolerance of the most skittish investors. So, what should the investor who can tolerate higher volatility in hopes of higher returns do?

Since target-date funds usually include a mix of the total stock market and bonds, you might think there's no way to be more diverse, but you'd be wrong. History shows that different parts of the stock market don't always move together and can have higher or lower long-term returns. The most widely available and affordable example of this is the part of the market occupied by smaller companies that are out of favor, also called "small-cap value." Funds made up of these stocks tend to perform better at different times from the overall market and have historically delivered significantly higher long-term returns. Consequently, they are a useful tuning tool for investors looking to get more out of a target-date fund. Yes, they can increase volatility, but the increase in returns can be more than worth it. So, the question is, how to combine them and how much difference do they make? That's what we'll explore in this book, but here's a teaser summary:

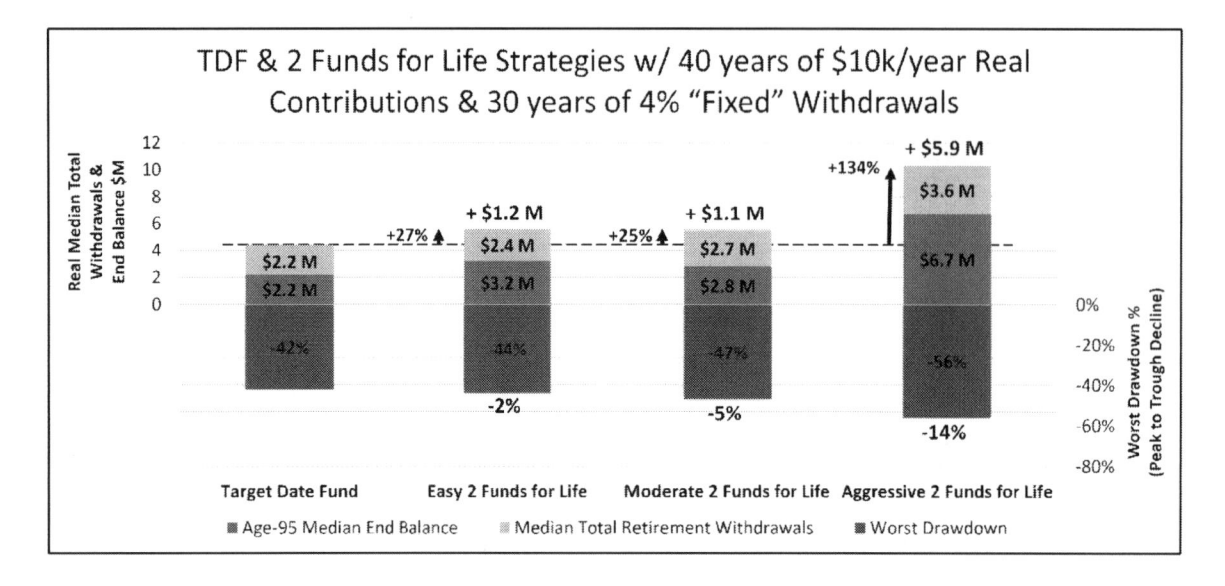

TDF & 2 Funds for Life Strategies w/ 40 years of $10k/year Real Contributions & 30 years of 4% "Fixed" Withdrawals

Strategy	Age-95 Median End Balance	Median Total Retirement Withdrawals	Worst Drawdown
Target Date Fund	$2.2 M	$2.2 M	-42%
Easy 2 Funds for Life	$3.2 M	$2.4 M (+27%, +$1.2 M)	-44% (-2%)
Moderate 2 Funds for Life	$2.8 M	$2.7 M (+25%, +$1.1 M)	-47% (-5%)
Aggressive 2 Funds for Life	$6.7 M	$3.6 M (+134%, +$5.9 M)	-56% (-14%)

Figure 1. Target-date fund and 2 Funds for Life strategies risk and reward

By adding just one fund to a target-date fund, we can increase the total real (inflation-adjusted) withdrawals and end balance an investor might expect over a lifetime by about 25% to more than 130%. For someone who invests $10k/year, increasing for inflation each year for 40 years, then takes out a "fixed" 4% for 30 years, that's an increased real lifetime benefit of over $1M to over $6M. To get that, they might have to tolerate 44% to 56% declines in the balance of their account instead of 42% declines, but they would also have a lower expected risk of running out of money before running out of life. In fact, the resilience of their portfolio in retirement would likely be better. So, what are these "Easy," "Moderate," and "Aggressive" 2 Funds for Life strategies?

The gist of the 2 Funds for Life strategies is this: (1) The Easy strategy is simply a 90% target-date fund, 10% US small-cap value fund allocation with no rebalancing; (2) the Moderate strategy invests 1.5 times the number of years to retirement (YTR) as a percentage in the US small-cap value fund, so it's 100% in the target-date fund in retirement; (3) the Aggressive strategy invests 2.5 times the YTR plus 20% in the

CHAPTER 1: INTRODUCTION — THE QUEST FOR SIMPLICITY

US small-cap value fund. You can see year-by-year allocation percentages for all three approaches in Appendix 12. These three portfolio glide paths (asset allocations over time) look like this:

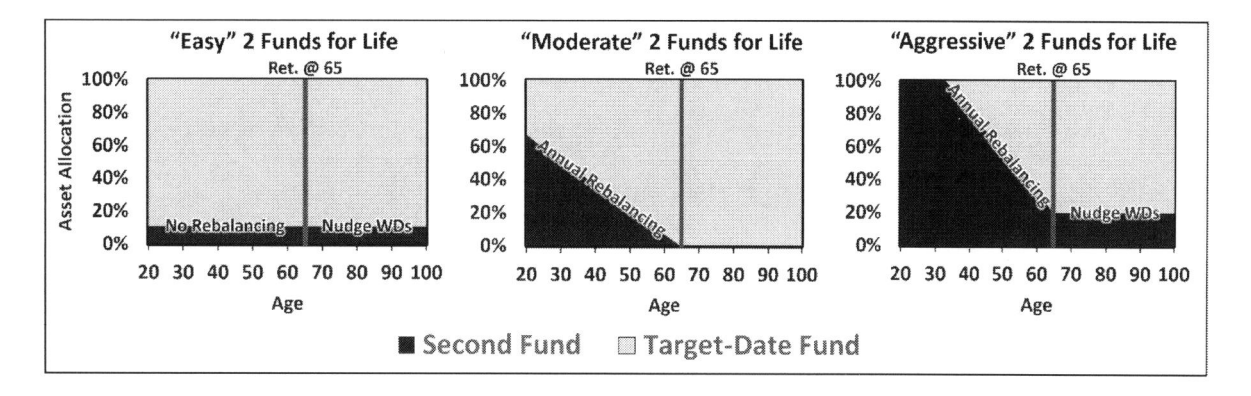

Figure 2. 2 Funds for Life strategy glide paths

The top area of the glide paths represents the target-date fund asset allocation. The bottom area is the investment in the second fund. Annual rebalancing means buying and selling some of the funds annually, so they get back to their desired allocations. Nudge withdrawals (WDs) mean taking the entire annual withdrawal from the fund that's bigger than its intended allocation.

If it's that simple, why did I write a whole book?

It's one thing to learn about a new investing approach and adopt it. It's another to invest with conviction and stick with it. The rest of the book will help investors choose the plan that's best for them and develop the conviction to follow it consistently over time. Here are some of the questions this book aims to address:

- How much should one save and when?
- Why does risk capacity change with age?
- How does a target-date fund work?
- What's the real difference between stocks and bonds?
- Why do some stocks perform differently than others?

- Why choose small-cap value over other diversifiers, such as momentum or low volatility?
- How much is enough international diversification?
- Can simple approaches be as effective as more complex ones?
- How long might a 2 Funds for Life approach lag the market?
- Wouldn't it be better to use an international small-cap value fund too?
- Which funds work best with these approaches?
- How did we do the analysis, and how likely is it the future will be like the past?
- How resilient are these approaches to surprises?
- How do things change for super savers planning to retire early?
- What happens if we tweak the age multiplier or minimum allocations?

I realize that not all of us learn the same way. Some of you just need the words and story. Some of you love tables of numbers. Some of you need to see *all* the charts and graphs. I've tried to offer something for all of you throughout this book. It might look intimidating, but there's no reason to dwell on the parts you don't need. Feel free to skip to what helps you most.

My dream is that this book will help you find a simple way to invest that's right for you. And if you do, I hope you learn enough to put that plan to work and stick with it through thick and thin. Since the approaches are simple, I hope they leave you more time to enjoy life and thrive along the way. In short, I hope this book improves your life and helps you improve the lives of those around you.

At the beginning of every chapter, I'll use images of long-lived plants and animals to help motivate and inspire our journey.

Throughout the book, I'll also highlight key messages like this:

CHAPTER 1: INTRODUCTION — THE QUEST FOR SIMPLICITY

2 Funds for Life strategies can improve retirement saving, retirement spending, retirement resilience, free time, and the wealth you pass on to others.

Here's the outline of the book: Chapters 2 through 9 cover foundational ideas; Chapters 10 through 13 develop and test the 2 Funds for Life strategies and variations; Chapter 14 provides a dose of humility; and Chapter 15 is the summary. Finally, the Appendices cover questions that more curious readers might have.

I've tried to avoid jargon, but it would be a disservice not to use the words readers will need to know when they begin to invest. To help readers with terms and phrases that might be less familiar, there's a glossary at the back of the book.

Hopefully, you're still with me and ready for our quest.

Just like great explorers of the past, we need to collect our tools before setting off. Since what we really want to know is how different investing approaches will work in the future, a crystal ball would be nice. Sadly, they're in short supply. The next best thing is to see how they would have done in the past and thus better understand how they might do in the future. The tool to do that is a backtester.

2 FUNDS FOR LIFE

Chapter 2
Backtesting — Our HMS Beagle

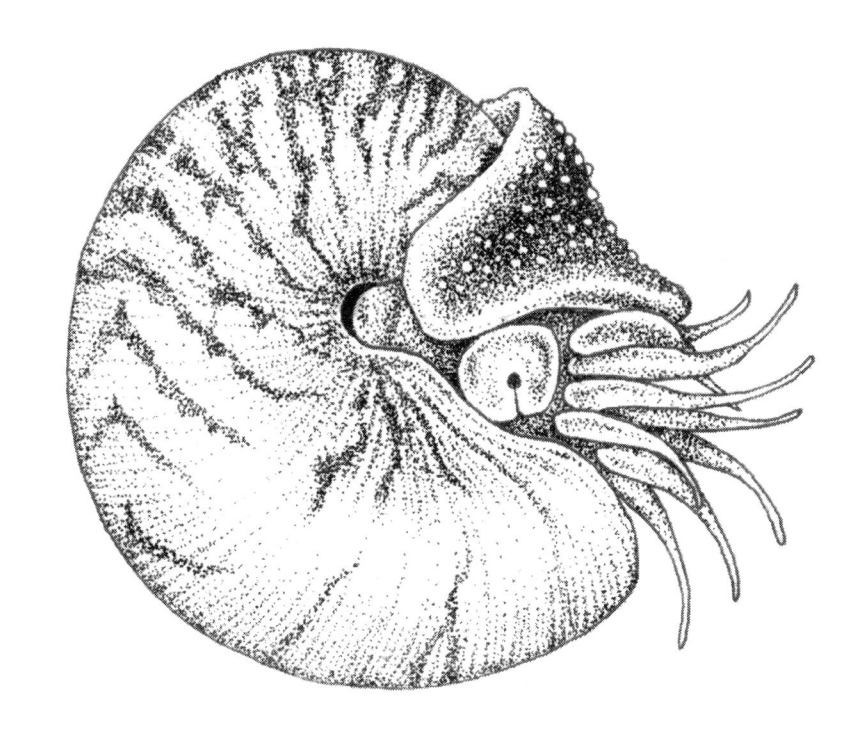

Nautilus pompilius — *The chambered nautilus is the longest-living cephalopod, with an estimated maximum lifespan of more than 20 years.*

The vehicle for Charles Darwin's voyage of discovery was the HMS Beagle. The vehicle for our quest is a backtester. Neither is perfect, but both can help us see things that would otherwise be hidden.

When it comes to backtesting, it helps to think of its analogy to weather forecasting. No one can guarantee any given day's weather forecast, but it's reasonable to expect that the broad climate patterns for any given area will repeat over time. Weather patterns tend to repeat annually with the seasons. Investing patterns tend to repeat over decades with economic cycles. And while no two cycles are the same, understanding how markets behaved during these different cycles may provide insight into how they may behave in the future.

So, how does an investing backtest work, and what does it show us?

Backtesting uses the historical information we have about the returns of different investments to see how an approach would have performed in the past. For a lump-sum investment in a single asset or fund, it's pretty simple. You multiply all the returns by the starting balance to get the result. It gets more complicated when we start changing things over time. If contributions or withdrawals are being made, or the investments are changing, like they do with a target-date fund, then some start dates and returns sequences will be better or luckier than others. How can we find out the full range of possibilities from unlucky to lucky? There are two ways to do this — Monte Carlo simulation or rolling start dates.

If you work with a financial planner or use a retirement planning website, you'll likely see results based on Monte Carlo simulations. The essence of the approach is to simulate a much longer history than what's available by random sampling or synthesizing sets of returns. It produces similar results to the rolling start date approach, but it assumes any year's returns could follow any other year's returns. Because rolling start dates produce similar results, make fewer assumptions, and preserve more of the sequential characteristics of the market, I've chosen to use them instead.

Backtesting with rolling start dates is a simple but powerful concept. Since we want to avoid being deceived by particularly lucky or unlucky start dates, we use them all. We start with the oldest date that has all the data needed (January 1970) and then use the rest of the years in sequence. Then we move to the next start month (February 1970) and repeat. If we run out of returns, we loop back to the beginning. This is also called "circular bootstrapping." So, instead of assuming any month's returns could be followed by any other month's returns, as in Monte Carlo simulations, we only assume that the first month's returns follow the last month's returns. It's not perfect, but backtesting never is.

The goal of backtesting isn't a perfect view of tiny differences in the past. Instead, we're looking for advantages that were so big or consistent that they're likely to help in the future.

Now that we have our method, let's describe the returns we'll use for testing.

Where possible, we use actual fund return histories, but not all of the asset classes have funds that go back to 1970. When actual fund returns aren't available, the next-best choice is index returns (see Appendix 8 for more detail). They don't include expenses, so we subtract an expense ratio from their returns to make them more realistic. Several asset classes don't even have indexes going back to 1970. For those, we've developed a proprietary model based on publicly available data, regression analysis, rhyming return substitution, and subtraction of representative expenses (see Appendix 12 for more detail). It helps us fill in gaps for several international funds and bond funds that would otherwise need to be filled in by substituting less-representative asset class returns. Once again, it's not perfect, but we hope it's indicative.

With a method and data behind it, we're ready to look at an example. We'll start with a simple portfolio recommended by Warren Buffett — the 90% S&P 500, 10% US short-term bond mix which we'll refer to as the "Buffett strategy." And since we're looking for lifetime solutions, let's look at an investor with no savings who starts investing $833 per month ($10k/year) at age 25 and increases their contributions with inflation through age 65. I chose $10k/year because it's a round number representing a 15% household savings rate for the 2020 median US household income of $68,400 per year. The actual monthly US household savings rates in 2020 varied widely due to the pandemic from a low of 7.6% to a high of 33.7%. If $10k/year sounds too high, divide the resulting balances by the amount that makes it more relevant to you. If you think saving $1,000 per year is more reasonable, divide all of the dollar values by 10. The rest of the metrics would be the same.

After 40 years of saving, when our investor reaches age 65, we'll assume they set a 4% fixed withdrawal amount based on the size of their nest egg. They'll then take out that amount annually starting at age 65, increasing the withdrawal for inflation every year until, after 30 years of retirement, they reach age 95. We'll also assume the portfolio is rebalanced annually. "Rebalancing" means the investor will buy and sell some of each fund as needed to get back to the desired 90%|10% allocations. Here's a summary of the assumptions:

1. Start saving and investing: age 25
2. End saving and start withdrawals: age 65
3. Finish withdrawals: age 95
4. Initial balance: $0
5. Contributions: ~$833/month, increasing with inflation till age 65
6. Withdrawals: 4% of the balance at age 65 taken annually, increasing with inflation till age 95
7. Rebalancing frequency: yearly
8. Target Asset Allocation: 90% S&P 500, 10% US Govt. Intermediate-Term Bonds
9. Returns History: 1970-2019, with circular bootstrapping

Inflation is clearly an important part of the returns and assumptions, especially over a 70-year lifetime. Even at a historically modest 3.4% inflation rate, a dollar at the end would only have the purchasing power of a dime at the beginning. To see things more clearly, we will look at results both with and without inflation. In the chart below, the big numbers that include the effects of inflation are "Nominal." The smaller numbers that reflect constant buying power throughout the scenario are "Real." Most of the time, we'll focus on the real results because they relate to what we think money is worth today.

Are you ready to see how this strategy did in the past? Here are the results. Don't be overwhelmed by the chart. We'll break it down and go over each part individually. Remember, we're sourcing tools for our quest. If you don't fully understand them now, that's okay. Some of the more obscure capabilities might come in handy once we're underway.

90% S&P 500, 10% US Govt. Bonds, 4% Fixed Withdrawals

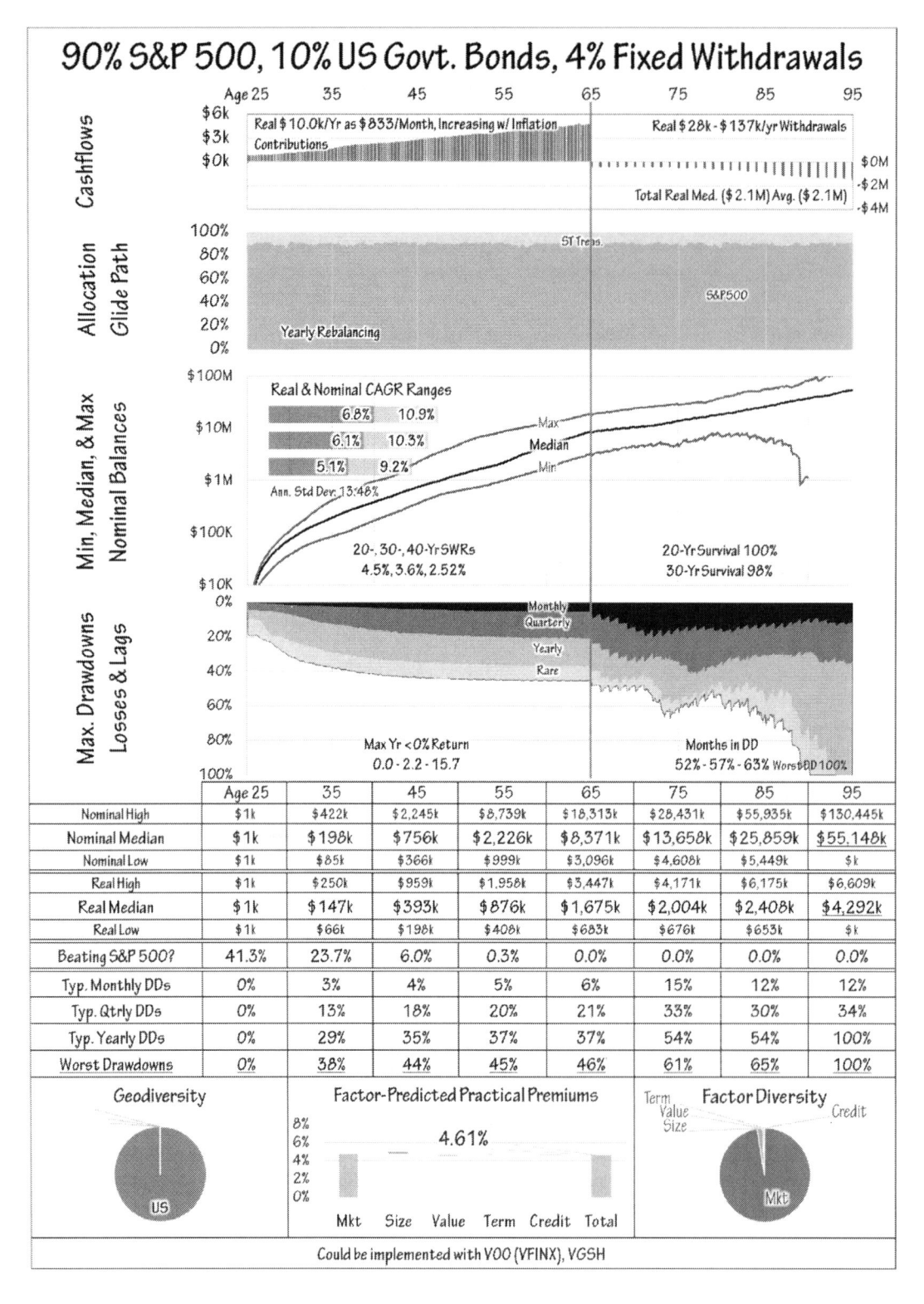

	Age 25	35	45	55	65	75	85	95
Nominal High	$1k	$422k	$2,245k	$8,739k	$18,313k	$28,431k	$55,935k	$130,445k
Nominal Median	$1k	$198k	$756k	$2,226k	$8,371k	$13,658k	$25,859k	$55,148k
Nominal Low	$1k	$85k	$366k	$999k	$3,096k	$4,608k	$5,449k	$k
Real High	$1k	$250k	$959k	$1,958k	$3,447k	$4,171k	$6,175k	$6,609k
Real Median	$1k	$147k	$393k	$876k	$1,675k	$2,004k	$2,408k	$4,292k
Real Low	$1k	$66k	$198k	$408k	$683k	$676k	$653k	$k
Beating S&P 500?	41.3%	23.7%	6.0%	0.3%	0.0%	0.0%	0.0%	0.0%
Typ. Monthly DDs	0%	3%	4%	5%	6%	15%	12%	12%
Typ. Qtrly DDs	0%	13%	18%	20%	21%	33%	30%	34%
Typ. Yearly DDs	0%	29%	35%	37%	37%	54%	54%	100%
Worst Drawdowns	0%	38%	44%	45%	46%	61%	65%	100%

Could be implemented with VOO (VFINX), VGSH

Figure 3. Backtest of the Buffett strategy

CHAPTER 2: BACKTESTING — OUR HMS BEAGLE

There is a chart of contribution and withdrawal cashflows in nominal and noninflation-adjusted dollars at the top of the page:

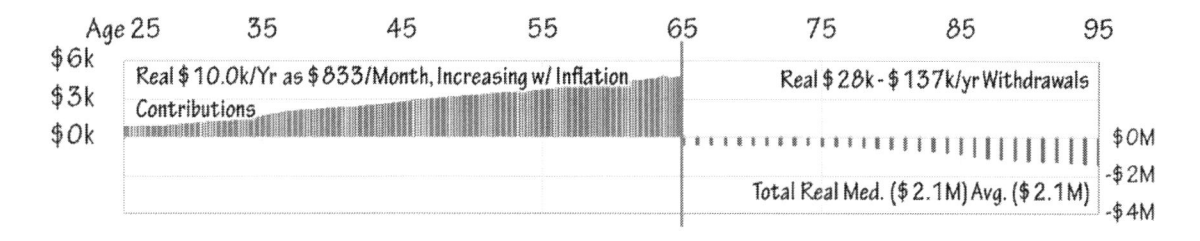

Figure 4. Cashflow graph from Buffett strategy backtest

The monthly contributions are scaled to the left-hand axis, and the withdrawals are scaled to the right-hand axis. The vertical line at age 65 indicates the transition from the contribution phase to the withdrawal phase and runs through all four graphs. Both the contributions and withdrawals increased with inflation over time so on a real inflation-adjusted basis both were constant. Note how the nominal annual withdrawals reached well over $1M per year by the end. Clearly, there was a lot of compounding and inflation over these 70 years. The chart also shows the range of annual real withdrawal rates and the real median and average total of all withdrawals. Remember, the *real* numbers are a way of seeing their buying power after correcting for inflation. Given that the scenario assumes a real contribution of only $10k × 40 years = $400k, it's fairly impressive that this investing approach delivered more than five times that much in median and average real withdrawals.

Below that, you can see the allocation glide path which shows how the asset allocation changed over one sequence of returns:

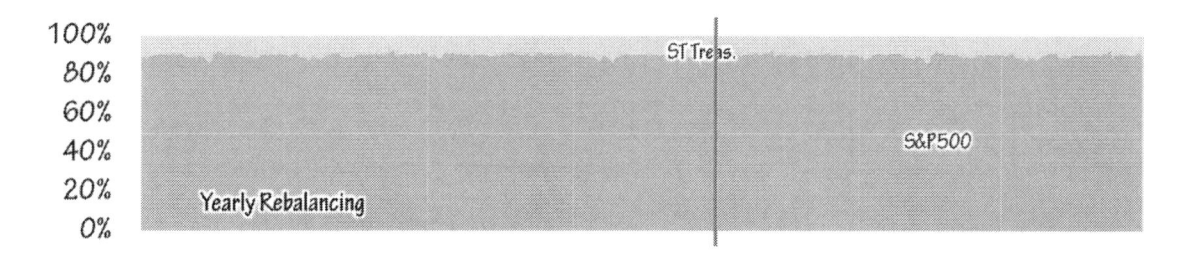

Figure 5. Allocation glide path from Buffett strategy backtest

Note how the asset allocation drifts a little up and down before being brought back to the desired allocation by annual rebalancing. In total, 600 periods of time (50 years times 12 months per year) were simulated and analyzed, but we show only the first scenario's cashflow and allocations, beginning with January 1970.

Figure 6 is the nominal balances chart. It shows the low, median, and high balances over time across the 600 different backtests. No one scenario follows any of these lines. Instead, each one zigzags up and down somewhere between the high and low. Throughout the book, we assume that any income received from investments (e.g., dividends and interest) is reinvested and that withdrawals are funded by selling investments.

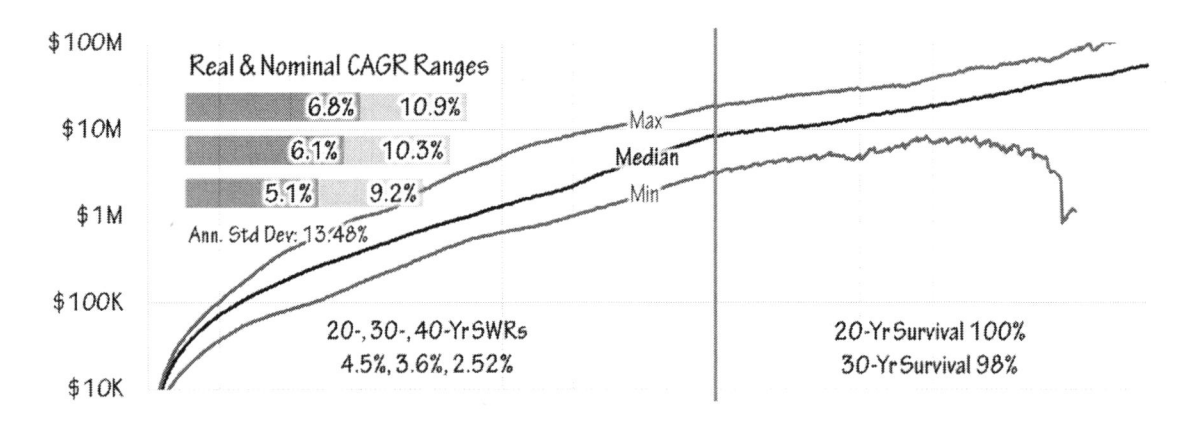

Figure 6. Growth, CAGR, SWR, Survival Rate graph from Buffett strategy backtest

This is a special kind of chart that lets us look at a vast range of numbers in a small space. It's called a "logarithmic chart." On this chart, exponential growth, the kind that happens when we keep multiplying something by the same number, shows up as a diagonal line heading up and to the right. We do that so we can see how the investments grew throughout the experience. If we plotted it on a normal linear scale, the first half of the experience would be near zero, and the last years would be very steep. Just look at the range of median values. We start on the left at age 25 with less than $10k and end up on the right at age 95 with between $10M and $100M. So don't be fooled if the line isn't as steep as you expected.

The top left bar chart shows the worst, median, and best real and nominal compound annual growth rates (CAGRs). In this case, the worst nominal CAGR was 9.2%, and the best was 10.9%. The median nominal return was 10.3%, and the median real return was 6.1%.

The annual standard deviation of nominal returns across all simulations is also shown below the bars. It was 13.48% for the Buffett strategy. "Standard deviation" is a statistical measure that indicates the volatility of returns. The higher the number, the more returns are likely to vary year-to-year.

At the bottom-left are the worst-case safe withdrawal rates (SWRs) the portfolio would have survived over 20, 30, and 40 years across every scenario tested. This is important because it indicates what initial percentage of your retirement portfolio you could have safely withdrawn annually to live on in retirement without running out of money.

In the bottom right of that chart are the 20- and 30-year survival rates. In this case, 100% of the scenarios survived to 20 years past retirement (age 85), but only 98% survived all 30 years to age 95.

Next is the drawdown (DD) graph, showing how drawdowns varied with age. Drawdowns are the amount our investments decline in value from a previous peak. This may be the most important chart on the page. You can think of it as a picture of the pain investors had to endure to earn their returns. Bigger numbers, shown lower on the graph, represent deeper drawdowns. The different shades reflect the frequency of different drawdown depths. The drawdowns that occur more frequently are less deep than the ones that occur rarely. The worst-case once-in-a-lifetime drawdowns across all scenarios are at the bottom of the "rare" shaded area.

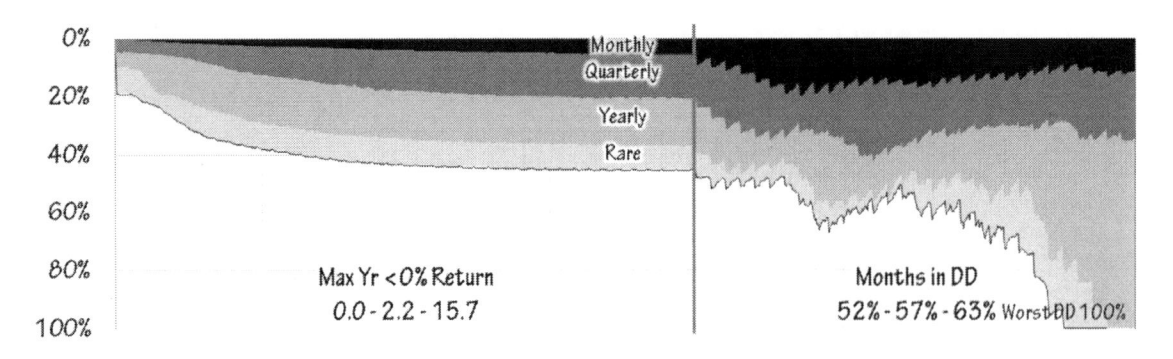

Figure 7. Drawdown graph from Buffett strategy backtest example

This relatively aggressive asset allocation had worst-case drawdowns of 40-46% in the saving years and then got worse in retirement. That means investors might have seen their account balance decline by almost 50% before starting to grow again at least once during accumulation. The lines get ragged after retirement because we're withdrawing money, and 2% of the scenarios didn't make it all the way to the end. Running out of money sounds scary, but remember that 98% of the scenarios survived. Those that did run out of money didn't run out until about age 87. If all of this sounds a little frightening, don't worry. We'll look at many ways to do better.

You can see the best, median, and worst durations from the start with a negative overall return at the bottom left of that graph. In this case, there was at least one scenario out of the 600 where you might have been invested for 15.7 years without having a positive return, which is sobering. On a more positive note, since the median was 2.2 years, more than half of the scenarios had a positive return in 2.2 years or less.

"Months in DD" numbers represent the low, median, and high percentages of months someone would have been below a previous all-time high. For this allocation, 52% to 63% of the months would have been below a previous high or in drawdown.

Next are the number tables. These are useful for seeing quantitative results along the way.

CHAPTER 2: BACKTESTING — OUR HMS BEAGLE

	Age 25	35	45	55	65	75	85	95
Nominal High	$1k	$422k	$2,245k	$8,739k	$18,313k	$28,431k	$55,935k	$130,445k
Nominal Median	$1k	$198k	$756k	$2,226k	$8,371k	$13,658k	$25,859k	$55,148k
Nominal Low	$1k	$85k	$366k	$999k	$3,096k	$4,608k	$5,449k	$k
Real High	$1k	$250k	$959k	$1,958k	$3,447k	$4,171k	$6,175k	$6,609k
Real Median	$1k	$147k	$393k	$876k	$1,675k	$2,004k	$2,408k	$4,292k
Real Low	$1k	$66k	$198k	$408k	$683k	$676k	$653k	$k
Beating S&P 500?	41.3%	23.7%	6.0%	0.3%	0.0%	0.0%	0.0%	0.0%
Typ. Monthly DDs	0%	3%	4%	5%	6%	15%	12%	12%
Typ. Qtrly DDs	0%	13%	18%	20%	21%	33%	30%	34%
Typ. Yearly DDs	0%	29%	35%	37%	37%	54%	54%	100%
Worst Drawdowns	0%	38%	44%	45%	46%	61%	65%	100%

Figure 8. Number tables from Buffett strategy backtest example

For example, at age 35, or 10 years into the experience, this approach had a 23.7% chance of being ahead of the S&P 500, but by age 55 that drops to under half of one percent. At age 95, this portfolio was never ahead of the S&P 500.

The final section includes diversification pies, factor-predicted premiums, and possible practical funds.

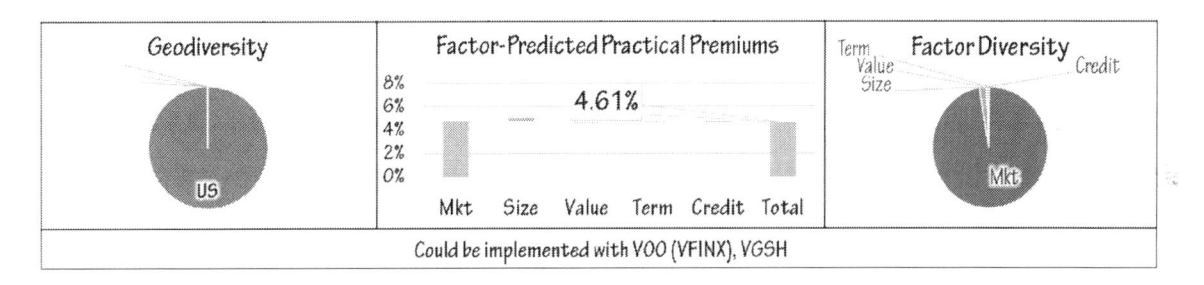

Figure 9. Diversification charts from Buffett strategy backtest example

The two pie charts show geographic and factor diversification across all scenarios based on data from the real-world funds listed at the bottom. This scenario is not geographically or factor diverse, so the pie charts are simple.

The "Factor-Predicted Practical Premiums" bar chart shows which market attributes are predicted to drive returns. Don't worry that the total doesn't match the nominal or real historical returns. Instead, view this as another indication of portfolio diversification. Well-diversified portfolios will be powered by multiple return engines. Poorly diversified portfolios will get almost all of their returns from one source. The Buffett strategy is poorly diversified, getting almost all of its returns from just the market risk factor. (We will explain factors and their impact on portfolios in more detail in Chapter 5.)

Finally, at the bottom of the chart is a list of suggested fund ticker symbols (just two here) for implementing the strategy. Appendix 4 includes a complete list of the funds and their ticker symbols.

I hope it's clear to you that this might help us move on in our quest. Since we're looking for simple and effective long-lived investing strategies, we need a way to compare them. This is it.

Some of you may have noticed we have only 50 years of history, and we're simulating 70-year scenarios. How does that work? I'll be the first to admit it is not ideal. I wish we had more history, but we don't. The biggest problem with this approach is that it underestimates the variability of returns around age 75. At that point in the backtests every scenario, regardless of the start date, has gone through the same 50 years of returns. Fortunately, the changing asset allocations, cashflows, and sequences of returns weighted by the resulting balances give us some variability. Though it's not perfect, it's still a meaningful way to compare how different approaches would have done in the past.

Let's look at one more example before moving on. We'll keep all the assumptions the same except for the portfolio asset allocation. Instead of using a 90% S&P 500 and a 10% US short-term bonds mix, we'll put everything in a Vanguard-like target-date fund (TDF). Here are the results:

CHAPTER 2: BACKTESTING — OUR HMS BEAGLE

100% Vanguard-Like Target-Date Fund, 4% Fixed Withdrawals

	Age 25	35	45	55	65	75	85	95
Nominal High	$1k	$479k	$2,010k	$7,379k	$12,900k	$15,480k	$23,900k	$64,532k
Nominal Median	$1k	$188k	$752k	$2,516k	$8,004k	$12,276k	$18,479k	$29,241k
Nominal Low	$1k	$102k	$422k	$1,120k	$3,360k	$5,421k	$10,435k	$10,142k
Real High	$1k	$256k	$810k	$1,646k	$2,393k	$2,271k	$2,655k	$3,569k
Real Median	$1k	$140k	$389k	$896k	$1,737k	$1,801k	$1,812k	$2,180k
Real Low	$1k	$79k	$231k	$461k	$748k	$795k	$1,050k	$588k
Beating S&P 500?	50.3%	54.3%	51.2%	39.8%	14.7%	2.8%	0.0%	0.0%
Typ. Monthly DDs	0%	1%	2%	2%	1%	1%	1%	1%
Typ. Qtrly DDs	0%	11%	14%	11%	7%	5%	5%	6%
Typ. Yearly DDs	0%	31%	34%	29%	22%	16%	14%	18%
Worst Drawdowns	0%	39%	41%	35%	27%	20%	19%	24%

Could be implemented with Vanguard-like target-date fund

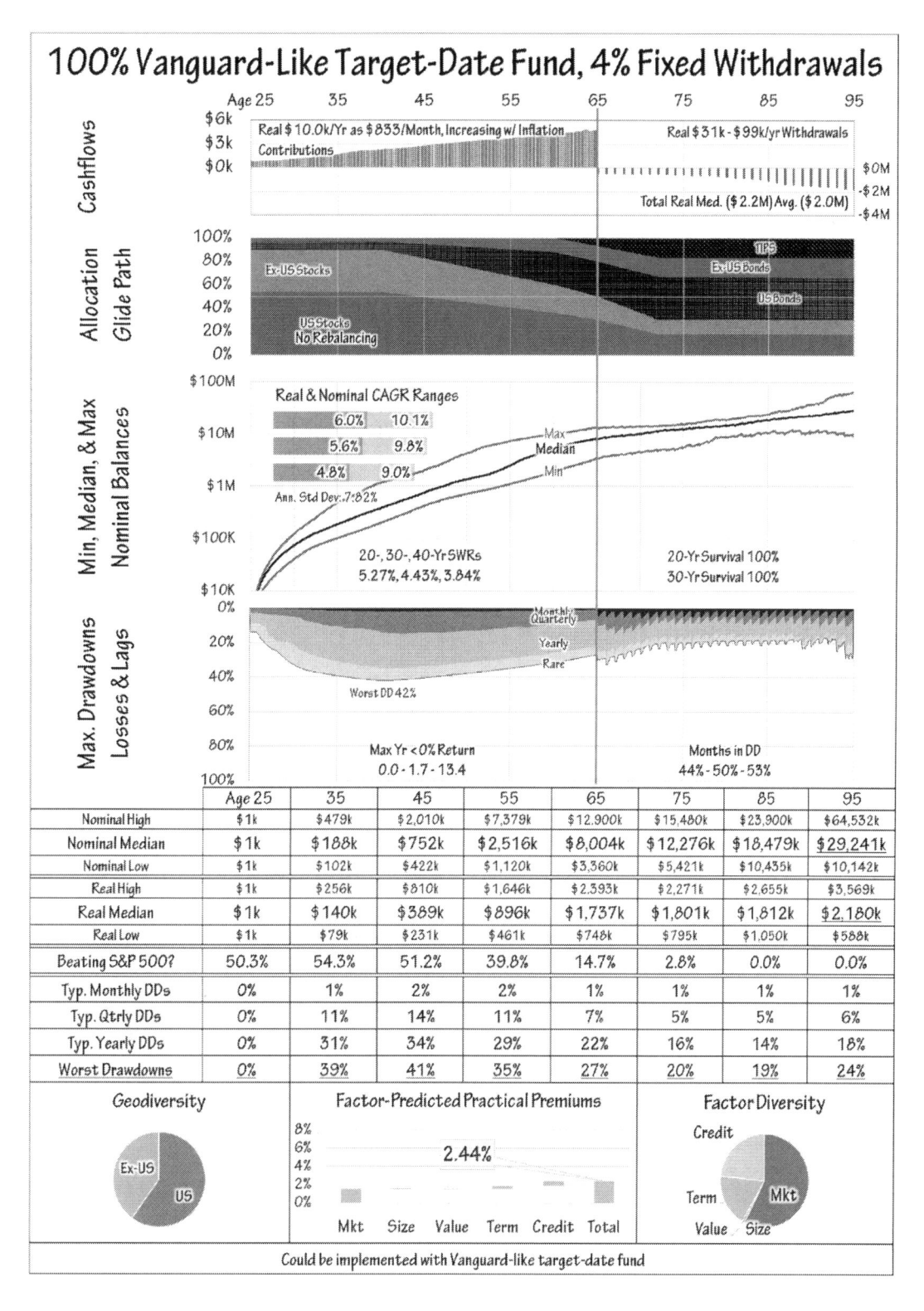

Figure 10. Backtest of Vanguard-like target-date fund

There are several big differences on this chart compared to the last.

The headline is that none of the scenarios ran out of money. They also experienced a lower worst-case drawdown of 42% at the relatively young age of 40. They then delivered a smoothly declining drawdown exposure well into retirement. Safe withdrawal rates are higher too. Total *real* median withdrawals are practically the same at $2.2M versus $2.1M for the Buffett strategy. The real median end balance was about 50% lower, but this was a much smoother ride. Remember, the Buffett strategy had worst-case drawdowns of more than 60% for most of the years in retirement compared to 24% or less for the target-date fund. For many people, the smaller drawdowns, higher confidence of not running out of money, and comparable spending in retirement would outweigh the risk of leaving a smaller legacy to their heirs.

There are some other amazing stories on this chart too.

Look at the nominal median end balance at age 95. It's over $29M. How is it possible that there could be $29M left over after contributing less than a million dollars and drawing out millions in retirement? There are two parts to the explanation: inflation and investing returns.

Regarding inflation, the differences in nominal and real CAGRs suggest a median historical inflation rate of about 4%. Over 40 years of accumulation, that reduced the value of a dollar by more than five times. Over the total 70-year scenario, it reduced the value of a dollar by 10 to 20 times. That's why the real median end balance is only $2,180k versus the nominal end balance of $29,241k.

Regarding investment returns, we assumed only $400k in *real* contributions ($10k/year × 40 years before adjusting for inflation). The investment returns turned that into $2.2M median real withdrawals plus a median real end balance of $2.2M at age 95. Even if someone had been saving only 10% per year, this $4.4M real benefit was more than the real $4M they would have earned in their lifetime. This reveals a shocking truth:

People who save and invest prudently across a lifetime are likely to earn more money from investing than they do from working.

It's also important to look at the worst-case scenarios. Look at the "Real Low" balance in the data table. At age 35, after 10 years of contributions, the worst-case real balance is less than $80k. Considering the real contributions to this point were $100k, that's not so good. At age 45, things are looking better. By then, the worst-case (low) *real* balance is $231k for $200k real invested. And by age 65, the worst-case scenario is that you have $748k real for $400k real invested. It's not great news if you're on that path, but it's a lot better than what you would have had without investing. Your $400k real investment would have eroded to less than $90k in real purchasing power without investing.

So, did this lead to a life of luxury?

We can see the real withdrawal rates in the top right corner of the cashflows chart, and they ranged from $31k/yr to $99k/yr. Since these are based on 4% withdrawals that are set at retirement, we can also calculate the median by multiplying the real median balance at age 65 ($1,737k) by 4% to get $69.48k/yr. Whether that's a comfortable retirement or not depends on the relationship of the $10k per year real savings rate to the spending rate of the investor. If that was a high percentage of an investor's income, these numbers might seem large. If it was a small percentage, these numbers might seem small. If an investor had an income of $40k/year and was saving $10k/year, even the worst case sounds fine because they were living on $30k/year ($40k - $10k) and would have that much to spend in retirement. If an investor had an income of $100k/year and saved $10k/year, the worst case sounds tight because they'd have been living on $90k/year leading up to retirement. In that case, even the median scenario might not be enough unless there's another source of income such as Social Security or a pension.

Of course, we'd really like to know how much we need to save based on our own circumstances. That's what we'll look at using our backtester in the next chapter.

Chapter 3
Setting Off — How Much to Save?

Pinus longaeva — *Bristlecone pines can live more than 5,000 years in desolate alpine conditions by frugally utilizing scarce resources.*

A ny successful quest starts with provisions. Savings are the essential provisions of investing. There's not much point in figuring out *how* to invest without having something *to* invest.

Most of us know intuitively that we should be saving for the future, but knowing how much and how soon to save can be perplexing. This chapter will explain why starting early and aiming for 10% to 15% makes sense.

The obvious reason for saving and investing is to accumulate some of what we have today so we can have more tomorrow. The two things that can derail this thought are easy credit and the notion that we need to have more today. This is a well-funded trap. There is no shortage of advertising money spent to encourage us to spend everything we earn and more because we deserve the good things in life today, but it's a path to endless catch-up that never achieves financial freedom. To avoid it, we need to cultivate an attitude of gratitude instead of envy and learn to be generous to our future selves. If we can focus on what we have instead of what we don't, it will help us defer some of today's gratification so our future selves can have the security and freedom we deserve. Economists have found that students who took a few minutes to look at an aged picture of themselves spent more time on, and did a better job of, financial planning. Look in the mirror or at a selfie. Who else is going to take care of future you? Saving money is often difficult, but it will be much easier if we're in touch with the reason we're doing it.

Now let's turn to the questions of "how much, and for how long?"

We can estimate a range of savings rates needed based on how different investing approaches have performed in the past. Using the backtester we described in the previous chapter, we can look back at the lucky, unlucky, and median results for a range of approaches. Here are the assumptions we'll use for those backtests.

- During our working years, we spend what we don't save. Spending includes expenses, donations, taxes — everything we don't save.
- In retirement, we maintain our standard of living and keep spending the same amount increasing with inflation. Things may not actually happen this way, but it's a reasonable place to start.

- We don't have access to Social Security or a pension when we retire. This is a conservative assumption but is likely true for people hoping to retire early.
- The total number of years we work and are retired is 60. This fits with starting work around age 20-25 and a life expectancy of about 80-85. It's not quite as conservative as the 70-years-to-age-95 scenarios we'll use in the rest of the book, but it's more realistic for estimating how much we need to save.
- Future portfolio investment returns and safe withdrawal rates will be similar to what they were from 1970 through 2019, the period we use for backtesting. This may or may not be true, but it's the best indicator we have.
- We invest in one of five options: the S&P 500, a Vanguard-like target-date fund, or one of the three 2 Funds for Life strategies described in Chapter 1.

We'll develop the rationale for the 2 Funds for Life strategies later. For now, consider them to be example approaches that are likely to produce better returns.

There are several factors at work here. The more we save, the less we spend. The less we spend, the less we need to spend in retirement to maintain our standard of living. The earlier we retire, the longer we need our money to last. The longer we need our money to last, the smaller the amount we can safely withdraw each year. And the more aggressive the approach, the higher the return. More aggressive approaches often have higher safe withdrawal rates too, but not always.

	Savings Rates Required So Retirement Withdrawals Match Pre-Retirement Spending								
	Work, Save & Invest 20 Yrs, Retire & Withdraw for 40 Yrs			Work, Save & Invest 30 Yrs, Retire & Withdraw for 30 Yrs			Work, Save & Invest 40 Yrs, Retire & Withdraw for 20 Yrs		
	Worst Case	Median	Best Case	Worst Case	Median	Best Case	Worst Case	Median	Best Case
S&P500	70.1%	53.0%	30.0%	41.6%	24.3%	11.8%	24.4%	11.3%	5.4%
V-Like TDF	53.5%	42.2%	28.9%	33.4%	20.6%	14.0%	19.4%	9.4%	7.1%
Simple 2FFL	51.4%	40.7%	27.3%	32.8%	19.7%	12.9%	16.7%	8.3%	5.8%
Mod. 2FFL	52.5%	40.9%	28.1%	32.1%	18.7%	11.8%	16.4%	7.6%	5.5%
Aggr. 2FFL	50.4%	34.8%	22.9%	28.4%	14.9%	8.5%	11.6%	5.5%	3.1%

Table 1. Savings rates required so retirement withdrawals match preretirement spending

Table 1 shows the savings-rate analysis results for three different timelines across the five different investing strategies. The timelines are all 60 years long but differ in the number of years working and retired. The left-hand columns show the amount someone would need to have saved over 20 years to fund 40 years of retirement. The middle columns are for 30 years of work and 30 years retired, and the right-hand columns are for 40 years of work and 20 years retired. The best-, worst-, and median-case results are shown for each scenario and portfolio.

Perhaps now you can see why a 15% savings rate is a reasonable starting point for the backtests. A 15% savings rate would enable someone to maintain their standard of living into retirement for most 40-year savings scenarios. A 10% savings rate would be fine for someone investing purely in a target-date fund for 40 years more than half the time, but it won't be enough to enable early retirement after 30 years of work except in the most aggressive best-case scenarios. If you're interested in retiring early, this table suggests saving between 20% and 50% depending on the age you want to quit working. It also suggests using a more aggressive strategy since it lowers the required savings rate for all scenarios.

This analysis is conservative by design because it doesn't consider any additional income sources such as Social Security or pensions. In 2020, the average percentage of retiree living expenses covered by Social Security in the US was between 30% and 40%. If we assume the Social Security benefit covers a third of the average retiree's expenses in the future, that's the equivalent of a 50% boost on top of their annual withdrawal. Here's a table reflecting the difference and its impact on required savings rates:

	Savings Rates Req'd so Ret. WD's Match Pre-Retirement Spending Less 33% for SS								
	Work, Save & Invest 20 Yrs, Retire & Withdraw for 40 Yrs			Work, Save & Invest 30 Yrs, Retire & Withdraw for 30 Yrs			Work, Save & Invest 40 Yrs, Retire & Withdraw for 20 Yrs		
	Very Unlucky	Median	Very Lucky	Very Unlucky	Median	Very Lucky	Very Unlucky	Median	Very Lucky
S&P500	61.0%	42.9%	22.2%	32.2%	17.6%	8.2%	17.7%	7.8%	3.7%
V-Like TDF	43.4%	32.7%	21.3%	25.0%	14.7%	9.8%	13.8%	6.5%	4.8%
Simple 2FFL	41.4%	31.4%	20.0%	24.5%	14.0%	9.0%	11.8%	5.7%	3.9%
Mod. 2FFL	42.5%	31.5%	20.7%	24.0%	13.3%	8.2%	11.6%	5.2%	3.8%
Aggr. 2FFL	40.3%	26.3%	16.5%	20.9%	10.4%	5.8%	8.0%	3.7%	2.1%

Table 2. Savings rates required so retirement withdrawals match preretirement spending less 33% for Social Security

This doesn't change anything for someone planning to retire early because they won't be eligible for Social Security, but it helps a lot for those who are able to take Social Security at retirement. The right-hand columns now show that a 10% savings rate would be sufficient more than half of the time for those willing to work 40 years followed by 20 years of retirement. It could also make a substantial difference for someone getting a late start on savings. Let's say you've put off starting to save for retirement, are now 50 years old, and wondering what you can do. If you're okay working another 20 years to age 70, the left-hand columns of the table suggest that saving 26% with an aggressive 2 Funds for Life strategy might be sufficient. Since that's the median required savings rate, it would give you about a 50% chance of being able to maintain your standard of living using investments and Social Security even if you live 40 years in retirement. That's a lot more doable than the 35% savings rate from the earlier table without Social Security.

Of course, the most difficult part of planning is the unexpected. We might think we're going to work for 40 years only to find we spend several years out of work and looking for a job. We might also find out we don't like our job as much as we thought we did and want to retire earlier. On the other hand, some people will find their perfect career and never want to quit. Because of the uncertainty, it's better to err on the side of over-saving if we can. If we don't go to an extreme that prevents enjoying life along the way, it's hard to imagine regretting it later. I've heard many people regret not starting to save earlier. I've never heard anyone say, "If only I'd spent more sooner!"

If you've been struggling to save at all and find this information discouraging, I get it. There are many good and necessary expenditures that can make it hard to start saving for retirement. Paying for food, housing, transportation, and school are just a few of the things that can get in the way.

The most important step in saving is getting started.

The second most important step is protecting and growing savings until they're where they need to be.

If you start by saving something, you can ramp it up over time until you get to your target. That will be much easier than trying to change your spending all at once. It won't get you to financial independence quite as quickly as jumping to a higher savings rate immediately, but it will get you there much faster than staying at a lower savings rate or not saving at all.

Remember, you're doing this for a very worthy cause. Future you will be grateful you did.

With some savings in hand, it's time to think of investing it. Before we get to specific approaches, let's look at the building blocks that make up our investing options. We'll start with stocks and bonds, or more specifically, stock and bond index funds.

Chapter 4
Elements— Stocks & Bonds

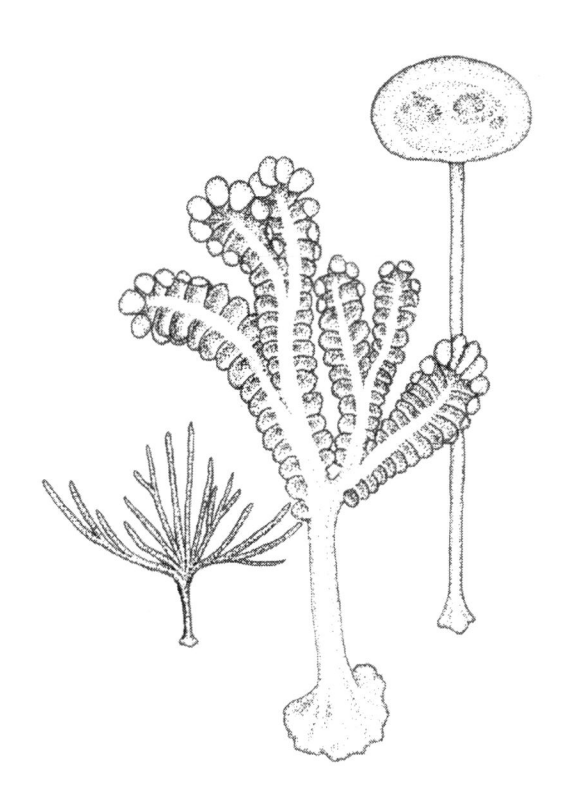

Hexactinellida — *Glass sponges are found in a wide variety at cold ocean depths, with some thought to be more than 15,000 years old.*

Life is full of risks. The trick is learning which are worth taking and which are not. When consequences are immediate and certain, we learn quickly. When they're not, it's easy to be deceived.

Most of us have heard that stocks are risky, and bonds are safe, but it would be more accurate to say that bond funds tend to protect capital better over days, months, or years, while stock funds tend to protect it better over decades.

Stocks (also called equities) and bonds (also called fixed income) are the two most important asset classes available to us, so let's look at them more closely.

A bond is a loan. It could be a relatively low-risk loan to the US Government or a high-risk loan to a down-on-its-luck business. It could be for a short term, such as a year, or a long term, such as 10 or 20 years. In exchange for the loan, the debtor agrees to pay us back interest and principal over time. Expected returns and volatility are usually lower than for stocks, so they serve as stabilizers or brakes in a portfolio. They do have some risk, though. If interest rates go up, bonds that were previously sold at lower rates will drop in value. If companies or governments default on their loans, failing to pay back principal and interest, bonds can lose all their value. Since we're looking to bonds for stability, it makes sense that they should be US government or investment-grade corporate bonds. This is what we usually find in target-date funds.

Equities are the ownership of part of a company. This is a higher-volatility, higher-return proposition. When we buy equities, whether through individual stocks, exchange-traded funds (ETFs), mutual funds, or target-date funds, we become part owners of one or more companies. If the companies we invest in grow or shrink their earnings, our investments will likely grow or shrink with them. If the companies go out of business, we could lose all of our money. That's one of the biggest reasons to buy a basket of companies through a mutual fund or ETF rather than stock in individual companies. When we combine the stocks of many companies with similar expected returns, the expected return stays the same, but the risk of failure declines dramatically. Because of that, we'll focus only on investing in equities through ETFs, mutual funds, or target-date funds for this asset class too.

What about commodities? Commodities are things like corn, oil, timber, and precious metals, including gold. They don't generate earnings, and their value fluctuates with supply and demand. Consequently, any expected return above the inflation rate is based on expectations of increasing scarcity or sophisticated trading strategies. Because of this and the fact that we get some commodities exposure by investing in companies that own commodities, we won't be including them in our analyses. For a much more thorough discussion of commodities, you might find this article useful, https://www.merriman.com/advanced-portfolio-management/why-we-still-dont-favor-commodities/

Because these two broad asset classes are the essential building blocks of most prudent investing strategies, let's look at how they have performed in the past over a short, medium, and long-term investing horizon. Here are the growth charts for the Vanguard US Total Stock Market Index fund (VTSAX) and the Vanguard US Total Bond Market Index Fund (VBTLX) for one, five, and 15 years:

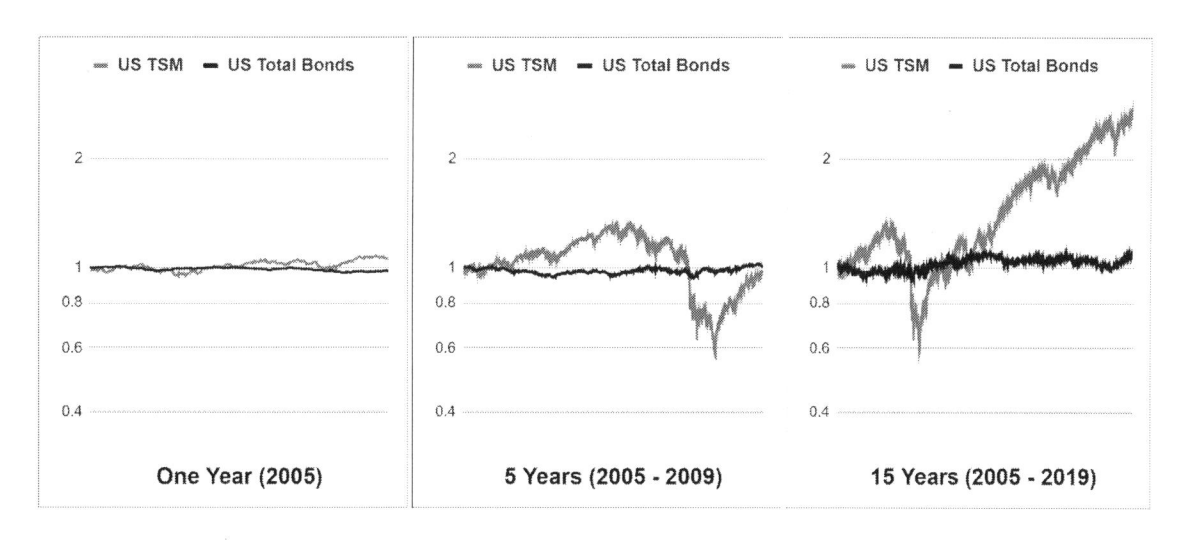

Figure 11. US total stocks and total bonds over one, five, and 15 years

Here are a few things to notice:

- Bonds were relatively stable with low growth.
- Stocks (US Total Stock Market, or TSM) were much more volatile and had much more growth.
- Stocks can lose a lot of their value very quickly. From October 2007 to February 2009, the Vanguard Total Stock Market Index fund lost over 50% of its value.
- Stocks did eventually bounce back.
- Both asset classes moved up and down at different times, which suggests combining them could smooth the ride.
- Finally, you might have to wait a long time to get a higher return from stocks.

Even at the end of five years on this chart, bonds were outperforming stocks. That's not unusual. The higher returns for equities can take decades to show up. To earn those higher returns, investors need to exercise patience and hope. This is also why it's not prudent to put the money you'll need in the short term, say within seven years, in the stock market.

You're probably starting to see some of the difficulties in learning to be a good investor. It's very different from learning other skills such as tennis or bike riding. Learning to ride a bike isn't necessarily easy, but it's intuitive. If we do the right things, we stay on the bike. If we don't, we fall. The feedback is immediate. In practically no time, most of us can master the basics of riding a bike. Investing is different.

> **One of the biggest challenges to becoming a good investor is that it can take decades to learn whether decisions were good or bad, and even then, we might confuse luck for skill.**

The delay between actions and results combined with their randomness makes it easy to learn the wrong lessons. Maybe you or someone you know invested in the stock market for a month, a year, or even a decade, only to lose money and then decide it doesn't pay to invest in the stock market. It's totally understandable, but it's also against all the long-term histories. Over the long term, societies and economies tend to grow. That growth fuels increased company earnings. For patient, persistent, hopeful investors who own a diversified portfolio of those companies, the increased earnings raise share prices and create great wealth. It's not magic, but it takes a shift in perspective that I hope this book will help you achieve.

So far, we've looked at stocks and bonds as broad categories, but both can be broken down into subclasses. Since we'll be relying on target-date funds for the bond portion of our portfolios, we'll focus next on stocks and ways to distinguish which ones have higher or lower expected risks and rewards.

Since some of you may be wondering how stocks or bonds would work on their own as lifetime savings portfolios, I'll insert the detailed backtests for the US total stock market and US total bonds here. Not surprisingly, the total stock market portfolio produced high returns and high volatility, while the total bond portfolio produced lower returns and lower volatility. There are many more attractive options coming, but these are useful reference points.

US Total Bond Market, 4% Fixed Withdrawals

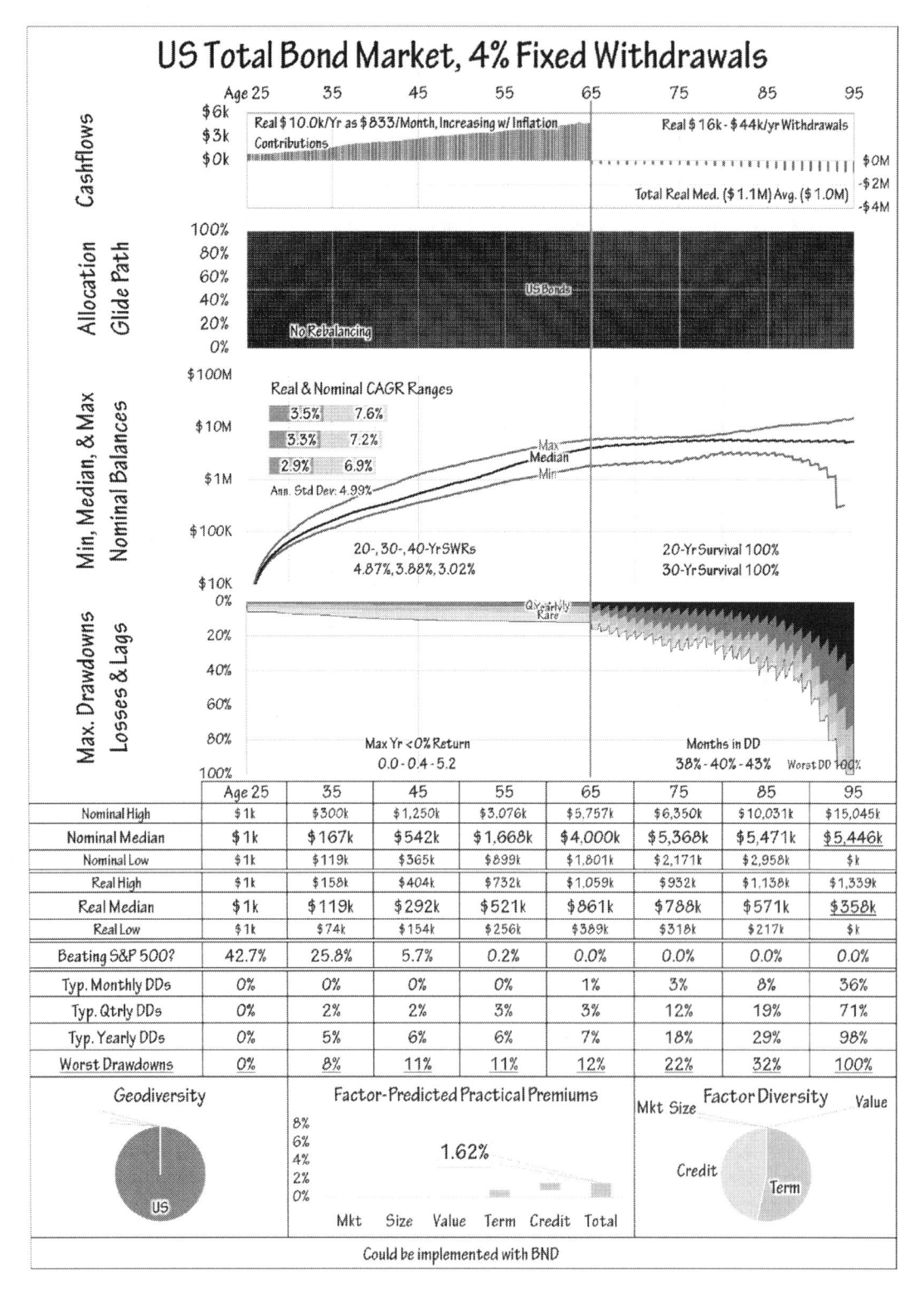

	Age 25	35	45	55	65	75	85	95
Nominal High	$1k	$300k	$1,250k	$3,076k	$5,757k	$6,350k	$10,031k	$15,045k
Nominal Median	$1k	$167k	$542k	$1,668k	$4,000k	$5,368k	$5,471k	$5,446k
Nominal Low	$1k	$119k	$365k	$899k	$1,801k	$2,171k	$2,958k	$k
Real High	$1k	$158k	$404k	$732k	$1,059k	$932k	$1,138k	$1,339k
Real Median	$1k	$119k	$292k	$521k	$861k	$788k	$571k	$358k
Real Low	$1k	$74k	$154k	$256k	$389k	$318k	$217k	$k
Beating S&P 500?	42.7%	25.8%	5.7%	0.2%	0.0%	0.0%	0.0%	0.0%
Typ. Monthly DDs	0%	0%	0%	0%	1%	3%	8%	36%
Typ. Qtrly DDs	0%	2%	2%	3%	3%	12%	19%	71%
Typ. Yearly DDs	0%	5%	6%	6%	7%	18%	29%	98%
Worst Drawdowns	0%	8%	11%	11%	12%	22%	32%	100%

Could be implemented with BND

Figure 12. Backtest of US Total Bond Market

CHAPTER 4: ELEMENTS — STOCKS & BONDS

US Total Stock Market, 100% Equities, 4% Fixed Withdrawals

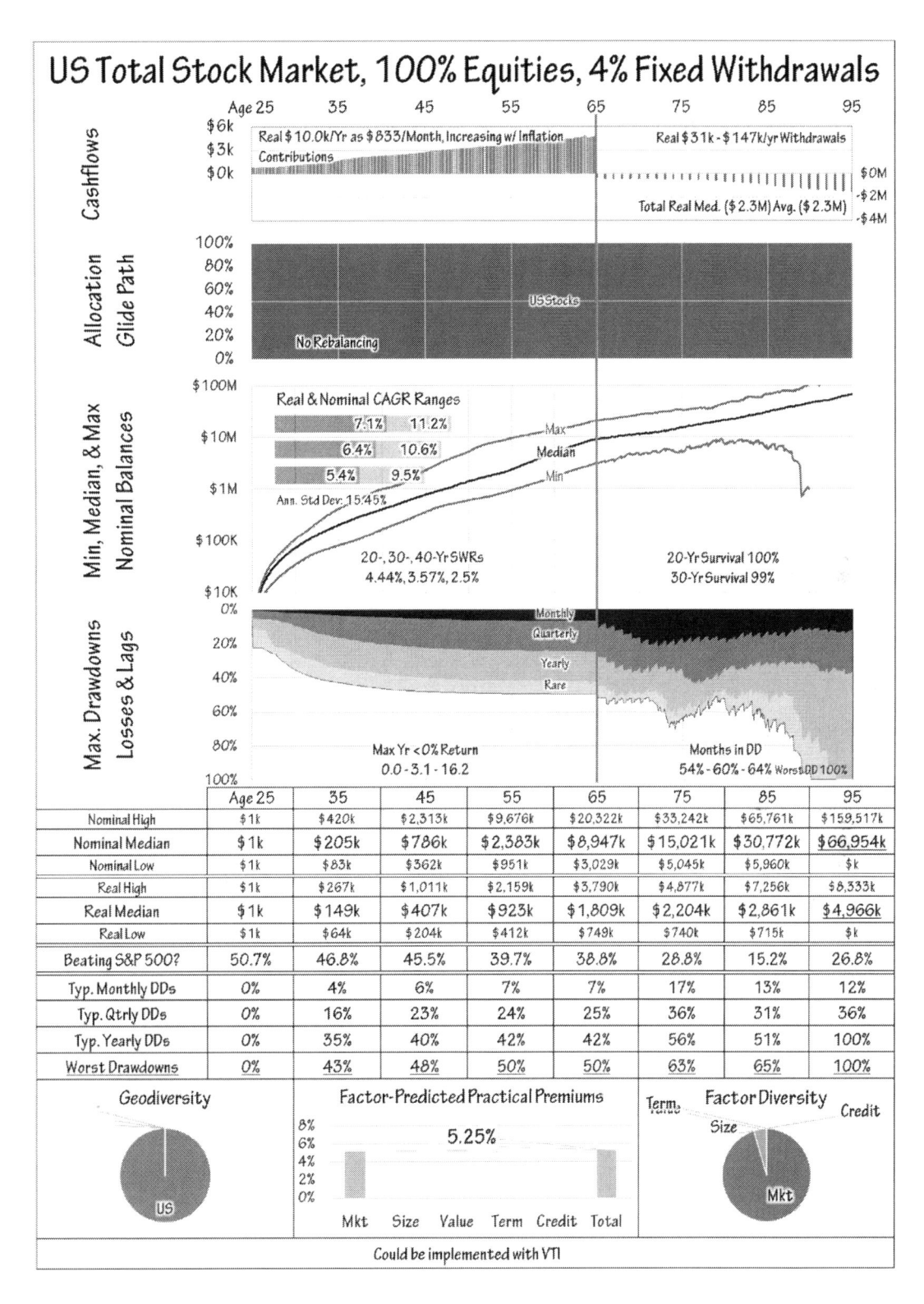

Cashflows: Real $10.0k/Yr as $833/Month, Increasing w/ Inflation Contributions; Real $31k - $147k/yr Withdrawals; Total Real Med. ($2.3M) Avg. ($2.3M)

Allocation Glide Path: US Stocks, No Rebalancing, 100%

Min, Median, & Max Nominal Balances:
Real & Nominal CAGR Ranges
- 7.1% / 11.2% (Max)
- 6.4% / 10.6% (Median)
- 5.4% / 9.5% (Min)

Ann. Std Dev: 15.45%

20-, 30-, 40-Yr SWRs: 4.44%, 3.57%, 2.5%

20-Yr Survival 100%
30-Yr Survival 99%

Max. Drawdowns Losses & Lags: Monthly / Quarterly / Yearly / Rare

Max Yr < 0% Return: 0.0 - 3.1 - 16.2

Months in DD: 54% - 60% - 64%   Worst DD 100%

	Age 25	35	45	55	65	75	85	95
Nominal High	$1k	$420k	$2,313k	$9,676k	$20,322k	$33,242k	$65,761k	$159,517k
Nominal Median	$1k	$205k	$786k	$2,383k	$8,947k	$15,021k	$30,772k	$66,954k
Nominal Low	$1k	$83k	$362k	$951k	$3,029k	$5,045k	$5,960k	$k
Real High	$1k	$267k	$1,011k	$2,159k	$3,790k	$4,877k	$7,256k	$8,333k
Real Median	$1k	$149k	$407k	$923k	$1,809k	$2,204k	$2,861k	$4,966k
Real Low	$1k	$64k	$204k	$412k	$749k	$740k	$715k	$k
Beating S&P 500?	50.7%	46.8%	45.5%	39.7%	38.8%	28.8%	15.2%	26.8%
Typ. Monthly DDs	0%	4%	6%	7%	7%	17%	13%	12%
Typ. Qtrly DDs	0%	16%	23%	24%	25%	36%	31%	36%
Typ. Yearly DDs	0%	35%	40%	42%	42%	56%	51%	100%
Worst Drawdowns	0%	43%	48%	50%	50%	63%	65%	100%

Geodiversity: US

Factor-Predicted Practical Premiums: 5.25% (Mkt, Size, Value, Term, Credit, Total)

Factor Diversity: Mkt, Size, Value, Term, Credit

Could be implemented with VTI

Figure 13. Backtest of US Total Stock Market

2 FUNDS FOR LIFE

Chapter 5
Discerning Differences —
Subclasses & Styles

Myotis brandti — *Brandt's bat is the longest-lived animal for its size, living up to 41 years while weighing only 4-8 grams.*

Perhaps Darwin's most famous observation was that differences in birds' beaks equipped them to thrive in different environments where they ate different foods. Small differences matter.

Though the average of all stock market investor returns can't exceed the overall market's return, it's not true that all investors must get less than that average. There are many ways to select and invest in stocks with higher expected returns and higher risks.

In the same way that 10 different people could come up with 10 different lists describing the attributes most likely to increase a car's gas mileage, academics have generated hundreds of attributes that contribute to the expected return and volatility of different stocks. They call these "risk factors." We can distill the most important ones to some common-sense observations about long-term performance:

1. Stocks have had higher risk and returns than bonds.
2. Stocks of smaller companies have had higher risk and returns than stocks of big companies.
3. Stocks of cheaper, out-of-favor "value" companies have had higher risk and returns than expensive high-flyers.
4. Stocks with momentum (going up in price) tend to keep going up.
5. Stocks of quality companies with good financials tend to outperform those with bad financials.
6. Stocks with low-to-average volatility (stable prices) have tended to outperform stocks with high volatility.

These observations have led to many "factor" funds that tilt their holdings toward one or more of these risk factors. Since higher returns (or premiums) for different factors show up at different times, combining them can produce higher returns with little additional risk because the ups and downs often cancel each other out.

That sounds easy, but which of these attributes should we choose, and why? The first thing to know is that they're not all widely available. By downloading and analyzing data from the Fund Factor Regressions page at the Portfolio Visualizer website, we can see which fund factor combinations were most available in mutual funds and ETFs over the past 20 years. Since individual funds can give us a little or a lot of exposure to each of these risk factors, we need to set a threshold. For this test, we'll only include funds with more than 30% (0.3) exposure to each of the factors in any given combination.

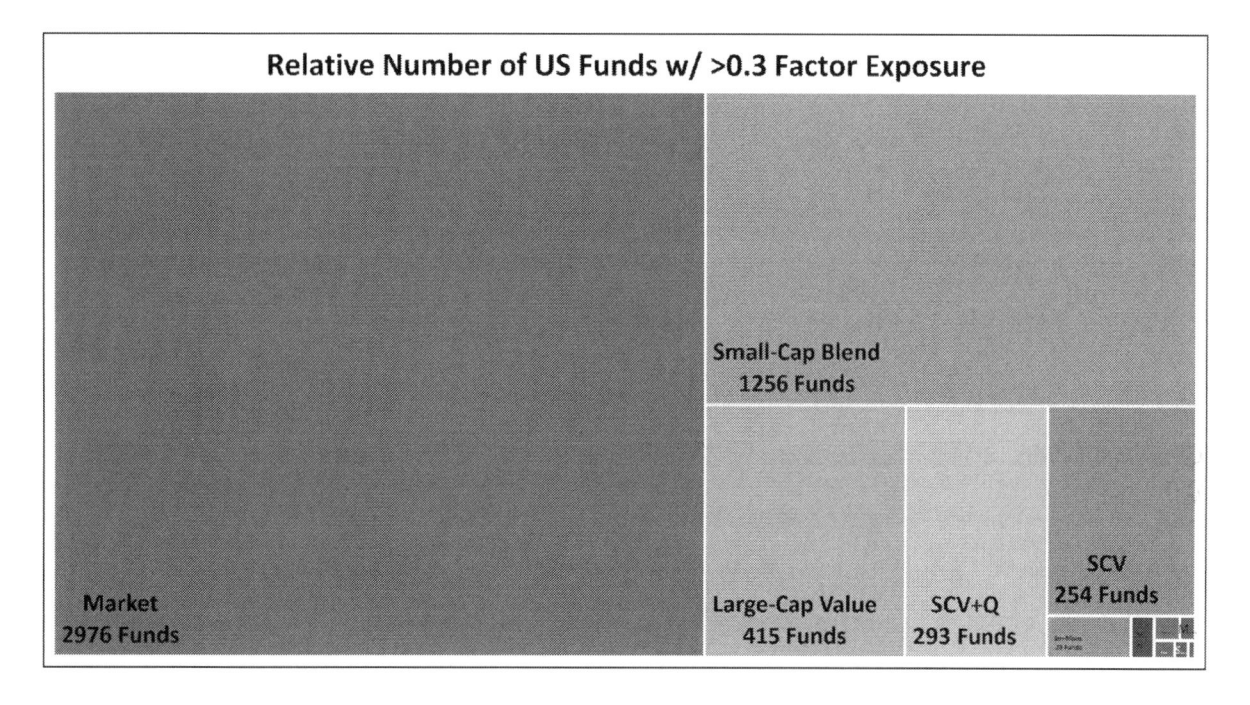

![Figure 14 treemap: Relative Number of US Funds w/ >0.3 Factor Exposure — Market 2976 Funds; Small-Cap Blend 1256 Funds; Large-Cap Value 415 Funds; SCV+Q 293 Funds; SCV 254 Funds]

Figure 14. Number of US ETF and mutual funds with >30% factor exposure to various factor combinations

So, what did we find?

First, broad market funds, such as S&P 500 funds or total market funds, are available by the thousands. Some of them are expensive and should be avoided. Still, intense competition has led to the creation of many near-zero-cost funds with meaningful exposure to market risk and its associated return premiums.

Small-cap blend and small-cap value funds are also widely available. There were 1,256 small-cap blend funds and 29 small-cap blend funds that added exposure to the momentum factor for a total of 1,285. There were 254 small-cap value funds and 293 small-cap value funds with added exposure to the quality factor for a total of 547. The exposure to momentum and quality may or may not be called out in the fund descriptions, so it's fair to say there were 1,285 small-cap blend funds and 547 small-cap value funds, some of which had exposure to other potentially beneficial factors.

Large-cap value funds were also widely available, with 415 funds in this timeframe, but because they didn't provide exposure to the small factor, they had lower expected returns. We'll look at historical returns for these different parts of the market shortly.

There wasn't much else after the market, large-cap value, and various flavors of small funds. In fact, there were fewer than 10 of any of the other factor combinations. The truth is that the other factors such as momentum, low-volatility, and quality are less available at similar levels of factor exposure in the US, and sometimes not at all internationally. Since the momentum, quality, and low-volatility factors are less widely available, it makes sense to use them as tiebreakers or extras for other funds. The small-cap value funds that also had exposure to the quality factor are a good example of this. The average fund in the SCV+Q category had an annual return 0.92% higher than the SCV-only category.

Since small-cap value funds are widely available in the US and international markets and have delivered good historical return premiums, we'll focus on using them as our diversifying second funds in the 2 Funds for Life strategies, recommending funds with exposure to quality where possible too.

Small-cap value funds are the most widely available, efficient, and cost-effective funds for diversifying a target-date fund in a 2 Funds for Life strategy.

Because the size and value factors are so widely available, they are often used to describe the entire stock market. If you visit the Morningstar website, you'll see their style box representation of the market, which looks like the chart below. "Growth" is used to describe the opposite of value, but the rest is self-explanatory.

CHAPTER 5: DISCERNING DIFFERENCES — SUBCLASSES & STYLES

	Value	Blend	Growth
Large		CAP-WEIGHTED CENTER	
Mid			
Small			

Table 3. Morningstar style box method of dividing US stock market

I've added "Cap-Weighted Center" to show where a total market or S&P 500 fund would land. A total market or S&P 500 fund is called "cap-weighted" because the percentage weighting of the individual stocks in those funds is proportional to the market capitalization (outstanding shares times price) of each stock. Why is the cap-weighted center in the top-middle box? Because the large companies are so much bigger than the small ones. Even though there are many more small and mid-sized companies, after adding them all up, they don't shift the center of the market below the middle of the top box.

Sometimes you'll hear people talk about "tilting" a portfolio toward small, value, growth, or a combination such as small value. That means owning more of one of those parts of the market than a cap-weighted portfolio of the whole market would own. A portfolio that owns the total market, such as the S&P 500 or most target-date funds, will have practically no tilt to small, value, or growth. That's because whatever they hold in small is offset by what they hold in large, and whatever they hold in value is offset by what they hold in growth. Adding an allocation to small, value, or growth would tilt the resulting portfolio, though, and the greater the allocation, the greater the tilt.

Since all of these style boxes represent parts of the stock market, they all provide exposure to the market risk, but some also provide varying degrees of exposure to the size and value risk factors. Those differences should produce different returns and levels of risk. Here are the style boxes with the historical returns and worst drawdowns from the Portfolio Visualizer website using January 1972 to February 2021 returns:

	Value	Blend	Growth
Large	11.19% -54.85%	10.55% -50.97%	10.70% -53.6%
Mid	12.87% -56.51%	12.15% -54.14%	10.81% -61.2%
Small	13.94% -56.13%	12.00% -53.95%	10.53% -64.07%

Table 4. US Stock market style boxes with CAGRs and drawdowns (January 1972– February 2021)

Because the bottom-left small-value corner provides exposure to three different risk factors (market, size, and value), we would expect it to have had the highest historical returns, and it did, with a CAGR of 13.94%. That's more than 3% higher than the large-cap blend, which is a good proxy for the S&P 500 or total market. This is one of the pieces of evidence that makes it reasonable to think that tilting a portfolio toward small and value will likely lead to increased returns. Because the small-value stocks had a worst-case drawdown of ~56% compared to ~51% for the large-blend part of the market, getting those returns required staying invested through those deeper drawdowns.

There are also some surprises.

Large-growth had a higher return than large-blend. It was only by 0.15 percentage point, but if more value-oriented stocks always outperformed more expensive ones, that's not what we'd expect. Since the difference is small, it might not be statistically significant. It's also possible that large-cap growth is at the end of an unusually good series of high returns. Maybe there will be a correction that brings it back in line with expectations. Academics work tirelessly to answer questions like these, but even they admit they don't know with certainty.

The other surprise is that small-cap growth and small-cap blend underperformed midcap growth and midcap blend, respectively. This is the opposite of what we'd expect if smaller was *always* better. A popular explanation for this discrepancy is that the penalty for investing in overpriced growth companies is higher in the small-company part of the market, where information is less available. We don't know for sure, but it seems reasonable that it would be easier to fool investors into spending too much to buy shares of an obscure small company promising a bright future than to do the same for a large-growth company with many analysts scrutinizing it daily.

Hopefully, that gives you an intuitive understanding of these important equity subclasses or styles. The real magic happens when we combine them, but before we get to that, let's look at another way to diversify — across geography.

For those wondering how US small-cap value would do in our lifetime backtest, here's the chart. It's no surprise that it produced a very high return and very high drawdowns. If there is a surprise, it's that it also had a high safe withdrawal rate and never ran out of money. It's also an asset that can take a lot of patience, with up to 15+-year runs of negative returns and 40+-year runs of lagging the S&P 500. We'll look at this challenge in more detail in Chapter 7.

100% US Small-Cap Value, 4% Fixed Withdrawals

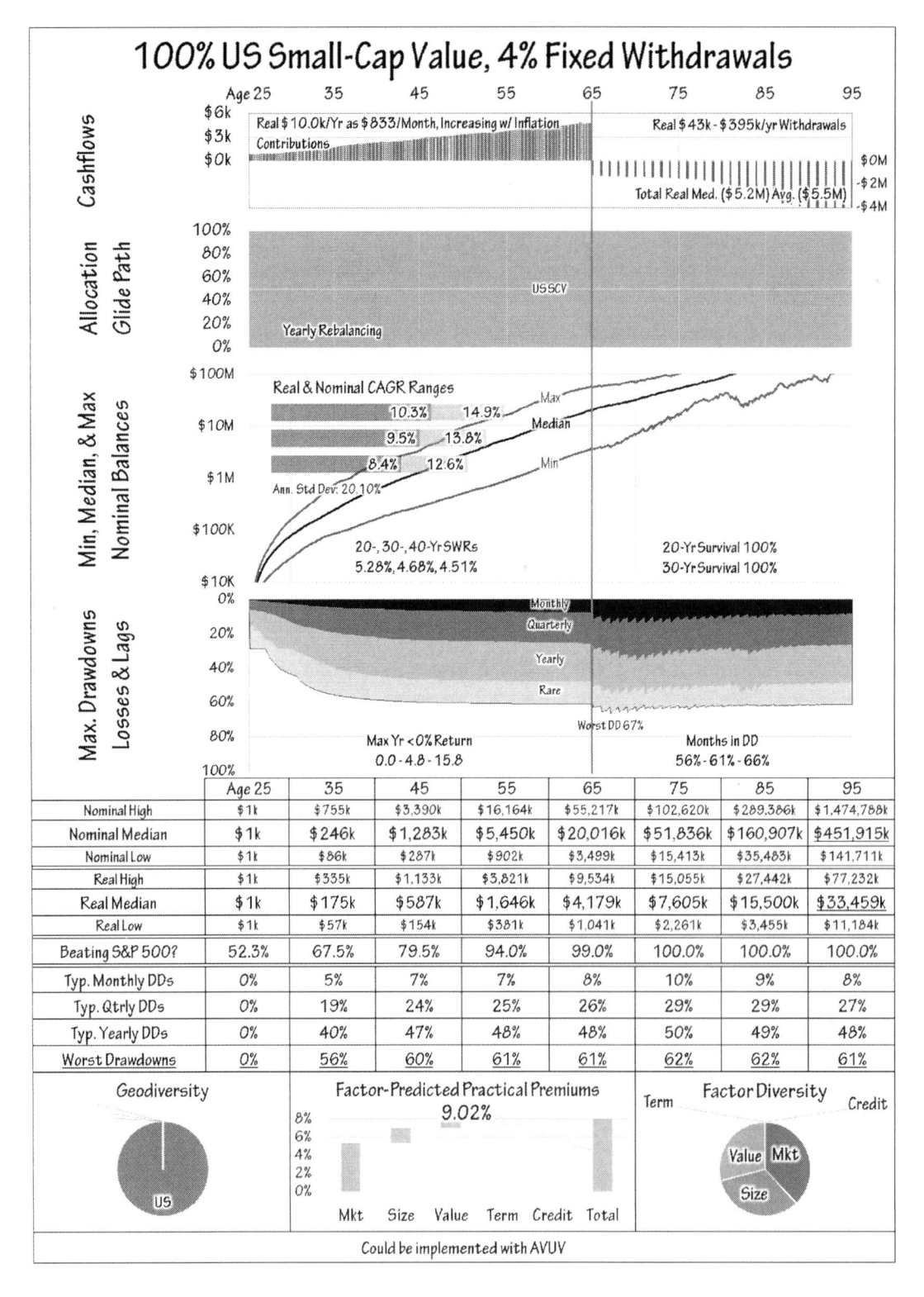

	Age 25	35	45	55	65	75	85	95
Nominal High	$1k	$755k	$3,390k	$16,164k	$55,217k	$102,620k	$289,386k	$1,474,788k
Nominal Median	$1k	$246k	$1,283k	$5,450k	$20,016k	$51,836k	$160,907k	$451,915k
Nominal Low	$1k	$86k	$287k	$902k	$3,499k	$15,413k	$35,483k	$141,711k
Real High	$1k	$335k	$1,133k	$3,821k	$9,534k	$15,055k	$27,442k	$77,232k
Real Median	$1k	$175k	$587k	$1,646k	$4,179k	$7,605k	$15,500k	$33,459k
Real Low	$1k	$57k	$154k	$381k	$1,041k	$2,261k	$3,455k	$11,184k
Beating S&P 500?	52.3%	67.5%	79.5%	94.0%	99.0%	100.0%	100.0%	100.0%
Typ. Monthly DDs	0%	5%	7%	7%	8%	10%	9%	8%
Typ. Qtrly DDs	0%	19%	24%	25%	26%	29%	29%	27%
Typ. Yearly DDs	0%	40%	47%	48%	48%	50%	49%	48%
Worst Drawdowns	0%	56%	60%	61%	61%	62%	62%	61%

Could be implemented with AVUV

Figure 15. Backtest of US small-cap value

Chapter 6
Geography — How Far to Go?

Aldabrachelys gigantea — *The world's largest tortoise, from the islands of the Aldabra atoll in Seychelles, has a maximum lifespan of over 200 years.*

Charles Darwin had to go to the ends of the earth on his voyage of discovery. Do we have to do the same to succeed as investors, or is an exclusive focus on our home market good enough?

Investors worldwide invest with a home country bias, ignoring the historical fact that individual country markets occasionally collapse, while the global market has always survived.

Markets in different parts of the world behave differently. The location of investments influences results and is a key characteristic of available ETFs, mutual funds, and target-date funds. For investing purposes, US investors usually look at the world in three broad categories: the US, international developed countries, and emerging markets. There are also many global or world funds that invest in the US and the rest of the world. Sometimes the term "ex-US" is used to indicate that the US market is excluded. Figure 16 shows how the relative total worth or market capitalization of these three markets has shifted over the past 120 years. Note how all the different regions contributed at different times without a clear long-term trend. Japan was classified initially as an emerging market but became an international developed market in 1967.

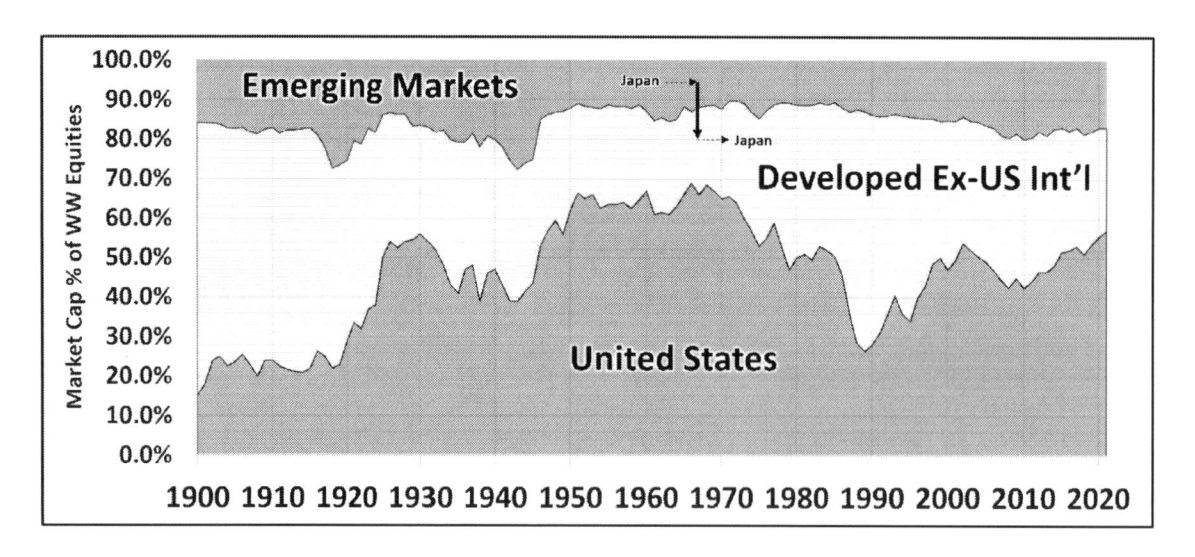

Figure 16. Approximate relative size of US, Developed Ex-US International, and Emerging Markets (1900-2020)

CHAPTER 6: GEOGRAPHY — HOW FAR TO GO?

Why do most of us invest with a home-country bias regardless of the size of our country? Because there's comfort and perceived safety in the familiar.

Stock market returns can vary significantly across different countries and regions, often to the great surprise of investors. Few people would have predicted in the year 1900 that the United States, which amounted to <20% of the total world stock market value at the time, would have the second-highest market return over the course of the next 120 years. Fewer still would have predicted that Australia would have the highest market return. That same period saw Japan rise from a single-digit percentage to over 45% of the world's stock market value around 1990, only to spend the next three decades well below that high. The Russian stock market went to zero when securities were declared invalid during the October Revolution of 1917. The Chinese stock market closed when the communists took over in 1949, and the German stock market lost more than 80% of its value when trading resumed after World War II. None of these were expected in 1900, but anyone who invested in many countries instead of only one would have avoided being wiped out by a single market failure.

If international investing is a form of protection or insurance against a single country's catastrophic failure, how expensive is it? Aren't international funds more expensive and less available? Aren't countries outside the US riskier? Don't they have higher taxes? And finally, don't we get enough international diversification by investing in US stocks when so much of their business is international anyway? Let's look at each of these questions individually.

1. Aren't international funds more expensive and less available?

Yes, international funds are more expensive in terms of expense ratio, but the difference varies a lot depending on the type of investment. The table below shows typical annual expense ratios and the number of funds available with meaningful (>30%) factor exposure for various regions and fund types. If you're buying a total-market fund, the expense ratio difference is only 0.02 to 0.07 percentage point, or $2 to $7 per $10,000 invested per year. For more specific fund types, the selection declines rapidly and the expense ratios go up. For the most specific small-cap value funds, the difference between a US fund and an emerging markets fund is 0.52 percentage point, or $52 per $10,000 invested per year. That could be substantial over a lifetime. Consequently, it's often more cost-effective to get more specific funds and factor tilts in US funds.

Example Expense Ratios & Relative Fund Selection for US & International Funds				
	US	Developed Markets	Emerging Markets	Global or World
Total Stock Market Funds	VTI -- 0.03% >6,000 Funds	VEA -- 0.05% >1,900 Funds	VWO -- 0.10% >500 Funds	VT -- 0.08% >800 Funds
Small Funds	IJR -- 0.07% >2,000 Funds	SCHC -- 0.11% ~100 Funds	EWX -- 0.65% ~40 Funds	SMCWX -- 1.06% >100 Funds
Value Funds	VONV -- 0.08% >1,400 Funds	EFV -- 0.40% >150 Funds	DFEVX -- 0.51% ~80 Funds	GVAL -- 0.65% ~70 Funds
Small-Cap Value Funds	VIOV -- 0.15% >600 Funds	AVDE -- 0.23% ~90 Funds	DEMSX -- 0.67% ~20 Funds	DGLIX -- 0.47% ~2 Funds

Table 5. Example expense ratios and relative fund selection for US and international funds

2. What about the risk of diversifying internationally?

Table 6 shows the backtested results for lump-sum investing in each of these major markets. The backtests used return sequences from 1970 through the end of 2019. I've listed the worst, median, and best compound annual growth rates (CAGRs), maximum drawdowns, and the likelihood of a 100% loss over a lifetime of investing. If we assume all developed countries are equally vulnerable to catastrophic failure, given two (Russia and China) examples of this kind of failure across the 22 major countries in the past 120 years, we can estimate the chance of any one country stock market failing in 70 years as 2/22 × 70/120 = 5.3%. Based on the same history and assumptions, the chance of all developed market countries or all emerging market countries experiencing catastrophic collapse simultaneously is essentially zero.

	US	Developed Markets	Emerging Markets	Global or World
Return and Risk Measures for US & International Funds				
CAGR (Best, Median, Worst)	14.1% 10.5% 8.2%	11.3% 9.1% 5.1%	15.0% 12.1% 8.6%	12.7% 10.4% 7.0%
Worst Drawdown (1970-2019)	50%	56%	59%	56%
Odds of 100% Loss Over 70 Years	5.3% (Single Country)	~0%	~0%	~0%

Table 6. Return and risk measures for US and international funds

So, investing internationally has been a little riskier. On a month-to-month or year-to-year basis, it has produced slightly lower or higher returns with more downside risk. Emerging markets have been the riskiest, but they've also delivered better returns over this 50-year period.

The biggest benefit of investing internationally is that it eliminates the risk of losing all our money in a single country market failure.

I suspect most of us would rather not have to spin a roulette wheel, where about one out of 20 possibilities means losing everything.

3. What about taxes? Don't many countries outside of the US have higher taxes, and won't that erode our returns?

Individual country taxes can vary dramatically, but they're not necessarily higher than in the US. Many countries have no capital gains tax. Some waive it for foreign investors. As of 2020, the IRS gives investors a tax credit or deduction up to the amount they would have paid in US taxes for taxes paid to another country for "qualified foreign taxes" on income, dividends, and interest in taxable accounts. Practically speaking, this means most investors using taxable accounts will not be substantially penalized from a tax perspective by diversifying internationally if they do their taxes correctly. Unfortunately, this is not the case for tax-advantaged accounts such as IRAs. This provides a small incentive to hold international equities in taxable accounts, but might easily be offset by other factors. For example, I wouldn't forego the chance to automatically invest in a 401k at work and get a company match just to save a little on the international taxes. For a more thorough look at how international fund taxes might impact returns in taxable and tax-advantaged accounts across various circumstances, I recommend reading this article *Where Should You Hold International Stocks: Taxable or Tax-Advantaged?* at the Physician on Fire website.

4. Don't we get enough international diversification through US-only funds since most US companies derive so much of their business through international trade?

The trend toward globalization means more interdependence and less diversification benefit in international investing today than in the past. Today's multinational companies in the S&P 500 derive about 30% of their revenue from international sales. So yes, it's reasonable to say that investing in the S&P 500 provides some exposure to markets outside the US, but investing solely in US companies still leaves a portfolio vulnerable to US-centric risk. Whether companies had significant sales outside of China, Russia, or Germany when their countries fell on hard times made little difference to their investors.

Most academics recommend following the wisdom of the crowd and investing the same percentage in each region or geography that the rest of the world does collectively. At the beginning of 2021, that would mean investing about 57% in the US, 26% in developed countries, and 17% in emerging markets. There are several rational reasons for US investors to tilt more towards the US market while still investing globally. First, US assets are cheaper in terms of fund expense ratios. Second, the selection of funds is greater in the US market. And third, due in part to that increased selection, the amount of exposure to investment factors available in the different asset classes or styles is greater for US funds. Finally, US funds are likely larger and more liquid, making them easier and cheaper to buy and sell.

The one counterargument to all of these is that the very qualities that make US funds attractive can attract so many investors that their prices are driven up in the market. To illustrate this point and provide one last nudge to consider diversifying internationally, here are the Research Affiliates Smart Beta Interactive estimated large-cap market benchmark recent and expected real (excluding inflation) returns for the three major regions we've discussed. These are based on the idea that returns following market highs tend to be lower, while returns following market lows tend to be higher. Given today's very high prices for US assets, diversifying internationally may be as important for the short term as it is for the long term.

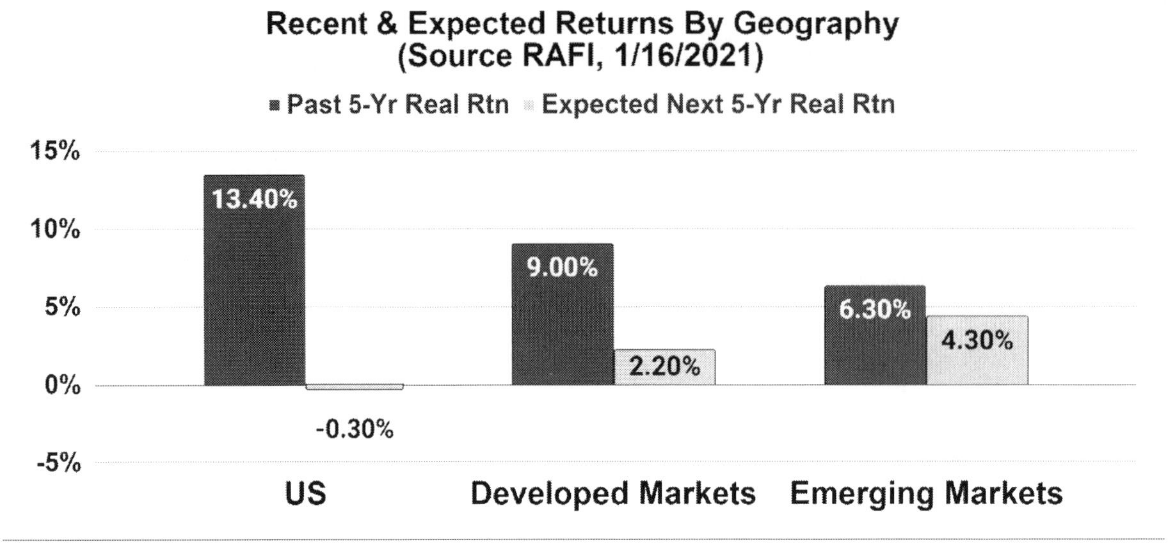

**Recent & Expected Returns By Geography
(Source RAFI, 1/16/2021)**

■ Past 5-Yr Real Rtn ■ Expected Next 5-Yr Real Rtn

	US	Developed Markets	Emerging Markets
Past 5-Yr Real Rtn	13.40%	9.00%	6.30%
Expected Next 5-Yr Real Rtn	-0.30%	2.20%	4.30%

Figure 17. Recent and expected returns by geography (source: RAFI, 1/16/2021)

Next, we'll look at how combinations of asset classes can be greater than the sum of their parts.

For those interested in more details, here are the backtests for the US total stock market, worldwide total stock market, and emerging markets:

CHAPTER 6: GEOGRAPHY — HOW FAR TO GO?

US Total Stock Market, 100% Equities, 4% Fixed Withdrawals

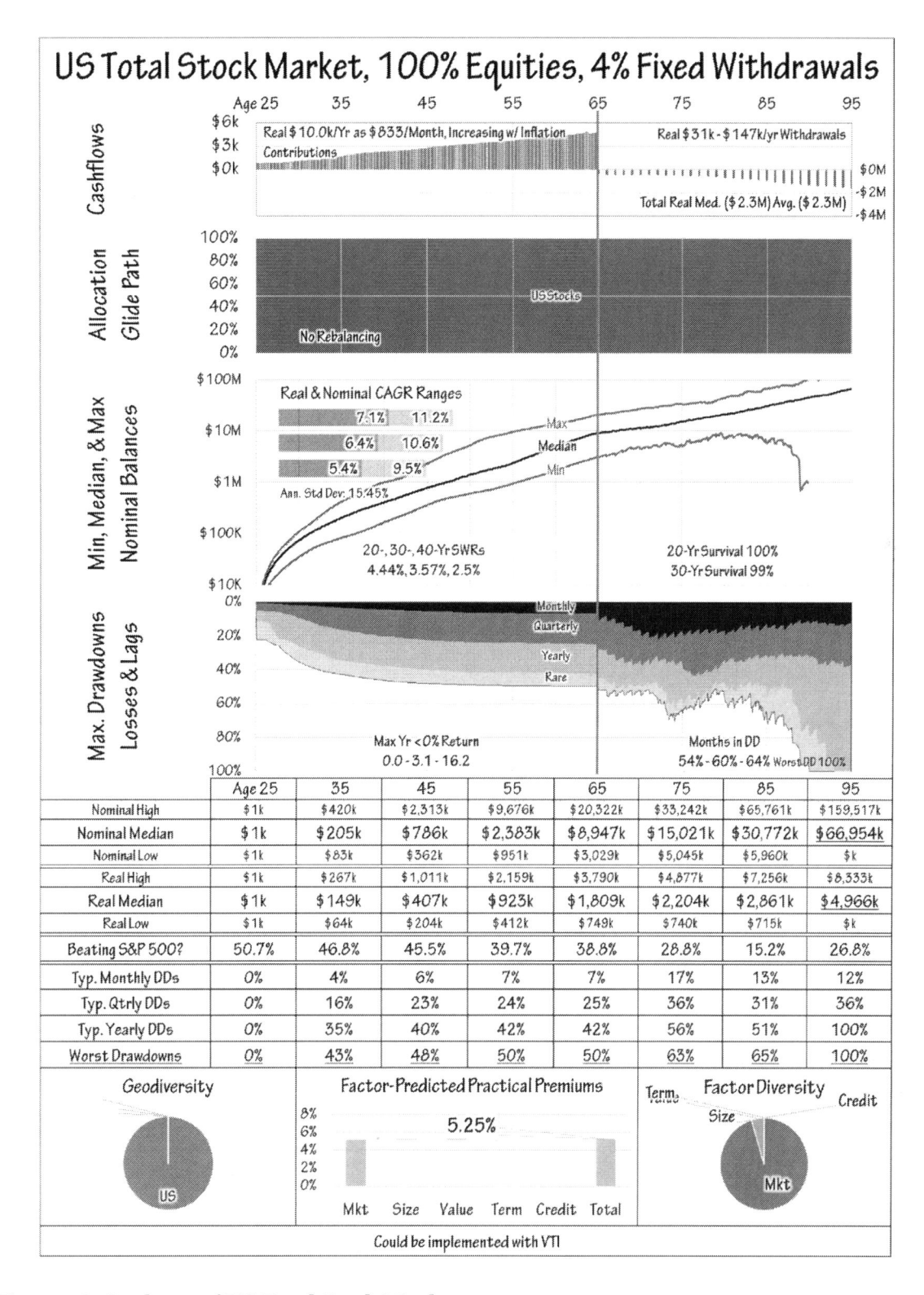

Cashflows: Real $10.0k/Yr as $833/Month, Increasing w/ Inflation Contributions | Real $31k - $147k/yr Withdrawals | Total Real Med. ($2.3M) Avg. ($2.3M)

Allocation Glide Path: US Stocks, No Rebalancing, 100%

Min, Median, & Max Nominal Balances:
Real & Nominal CAGR Ranges
- 7.1% — 11.2% (Max)
- 6.4% — 10.6% (Median)
- 5.4% — 9.5% (Min)

Ann. Std Dev: 15.45%

20-, 30-, 40-Yr SWRs: 4.44%, 3.57%, 2.5%

20-Yr Survival 100%
30-Yr Survival 99%

Max. Drawdowns Losses & Lags: Monthly, Quarterly, Yearly, Rare

Max Yr <0% Return: 0.0 - 3.1 - 16.2

Months in DD: 54% - 60% - 64% Worst DD 100%

	Age 25	35	45	55	65	75	85	95
Nominal High	$1k	$420k	$2,313k	$9,676k	$20,322k	$33,242k	$65,761k	$159,517k
Nominal Median	$1k	$205k	$786k	$2,383k	$8,947k	$15,021k	$30,772k	$66,954k
Nominal Low	$1k	$83k	$362k	$951k	$3,029k	$5,045k	$5,960k	$k
Real High	$1k	$267k	$1,011k	$2,159k	$3,790k	$4,877k	$7,256k	$8,333k
Real Median	$1k	$149k	$407k	$923k	$1,809k	$2,204k	$2,861k	$4,966k
Real Low	$1k	$64k	$204k	$412k	$749k	$740k	$715k	$k
Beating S&P 500?	50.7%	46.8%	45.5%	39.7%	38.8%	28.8%	15.2%	26.8%
Typ. Monthly DDs	0%	4%	6%	7%	7%	17%	13%	12%
Typ. Qtrly DDs	0%	16%	23%	24%	25%	36%	31%	36%
Typ. Yearly DDs	0%	35%	40%	42%	42%	56%	51%	100%
Worst Drawdowns	0%	43%	48%	50%	50%	63%	65%	100%

Geodiversity: US

Factor-Predicted Practical Premiums: 5.25% (Mkt, Size, Value, Term, Credit, Total)

Factor Diversity: Mkt, Size, Term, Credit

Could be implemented with VTI

Figure 18. Backtest of US Total Stock Market

Worldwide Total Stock Market, 4% Fixed Withdrawals

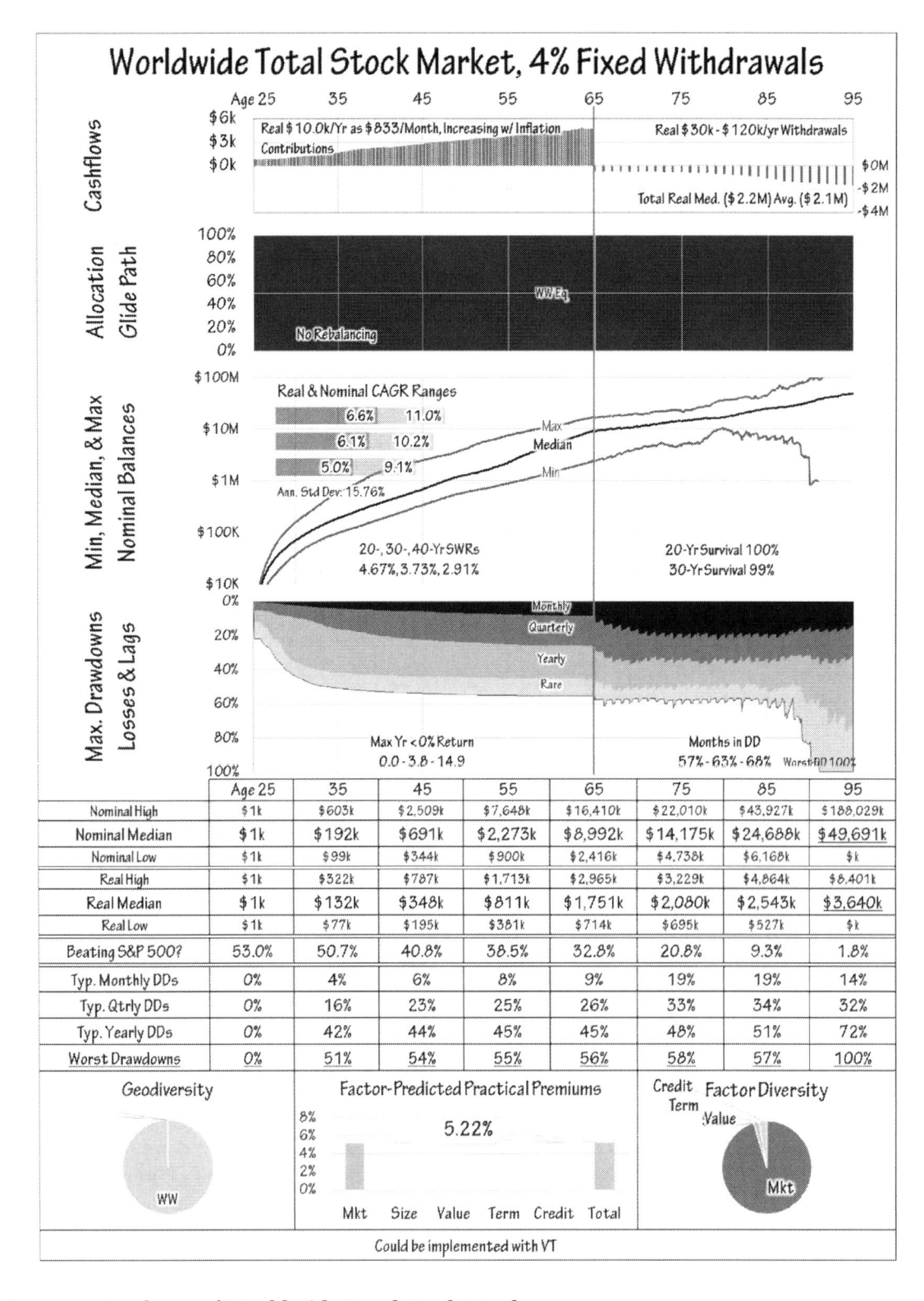

	Age 25	35	45	55	65	75	85	95
Nominal High	$1k	$603k	$2,509k	$7,648k	$16,410k	$22,010k	$43,927k	$188,029k
Nominal Median	$1k	$192k	$691k	$2,273k	$8,992k	$14,175k	$24,688k	$49,691k
Nominal Low	$1k	$99k	$344k	$900k	$2,416k	$4,738k	$6,168k	$k
Real High	$1k	$322k	$787k	$1,713k	$2,965k	$3,229k	$4,864k	$8,401k
Real Median	$1k	$132k	$348k	$811k	$1,751k	$2,080k	$2,543k	$3,640k
Real Low	$1k	$77k	$195k	$381k	$714k	$695k	$527k	$k
Beating S&P 500?	53.0%	50.7%	40.8%	38.5%	32.8%	20.8%	9.3%	1.8%
Typ. Monthly DDs	0%	4%	6%	8%	9%	19%	19%	14%
Typ. Qtrly DDs	0%	16%	23%	25%	26%	33%	34%	32%
Typ. Yearly DDs	0%	42%	44%	45%	45%	48%	51%	72%
Worst Drawdowns	0%	51%	54%	55%	56%	58%	57%	100%

Geodiversity: WW

Factor-Predicted Practical Premiums: 5.22% (Mkt, Size, Value, Term, Credit, Total)

Factor Diversity: Mkt (Credit, Term, Value)

Could be implemented with VT

Figure 19. Backtest of Worldwide Total Stock Market

CHAPTER 6: GEOGRAPHY — HOW FAR TO GO?

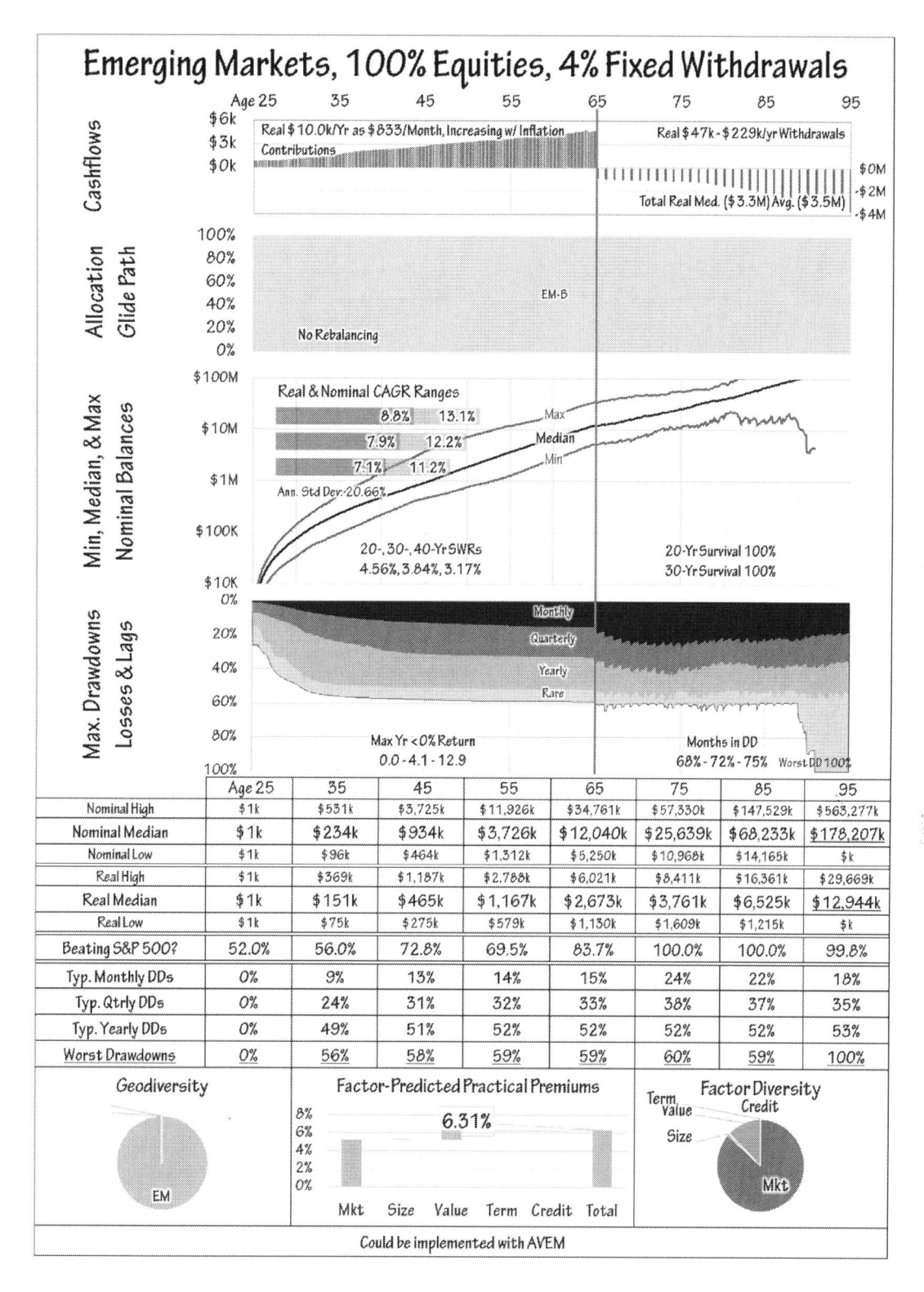

Emerging Markets, 100% Equities, 4% Fixed Withdrawals

	Age 25	35	45	55	65	75	85	95
Nominal High	$1k	$531k	$3,725k	$11,926k	$34,761k	$57,330k	$147,529k	$563,277k
Nominal Median	$1k	$234k	$934k	$3,726k	$12,040k	$25,639k	$68,233k	$178,207k
Nominal Low	$1k	$96k	$464k	$1,312k	$5,250k	$10,968k	$14,165k	$k
Real High	$1k	$369k	$1,187k	$2,788k	$6,021k	$8,411k	$16,361k	$29,669k
Real Median	$1k	$151k	$465k	$1,167k	$2,673k	$3,761k	$6,525k	$12,944k
Real Low	$1k	$75k	$275k	$579k	$1,130k	$1,609k	$1,215k	$k
Beating S&P 500?	52.0%	56.0%	72.8%	69.5%	83.7%	100.0%	100.0%	99.8%
Typ. Monthly DDs	0%	9%	13%	14%	15%	24%	22%	18%
Typ. Qtrly DDs	0%	24%	31%	32%	33%	38%	37%	35%
Typ. Yearly DDs	0%	49%	51%	52%	52%	52%	52%	53%
Worst Drawdowns	0%	56%	58%	59%	59%	60%	59%	100%

Could be implemented with AVEM

Figure 20. Backtest of Emerging Markets

2 FUNDS FOR LIFE

Chapter 7
Ecosystems — Diversification & Combinations

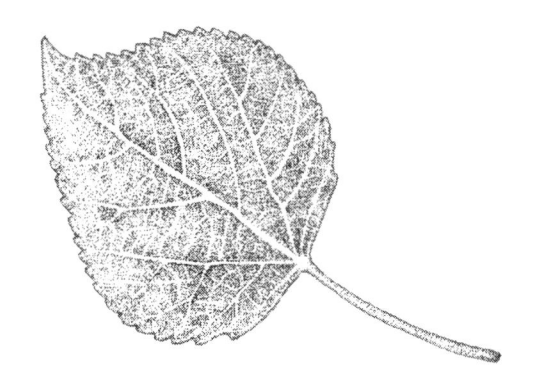

Populus tremuloides — *Quaking aspens live in clonal colonies that can survive for thousands of years and weigh millions of kilograms, making them the heaviest known organisms in the world.*

Where life is abundant, diversity is too. The African savanna, coral reefs, wetlands, and rain forests are marked by an immense variety of life, from tiny microbes to mammals, fish, reptiles, and birds. That variety creates resilience against calamity. So far, we've looked at bonds, stocks, small-cap value stocks, and geography as separate things with different levels of risk and reward, but the real magic happens when we combine them.

We've all heard the expression "don't put all your eggs in one basket."

Concentrated risk is intuitively bad. We've already learned about three meaningful ways we can diversify. We can combine stocks and bonds. We can invest in more than one equity factor. And we can invest in more than one geographic market. That's a lot of moving parts. Let's look at how they interact, starting with stocks and bonds.

As we saw earlier, bonds are less volatile than stocks, but stocks have had higher long-term returns. If we invest in a mix of stocks and bonds, we can get something in between. Figure 21 shows how the return, drawdown risk, and safe withdrawal rates vary for different mix percentages based on a rolling start date analysis of data from 1970 through 2019. In this chapter, we'll assume lump-sum investments with annual rebalancing.

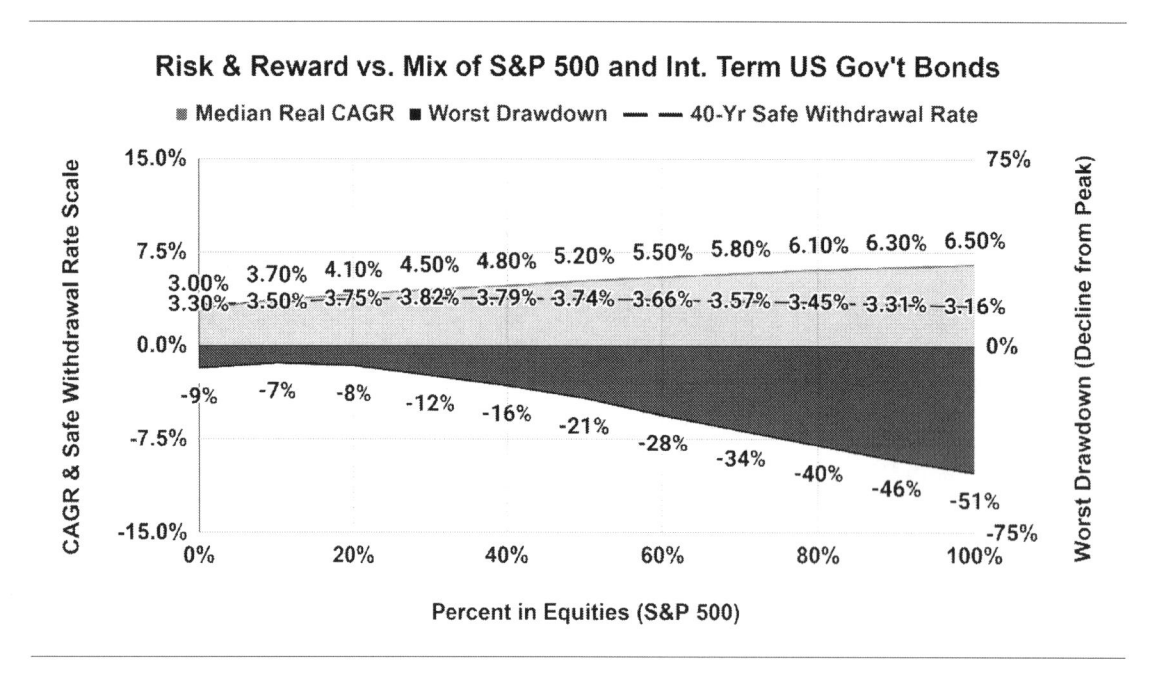

Figure 21. Risk and reward versus a mix of S&P 500 and intermediate-term US government bonds

As expected, higher percentages of stocks produced higher returns and higher risk in the form of greater worst-case drawdowns. Investing 100% in bonds had only a 3%

CHAPTER 7: ECOSYSTEMS — DIVERSIFICATION & COMBINATIONS

median real compound annual growth rate, but it also had only a 9% worst-case drawdown. Investing 100% in the S&P 500 raised the median real return to 6.5%, but it had a 51% worst-case drawdown. For a long-term investor, tolerating the bumpier ride could be well worth it because the deepest drawdowns only occur rarely and the effects of compounding accrue over time. There are two things I find surprising on the chart. The first is that going from 100% bonds to 90% or 80% bonds actually reduces the worst drawdowns from 9% to 7% or 8%. This is because stocks and bonds tend to perform better or worse at different times. The second surprise is that the highest 40-year safe withdrawal rate for a mix of intermediate-term US Government Bonds and the S&P 500 happened at 30% in equities and was only 3.82%. As we'll see next, diversifying with additional equity factors has helped increase both the total safe withdrawal rate and the median real CAGR.

If adding stocks to bonds increases return and risk, what happens if we add a tilt to higher-risk equity factors such as size and value to the S&P 500? Figure 22 extends the previous chart to show how the return, drawdown risk, and safe withdrawal rates vary when we shift some of the S&P 500 allocation into a US small-cap value fund. Note the portfolio asset allocation along the bottom axis.

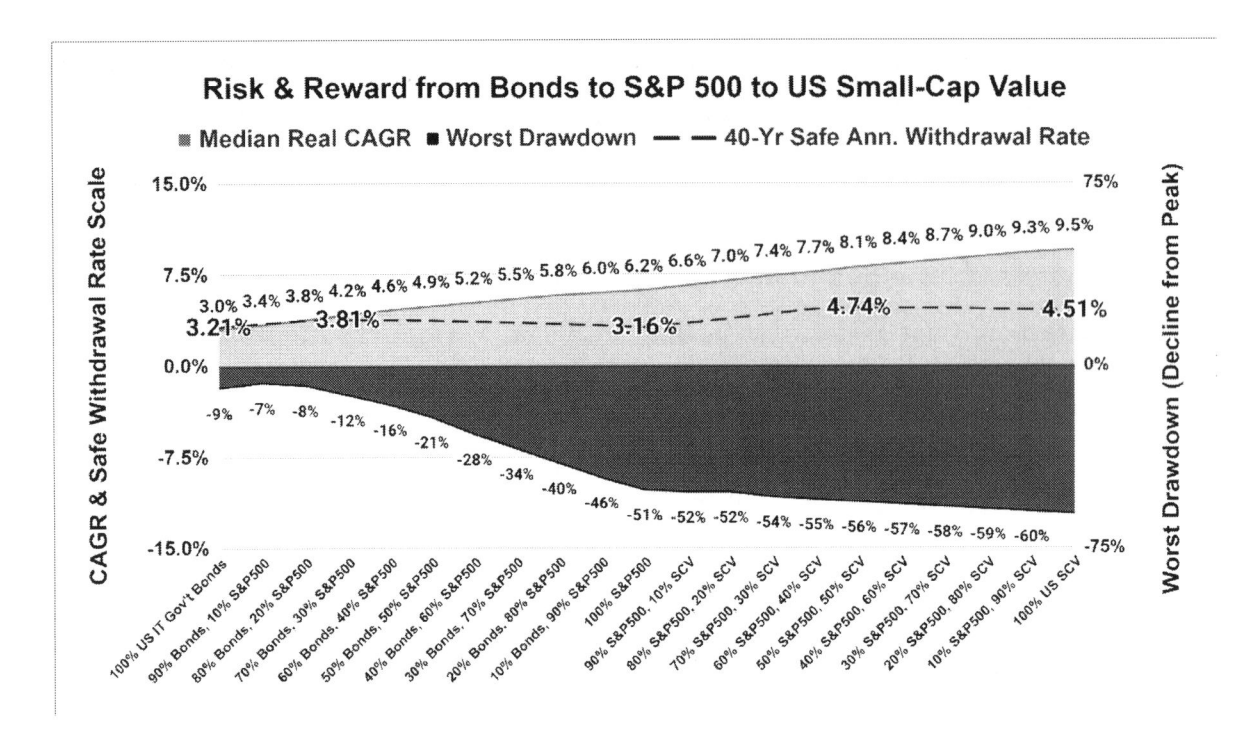

Figure 22. Risk and reward from intermediate-term US government bonds to S&P 500 to US small-cap value

As expected, increased tilts to small and value have produced significantly higher returns with some increased risk. This was because the small and value returns came at different times from the broad market returns. Shifting 10% of the S&P 500 allocation to US small-cap value produced 0.4 percentage point higher compound annual return (from 6.2% to 6.6%) while only increasing worst-case drawdowns by 1 percentage point (from -51% to -52%). Perhaps the most surprising thing about this chart is that the highest 40-year safe withdrawal rate was for a 50|50 mix of the S&P 500 and US small-cap value, and it was 4.74%. Even at 100% in small-cap value, the 40-year safe withdrawal rate was 4.51%.

> **Adding small-cap value to the S&P 500 produced higher safe withdrawal rates, suggesting it could be beneficial for retirees — especially those who retire early.**

To finish this exploration of mixing bonds, the S&P 500, and US small-cap value, we need to look at what happens with combinations of small-cap value and bonds. You can think of this as the third side of the triangle, with the three asset classes at the corners. Figure 23 shows the complete picture:

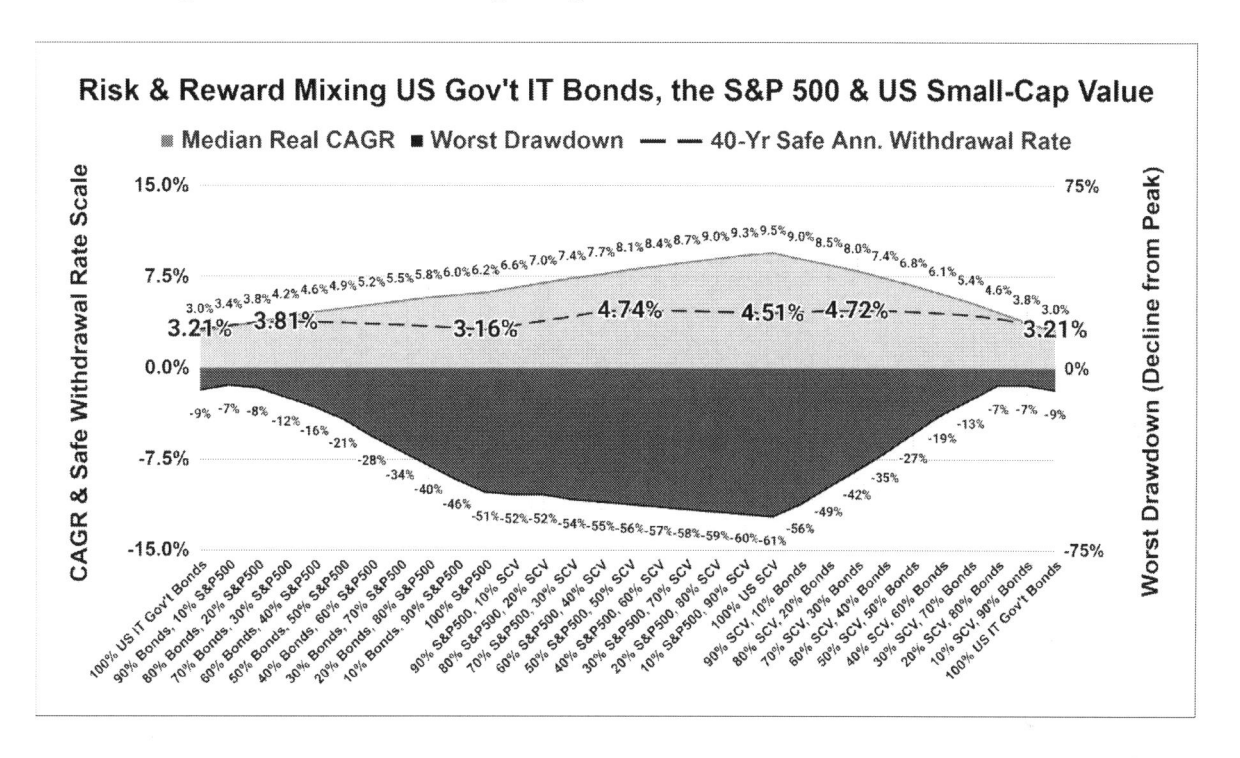

Figure 23. Risk and reward versus a mix of intermediate-term US government bonds, S&P 500, and US small-cap value

This last section of the chart is perhaps the most surprising of all. By combining such different assets, we ended up with options that have had relatively high historical returns and safe withdrawal rates with relatively low drawdowns. For example, a classic 50|50 S&P 500 and bonds combination had a 4.9% real return and -21% worst drawdown. In contrast, a 30|70 small-cap value and bonds combination had a 5.4% real return and only a -13% worst drawdown. These are sometimes called "barbell" portfolios because they bring together relative opposite asset classes.

For any given return, the lowest associated drawdown was for a combination of small-cap value and intermediate-term US government bonds.

There is another important risk that's not captured in the previous charts. It's the risk of falling behind the S&P 500, sometimes called "tracking error." Although including some small and value assets in portfolios has increased median real returns in the past, those returns came at different times than the broader market returns. Consequently, there's a risk of spending many years or even decades in a historically superior strategy that's not "winning." Since we tend to judge our success or failure relative to those around us, this can be a bitter pill to swallow. When markets are zooming higher, and our neighbors and coworkers are all excited, we want to be doing well too. If we've chosen to invest differently for a better long-term return, it's easy to doubt we've made the right choice. If we give up on our different strategy too soon, we'll lock in the period of underperformance and never get the higher return we were seeking. So, how long might we have to wait?

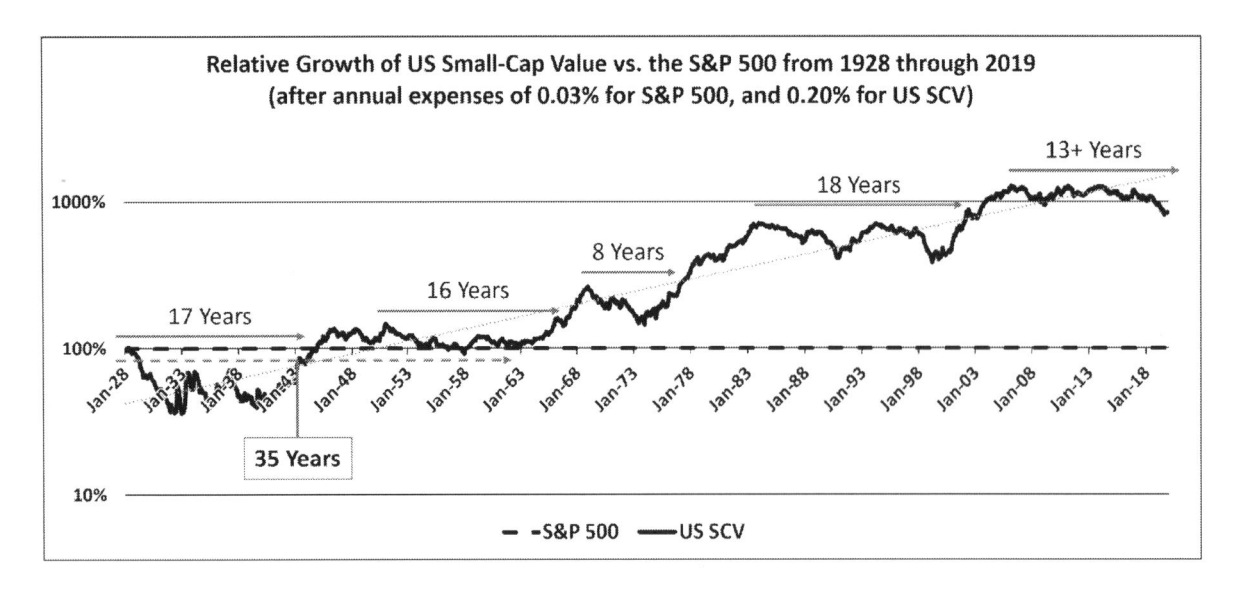

Figure 24. Relative growth of US small-cap value vs. the S&P 500 from 1928 through 2019

Figure 24 is a relative growth or "telltale" chart. It shows how fast US small-cap value grew compared to the S&P 500. Although there's a long-term up-and-to-the-right trend, it's far from steady. Had someone invested 100% in small and value stocks from 1928 through 2019, they would have ended up with about 10 times as much money as someone who invested in just the S&P 500, but their patience would have been tried many times along the way. There were five times that their strategy would have been underperforming the market for between eight and 18 years. There was even a 35-year period ending in 1963 in which small-cap value had essentially the same total return as the S&P 500. During those decades, countless articles would have been written about how investing in small and value stocks no longer worked—that it was different this time. For the lucky investor who ignored them, the reward was great. During this lag period, they would have still seen a return comparable to the S&P 500, and after the lag, they would have seen a higher return. For those who changed course one or more times along the way, the outcome was likely much worse than just investing in the S&P 500 after expenses.

The last mix we'll consider is US versus worldwide. As we learned in the last chapter, the primary reason to invest in multiple countries is to protect against catastrophic failure in a single market. Although there are some costs, the benefits justify at least some geographic diversification. Let's look at what happens when we go from one extreme to another — from an all-US total stock market portfolio to one that's everything but the US or ex-US. Since there wasn't a catastrophic failure of the US stock market in the time period (1970 through 2019) we're using for these backtests, this will slightly understate the risk of investing in a single market, but that's the best data we have. Figure 25 shows the results. The data for this and prior tests are based on actual fund returns, if available, or indexes with subtracted expense ratios to make the analysis as realistic as possible.

Risk & Reward vs. Mix of US and Ex-US Total Stock Market

▪ Median Real CAGR ▪ Worst Drawdown — — 40-Yr Safe Withdrawal Rate

% Ex-US	0%	10%	20%	30%	40%	50%	60%	70%	80%	90%	100%
Median Real CAGR	6.50%	6.60%	6.70%	6.70%	6.80%	6.80%	6.80%	6.70%	6.60%	6.40%	6.30%
40-Yr SWR	3.23%	3.32%	3.40%	3.47%	3.54%	3.60%	3.65%	3.64%	3.51%	3.33%	3.15%
Worst Drawdown	-50%	-50%	-50%	-50%	-50%	-51%	-52%	-54%	-55%	-56%	-57%

Percent in Ex-US Total Stock Market -- Balance is in US Total Stock Market

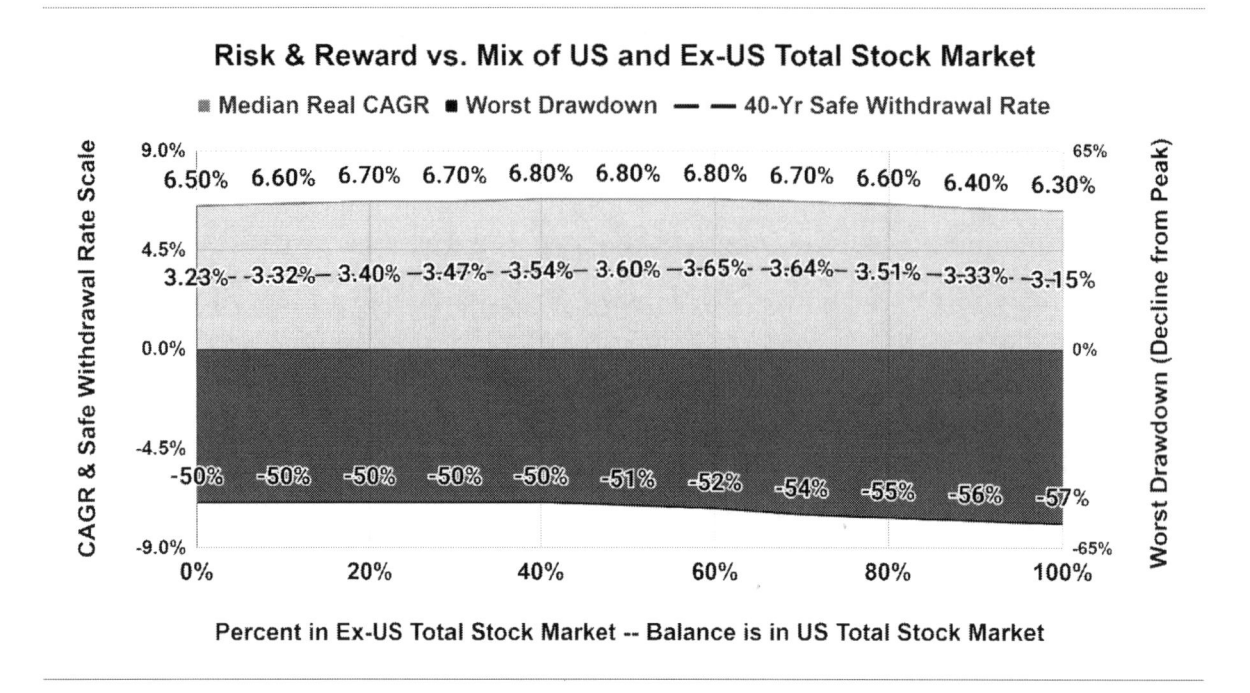

Figure 25. Risk and reward versus a mix of the US and ex-US Total Stock Market

Since US and ex-US stocks are such similar assets, the differences here are small. The median real rate of return and safe withdrawal rates increased slightly with no increase in worst drawdowns as we go from 0% in ex-US stocks to about 50%. So, not only do we avoid the risk of a single country catastrophic failure by diversifying geographically, but we are also likely to get a small bump in annual returns (e.g., 0.3%) for doing it. Whether you invest 20%, 30%, 40%, or 50% in international stocks, you'll be getting some helpful diversification and protecting yourself from the risk of your home country falling on disastrous times.

We've validated five helpful diversification ingredients: stocks, bonds, the small and value factors, and geography. In combination, they can produce something better than the average of their individual characteristics because they tend to perform better or worse at different times. Does that mean we need to purchase them separately in a complex portfolio? Not at all. Because there are so many different funds available today, we can build portfolios that are well diversified across all five

CHAPTER 7: ECOSYSTEMS — DIVERSIFICATION & COMBINATIONS

of these with only one or two funds. Before we get to that, though, let's look at another crucial variable in the mix. Let's look at you.

Chapter 8
Individual Variation — Risk, Age & Temperament

Sphenodon punctatus — *The tuatara is the sole surviving member of its order, which originated around 250 million years ago.*

Our appetite and capacity for risk change throughout life. Too little or too much risk can torpedo our chances of success. The good news is that there is a wide range of acceptable risks to get us where we need to go.

The drawings in this book feature long-lived plants and animals. Though all of them are long-lived or relatively long-lived, not all of them are long-term investors. Scientists categorize the animals that make long-term investments as "K-strategists" or "K-selected." K-selected species typically mature more slowly, reproduce later, have longer life spans, produce fewer offspring at a time and, among other things, invest more in the nurture and development of those offspring. Not surprisingly, humans are a K-selected species. That means at some level, deep down, we are all wired for long-term investing.

Sadly, our long-term investor wiring is a little out of date. Yes, it does a good job of getting us to invest in family, children, and social connections, but it does little to help with 401(k)s, IRAs, mutual funds, and ETFs. How could it? It took millions of years to evolve, and our modern personal finance investing environment changes almost daily. There is hope, though. We are nothing if not flexible and adaptive. The trick is in making the connections. Once we see how personal finance decisions are key to our future security, freedom, and happiness, investing becomes natural again.

One of the best ways to start seeing those connections is to zoom out and think about the whole of our lives from beginning to end. We're all different, but many things are the same. We're born, we live, we die. In between, we work, we play, we rest, and as we gain experience, we develop. Individually, we all develop different talents, skills, and abilities, but the cumulative effect is similar. As babies, we depend on others for everything, but as we grow, we become more independent, more resilient, more risk tolerant.

In our early years, the environment we're born into is one of chance. If we're lucky, parents and extended family teach us by example and nurture. If we're luckier still, we go to a school where motivated teachers help us develop a love of learning and good study habits. For most of us, luck soon gives way to choice. Even in difficult environments, we make choices that lead to increased or decreased resilience. The choices will be easier for some and harder for others, but the consequences will be similar.

What if we, or someone we know, were extremely unlucky and were born into challenging circumstances with headwinds instead of tailwinds? Recent research by Edith Chen and colleagues suggests that good predictors of better outcomes for low socioeconomic status adolescents are a "shift-and-persist" strategy coupled with the presence of a supportive, positive role model. Shifting is an ability to accept and reframe the meaning of daily stressors as less threatening or potentially positive — perceiving them as learning or growth opportunities. Persisting means finding ways to endure adversity with strength by developing purpose in life and holding on to hope that, despite adversity, the future may be better. It's not clear whether shift-and-persist can be taught, but the helpful influence of positive role models suggests that at least it can be fostered. There's no simple cure for bad circumstances, but it can't hurt to have a caring role model or finding one and developing our own shift-and-persist capabilities.

It's ironic, but many of the most impactful choices we'll make happen in our teens and twenties. If we choose to learn more marketable skills or are lucky enough to find a calling we care so passionately about that we'll move heaven and earth to make it happen, our resilience goes up. If we drop out of school too early, our resilience goes down. Starting a job or career and gaining work experience improves it. Choosing to establish frugal habits, saving early, and investing regularly are hugely important early steps to increasing our resilience. Conversely, spending too much, taking on debt, and delaying investing will lower our resilience. These choices are crucial because many will last a lifetime. It's not that we can't change, but most of us won't.

Once we're working, our resilience depends in large part on consistency. Consistently contributing to a retirement program. Consistently investing well. Consistently ignoring the ups and downs of the market to stay invested. And consistently working.

Unfortunately, many of us will experience unanticipated and unwanted years of unemployment. That reduces our risk tolerance, but as long as it's not too many of our working years, it won't wipe it out altogether. There are things we can do to overcome these resilience-reducing events. We can work longer, plan better, economize, delay taking Social Security, or even change where we live to lower living expenses.

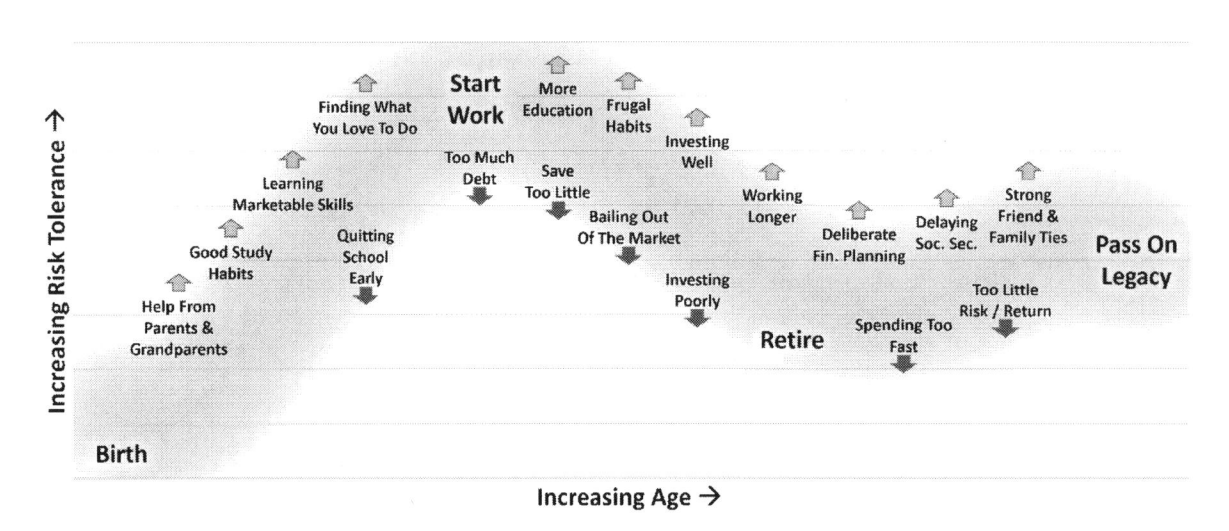

Figure 26. Financial risk tolerance changes with age and circumstances.

With all these opportunities to increase our risk tolerance over time, you might expect that it would only increase throughout our lives, but that's not so. Instead, it tends to increase until we start working and then decreases until we retire. The reason is simple — time. At the start of our careers, we have all our working and investing years in front of us. That's 40-plus years to work and have markets compound. If we invest $1 and get an 8% return for 40 years, it will be worth more than $20 in the end. Over 30 years, it only grows to $10. Over 20 years, it grows to less than $5. Over 10 years, it grows to just over $2.

Our total earning potential doesn't decline evenly. It declines much faster in the early years and slower in the later years.

Once we see how every passing year erodes our earning potential and ability to grow investments, the motivation to save and invest becomes clear. This isn't about putting off living today so we can live better tomorrow. It's the opposite. It's living every day like it matters so tomorrow is better. When we develop our talents, find ways to contribute that are valued, and live within our means while saving to be generous to our future selves, we thrive. For some, this is a culture they will have inherited from their parents. For others, it's a culture they'll need to pioneer. Regardless of which path you find yourself on, increasing your resilience and risk tolerance will help you spiral up instead of down.

Now that we understand how our resilience or risk tolerance changes through life, let's look at how we can assess where we're at individually at any point along the way.

One way to determine our individual risk tolerance is to take an investor risk survey. Vanguard has one that's free, quick, and easy, and it's a good place to start.

Another approach is to ponder similar questions on your own. Here are some I think are worth considering:

1. **What did I learn about investing growing up?** A history of family exemplars and mentors can help you stick to a strategy. If investing isn't part of your family culture, it may be harder to weather storms.

2. **Who do I know that can help coach me through tough times?** A knowledgeable friend could be a good resource. A misinformed friend might do more harm than good.

3. **How much do I know about my investing approach?** Knowledge helps inoculate us against misinformation, emotion, and fear. Ignorance makes us more vulnerable to panic selling at the wrong time.

4. **How important is it to me to keep up with the market?** If it's very important, investing in the S&P 500 might be your best bet. If you're willing to underperform for long periods in hopes of a better outcome, then investing in other parts of the market (e.g., small-cap value) might be for you.

5. **Do I want to lower risk as I get older?** A target-date fund or robo-advisor can accomplish this, but target-date funds are cheaper. Not doing this brings added risks (more on that later).

6. **Am I ahead or behind on saving for my goals?** Being ahead lets you take more risks, which, over time, puts you further ahead. Being behind leaves less room for error, requires taking less risk, and keeps you from getting ahead faster.

7. **How much am I willing to see my accounts drop in value before losing sleep or selling?** If you can tolerate a 50% or more drawdown, investing in 100% stocks might be fine. If you have less tolerance, you'll probably need to own a lower percentage of stocks.

8. **How often do I check my account balances, and how much does it move my emotions?** If you look daily, and it affects you a lot, then investing in an S&P 500 or TDF might be best. If you look infrequently, or it doesn't much affect your mood, you might want to invest in a more diversified portfolio.

9. **How much do I need compared to what I have?** If you already have what you need, you can take less risk. If you have much less than you need and have years for compounding to help, you can take more risk. If you have much less than you need and don't have years for compounding to help, it might be time to seek help from a financial planner.

10. **What's the rough, relative size of my financial needs over three, seven, and 10+ years?** It makes sense to keep money for short-term needs in less volatile assets. Money for medium and longer-term needs can be in more volatile assets. Thinking this out helps avoid all-or-nothing emotional extremes.

Hopefully, after pondering these questions, you'll have a better idea of the type of investor you are today and the kind of risk tolerance you have. Regardless of where you are, remember that it can change over time due to age, luck, choice, and circumstance.

Now that we have a feel for our risk tolerance and how it declines with age, let's start considering ways to invest. To keep things simple, let's start with the target-date fund.

Chapter 9
Elegant Simplicity — Target-Date Funds

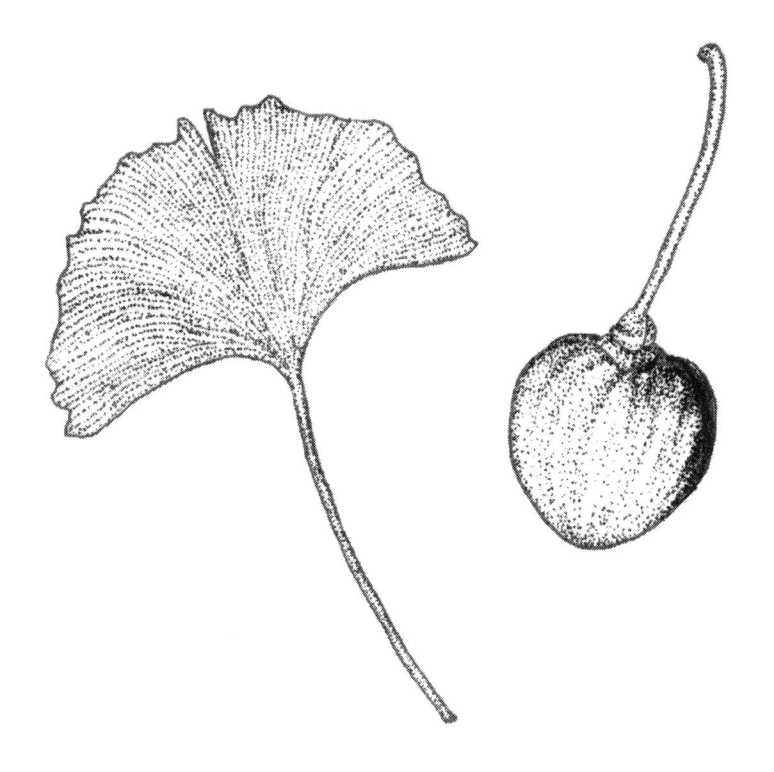

Ginkgo biloba — *Ginkgo trees have disease and insect-resistant wood and form aerial roots and sprouts, helping some to live more than 1,000 years.*

It's not surprising that we yearn for simplicity. Simple is easy and fast. Complex is hard and slow. Our family tree was pruned of those that valued complex and slow paths more highly long ago.

Wouldn't it be great if there was a single fund that included US and international stocks and a bond allocation that adjusts with age, so it's appropriate all the way from our early investing years through retirement till death? There is. It's the target-date fund.

Target-date funds are rapidly coming to dominate the retirement savings landscape in the US, and for good reason. They are often the default investment in employer 401(k) retirement savings programs, and they provide access to broad, globally diversified portfolios of age-appropriate, risk-adjusted investments at low cost. What's more, investors who use them have higher expected returns than those who don't. In a 2020 study, Professors Mitchell and Utkus from The Wharton School of the University of Pennsylvania found that investors who invested solely in target-date funds had a 2.3% higher expected annual portfolio return than investors who didn't use target-date funds. The reason was simple. Target-date funds nudged investors to hold more of their portfolio in stocks at younger ages.

Let's look at how a target-date fund is constructed, what it's supposed to do, and what it actually does.

As the name suggests, target-date funds are built around the year an investor targets to retire. If someone plans to retire on or around 2055, using Vanguard's funds, they should choose the Vanguard Target Retirement 2055 Fund (VFFVX). Since Vanguard is by far the market leader in this space, we'll use them as our reference. Figure 27 shows how they change their fund investments over time. This is called their "glide path." I've assumed a retirement age of 65 to make this more relatable, but their actual glide path is tied to the retirement year regardless of age.

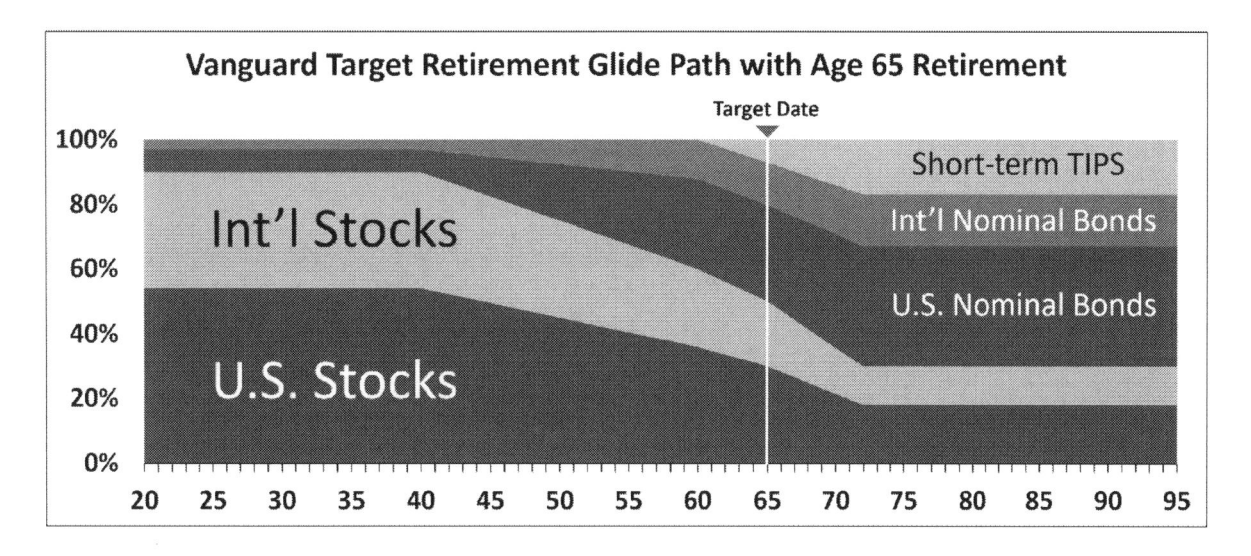

CHAPTER 9: ELEGANT SIMPLICITY — TARGET-DATE FUNDS

Figure 27. Vanguard target retirement glide path

Until 25 years before retirement, or age 40 in this example, the glide path is 90% in stocks and 10% in bonds. At that point, the bond percentage increases until they are 50% bonds at retirement and 70% bonds seven years later. There is also a shift to inflation-protected bonds in the later years, but the headline is that the more volatile stock percentage is declines while the less-volatile bond percentage increases. The genius bit is that these changes happen automatically in the background with no investor involvement. With a single investment decision, you can set yourself up for a lifetime of prudent investing.

So, let's see if the glide path maximizes risk in the early years and lowers it in the later years like it's supposed to.

To check, we'll look at two different examples: an investor who starts with a lump-sum investment in a Vanguard-like target-date fund and adds nothing to it, and an investor who starts with nothing and makes regular monthly contributions to the same target-date fund. Using the 1970 through 2019 return history with rolling start dates, how did the drawdown risks vary with age?

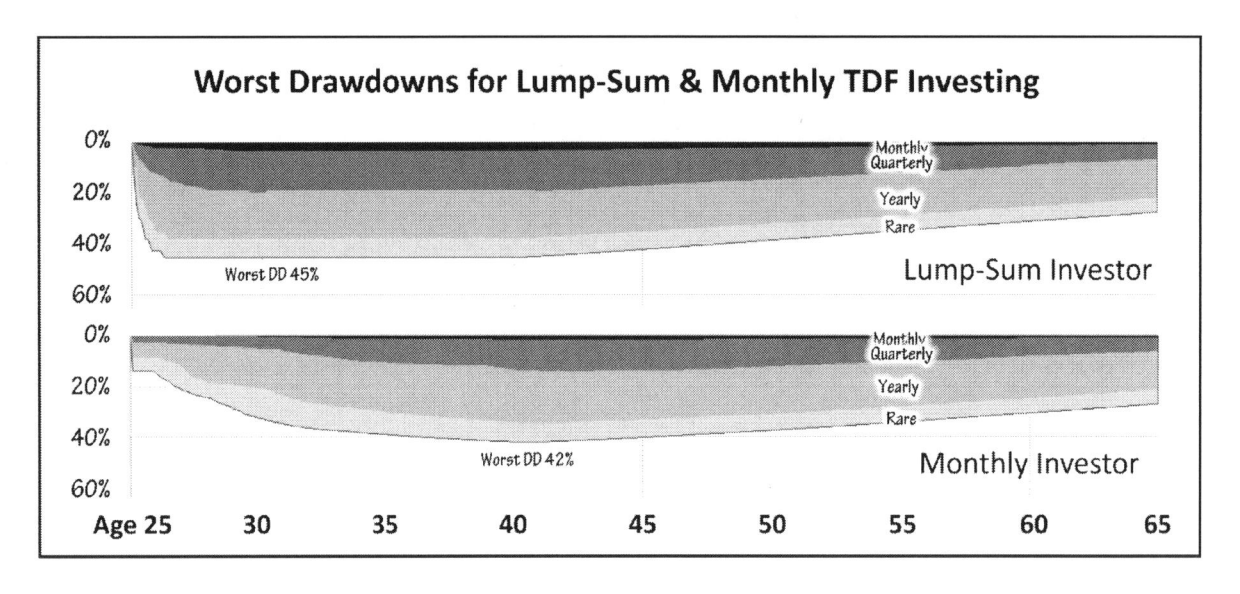

Figure 28. Worst drawdowns for lump-sum and monthly investing in Vanguard-like target-date fund (1970-2019)

For the lump-sum investor, the target-date glide path seems to be doing what it's supposed to. Risk starts high at age 25, stays high until about age 40, then declines until retirement. The worst drawdown is about 45% early on, and drawdown risk by retirement age is only about 28%. The problem is that most of us aren't lump-sum investors. Most of us start with little and save gradually. The bottom graph shows this monthly investor experience, and it's *very* different. Instead of risk starting high, it actually starts low. So low, in fact, that it's less than the risk we'll experience nearing retirement. For a young investor, that's a squandered opportunity. Instead of having some bonds in the early years, a young investor would do well to take more risk. The great news for young investors is that their investing experience starts with training wheels. Since they are always buying, they are always growing their investment. Since they buy every month, they are averaging prices over time, which reduces risk. And since they're buying roughly the same dollar amount every month, they're buying more shares when prices are low and fewer when prices are high.

If you still doubt this difference in drawdowns, let's look at what a lump-sum and monthly investor would have experienced had they invested in the Worldwide Total Stock Market starting in 1970:

CHAPTER 9: ELEGANT SIMPLICITY — TARGET-DATE FUNDS

Figure 29. Worldwide Total Stock Market drawdowns for lump-sum and monthly investments (1970-2019)

Figure 29 shows how much deeper the drawdowns were for a lump-sum investor than a monthly investor. Why does the monthly investor see so much shallower drawdowns? The answer is simple: contributions. When contributions are large relative to the size of the account, then the market's ups and downs become hard to see against the rising balance driven by contributions. If an investor has an account balance of $1,000, the market declines by 20%, and then they contribute $200, they might not even notice a market downturn. (For a more detailed discussion of the impact of contribution frequency on drawdowns, see Appendix 9.)

The other concern with the target-date fund glide path is that it has no exposure to the diversifying equity risk factors we looked at previously. All the stocks are in cap-weighted total stock market funds.

> **Target-date funds provide a globally diversified, risk-adjusted portfolio in a single fund, but they tend to be conservative and are weakly diversified across equity risk factors such as size and value.**

Target-date fund providers must be aware of these limitations, so why don't they change? It's probably for the same reason that they only offer target-date funds in five- or 10-year target-date increments. Customization costs money, so it's more practical to offer a one-size-fits-all solution, especially when they don't know anything about individual investors' risk tolerance. The good news is that we can address these concerns in a customized way by adding just one or two funds.

Chapter 10
Symbiosis — 2 Funds Combinations

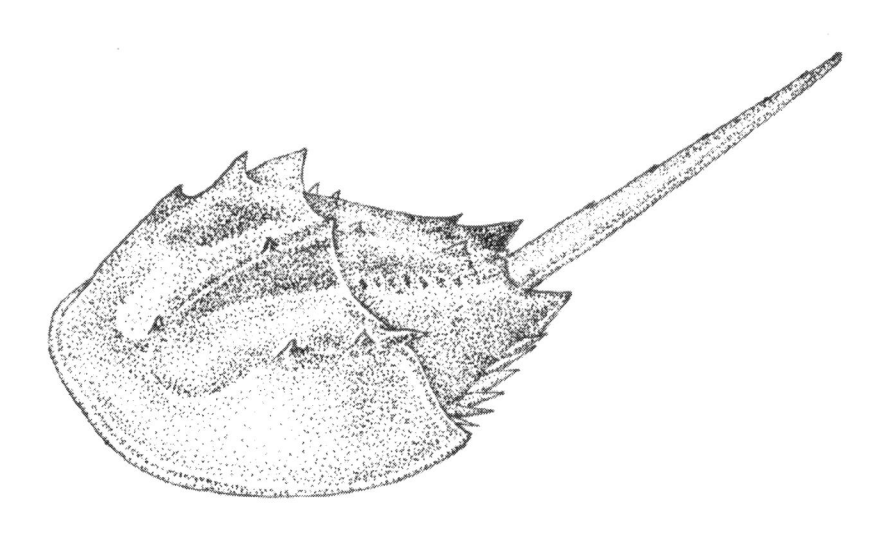

Family Limulidae — The horseshoe crab is recognizably similar to fossils more than 400 million years old, a testament to the fitness of its body plan.

Symbiosis is the mutually beneficial interaction of different organisms. For example, bees and birds harvest nectar from flowers while pollinating them in the process. Asset classes can be symbiotic too.

By combining conservative target-date funds with more aggressive and factor-diverse small-cap value funds, we can increase expected returns per unit of risk, control when that risk occurs, increase safe withdrawal rates, and decrease the chance of running out of money in retirement.

Since we know that different strategies can lag the market for a long time (see Figure 24), let's start small and see what happens if we only invest 10% in small-cap value and the remaining 90% in the target-date fund.

To keep things simple and accommodate investors who don't have access to a good small-cap value fund in their retirement savings account, let's assume there is no rebalancing during accumulation. Since rebalancing requires selling one asset to buy another, that would require transferring money between accounts, which might not be possible.

In an ideal world, the investor would set up paycheck withdrawals so that 90% of their total annual retirement savings goes into the primary retirement account where it's automatically invested in a target-date fund, and the other 10% of the retirement savings goes into a second account where it's automatically invested in a US small-cap value fund. To keep things comparable, we'll assume that total contributions are $10k/year (made in monthly contributions) and increase with inflation for 40 years.

Once the investor retires, we'll assume they multiply the account balance by 4% and use that as their fixed withdrawal rate, increasing it each year for inflation through 30 years of retirement. These are called "fixed withdrawals" in the world of finance, even though they increase with inflation.

During retirement, they'll use nudge withdrawals, taking their annual withdrawals from whichever fund is over its intended allocation. If the target-date fund is over 90%, they'll take from it. If the small-cap value fund is over 10%, they'll take from it. It's not as complicated as rebalancing, but it nudges things back toward their desired allocations over time. Not only is it simpler than traditional rebalancing, but it's also less emotional because there's no need to sell what's been winning lately to buy

CHAPTER 10: SYMBIOSIS — 2 FUNDS COMBINATIONS

what's been losing. (See Appendix 10 for more on nudge withdrawals versus annual rebalancing).

Here's the backtest for this *Easy* 2 Funds for Life strategy:

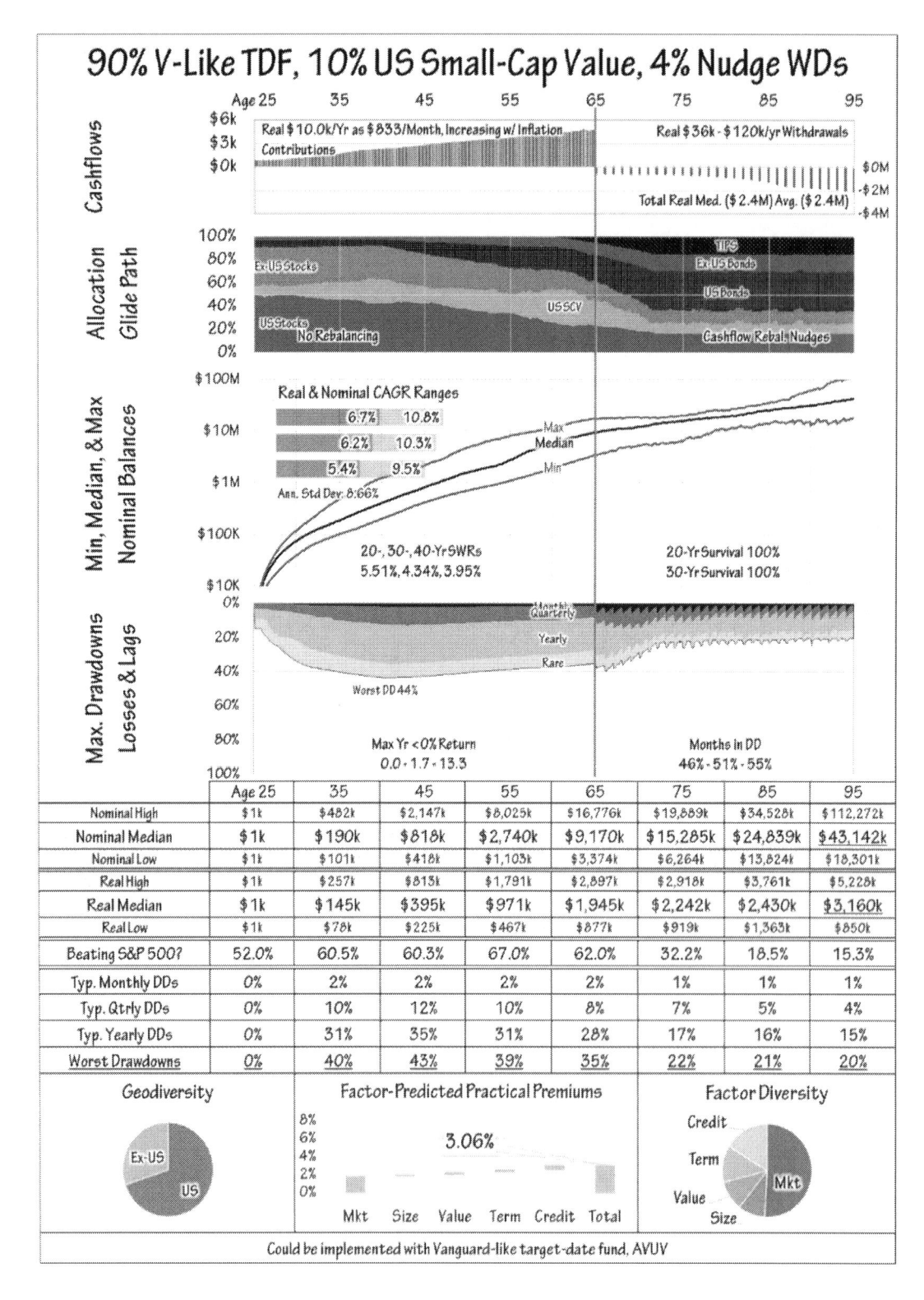

Figure 30. Backtest of Easy 2 Funds for Life strategy

This 90% TDF|10% US-SCV approach is quite a bit better than either the 100% TDF or Buffett approach. In many respects, it's the best of both worlds. It has a 100% 30-year survival rate, keeps risk decreasing with age into retirement, and improves on both approaches in terms of factor diversification, minimum end balances, and total dollars withdrawn. Yes, the median real end balance for this approach was about $3.16M instead of $4.29M for the Buffett strategy, but this approach never ran out of money and had a 15% chance of beating the S&P 500 at age 95, compared to a 0% chance for the Buffett strategy and all-TDF strategy. A 15% chance of beating the S&P 500 might not sound like much, but the S&P 500 is much more volatile, with worst-case drawdowns of 50% to 100% between ages 55 and 95. If someone pressed me to offer a solution as simple and relevant as Buffet's, I think this would be it.

As inspiring and exciting as the nominal inflated end balances are, we'll see our future more clearly if we continue to focus on the real end balance ranges and real withdrawals, so that's what's included in the summary tables.

	Real End Balance Range	Median Real WDs	Worst Peak DD & Age	Worst DD @ 65, 95	40-Year SWR	30-Year, Survival %	% of Times > S&P 500
Buffett strategy Fixed 90 | 10 S&P 500 | ST Bonds	$6.61M $4.29M $0k	$2.1M 70k/yr	100% @ 90	46% 100%	2.52%	98%	0%
Vanguard-Like Target-Date Fund	$3.57M $2.18M $588k	$2.2M $73k/yr	42% @ 40	27% 24%	3.84%	100%	0%
Easy 2FFL Fixed 90 | 10 TDF | US SCV	$5.23M $3.16M $850k	$2.4M $80k/yr	44% @ 40	35% 20%	3.95%	100%	15%

Table 7. Comparison of Buffett strategy, Vanguard-like target-date fund, and easy 2 Funds for Life strategies

Looking at Table 7, it's clear that the downside to the unrebalanced 90|10 2 Funds for Life approach is that risk can grow nearing retirement. Since we're not rebalancing, there's a good chance that the 10% allocation to US small-cap value will grow faster than the rest of the portfolio, leading to increased volatility. One way to deal with this is to vary the allocation to this second fund with age or the remaining years to retirement.

A good place to start would be a multiplier that puts a newborn 100% in the second fund and a retiree 100% in the target-date fund. Since traditional retirement is around age 65, a 1.5× multiplier comes close. If we put 1.5 × YTR as a percentage in the small-cap value fund, at 40 years to retirement (around age 25), that would be 60%. At 20 years to retirement (age 45), it would be 30%, and at retirement (age 65), it would be 0%.

If we assume traditional annual rebalancing until the second fund goes to zero, we get the glide path shown in Figure 31:

CHAPTER 10: SYMBIOSIS — 2 FUNDS COMBINATIONS

"Moderate" 2 Funds for Life — Ret. @ 65

[Glide path chart: Second Fund starts at 60% at age 20, declining linearly to 0% at age 65; Target-Date Fund is the complement. Annual Rebalancing.]

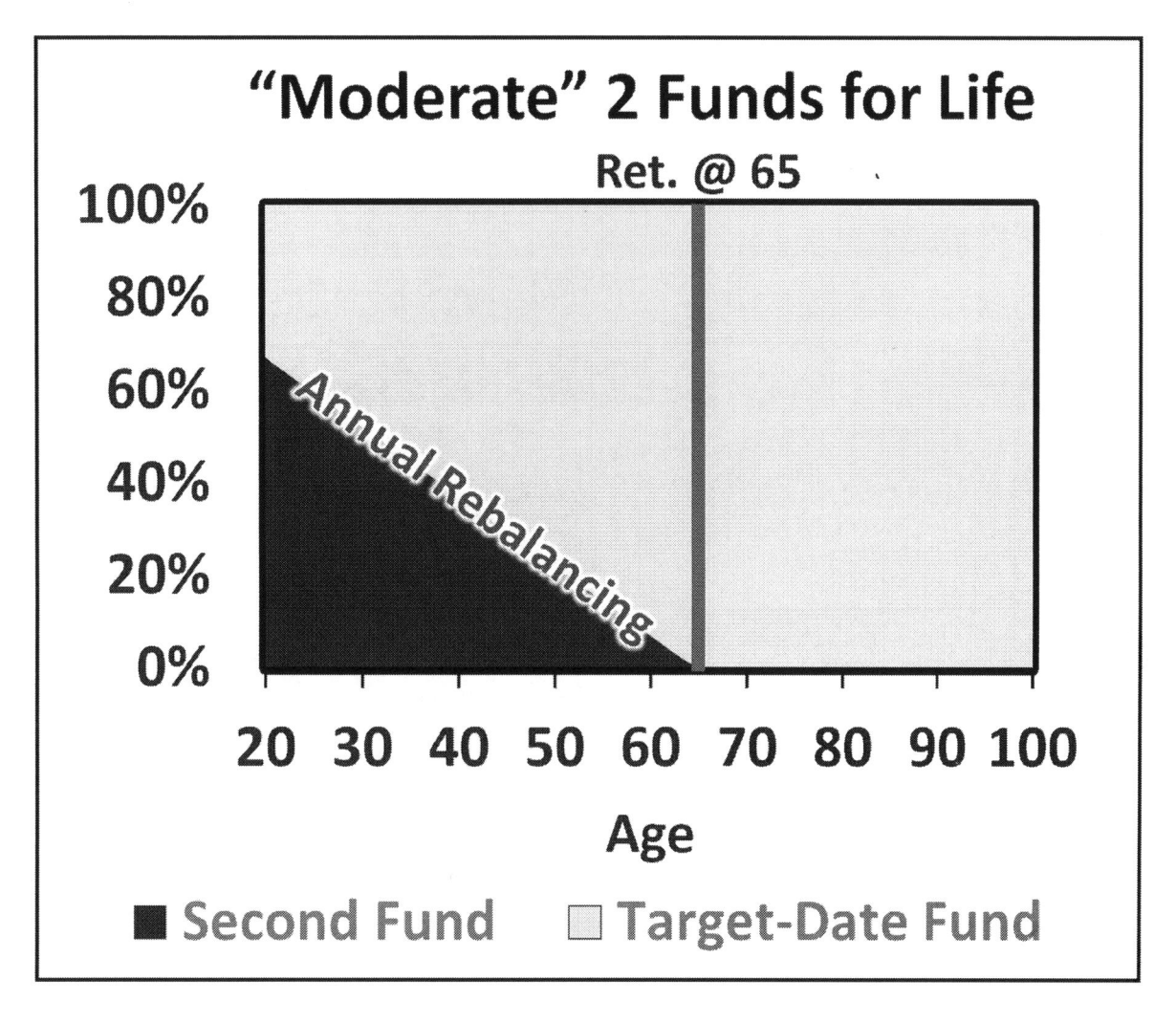

Figure 31. Moderate 2 Funds for Life glide path

If you don't want to do the math, you can find year-by-year allocations for this and the other age-based strategies in Appendix 12.

Let's see how this Moderate 2 Funds for Life approach would have done in the past:

1.5 × YTR in US SCV, Rest in V-Like TDF, 4% Fixed WDs

Cashflows: Real $10.0k/Yr as $833/Month, increasing w/ Inflation Contributions; Real $38k - $130k/yr Withdrawals; Total Real Med. ($2.7M) Avg. ($2.6M)

Allocation Glide Path: US SCV, Ex-US Stocks, US Stocks, Yearly Rebalancing, US Bonds, Ex-US Bonds, TIPS

Min, Median, & Max Nominal Balances: Real & Nominal CAGR Ranges 6.9% / 10.9%, 6.2% / 10.3%, 5.3% / 9.5%; Ann. Std Dev: 9.51%; 20-, 30-, 40-Yr SWRs 5.27%, 4.43%, 3.84%; 20-Yr Survival 100%; 30-Yr Survival 100%

Max. Drawdowns Losses & Lags: Monthly, Quarterly, Yearly, Rare; Worst DD 47%; Max Yr <0% Return 0.0 - 2.1 - 12.4; Months in DD 48% - 52% - 55%

	Age 25	35	45	55	65	75	85	95
Nominal High	$1k	$512k	$2,625k	$9,798k	$17,990k	$21,793k	$33,456k	$93,104k
Nominal Median	$1k	$218k	$943k	$3,150k	$10,206k	$15,624k	$23,519k	$36,744k
Nominal Low	$1k	$101k	$386k	$1,192k	$4,079k	$6,627k	$12,717k	$13,010k
Real High	$1k	$274k	$892k	$2,186k	$3,104k	$3,197k	$3,308k	$4,344k
Real Median	$1k	$158k	$446k	$1,120k	$2,186k	$2,292k	$2,330k	$2,828k
Real Low	$1k	$69k	$208k	$504k	$916k	$972k	$1,280k	$754k
Beating S&P 500?	52.8%	60.8%	74.0%	89.2%	77.0%	58.5%	29.7%	25.5%
Typ. Monthly DDs	0%	2%	2%	2%	1%	1%	1%	1%
Typ. Qtrly DDs	0%	11%	12%	10%	6%	5%	5%	6%
Typ. Yearly DDs	0%	33%	36%	30%	22%	16%	14%	18%
Worst Drawdowns	0%	46%	45%	38%	28%	20%	19%	24%

Geodiversity: Ex-US, US

Factor-Predicted Practical Premiums: 2.53% (Mkt, Size, Value, Term, Credit, Total)

Factor Diversity: Credit, Mkt, Term, Value, Size

Could be implemented with Vanguard-like target-date fund, AVUV

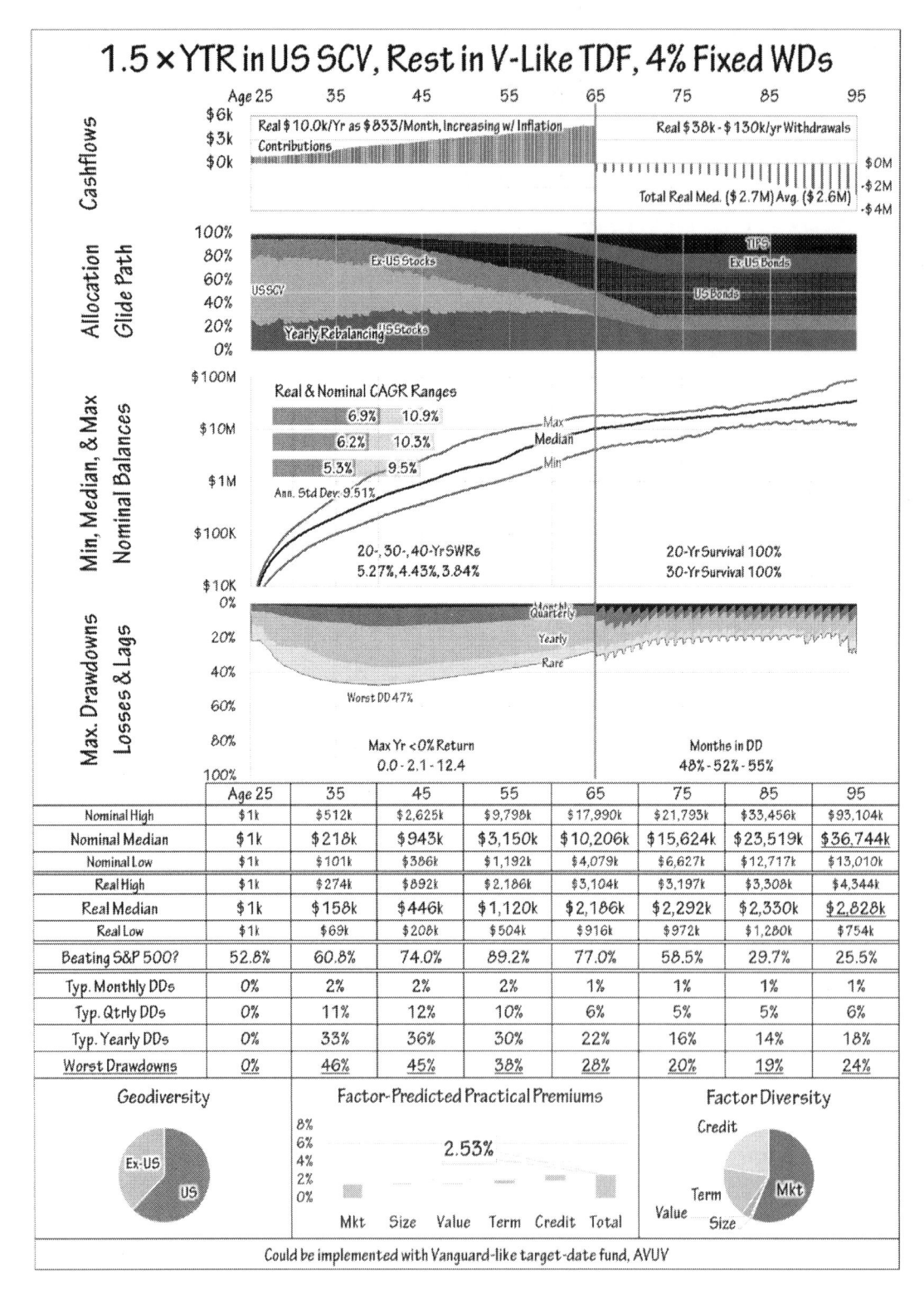

Figure 32. Backtest of Moderate 2 Funds for Life strategy

Using 1.5 × YTR as a percentage to scale the amount invested in the target-date fund worked as intended. Instead of having our worst-case drawdowns occurring near retirement, they now occur around age 40. The approach outperformed the plain target-date fund in every respect except drawdowns, where it's 5% worse in the early-year peak and 1% worse around retirement. Those slightly larger drawdowns produced a 30% higher median end balance, 23% higher median withdrawals, and a 26% chance of having a final end balance that beat the much riskier S&P 500. The end balances are much lower than the easy 2 Funds for Life strategy, though. That's because the Vanguard target-date retirement glide path is very conservative in retirement, with only 30% in equities and no exposure to diversifying risk factors such as small and value.

Something surprising is that the factor diversity pie shows very little exposure to size and value. The reason is that it reflects the dollar-weighted total, and the heavy tilts to small and value are in the early years when the size of the portfolio is small. By the time the account balance is large, we're ramping down the small-cap value fund and only getting market risk from the equities and credit and term risk from the bonds in the target-date fund.

	Real End Balance Range	Median Real WDs	Worst Peak DD & Age	Worst DD @ 65, 95	40-Year SWR	30-Year, Survival %	% of Times > S&P 500
Buffett strategy Fixed 90 | 10 S&P 500 | ST Bonds	$6.61M $4.29M $0k	$2.1M 70k/yr	100% @ 90	46% 100%	2.52%	98%	0%
Vanguard-Like Target-date Fund	$3.57M $2.18M $588k	$2.2M $73k/yr	42% @ 40	27% 24%	3.84%	100%	0%
Easy 2FFL Fixed 90 | 10 TDF | US SCV	$5.23M $3.16M $850k	$2.4M $80k/yr	44% @ 40	35% 20%	3.95%	100%	15%
Moderate 2FFL 1.5 X YTR in US SCV, Rest in V-Like TDF	$4.34M $2.83M $754k	$2.7M $90k/yr	47% @ 40	28% 24%	3.84%	100%	26%

Table 8. Comparison of Buffett strategy, Vanguard-like target-date fund, Easy 2 Funds for Life, and Moderate 2 Funds for Life strategies

So, how can we compensate for the conservatism of the target-date fund in the later years and the limited factor exposure from the small balances in the early years?

The answer is simple. Instead of letting the small-cap value fund allocation go to zero at retirement, we set a minimum percentage floor for the second fund. Instead of multiplying YTR by 1.5, we multiply it by 2.5. The allocation floor should compensate for the conservatism of the target-date fund in the later years, and the steeper age-scaled ramp will give us higher exposure to the second fund in the early years. Since we'll have two funds in retirement, we'll use nudge withdrawals. Here's how all three approaches look:

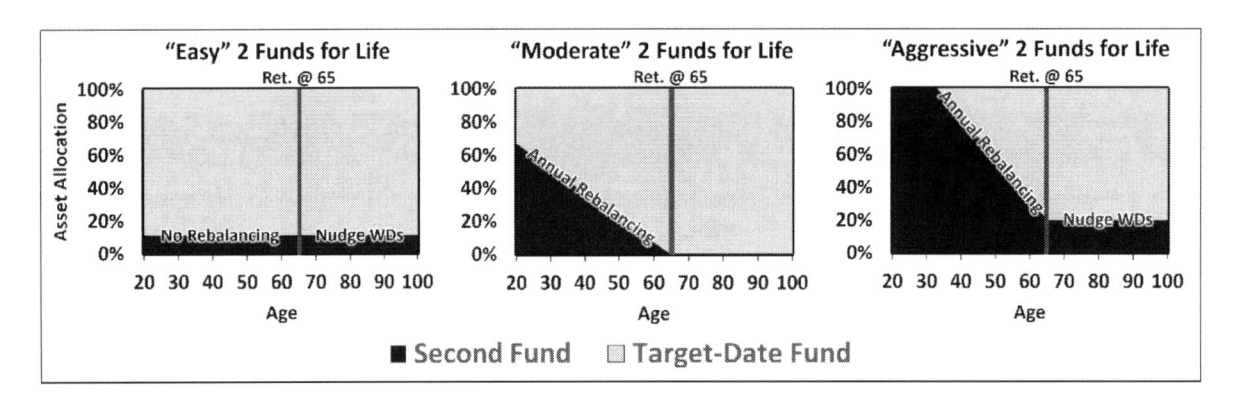

Figure 33. Easy, Moderate, and Aggressive 2 Funds for Life glide paths

Let's see how this *Aggressive* 2 Funds for Life strategy did in the backtest:

CHAPTER 10: SYMBIOSIS — 2 FUNDS COMBINATIONS

2.5 × YTR + 20% in US SCV, Rest in V-Like TDF, 4% Nudge WDs

Cashflows: Real $10.0k/Yr as $833/Month, Increasing w/ Inflation Contributions. Real $52k-$213k/yr Withdrawals. Total Real Med. ($3.6M) Avg. ($3.8M)

Allocation Glide Path: US SCV, Yearly Rebalancing, Ex-US Stocks, US Stocks, US Bonds, Ex-US Bonds, TIPS, Cashflow Rebal. Nudges

Min, Median, & Max Nominal Balances: Real & Nominal CAGR Ranges: 8.5%–12.6%, 7.3%–11.4%, 6.5%–10.7%. Ann. Std Dev: 13.31%. 20-, 30-, 40-Yr SWRs: 5.89%, 4.71%, 4.36%. 20-Yr Survival 100%, 30-Yr Survival 100%.

Max. Drawdowns Losses & Lags: Monthly, Quarterly, Yearly, Rare. Worst DD 56%. Max Yr <0% Return 0.0 - 4.5 - 15.3. Months in DD 52% - 57% - 61%.

	Age 25	35	45	55	65	75	85	95
Nominal High	$1k	$750k	$3,329k	$13,279k	$30,010k	$38,167k	$74,105k	$279,067k
Nominal Median	$1k	$246k	$1,169k	$4,043k	$13,605k	$24,683k	$45,459k	$89,037k
Nominal Low	$1k	$86k	$325k	$1,161k	$4,712k	$10,762k	$29,143k	$46,637k
Real High	$1k	$333k	$1,054k	$2,963k	$5,182k	$5,599k	$6,478k	$15,955k
Real Median	$1k	$175k	$567k	$1,430k	$2,901k	$3,621k	$4,686k	$6,713k
Real Low	$1k	$57k	$175k	$491k	$1,282k	$1,579k	$2,928k	$2,727k
Beating S&P 500?	52.3%	67.3%	78.8%	99.3%	100.0%	98.5%	100.0%	100.0%
Typ. Monthly DDs	0%	5%	5%	3%	2%	2%	1%	1%
Typ. Qtrly DDs	0%	19%	18%	14%	8%	8%	7%	7%
Typ. Yearly DDs	0%	40%	42%	36%	27%	21%	20%	21%
Worst Drawdowns	0%	55%	54%	46%	34%	27%	27%	29%

Geodiversity: Ex-US, US

Factor-Predicted Practical Premiums: 3.99% — Mkt, Size, Value, Term, Credit, Total

Factor Diversity: Credit, Term, Value, Size, Mkt

Could be implemented with Vanguard-like target-date fund, AVUV

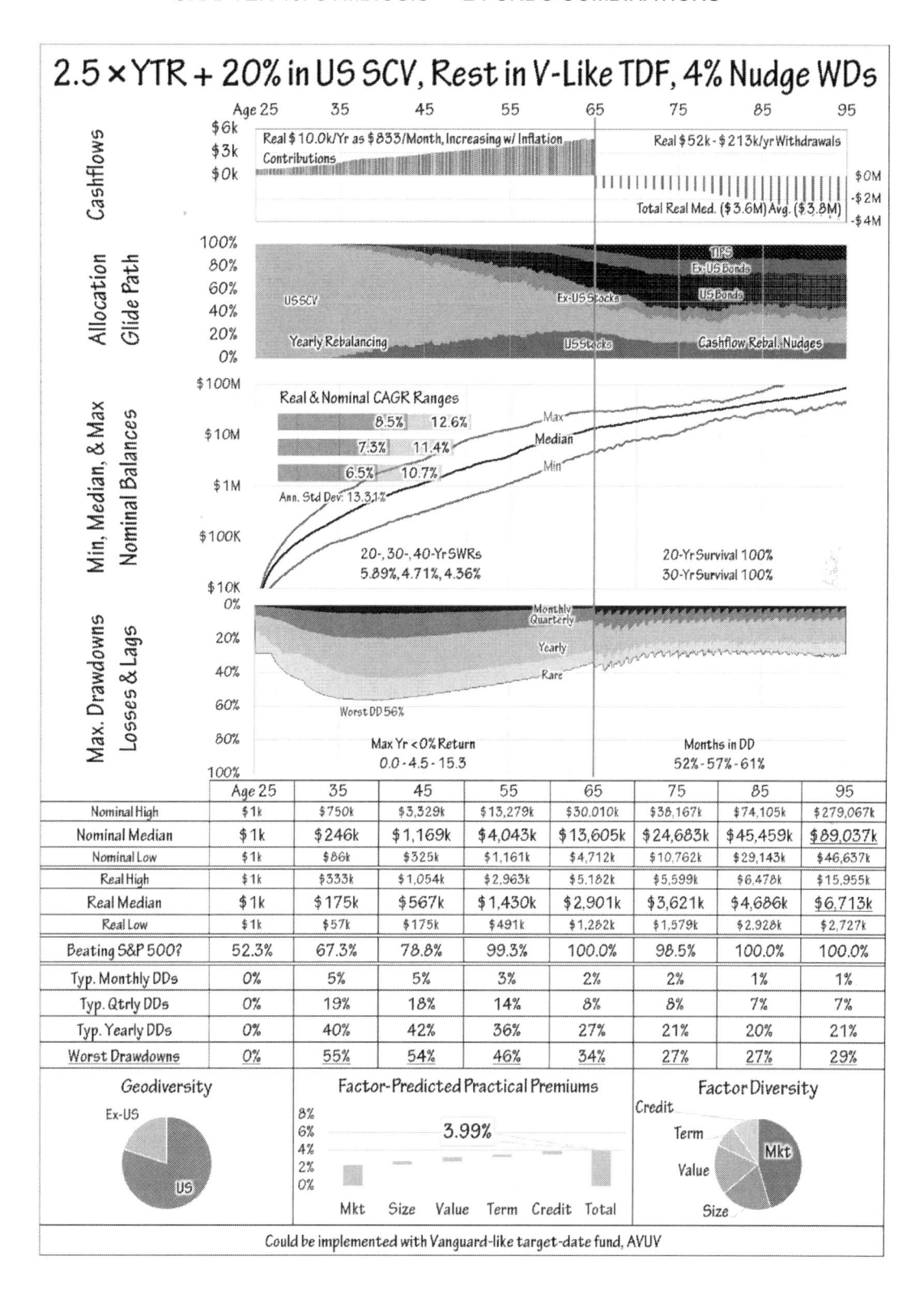

Figure 34. Backtest of Aggressive 2 Funds for Life strategy

Adding the minimum allocation floor of 20% and a steeper 2.5 × YTR ramp looks to have had the desired effects. Factor diversification increased substantially along with the real median end balance range, total withdrawals, and safe withdrawal rate; and the chance of beating the much riskier S&P 500 at age 95 increased to 100%. Of course, those benefits came at the cost of having to tolerate a bumpier ride. The worst peak drawdowns increased from 47% to 56% at age 40, from 28% to 34% at age 65, and from 24% to 29% at age 95. Would it have been worth it? For the investor who could stick with it, I think the answer is a decisive yes. There are definite rewards to be had for investors who can learn to ignore short-term ups and downs, but if that's not you, it's critical to pick something that's a better fit.

We now have three different 2 Funds for Life strategies. The 90|10 is *Easy*, the 1.5 × YTR is *Moderate*, and the 2.5 × YTR + 20% is *Aggressive*. We could explore infinite variations, but we'll use these three for the rest of the book. You'll find a wider range of options explored in Appendix 1.

	Real End Balance Range	Median Real WDs	Worst Peak DD & Age	Worst DD @ 65, 95	40-Year SWR	30-Year, Survival %	% of Times > S&P 500
Buffett strategy Fixed 90 | 10 S&P 500 | ST Bonds	$6.61M $4.29M $0k	$2.1M 70k/yr	100% @ 90	46% 100%	2.52%	98%	0%
Vanguard-Like Target-date Fund	$3.57M $2.18M $588k	$2.2M $73k/yr	42% @ 40	27% 24%	3.84%	100%	0%
Easy 2FFL Fixed 90 | 10 TDF | US SCV	$5.23M $3.16M $850k	$2.4M $80k/yr	44% @ 40	35% 20%	3.95%	100%	15%
Moderate 2FFL 1.5 X YTR in US SCV, Rest in V-Like TDF	$4.34M $2.83M $754k	$2.7M $90k/yr	47% @ 40	28% 24%	3.84%	100%	26%
Aggressive 2FFL 2.5 X YTR + 20% in US SCV, Rest in V-Like TDF	$15.96 $6.71M $2.73M	$3.6M $120k/yr	56% @ 40	34% 29%	4.36%	100%	100%

Table 9. Comparison of Buffett strategy; Vanguard-like target-date fund; Easy, Moderate, and Aggressive 2 Funds for Life strategies

These examples show how tolerating higher early drawdowns would have increased retirement income and tolerating higher later drawdowns would have increased retirement resilience and end balances.

One concern with the 2 Funds for Life approaches as described is that they are only weakly diversified across countries. By taking a 60% US target-date fund such as Vanguard and then adding a US small-cap value fund to it, we end up with little international exposure in the overall investor experience. In the next chapter, we'll explore ways to get more international diversification by using an international small-cap value fund or a combination of US and international funds.

Chapter 11
Intermediates — 3-Fund Combinations

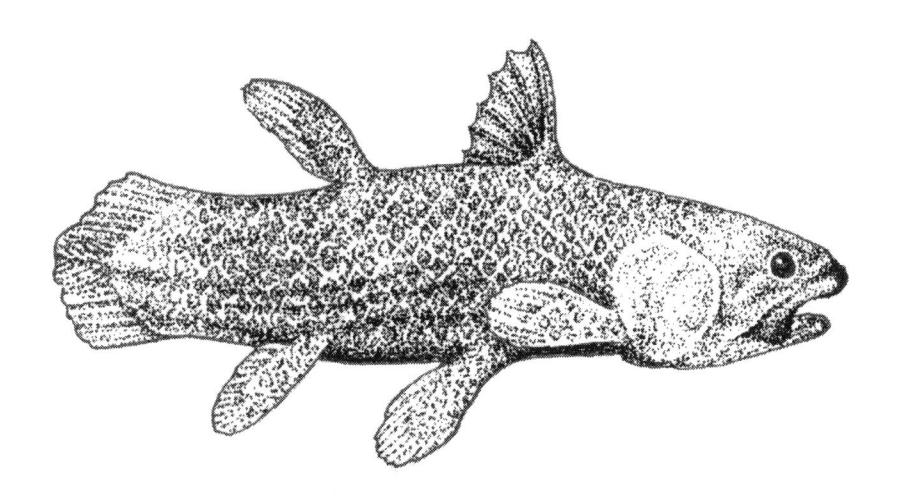

Coelacanth *— This order can live 60+ years and is an intermediate form more closely related to terrestrial vertebrates than to ray-finned fish.*

As animals are hemmed in by the loss of habitat, their likelihood of extinction increases. Do the US-centric 2 Funds for Life strategies we just developed increase our chances of financial extinction? Would including a third fund reduce the risk?

For investors interested in broad geographic diversification, using an international small-cap value fund in addition to a US small-cap value fund makes sense.

To see how, we'll redo the backtests of our 2 Funds for Life strategies using a combination of both US and international small-cap value funds.

We'll use the same scenario assumptions as before with a slight modification to the nudge withdrawals to accommodate three funds. If the target-date fund is above its desired allocation, we'll still take from it the entire withdrawal. But if the target-date fund is below its desired allocation, we'll take the entire withdrawal from the larger of the two small-cap value funds. We'll use a 50|50 split for the US and international small-cap value funds. Since the safe withdrawal rates and drawdowns are remarkably similar, we'll focus on the changes to the median real end balance ranges, real total withdrawals, and geographic splits. Table 10 compares the US small-cap-value-only approach to the 3-fund solution using the US and international (WW, or worldwide) small-cap value funds.

	US-Only SCV Median Real End Balances	US | Int'l SCV Median Real End Balances	US-Only SCV Median Real WDs	US | Int'l SCV Median Real WDs	US-Only SCV Lifetime Portfolio US %	US | Int'l SCV Lifetime Portfolio US %
Easy 2FFL Fixed 90 | 10 TDF | US or WW SCV	$5.23M $3.16M $850k	$5.90M $3.34M $639K	$2.4M $80k/yr	$2.6M ~$87k/yr	<u>72%</u>	<u>57%</u>
Moderate 2FFL 1.5 X YTR in US or WW SCV, Rest in Vanguard-Like TDF	$4.34M $2.83M $754k	$4.31M $2.86M $823k	$2.7M $90k/yr	$2.8M ~$93k/yr	<u>65%</u>	<u>60%</u>
Aggressive 2FFL 2.5 X YTR + 20% in US or WW SCV, Rest in Vanguard-Like TDF	$15.96 $6.71M $2.73M	$17.5M $7.51M $3.85M	$3.6M $120k/yr	$4.2M ~$140k/yr	<u>81%</u>	<u>57%</u>

Table 10. Comparison of 2 Funds for Life strategies utilizing US small-cap value versus a combination of US and international small-cap value for the second fund

Splitting the second fund into 50% US small-cap value and 50% international small-cap value reduced the average lifetime US allocation significantly, but not to the point of eliminating the US tilt of the target-date fund. Instead of 65% to 81% US equities when using US-only small-cap value, we get a range of 57% to 62% US equities using the combination of US and international small-cap value. The combination also increased median real end balances and total withdrawals by about 1% to 15% without substantially increasing drawdown risks.

Using the US and international small-cap value combination increased geographic diversification and returns without increasing drawdowns significantly.

Although we've only modeled the all-US and 50|50 US-international combinations for second funds, investors could adopt combinations that are in between to fine-tune their desired level of geographic diversification. The one thing to be careful of is using nudge withdrawals when the allocation percentage of any given fund at retirement is near the withdrawal percentage. If that's the case, you can end up unintentionally driving a fund allocation to zero. That's why we've only used the 4% nudge withdrawals with strategies that have at least a 5%, and ideally 10%, or greater minimum allocation.

Today, these approaches require three funds to implement. With the rapid growth in funds, we might not have to wait long for a low-cost, recommendable, global small-cap value fund to appear. At that point, this becomes a feasible 2 Funds for Life solution. In the meantime, some of you are probably asking, "What would happen if we just used international small-cap value for the second fund?" Would it tilt too much toward international or just compensate for the US-centric tilt of the target-date fund? Table 11 summarizes the backtests of these options:

	US-Only SCV Real End Balance Range	Int'l-Only SCV Real End Balance Range	US-Only SCV Median Real WDs	Int'l-Only SCV Median Real WDs	US-Only SCV Lifetime Portfolio US %	Int'l-Only SCV Lifetime Portfolio US %
Easy 2FFL Fixed 90 | 10 TDF | US or Int'l SCV	$5.23M **$3.16M** $850k	$5.93M **$3.25M** $677K	**$2.4M** $80k/yr	**$2.6M** $87k/yr	<u>72%</u>	<u>44%</u>
Moderate 2FFL 1.5 X YTR in US or Int'l SCV, Rest in V-Like TDF	$4.34M **$2.83M** $754k	$4.84M **$2.77M** $875k	**$2.7M** $90k/yr	**$2.8M** $93k/yr	<u>65%</u>	<u>57%</u>
Aggressive 2FFL 2.5 X YTR + 20% in US or Int'l SCV, Rest in V-Like TDF	$15.96 **$6.71M** $2.73M	$19.4M **$6.87M** $3.33M	**$3.6M** $120k/yr	**$4.6M** $153k/yr	<u>81%</u>	<u>29%</u>

Table 11. Comparison of 2 Funds for Life strategies utilizing US small-cap value versus international small-cap value for the second fund

Using an international small-cap value fund for the Easy 2 Funds for Life strategy produced a 44% median lifetime allocation to the US. Using the same approach for the Moderate 2 Funds for Life strategy reduced the US allocation to 59%. The reason it made a smaller difference for the moderate approach is that the second fund allocation is largest in the early years when the account balance is relatively small. The opposite is true for the Aggressive 2 Funds for Life strategy. Using an all-international small-cap value fund for the Aggressive strategy reduced the median lifetime US allocation to only 29%. Using a mix of US and international small-cap value funds for the Aggressive strategy produced a median lifetime US allocation of 57% (see Table 10), which is probably more palatable to most US investors.

Moving all of the US small-cap value allocation to an international fund also increased overall returns. The real end balance ranges and median real withdrawals increased across the board. Since we have no reason to believe that international developed markets should outperform the US or vice versa, over the long term, it's probably best to see this outperformance as a quirk of the timeframe tested. Still, it's good to see that we wouldn't have been penalized for having been more geographically diversified.

CHAPTER 11: INTERMEDIATES — 3-FUND COMBINATIONS

It's also good to see how we can diversify across both factors and geography with only two or three funds.

The 2 Funds for Life strategies are looking good, but so far we've only compared them to other simple strategies. How would they compare to more complex approaches? Are we sacrificing a lot of performance for simplicity, or is complexity unnecessary? That's what we'll explore next.

Here are the detailed backtests for the scenarios discussed in this chapter:

90% in V-Like TDF, 10% in US|Int'l SCV, 4% Nudge WDs

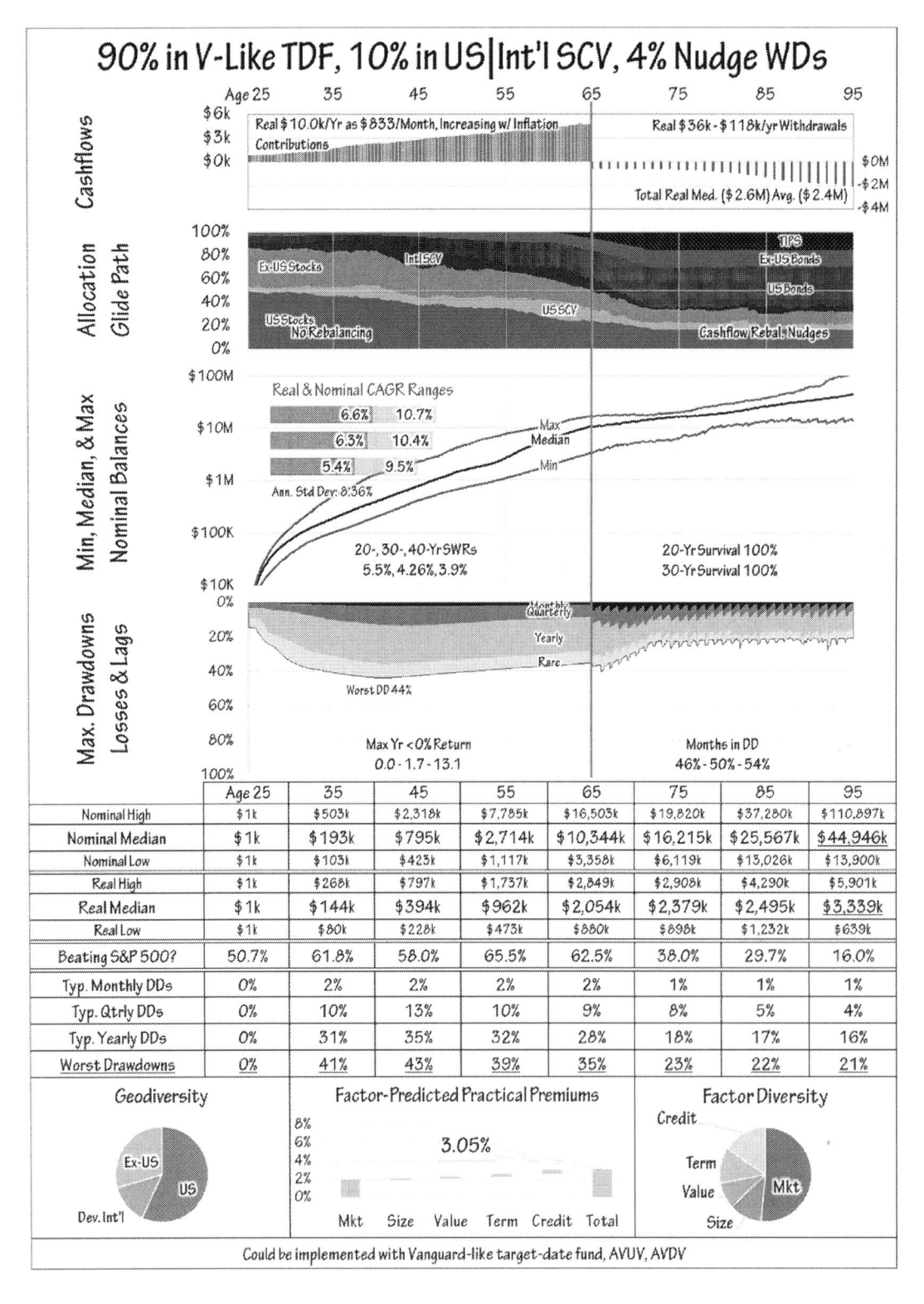

	Age 25	35	45	55	65	75	85	95
Nominal High	$1k	$503k	$2,318k	$7,785k	$16,503k	$19,820k	$37,280k	$110,897k
Nominal Median	$1k	$193k	$795k	$2,714k	$10,344k	$16,215k	$25,567k	$44,946k
Nominal Low	$1k	$103k	$423k	$1,117k	$3,358k	$6,119k	$13,026k	$13,900k
Real High	$1k	$268k	$797k	$1,737k	$2,849k	$2,908k	$4,290k	$5,901k
Real Median	$1k	$144k	$394k	$962k	$2,054k	$2,379k	$2,495k	$3,339k
Real Low	$1k	$80k	$228k	$473k	$880k	$898k	$1,232k	$639k
Beating S&P 500?	50.7%	61.8%	58.0%	65.5%	62.5%	38.0%	29.7%	16.0%
Typ. Monthly DDs	0%	2%	2%	2%	2%	1%	1%	1%
Typ. Qtrly DDs	0%	10%	13%	10%	9%	8%	5%	4%
Typ. Yearly DDs	0%	31%	35%	32%	28%	18%	17%	16%
Worst Drawdowns	0%	41%	43%	39%	35%	23%	22%	21%

Could be implemented with Vanguard-like target-date fund, AVUV, AVDV

Figure 35. Backtest of Easy 2 Funds for Life strategy using a combination of US and international small-cap value

CHAPTER 11: INTERMEDIATES — 3-FUND COMBINATIONS

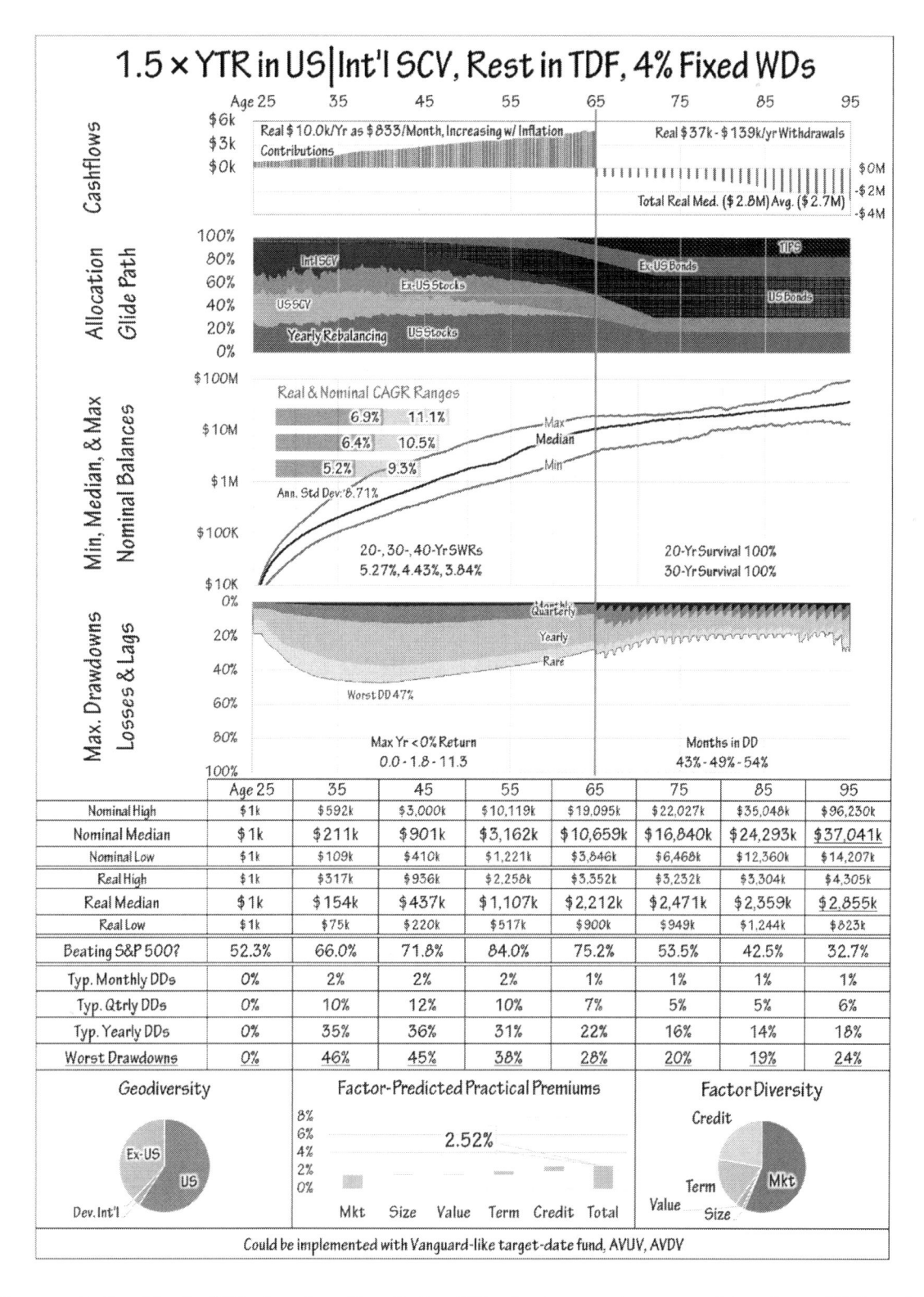

1.5 × YTR in US|Int'l SCV, Rest in TDF, 4% Fixed WDs

	Age 25	35	45	55	65	75	85	95
Nominal High	$1k	$592k	$3,000k	$10,119k	$19,095k	$22,027k	$35,048k	$96,230k
Nominal Median	$1k	$211k	$901k	$3,162k	$10,659k	$16,840k	$24,293k	$37,041k
Nominal Low	$1k	$109k	$410k	$1,221k	$3,846k	$6,468k	$12,360k	$14,207k
Real High	$1k	$317k	$936k	$2,258k	$3,552k	$3,252k	$3,304k	$4,305k
Real Median	$1k	$154k	$437k	$1,107k	$2,212k	$2,471k	$2,359k	$2,855k
Real Low	$1k	$75k	$220k	$517k	$900k	$949k	$1,244k	$823k
Beating S&P 500?	52.3%	66.0%	71.8%	84.0%	75.2%	53.5%	42.5%	32.7%
Typ. Monthly DDs	0%	2%	2%	2%	1%	1%	1%	1%
Typ. Qtrly DDs	0%	10%	12%	10%	7%	5%	5%	6%
Typ. Yearly DDs	0%	35%	36%	31%	22%	16%	14%	18%
Worst Drawdowns	0%	46%	45%	38%	28%	20%	19%	24%

Could be implemented with Vanguard-like target-date fund, AVUV, AVDV

Figure 36. Backtest of Moderate 2 Funds for Life strategy using a combination of US and international small-cap value

2.5 × YTR + 20% in US|Int'l SCV, Rest in TDF, 4% Nudge WDs

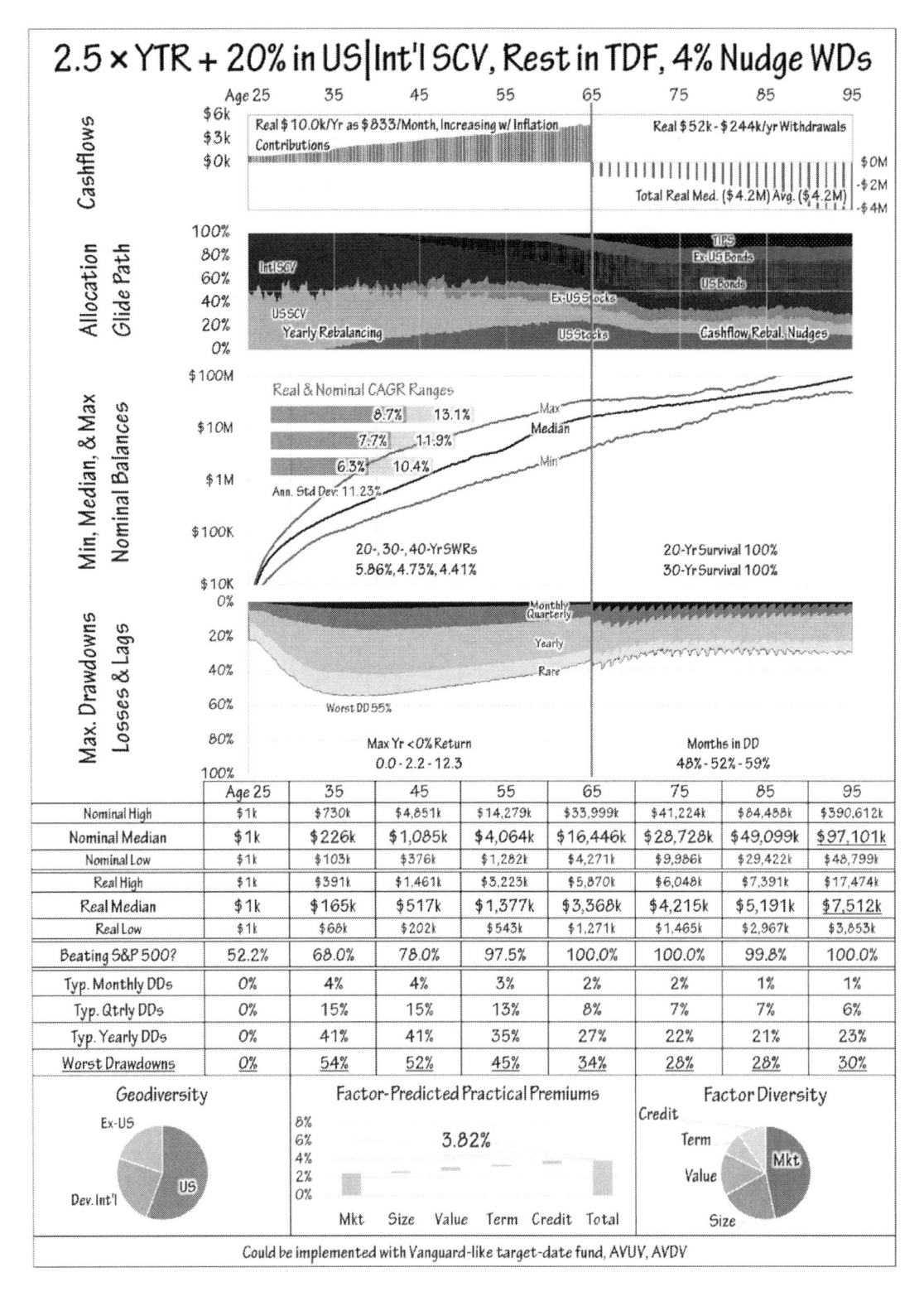

	Age 25	35	45	55	65	75	85	95
Nominal High	$1k	$730k	$4,851k	$14,279k	$33,999k	$41,224k	$84,488k	$390,612k
Nominal Median	$1k	$226k	$1,085k	$4,064k	$16,446k	$28,728k	$49,099k	$97,101k
Nominal Low	$1k	$103k	$376k	$1,282k	$4,271k	$9,986k	$29,422k	$48,799k
Real High	$1k	$391k	$1,461k	$3,223k	$5,870k	$6,048k	$7,391k	$17,474k
Real Median	$1k	$165k	$517k	$1,377k	$3,368k	$4,215k	$5,191k	$7,512k
Real Low	$1k	$68k	$202k	$543k	$1,271k	$1,465k	$2,967k	$3,853k
Beating S&P 500?	52.2%	68.0%	78.0%	97.5%	100.0%	100.0%	99.8%	100.0%
Typ. Monthly DDs	0%	4%	4%	3%	2%	2%	1%	1%
Typ. Qtrly DDs	0%	15%	15%	13%	8%	7%	7%	6%
Typ. Yearly DDs	0%	41%	41%	35%	27%	22%	21%	23%
Worst Drawdowns	0%	54%	52%	45%	34%	28%	28%	30%

Could be implemented with Vanguard-like target-date fund, AVUV, AVDV

Figure 37. Backtest of Aggressive 2 Funds for Life strategy using a combination of US and international small-cap value

CHAPTER 11: INTERMEDIATES — 3-FUND COMBINATIONS

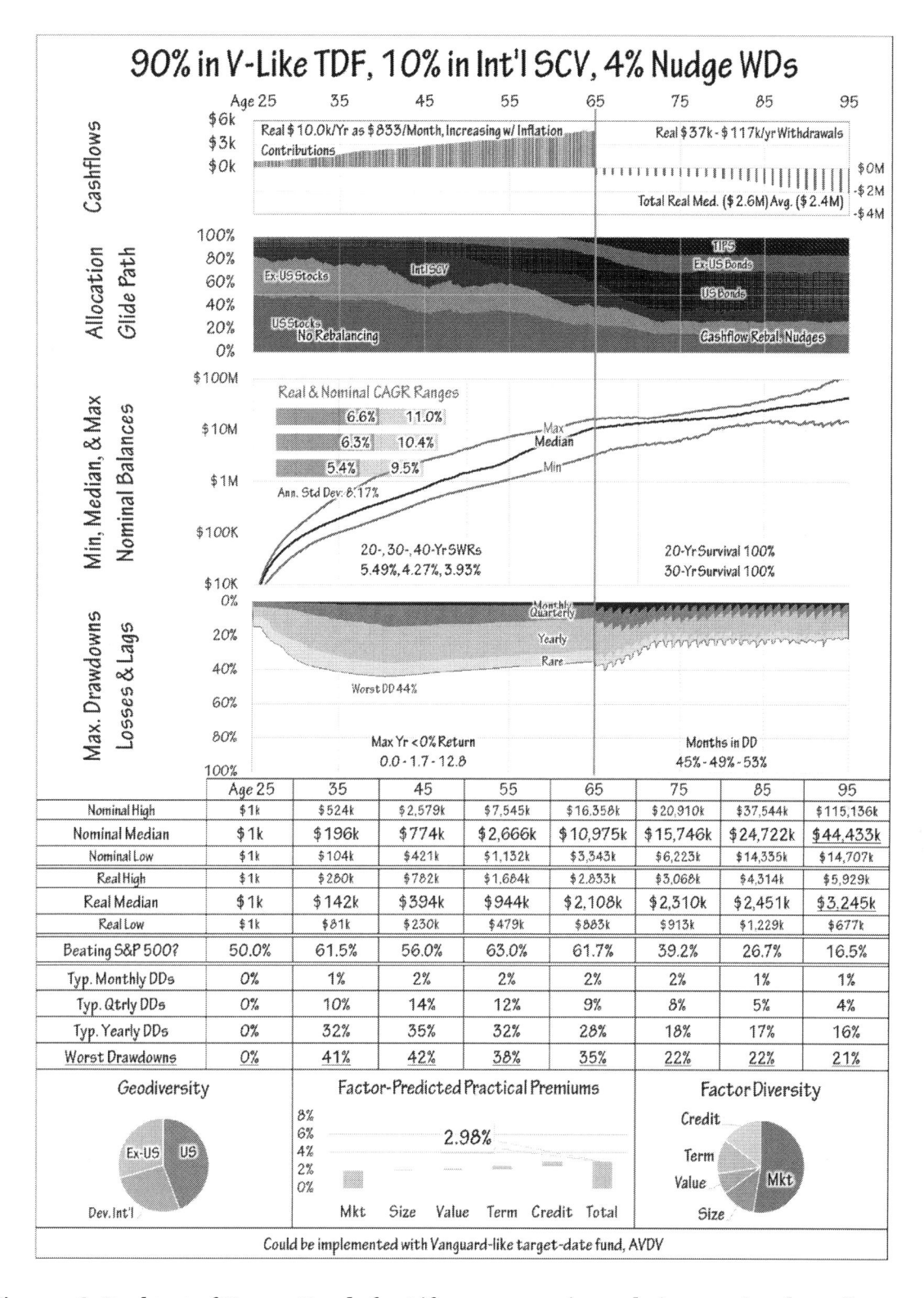

90% in V-Like TDF, 10% in Int'l SCV, 4% Nudge WDs

Cashflows: Real $10.0k/Yr as $833/Month, Increasing w/ Inflation Contributions; Real $37k - $117k/yr Withdrawals; Total Real Med. ($2.6M) Avg. ($2.4M)

Allocation Glide Path: Ex-US Stocks, Int'l SCV, US Stocks, TIPS, Ex-US Bonds, US Bonds; No Rebalancing; Cashflow Rebal. Nudges

Min, Median, & Max Nominal Balances:
Real & Nominal CAGR Ranges: 6.6% – 11.0%; 6.3% – 10.4%; 5.4% – 9.5%
Ann. Std Dev: 8.17%
20-, 30-, 40-Yr SWRs: 5.49%, 4.27%, 3.93%
20-Yr Survival 100%
30-Yr Survival 100%

Max. Drawdowns Losses & Lags: Worst DD 44%; Max Yr <0% Return 0.0 - 1.7 - 12.8; Months in DD 45% - 49% - 53%

	Age 25	35	45	55	65	75	85	95
Nominal High	$1k	$524k	$2,579k	$7,545k	$16,358k	$20,910k	$37,544k	$115,136k
Nominal Median	$1k	$196k	$774k	$2,666k	$10,975k	$15,746k	$24,722k	$44,433k
Nominal Low	$1k	$104k	$421k	$1,132k	$3,343k	$6,223k	$14,335k	$14,707k
Real High	$1k	$280k	$782k	$1,684k	$2,833k	$3,068k	$4,314k	$5,929k
Real Median	$1k	$142k	$394k	$944k	$2,108k	$2,310k	$2,451k	$3,245k
Real Low	$1k	$81k	$230k	$479k	$883k	$913k	$1,229k	$677k
Beating S&P 500?	50.0%	61.5%	56.0%	63.0%	61.7%	39.2%	26.7%	16.5%
Typ. Monthly DDs	0%	1%	2%	2%	2%	2%	1%	1%
Typ. Qtrly DDs	0%	10%	14%	12%	9%	8%	5%	4%
Typ. Yearly DDs	0%	32%	35%	32%	28%	18%	17%	16%
Worst Drawdowns	0%	41%	42%	38%	35%	22%	22%	21%

Geodiversity: Ex-US, US, Dev. Int'l

Factor-Predicted Practical Premiums: 2.98% (Mkt, Size, Value, Term, Credit, Total)

Factor Diversity: Credit, Term, Value, Size, Mkt

Could be implemented with Vanguard-like target-date fund, AVDV

Figure 38. Backtest of Easy 2 Funds for Life strategy using only international small-cap value for the second fund

1.5 × YTR in Int'l SCV, Rest in TDF, 4% Fixed WDs

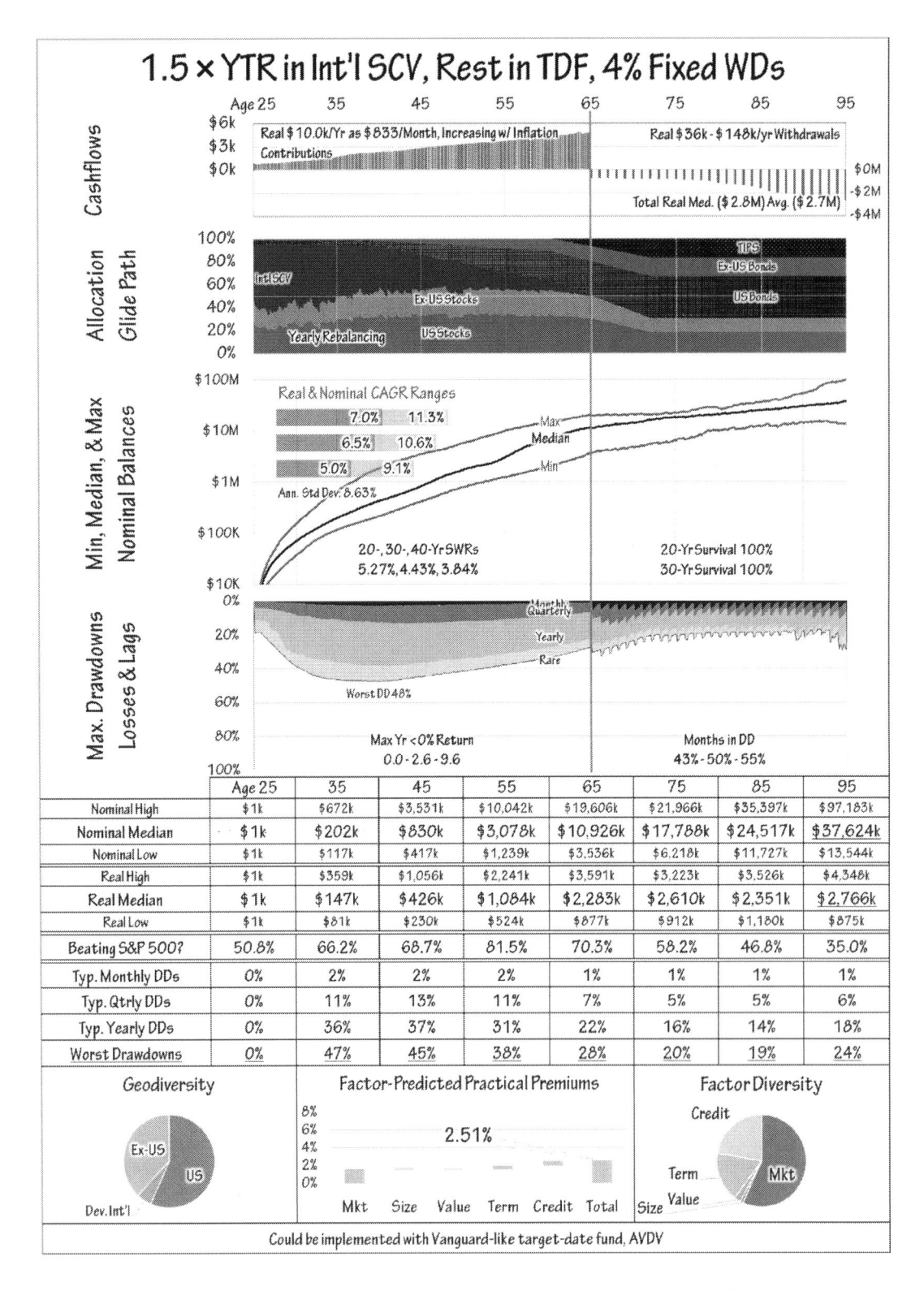

	Age 25	35	45	55	65	75	85	95
Nominal High	$1k	$672k	$3,531k	$10,042k	$19,606k	$21,966k	$35,397k	$97,183k
Nominal Median	$1k	$202k	$830k	$3,078k	$10,926k	$17,788k	$24,517k	$37,624k
Nominal Low	$1k	$117k	$417k	$1,239k	$3,536k	$6,218k	$11,727k	$13,544k
Real High	$1k	$359k	$1,056k	$2,241k	$3,591k	$3,223k	$3,526k	$4,348k
Real Median	$1k	$147k	$426k	$1,084k	$2,283k	$2,610k	$2,351k	$2,766k
Real Low	$1k	$81k	$230k	$524k	$877k	$912k	$1,180k	$875k
Beating S&P 500?	50.8%	66.2%	68.7%	81.5%	70.3%	58.2%	46.8%	35.0%
Typ. Monthly DDs	0%	2%	2%	2%	1%	1%	1%	1%
Typ. Qtrly DDs	0%	11%	13%	11%	7%	5%	5%	6%
Typ. Yearly DDs	0%	36%	37%	31%	22%	16%	14%	18%
Worst Drawdowns	0%	47%	45%	38%	28%	20%	19%	24%

Factor-Predicted Practical Premiums: 2.51%

Could be implemented with Vanguard-like target-date fund, AVDV

Figure 39. Backtest of Moderate 2 Funds for Life strategy using only international small-cap value for the second fund

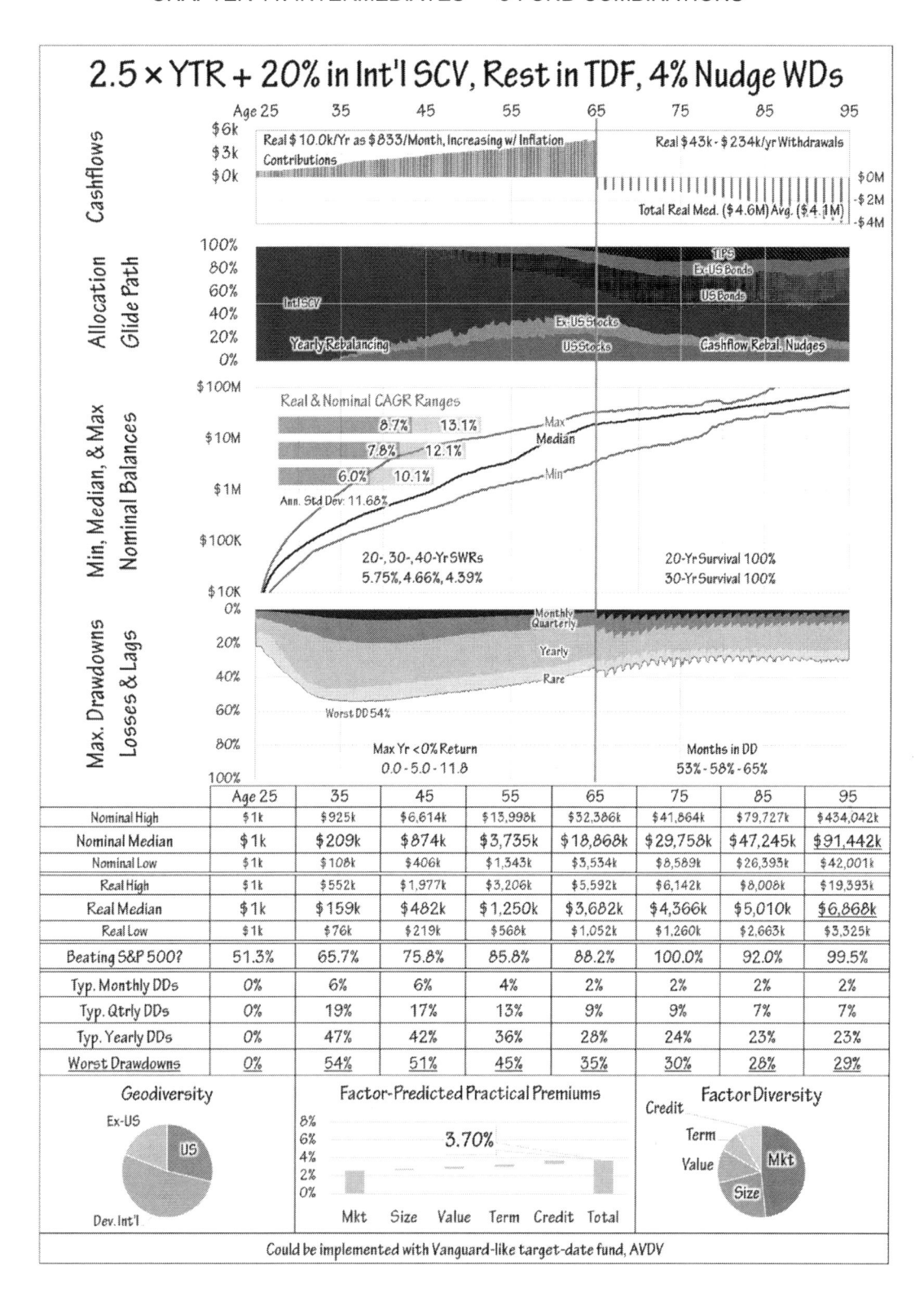

Figure 40. Backtest of Aggressive 2 Funds for Life strategy using only international small-cap value for the second fund

Chapter 12
Complexity — 4- to 13-Fund Combinations

Balaena mysticetus *— The bowhead whale is thought to be the longest-living mammal, with a maximum lifespan of over 200 years.*

We sometimes mistake complexity for excellence, but the most ubiquitous forms of life on earth are the simplest. In terms of sheer numbers, bacteria rule the world.

In this chapter, we'll see whether 2- and 3-fund portfolios can compete with complex ones.

We'll look at complex and simple *fixed* allocation portfolios first, then see if the Aggressive 2 Funds for Life strategy can match or beat a customizable complex glide path.

Readers who've followed our work at The Merriman Financial Education Foundation will be familiar with several more complex portfolios. Paul's Ultimate Buy-and-Hold portfolio is the best known. It includes 10 equity funds and three fixed income funds. We've also introduced US and Worldwide 4-Fund, All-Value, and All-Small-Cap-Value portfolios. We even created a customizable Merriman Aggressive Target-Date Glide Path. The question is how well they perform compared to the simpler approaches.

The fixed allocation portfolios we'll be testing are shown in Table 12. Emerging markets allocations are added to the All-Value and All-Small-Cap-Value funds to provide an added level of diversification. The percentages in the top part of the chart are for a 100% equities portfolio. Investors usually fine-tune their risk by combining the equity portfolio with some percentage of bonds. The recommended relative allocation to each type of bond fund is given in the table's bottom section.

CHAPTER 12: COMPLEXITY — 4- TO 13-FUND COMBINATIONS

	Ultimate Buy and Hold	US 4-Fund Combo	Worldwide 4-Fund Combo	All-Value	All Small-cap Value
US Large-Cap Blend	10%	25%	25%	--	--
US Large-Cap Value	10%	25%	--	25%	--
US Small-cap Blend	10%	25%	--	--	--
US Small-cap Value	10%	25%	25%	25%	50%
US REIT	10%	--	--	--	--
Int'l Large-Cap Blend	10%	--	--	--	--
Int'l Large-Cap Value	10%	--	25%	20%	--
Int'l Small-Cap Blend	10%	--	25%	--	--
Int'l Small-Cap Value	10%	--	--	20%	30%
Emerging Markets	10%	--	--	10%	20%
US Short-Term Gov't Bonds	30% of total fixed income allocation				
US Int.-Term Gov't Bonds	50% of total fixed income allocation				
US Treas. Infl. Prot. Securities	20% of total fixed income allocation				

Table 12. Complex portfolio asset allocations

The Merriman Aggressive Target-Date Glide Path is a dynamic allocation that varies over time. By default, it's a 70% US, 30% Ex-US equity distribution, but investors can customize it using the Custom Merriman Aggressive Target-Date Allocation Google sheet. Here's the default glide path. It starts as an all-small-cap-value portfolio with some emerging markets for diversification and transitions to a 50% all-Ultimate-Buy-and-Hold portfolio with 50% fixed income by age 65.

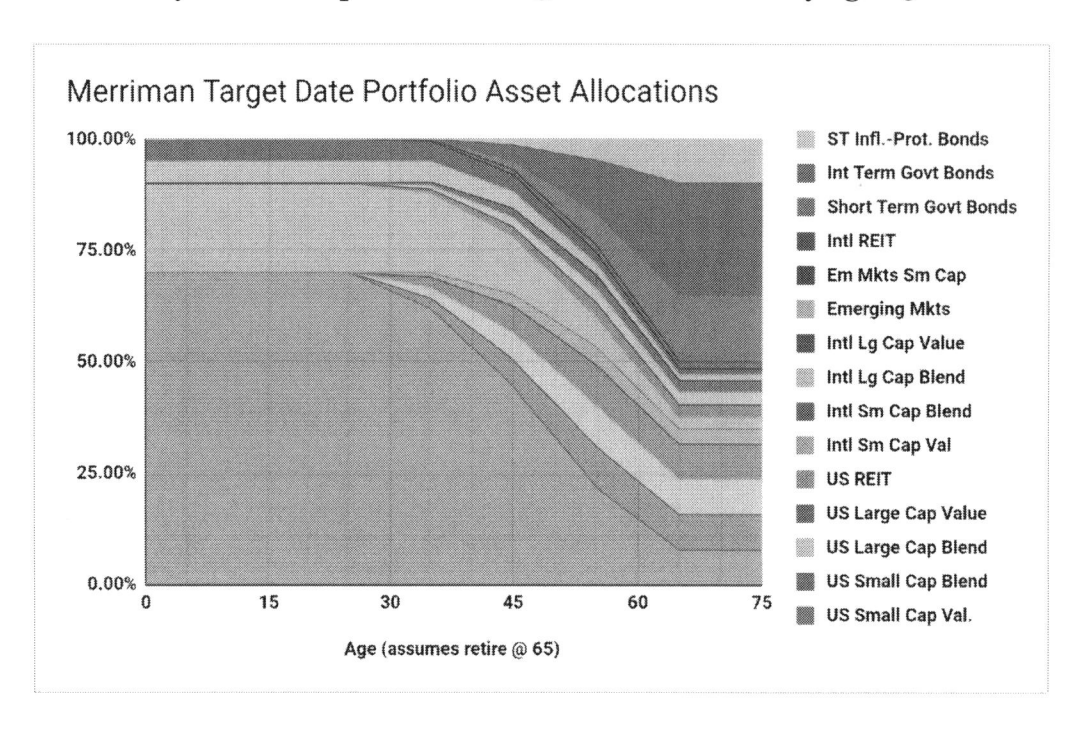

Figure 41. Merriman Aggressive Target-Date Portfolio asset allocation

As you can see, these options are much more complex than a 2- or 3-fund solution. The biggest benefit of this complexity is control. By having many funds, we can independently control how much of the portfolio is invested in large and small, growth and value, US and international or emerging markets, or even real estate investment trusts (REITs). The 2 Funds for Life portfolios give up some of these controls because each fund represents multiple aspects of the portfolio. For many investors, these fine controls are not necessary and might even be a distraction. On the other hand, if we have to give up significant returns or take on more risk to have a simpler portfolio, most investors will object.

CHAPTER 12: COMPLEXITY — 4- TO 13-FUND COMBINATIONS

So, is there a cost in terms of return per unit of risk in going with a simpler portfolio?

Let's find out by comparing the fixed allocation complex portfolios to a simple alternative made up of just three funds: intermediate-term US government bonds and a 50|50 mix of US small-cap value and international small-cap value. Since the fixed allocation portfolios are often combined with bonds, we'll look at them with 50%, 70%, and 100% equities. To make the comparison fair, we'll use whatever percentage of bonds is necessary for the 3-Fund combos to deliver approximately the same total of real withdrawals and real end balances. The rest of our scenario assumptions will be the same as we've used before — 40 years of steady savings followed by 30 years of 4% fixed withdrawals. Figure 42 summarizes the results:

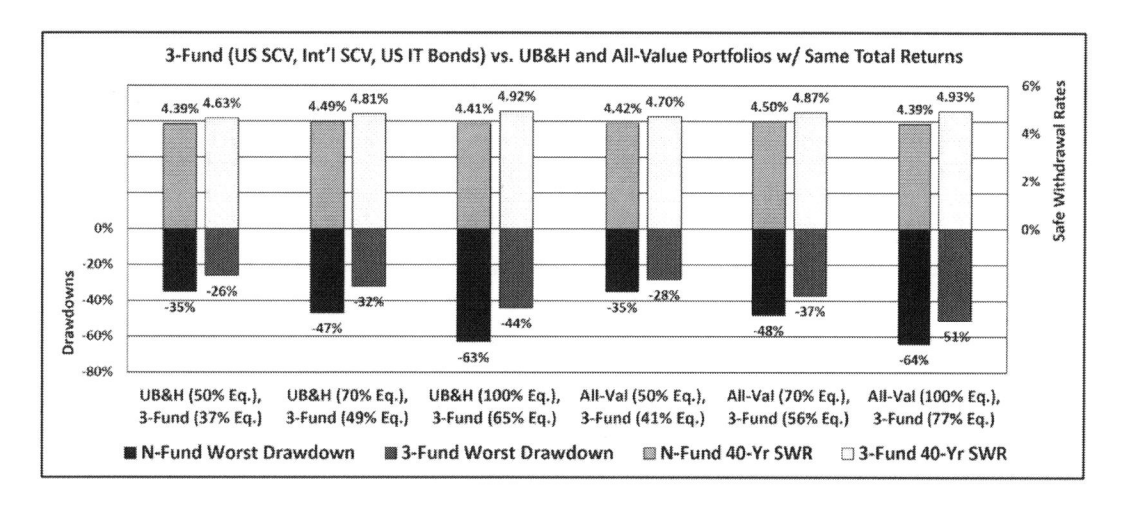

Figure 42. Comparison of Ultimate Buy-and-Hold, All-Value, and 3-Fund (US SCV, Int'l SCV, US IT Bonds) portfolios

The three pairs of columns on the left compare the Ultimate Buy-and-Hold portfolio to the 3-Fund alternative, and the three column pairs on the right compare the All-Value portfolio to the 3-Fund alternative. All the comparisons show the simpler portfolio had shallower drawdowns and higher safe withdrawal rates across all the equity percentages tested.

113

In short, the 3-Fund portfolios delivered the same total financial benefit as the more complex portfolios, but with less time, less pain, and less risk.

To many people, I suspect these results are counterintuitive. Wouldn't the Ultimate Buy-and-Hold or All-Value portfolios, which have many more kinds of funds, be more diversified? And wouldn't that make them less volatile or risky than the 3-Fund portfolios that have only small-cap value equities? The reason that's not the case is that meaningful diversification comes from combining things that behave differently. Although the complex portfolios have a larger number of funds, those funds behave more alike, providing weaker diversification benefits. In contrast, the 3-Fund combos are built from two asset classes that are more different — bonds and small-cap value. In terms of the factors or attributes that academics say drive returns, such as market, size, and value, the 3-Fund portfolios are more diverse, not less, than the more complex portfolios. You can see that in the factor diversity pie charts from the backtests, summarized in Figure 43:

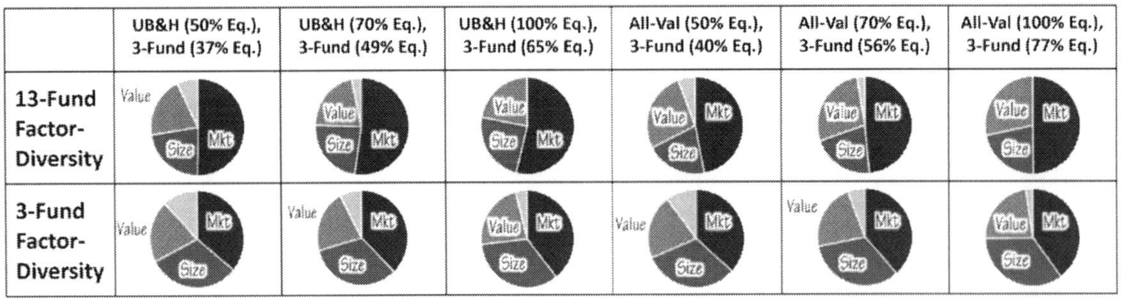

	UB&H (50% Eq.), 3-Fund (37% Eq.)	UB&H (70% Eq.), 3-Fund (49% Eq.)	UB&H (100% Eq.), 3-Fund (65% Eq.)	All-Val (50% Eq.), 3-Fund (40% Eq.)	All-Val (70% Eq.), 3-Fund (56% Eq.)	All-Val (100% Eq.), 3-Fund (77% Eq.)
13-Fund Factor-Diversity						
3-Fund Factor-Diversity						

Figure 43. Factor diversification pies from backtests of Ultimate Buy-and-Hold, All-Value, and 3-Fund portfolios

In the spirit of openness, completeness, and transparency, I'll insert all 12 of the comparison backtests in the same order as they appear in the chart going from left to right. The factor diversity pie charts also appear in the bottom right-hand corner of each chart.

Following those backtests, we'll see if the Aggressive 2 Funds for Life approach can match or beat the Merriman Aggressive Target-Date Glide Path.

WW UB&H, 50% Equities, 4% Fixed Withdrawals

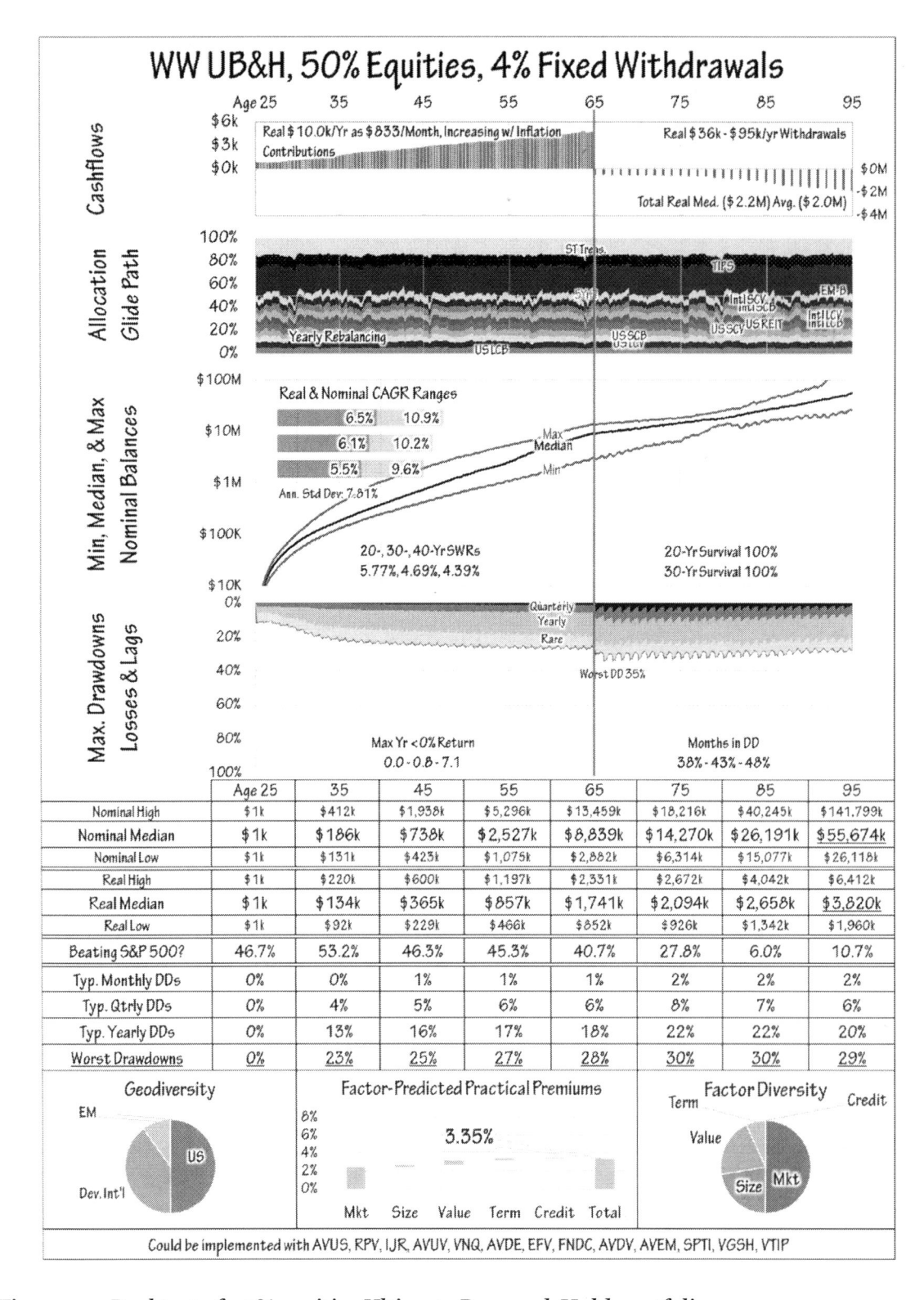

	Age 25	35	45	55	65	75	85	95
Nominal High	$1k	$412k	$1,938k	$5,296k	$13,459k	$18,216k	$40,245k	$141,799k
Nominal Median	$1k	$186k	$738k	$2,527k	$8,839k	$14,270k	$26,191k	$55,674k
Nominal Low	$1k	$131k	$423k	$1,075k	$2,882k	$6,314k	$15,077k	$26,118k
Real High	$1k	$220k	$600k	$1,197k	$2,331k	$2,672k	$4,042k	$6,412k
Real Median	$1k	$134k	$365k	$857k	$1,741k	$2,094k	$2,658k	$3,820k
Real Low	$1k	$92k	$229k	$466k	$852k	$926k	$1,342k	$1,960k
Beating S&P 500?	46.7%	53.2%	46.3%	45.3%	40.7%	27.8%	6.0%	10.7%
Typ. Monthly DDs	0%	0%	1%	1%	1%	2%	2%	2%
Typ. Qtrly DDs	0%	4%	5%	6%	6%	8%	7%	6%
Typ. Yearly DDs	0%	13%	16%	17%	18%	22%	22%	20%
Worst Drawdowns	0%	23%	25%	27%	28%	30%	30%	29%

Could be implemented with AVUS, RPV, IJR, AVUV, VNQ, AVDE, EFV, FNDC, AVDV, AVEM, SPTI, VGSH, VTIP

Figure 44. Backtest of 50% equities Ultimate Buy-and-Hold portfolio

CHAPTER 12: COMPLEXITY — 4- TO 13-FUND COMBINATIONS

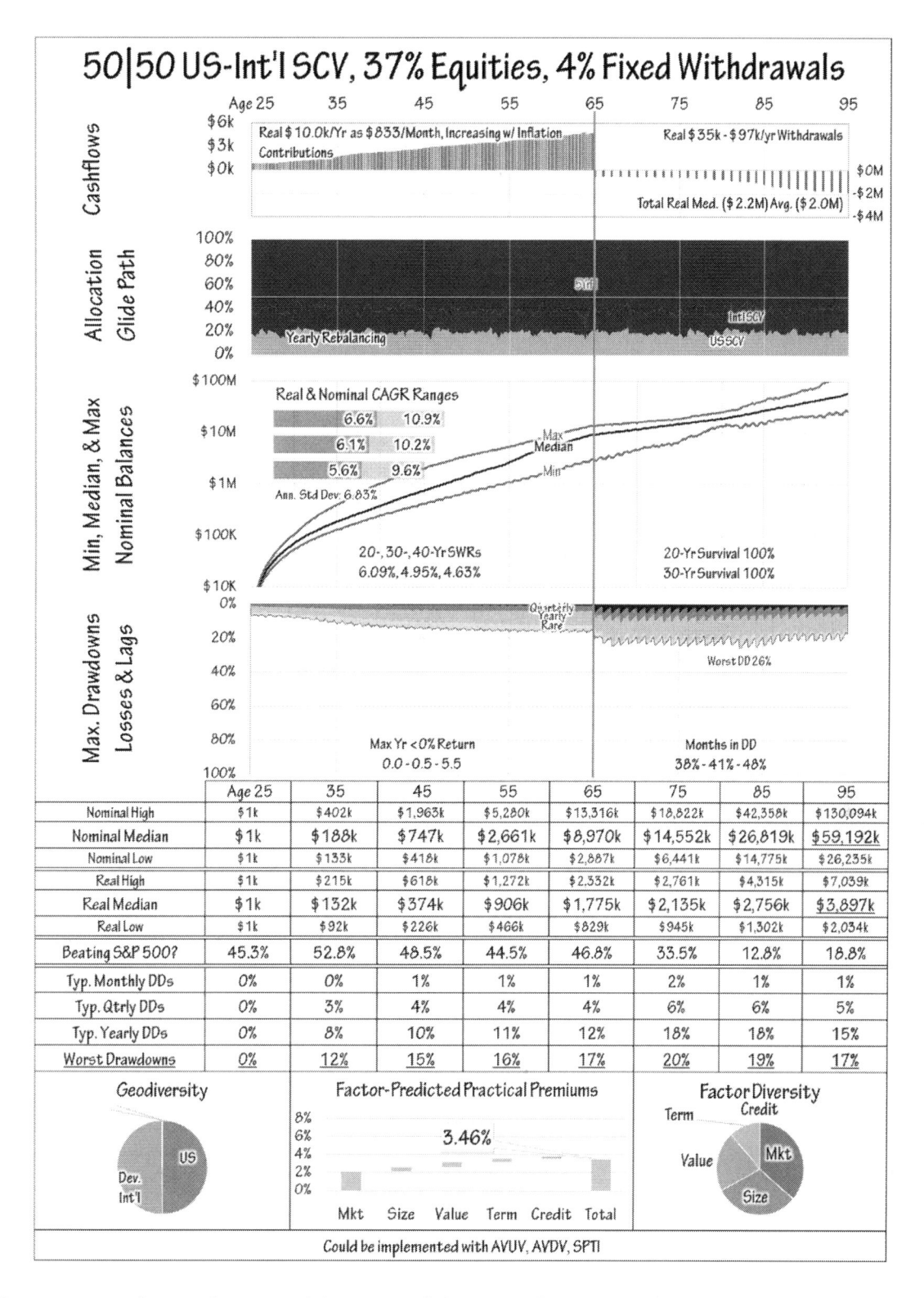

50|50 US-Int'l SCV, 37% Equities, 4% Fixed Withdrawals

	Age 25	35	45	55	65	75	85	95
Nominal High	$1k	$402k	$1,963k	$5,280k	$13,316k	$18,822k	$42,358k	$130,094k
Nominal Median	$1k	$188k	$747k	$2,661k	$8,970k	$14,552k	$26,819k	$59,192k
Nominal Low	$1k	$133k	$418k	$1,078k	$2,887k	$6,441k	$14,775k	$26,235k
Real High	$1k	$215k	$618k	$1,272k	$2,532k	$2,761k	$4,315k	$7,039k
Real Median	$1k	$132k	$374k	$906k	$1,775k	$2,135k	$2,756k	$3,897k
Real Low	$1k	$92k	$226k	$466k	$829k	$945k	$1,302k	$2,034k
Beating S&P 500?	45.3%	52.8%	48.5%	44.5%	46.8%	33.5%	12.8%	18.8%
Typ. Monthly DDs	0%	0%	1%	1%	1%	2%	1%	1%
Typ. Qtrly DDs	0%	3%	4%	4%	4%	6%	6%	5%
Typ. Yearly DDs	0%	8%	10%	11%	12%	18%	18%	15%
Worst Drawdowns	0%	12%	15%	16%	17%	20%	19%	17%

Could be implemented with AVUV, AVDV, SPTI

Figure 45. Backtest of 37% equities 3-Fund (US & Int'l SCV, US IT Govt. Bonds) portfolio

117

WW UB&H, 70% Equities, 4% Fixed Withdrawals

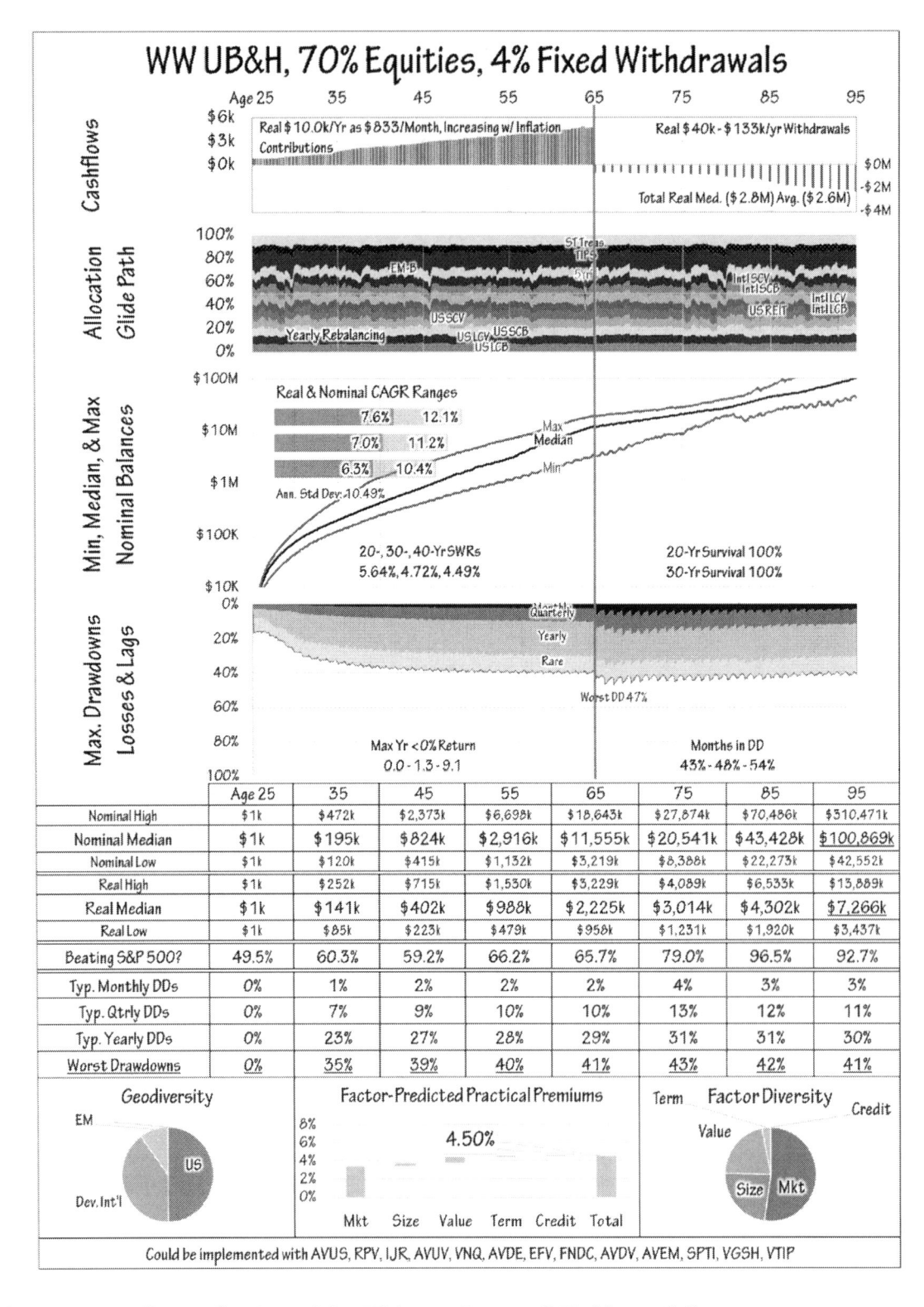

	Age 25	35	45	55	65	75	85	95
Nominal High	$1k	$472k	$2,373k	$6,698k	$18,643k	$27,874k	$70,486k	$310,471k
Nominal Median	$1k	$195k	$824k	$2,916k	$11,555k	$20,541k	$43,428k	$100,869k
Nominal Low	$1k	$120k	$415k	$1,132k	$3,219k	$8,388k	$22,273k	$42,552k
Real High	$1k	$252k	$715k	$1,530k	$3,229k	$4,089k	$6,533k	$13,889k
Real Median	$1k	$141k	$402k	$988k	$2,225k	$3,014k	$4,302k	$7,266k
Real Low	$1k	$85k	$223k	$479k	$958k	$1,231k	$1,920k	$3,437k
Beating S&P 500?	49.5%	60.3%	59.2%	66.2%	65.7%	79.0%	96.5%	92.7%
Typ. Monthly DDs	0%	1%	2%	2%	2%	4%	3%	3%
Typ. Qtrly DDs	0%	7%	9%	10%	10%	13%	12%	11%
Typ. Yearly DDs	0%	23%	27%	28%	29%	31%	31%	30%
Worst Drawdowns	0%	35%	39%	40%	41%	43%	42%	41%

Could be implemented with AVUS, RPV, IJR, AVUV, VNQ, AVDE, EFV, FNDC, AVDV, AVEM, SPTI, VGSH, VTIP

Figure 46. Backtest of 70% equities Ultimate Buy-and-Hold portfolio

CHAPTER 12: COMPLEXITY — 4- TO 13-FUND COMBINATIONS

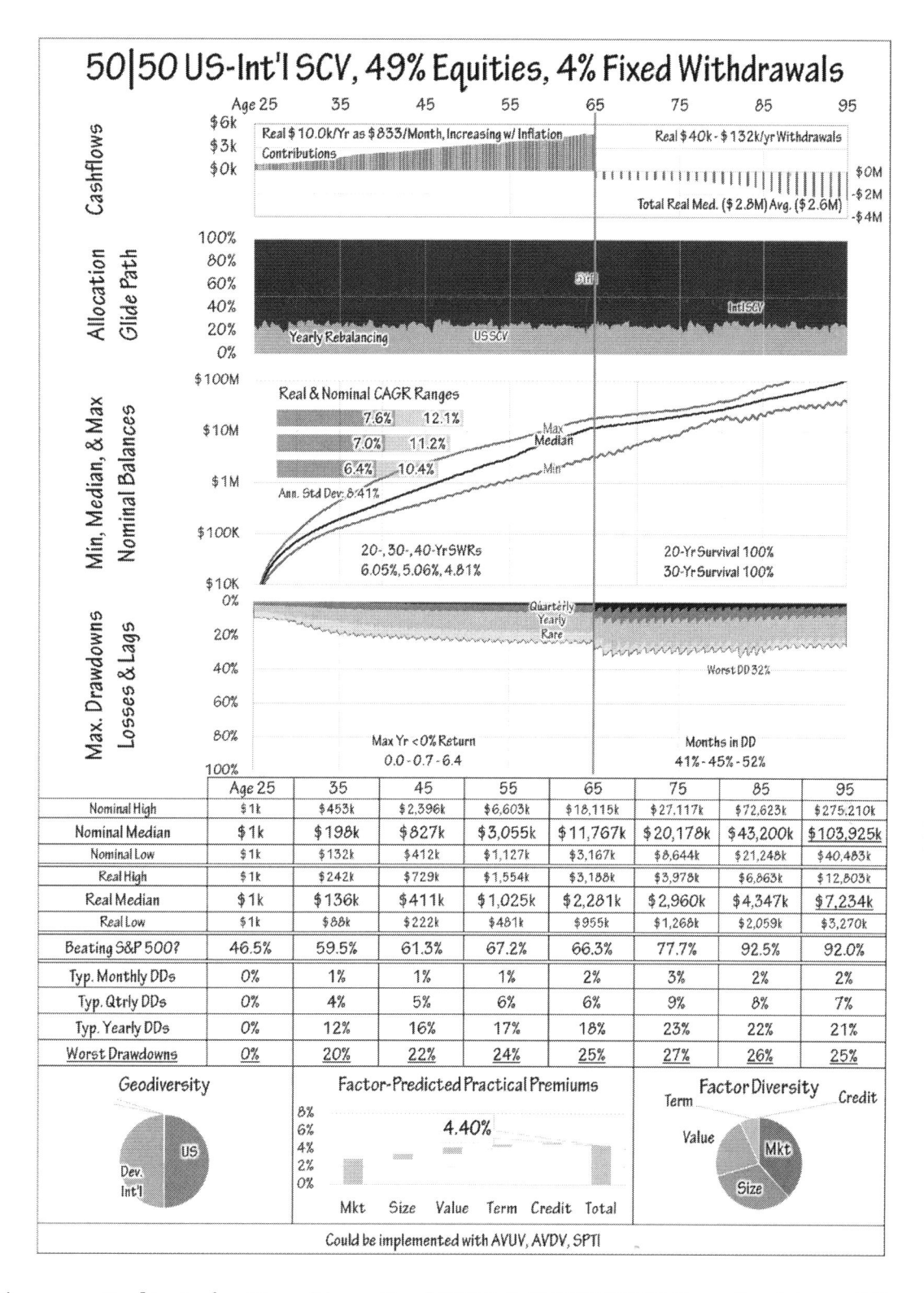

50|50 US-Int'l SCV, 49% Equities, 4% Fixed Withdrawals

	Age 25	35	45	55	65	75	85	95
Nominal High	$1k	$453k	$2,396k	$6,603k	$18,115k	$27,117k	$72,623k	$275,210k
Nominal Median	$1k	$198k	$827k	$3,055k	$11,767k	$20,178k	$43,200k	$103,925k
Nominal Low	$1k	$132k	$412k	$1,127k	$3,167k	$8,644k	$21,248k	$40,483k
Real High	$1k	$242k	$729k	$1,554k	$3,188k	$3,978k	$6,863k	$12,803k
Real Median	$1k	$136k	$411k	$1,025k	$2,281k	$2,960k	$4,347k	$7,234k
Real Low	$1k	$88k	$222k	$481k	$955k	$1,268k	$2,059k	$3,270k
Beating S&P 500?	46.5%	59.5%	61.3%	67.2%	66.3%	77.7%	92.5%	92.0%
Typ. Monthly DDs	0%	1%	1%	1%	2%	3%	2%	2%
Typ. Qtrly DDs	0%	4%	5%	6%	6%	9%	8%	7%
Typ. Yearly DDs	0%	12%	16%	17%	18%	23%	22%	21%
Worst Drawdowns	0%	20%	22%	24%	25%	27%	26%	25%

Could be implemented with AVUV, AVDV, SPTI

Figure 47. Backtest of 49% equities 3-Fund (US & Int'l SCV, US IT Govt. Bonds) portfolio

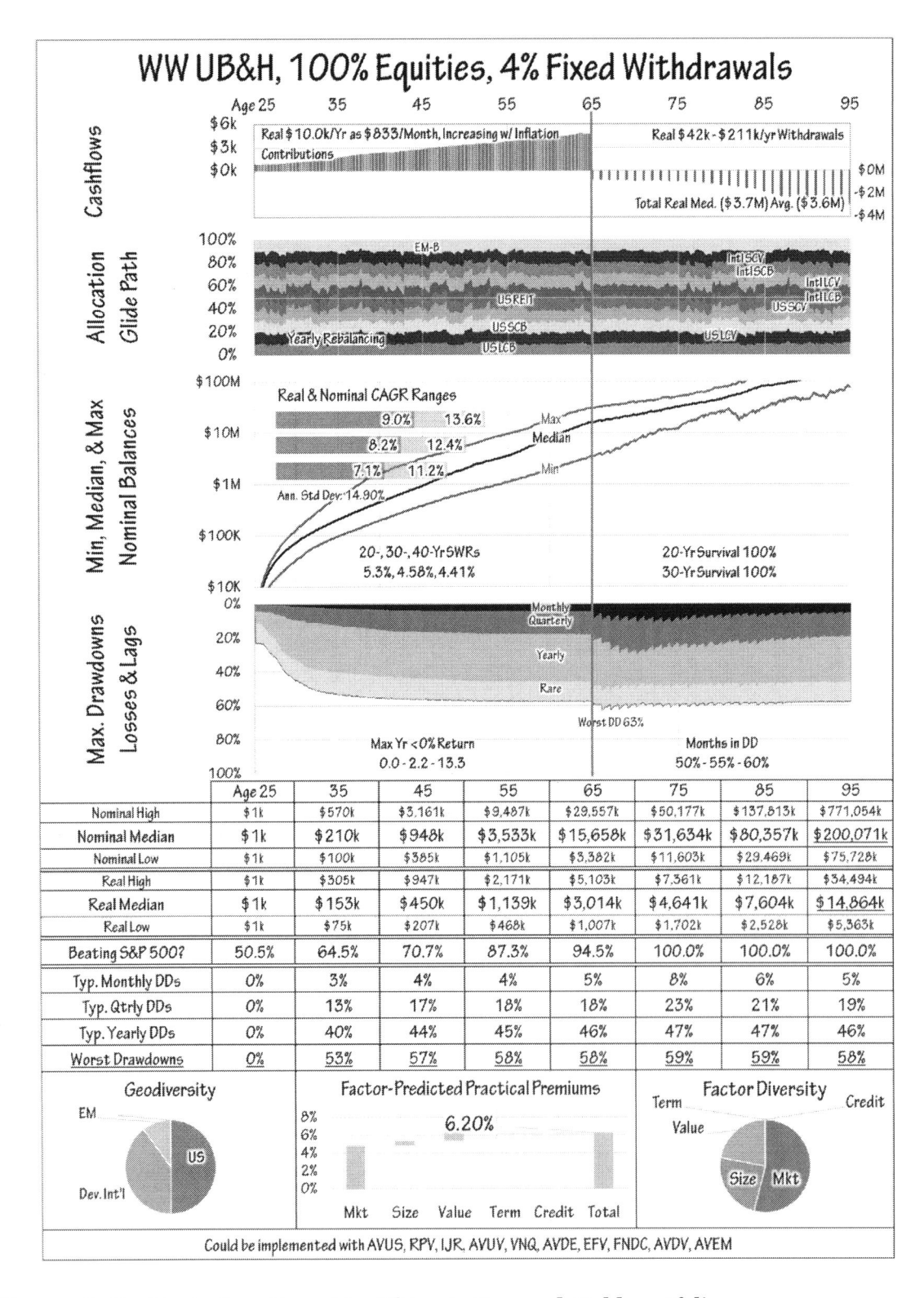

Figure 48. Backtest of 100% equities Ultimate Buy-and-Hold portfolio

CHAPTER 12: COMPLEXITY — 4- TO 13-FUND COMBINATIONS

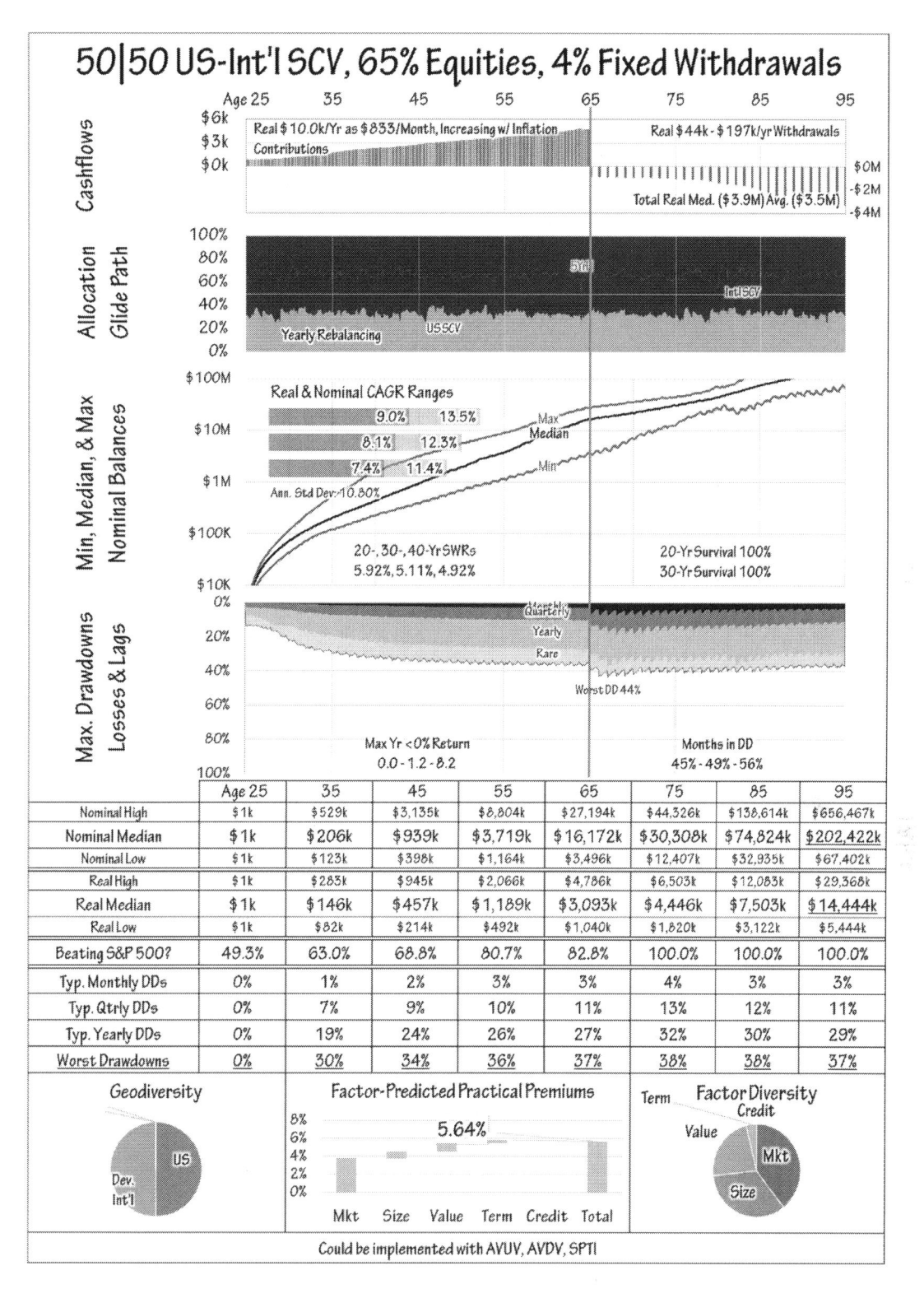

50|50 US-Int'l SCV, 65% Equities, 4% Fixed Withdrawals

Cashflows: Real $10.0k/Yr as $833/Month, Increasing w/ Inflation Contributions; Real $44k - $197k/yr Withdrawals; Total Real Med. ($3.9M) Avg. ($3.5M)

Allocation Glide Path: Yearly Rebalancing; US SCV; Int'l SCV

Min, Median, & Max Nominal Balances: Real & Nominal CAGR Ranges 9.0% 13.5%, 8.1% 12.3%, 7.4% 11.4%; Ann. Std Dev: 10.80%; 20-, 30-, 40-Yr SWRs: 5.92%, 5.11%, 4.92%; 20-Yr Survival 100%; 30-Yr Survival 100%

Max. Drawdowns Losses & Lags: Monthly, Quarterly, Yearly, Rare; Worst DD 44%; Max Yr <0% Return 0.0 - 1.2 - 8.2; Months in DD 45% - 49% - 56%

	Age 25	35	45	55	65	75	85	95
Nominal High	$1k	$529k	$3,135k	$8,804k	$27,194k	$44,326k	$138,614k	$656,467k
Nominal Median	$1k	$206k	$939k	$3,719k	$16,172k	$30,308k	$74,824k	$202,422k
Nominal Low	$1k	$123k	$398k	$1,164k	$3,496k	$12,407k	$32,935k	$67,402k
Real High	$1k	$283k	$945k	$2,066k	$4,786k	$6,503k	$12,083k	$29,368k
Real Median	$1k	$146k	$457k	$1,189k	$3,093k	$4,446k	$7,503k	$14,444k
Real Low	$1k	$82k	$214k	$492k	$1,040k	$1,820k	$3,122k	$5,444k
Beating S&P 500?	49.3%	63.0%	68.8%	80.7%	82.8%	100.0%	100.0%	100.0%
Typ. Monthly DDs	0%	1%	2%	3%	3%	4%	3%	3%
Typ. Qtrly DDs	0%	7%	9%	10%	11%	13%	12%	11%
Typ. Yearly DDs	0%	19%	24%	26%	27%	32%	30%	29%
Worst Drawdowns	0%	30%	34%	36%	37%	38%	38%	37%

Geodiversity: US, Dev. Int'l

Factor-Predicted Practical Premiums: 5.64% — Mkt, Size, Value, Term, Credit, Total

Factor Diversity Credit: Term, Value, Mkt, Size

Could be implemented with AVUV, AVDV, SPTI

Figure 49. Backtest of 65% equities 3-Fund (US & Int'l SCV, US IT Govt. Bonds) portfolio

WW All-Value, 50% Equities, 4% Fixed Withdrawals

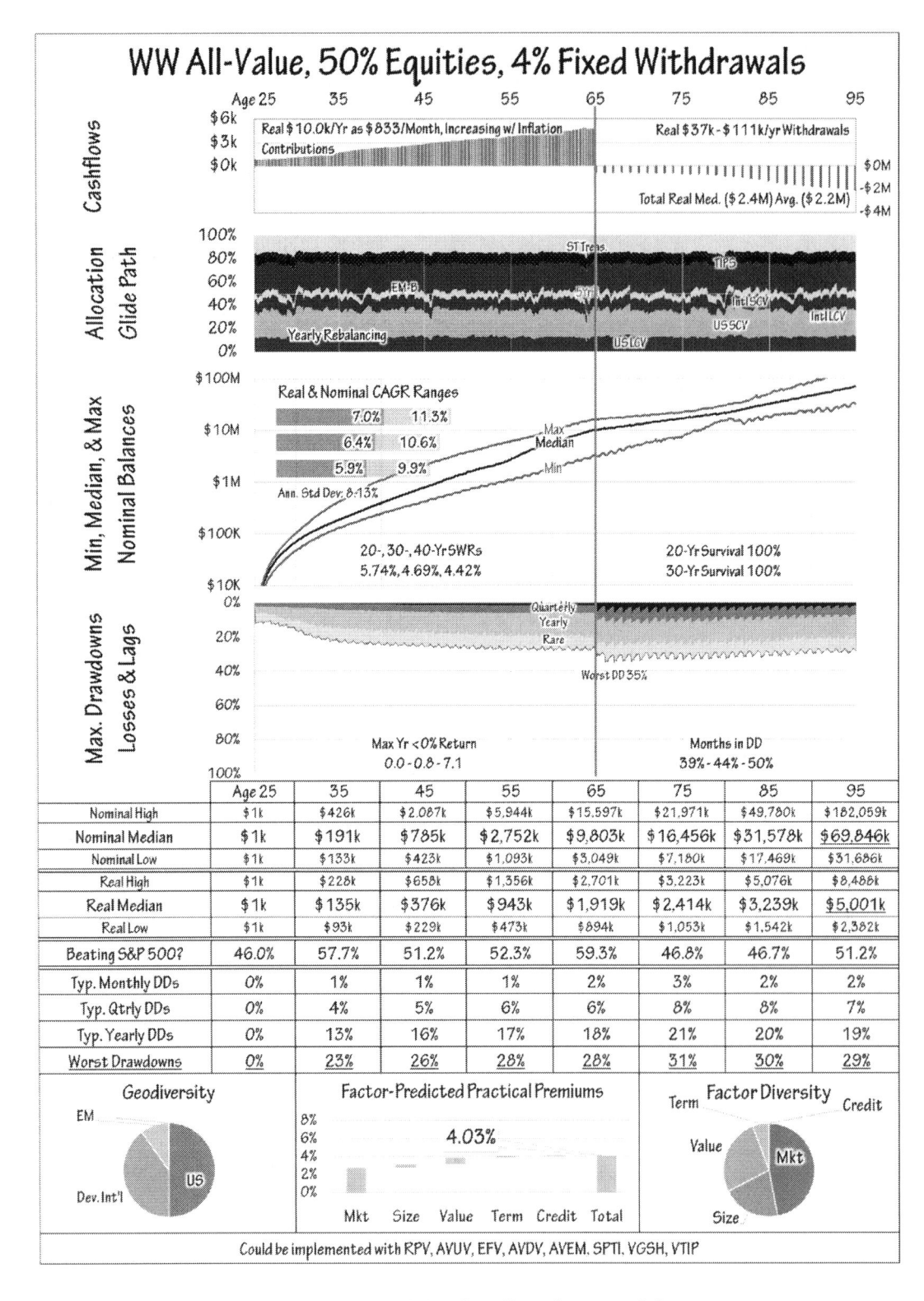

	Age 25	35	45	55	65	75	85	95
Nominal High	$1k	$426k	$2,087k	$5,944k	$15,597k	$21,971k	$49,780k	$182,059k
Nominal Median	$1k	$191k	$785k	$2,752k	$9,803k	$16,456k	$31,578k	$69,846k
Nominal Low	$1k	$133k	$423k	$1,093k	$3,049k	$7,180k	$17,469k	$31,686k
Real High	$1k	$228k	$658k	$1,356k	$2,701k	$3,223k	$5,076k	$8,488k
Real Median	$1k	$135k	$376k	$943k	$1,919k	$2,414k	$3,239k	$5,001k
Real Low	$1k	$93k	$229k	$473k	$894k	$1,053k	$1,542k	$2,382k
Beating S&P 500?	46.0%	57.7%	51.2%	52.3%	59.3%	46.8%	46.7%	51.2%
Typ. Monthly DDs	0%	1%	1%	1%	2%	3%	2%	2%
Typ. Qtrly DDs	0%	4%	5%	6%	6%	8%	8%	7%
Typ. Yearly DDs	0%	13%	16%	17%	18%	21%	20%	19%
Worst Drawdowns	0%	23%	26%	28%	28%	31%	30%	29%

Could be implemented with RPV, AVUV, EFV, AVDV, AVEM, SPTI, VGSH, VTIP

Figure 50. Backtest of 50% equities Worldwide All-Value portfolio

CHAPTER 12: COMPLEXITY — 4- TO 13-FUND COMBINATIONS

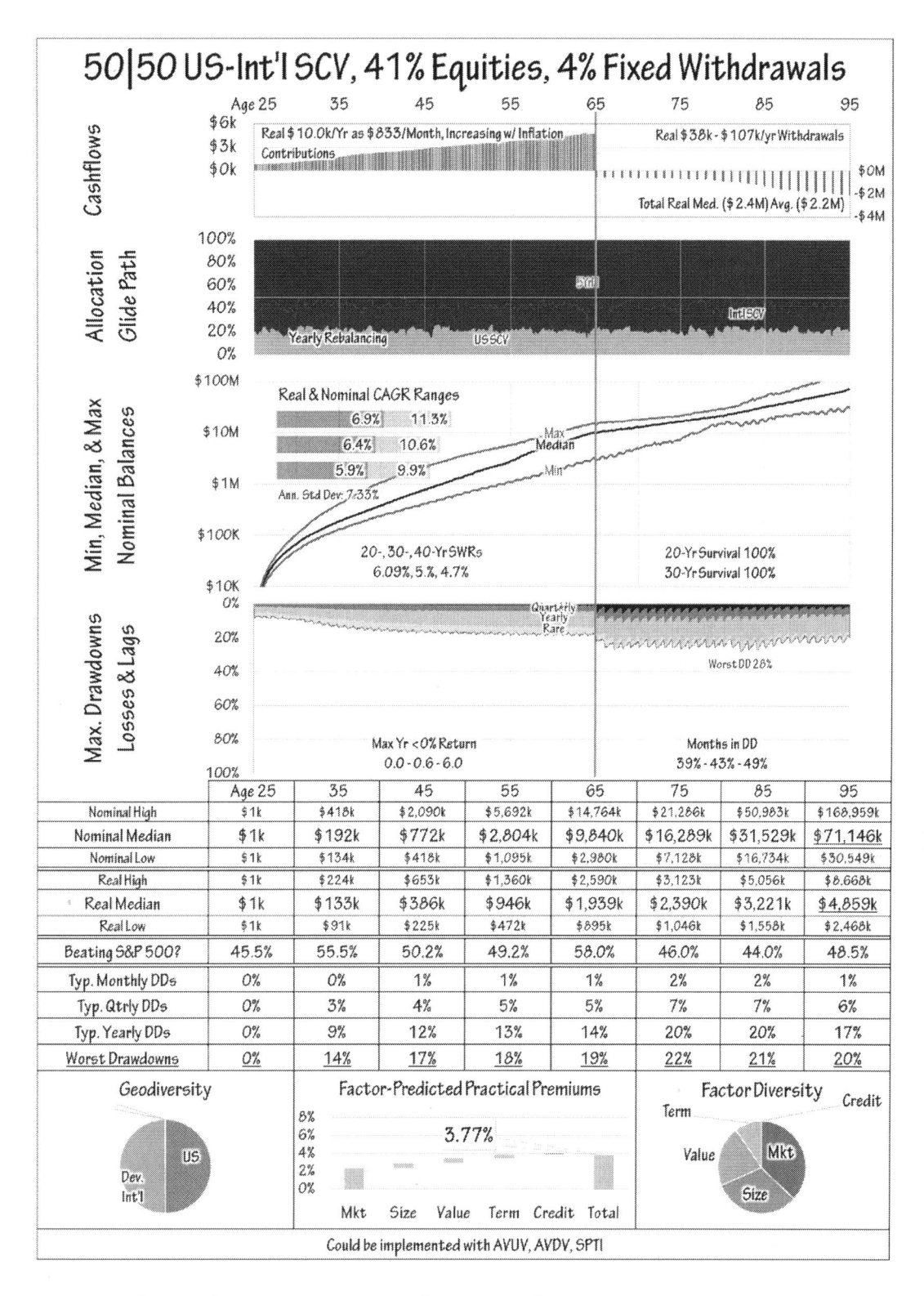

50|50 US-Int'l SCV, 41% Equities, 4% Fixed Withdrawals

	Age 25	35	45	55	65	75	85	95
Nominal High	$1k	$418k	$2,090k	$5,692k	$14,764k	$21,286k	$50,983k	$168,959k
Nominal Median	$1k	$192k	$772k	$2,804k	$9,840k	$16,289k	$31,529k	$71,146k
Nominal Low	$1k	$134k	$418k	$1,095k	$2,980k	$7,128k	$16,734k	$30,549k
Real High	$1k	$224k	$653k	$1,360k	$2,590k	$3,123k	$5,056k	$8,668k
Real Median	$1k	$133k	$386k	$946k	$1,939k	$2,390k	$3,221k	$4,859k
Real Low	$1k	$91k	$225k	$472k	$895k	$1,046k	$1,558k	$2,468k
Beating S&P 500?	45.5%	55.5%	50.2%	49.2%	58.0%	46.0%	44.0%	48.5%
Typ. Monthly DDs	0%	0%	1%	1%	1%	2%	2%	1%
Typ. Qtrly DDs	0%	3%	4%	5%	5%	7%	7%	6%
Typ. Yearly DDs	0%	9%	12%	13%	14%	20%	20%	17%
Worst Drawdowns	0%	14%	17%	18%	19%	22%	21%	20%

Factor-Predicted Practical Premiums: 3.77%

Could be implemented with AVUV, AVDV, SPTI

Figure 51. Backtest of 41% equities 3-Fund (US & Int'l SCV, US IT Govt. Bonds) portfolio

WW All-Value, 70% Equities, 4% Fixed Withdrawals

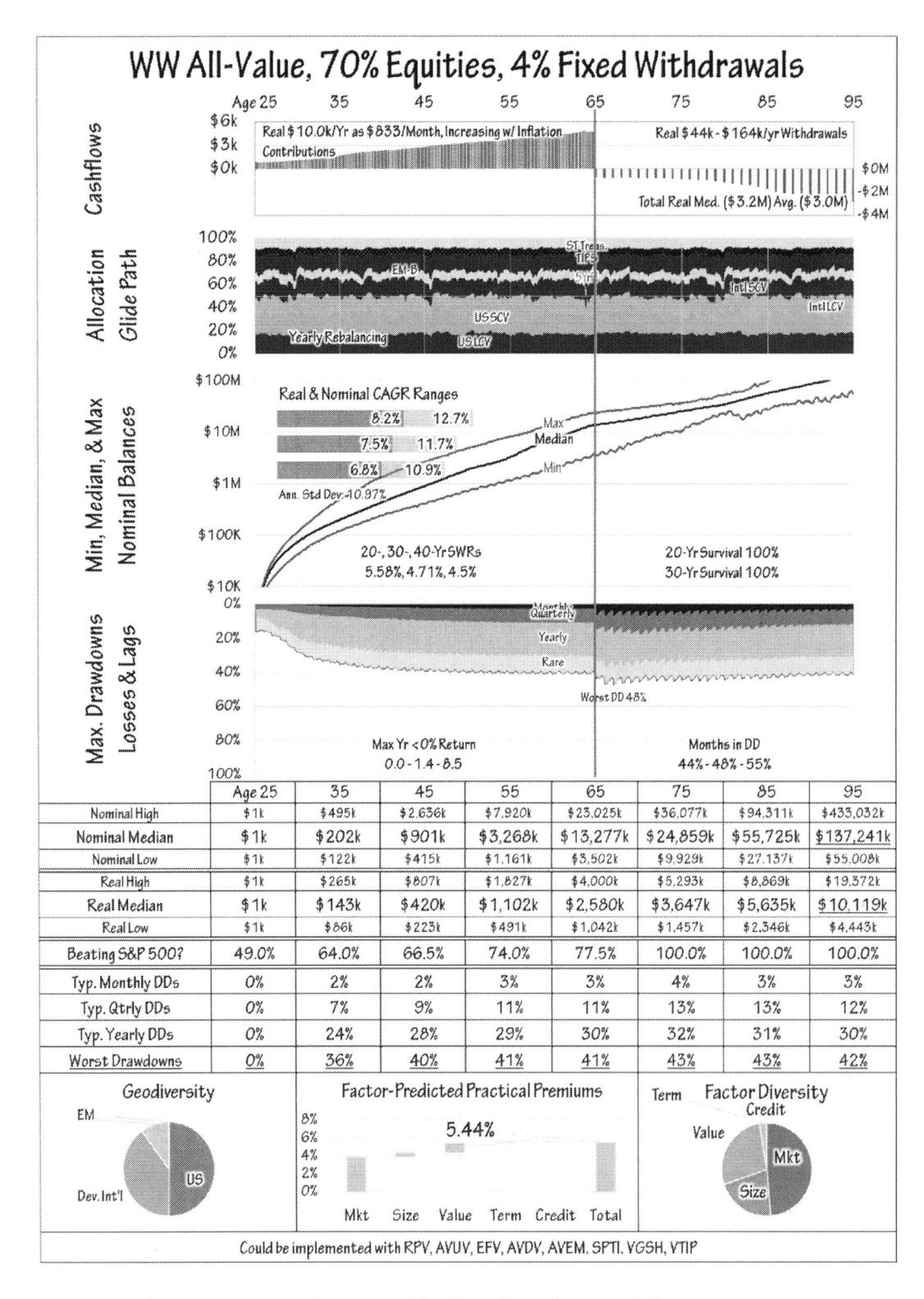

	Age 25	35	45	55	65	75	85	95
Nominal High	$1k	$495k	$2,636k	$7,920k	$23,025k	$36,077k	$94,311k	$433,032k
Nominal Median	$1k	$202k	$901k	$3,268k	$13,277k	$24,859k	$55,725k	$137,241k
Nominal Low	$1k	$122k	$415k	$1,161k	$3,502k	$9,929k	$27,137k	$55,008k
Real High	$1k	$265k	$807k	$1,827k	$4,000k	$5,293k	$8,869k	$19,372k
Real Median	$1k	$143k	$420k	$1,102k	$2,580k	$3,647k	$5,635k	$10,119k
Real Low	$1k	$86k	$223k	$491k	$1,042k	$1,457k	$2,346k	$4,443k
Beating S&P 500?	49.0%	64.0%	66.5%	74.0%	77.5%	100.0%	100.0%	100.0%
Typ. Monthly DDs	0%	2%	2%	3%	3%	4%	3%	3%
Typ. Qtrly DDs	0%	7%	9%	11%	11%	13%	13%	12%
Typ. Yearly DDs	0%	24%	28%	29%	30%	32%	31%	30%
Worst Drawdowns	0%	36%	40%	41%	41%	43%	43%	42%

Could be implemented with RPV, AVUV, EFV, AVDV, AVEM, SPTI, VGSH, VTIP

Figure 52. Backtest of 70% equities Worldwide All-Value portfolio

CHAPTER 12: COMPLEXITY — 4- TO 13-FUND COMBINATIONS

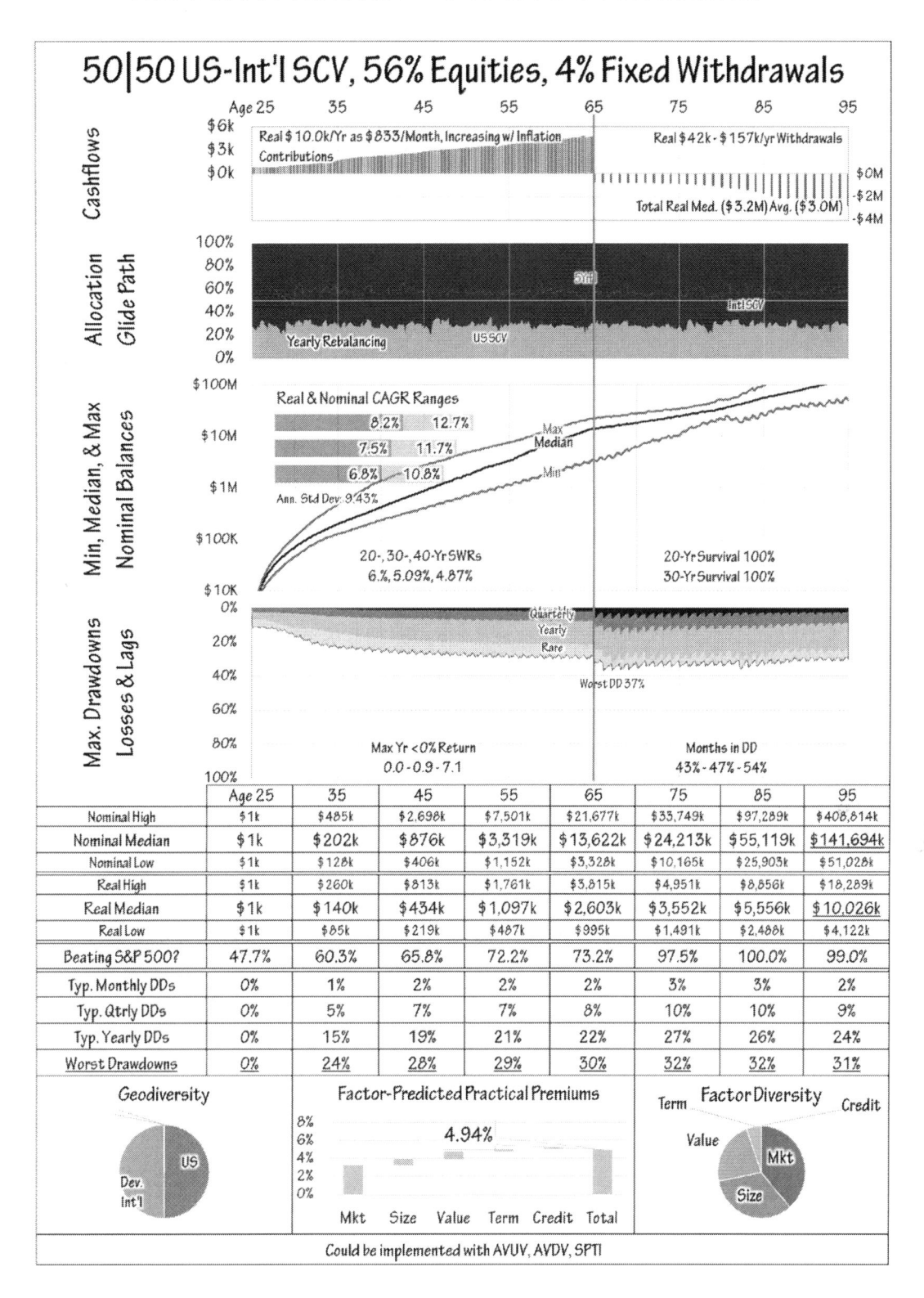

50|50 US-Int'l SCV, 56% Equities, 4% Fixed Withdrawals

	Age 25	35	45	55	65	75	85	95
Nominal High	$1k	$485k	$2,698k	$7,501k	$21,677k	$33,749k	$97,289k	$408,814k
Nominal Median	$1k	$202k	$876k	$3,319k	$13,622k	$24,213k	$55,119k	$141,694k
Nominal Low	$1k	$128k	$406k	$1,152k	$3,328k	$10,165k	$25,903k	$51,028k
Real High	$1k	$260k	$813k	$1,761k	$3,815k	$4,951k	$8,856k	$18,289k
Real Median	$1k	$140k	$434k	$1,097k	$2,603k	$3,552k	$5,556k	$10,026k
Real Low	$1k	$85k	$219k	$487k	$995k	$1,491k	$2,488k	$4,122k
Beating S&P 500?	47.7%	60.3%	65.8%	72.2%	73.2%	97.5%	100.0%	99.0%
Typ. Monthly DDs	0%	1%	2%	2%	2%	3%	3%	2%
Typ. Qtrly DDs	0%	5%	7%	7%	8%	10%	10%	9%
Typ. Yearly DDs	0%	15%	19%	21%	22%	27%	26%	24%
Worst Drawdowns	0%	24%	28%	29%	30%	32%	32%	31%

Could be implemented with AVUV, AVDV, SPTI

Figure 53. Backtest of 56% equities 3-Fund (US & Int'l SCV, US IT Govt. Bonds) portfolio

WW All-Value, 100% Equities, 4% Fixed Withdrawals

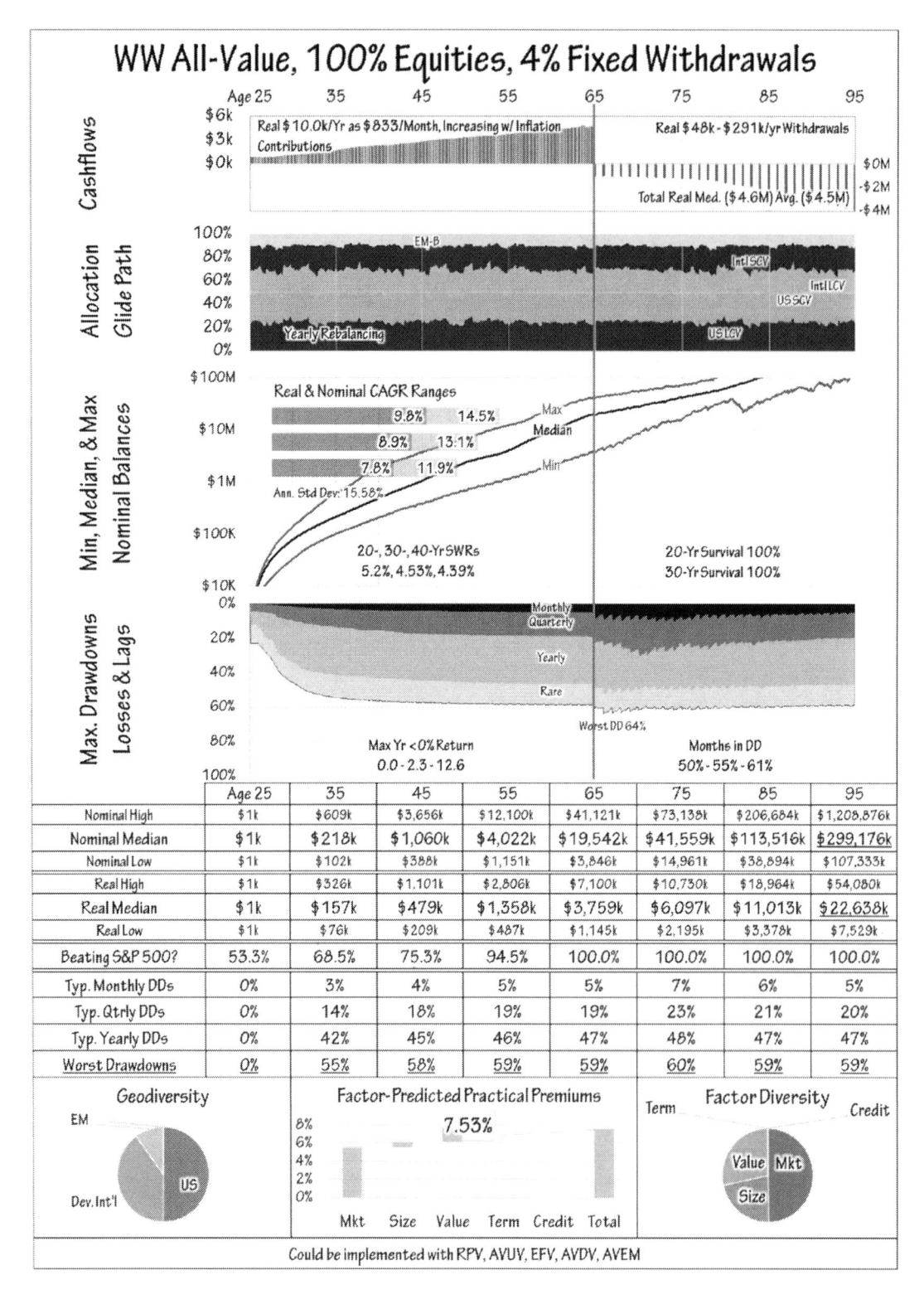

	Age 25	35	45	55	65	75	85	95
Nominal High	$1k	$609k	$3,656k	$12,100k	$41,121k	$73,138k	$206,684k	$1,208,876k
Nominal Median	$1k	$218k	$1,060k	$4,022k	$19,542k	$41,559k	$113,516k	$299,176k
Nominal Low	$1k	$102k	$388k	$1,151k	$3,846k	$14,961k	$38,894k	$107,333k
Real High	$1k	$326k	$1,101k	$2,806k	$7,100k	$10,730k	$18,964k	$54,080k
Real Median	$1k	$157k	$479k	$1,358k	$3,759k	$6,097k	$11,013k	$22,638k
Real Low	$1k	$76k	$209k	$487k	$1,145k	$2,195k	$3,378k	$7,529k
Beating S&P 500?	53.3%	68.5%	75.3%	94.5%	100.0%	100.0%	100.0%	100.0%
Typ. Monthly DDs	0%	3%	4%	5%	5%	7%	6%	5%
Typ. Qtrly DDs	0%	14%	18%	19%	19%	23%	21%	20%
Typ. Yearly DDs	0%	42%	45%	46%	47%	48%	47%	47%
Worst Drawdowns	0%	55%	58%	59%	59%	60%	59%	59%

Could be implemented with RPV, AVUV, EFV, AVDV, AVEM

Figure 54. Backtest of 100% equities Worldwide All-Value portfolio

CHAPTER 12: COMPLEXITY — 4- TO 13-FUND COMBINATIONS

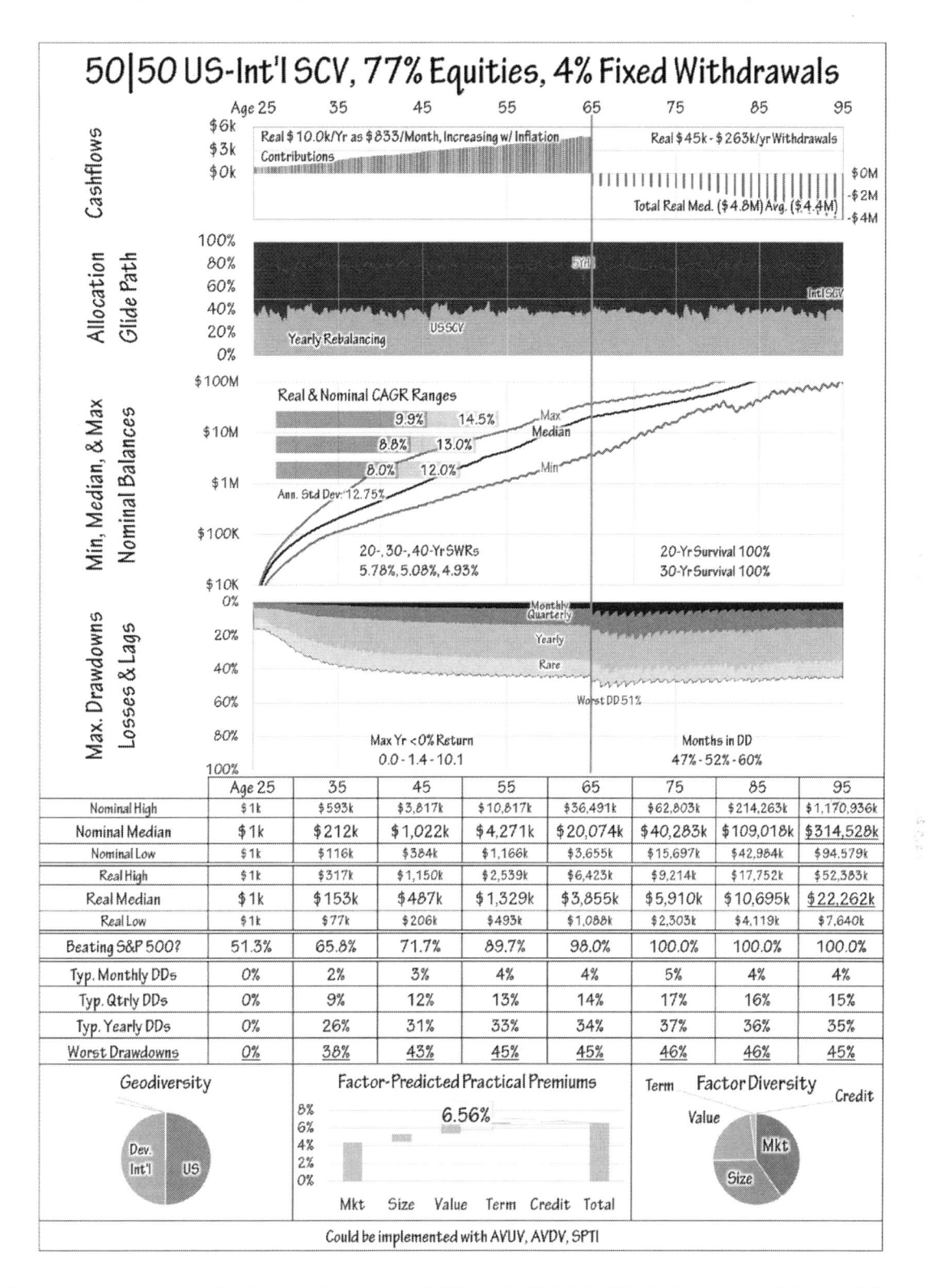

50|50 US-Int'l SCV, 77% Equities, 4% Fixed Withdrawals

	Age 25	35	45	55	65	75	85	95
Nominal High	$1k	$593k	$3,817k	$10,817k	$36,491k	$62,803k	$214,263k	$1,170,936k
Nominal Median	$1k	$212k	$1,022k	$4,271k	$20,074k	$40,283k	$109,018k	$314,528k
Nominal Low	$1k	$116k	$384k	$1,166k	$3,655k	$15,697k	$42,984k	$94,579k
Real High	$1k	$317k	$1,150k	$2,539k	$6,423k	$9,214k	$17,752k	$52,383k
Real Median	$1k	$153k	$487k	$1,329k	$3,855k	$5,910k	$10,695k	$22,262k
Real Low	$1k	$77k	$206k	$493k	$1,088k	$2,303k	$4,119k	$7,640k
Beating S&P 500?	51.3%	65.8%	71.7%	89.7%	98.0%	100.0%	100.0%	100.0%
Typ. Monthly DDs	0%	2%	3%	4%	4%	5%	4%	4%
Typ. Qtrly DDs	0%	9%	12%	13%	14%	17%	16%	15%
Typ. Yearly DDs	0%	26%	31%	33%	34%	37%	36%	35%
Worst Drawdowns	0%	38%	43%	45%	45%	46%	46%	45%

Could be implemented with AVUV, AVDV, SPTI

Figure 55. Backtest of 77% equities 3-Fund (US & Int'l SCV, US IT Govt. Bonds) portfolio

We've shown that we don't need complexity to get the highest return per unit of risk for fixed allocations, but what about the Merriman Aggressive Target-Date Glide Path? Do we need a complex portfolio to get the highest return per unit of risk from dynamic allocations?

Here again, the real benefit of complexity is control. If you want independent fine control over how much is in large and small, growth and value, US and international, all varying with time, then a complex solution is necessary. If, on the other hand, you're primarily concerned with performance in terms of return per unit of risk, it's not. To prove the point, let's look at how the Merriman Aggressive Target-Date Glide Path compared to the Aggressive 2 Funds for Life approach and the 3-Fund alternative that uses a mix of US and international small-cap value.

CHAPTER 12: COMPLEXITY — 4- TO 13-FUND COMBINATIONS

Merriman Aggressive Target-Date Glide Path, 4% Fixed WDs

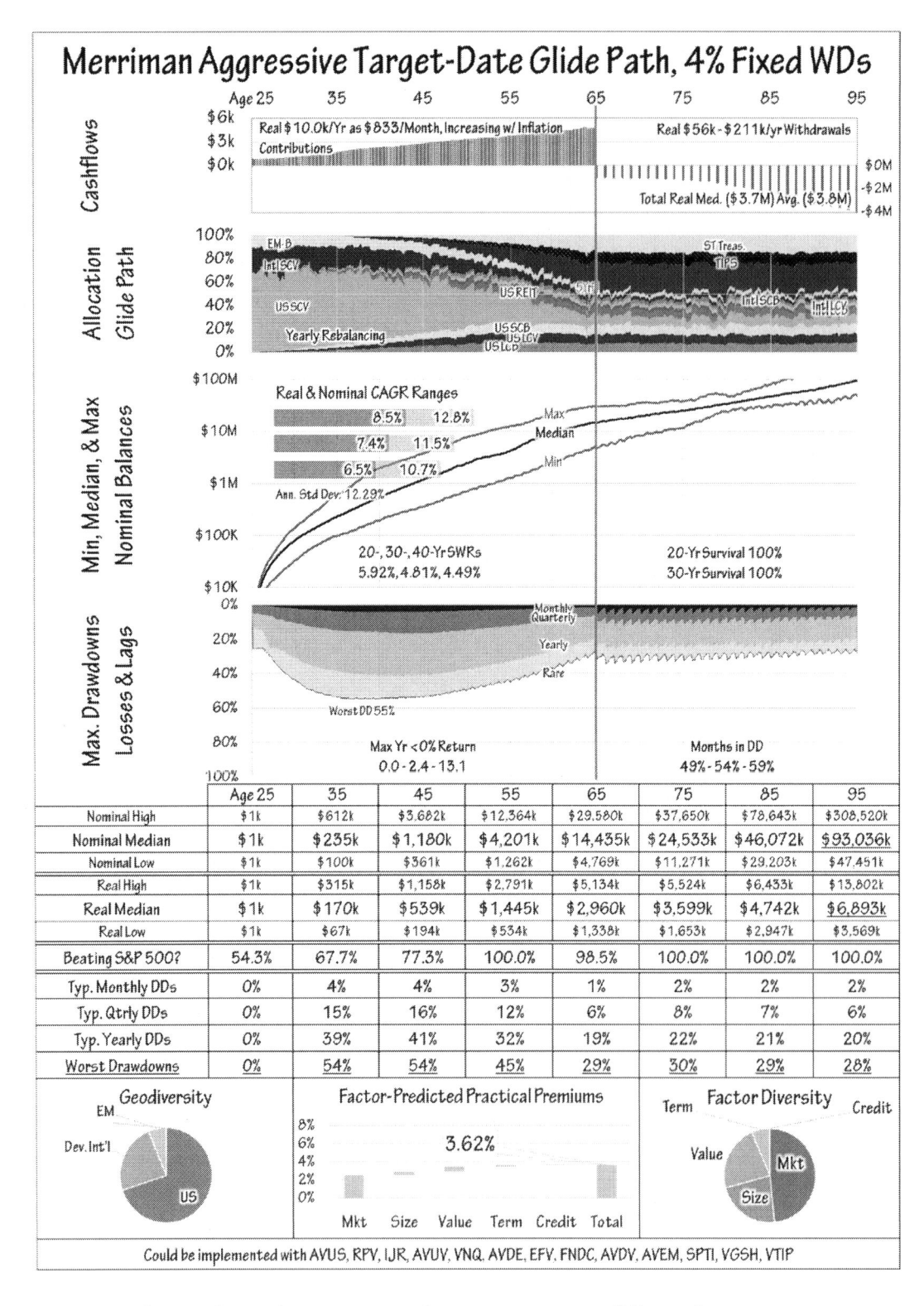

	Age 25	35	45	55	65	75	85	95
Nominal High	$1k	$612k	$3,682k	$12,364k	$29,580k	$37,650k	$78,643k	$308,520k
Nominal Median	$1k	$235k	$1,180k	$4,201k	$14,435k	$24,533k	$46,072k	$93,036k
Nominal Low	$1k	$100k	$361k	$1,262k	$4,769k	$11,271k	$29,203k	$47,451k
Real High	$1k	$315k	$1,158k	$2,791k	$5,134k	$5,524k	$6,433k	$13,802k
Real Median	$1k	$170k	$539k	$1,445k	$2,960k	$3,599k	$4,742k	$6,893k
Real Low	$1k	$67k	$194k	$534k	$1,338k	$1,653k	$2,947k	$3,569k
Beating S&P 500?	54.3%	67.7%	77.3%	100.0%	98.5%	100.0%	100.0%	100.0%
Typ. Monthly DDs	0%	4%	4%	3%	1%	2%	2%	2%
Typ. Qtrly DDs	0%	15%	16%	12%	6%	8%	7%	6%
Typ. Yearly DDs	0%	39%	41%	32%	19%	22%	21%	20%
Worst Drawdowns	0%	54%	54%	45%	29%	30%	29%	28%

Could be implemented with AVUS, RPV, IJR, AVUV, VNQ, AVDE, EFV, FNDC, AVDV, AVEM, SPTI, VGSH, VTIP

Figure 56. Backtest of Merriman Aggressive Target-Date Glide Path

CHAPTER 12: COMPLEXITY — 4- TO 13-FUND COMBINATIONS

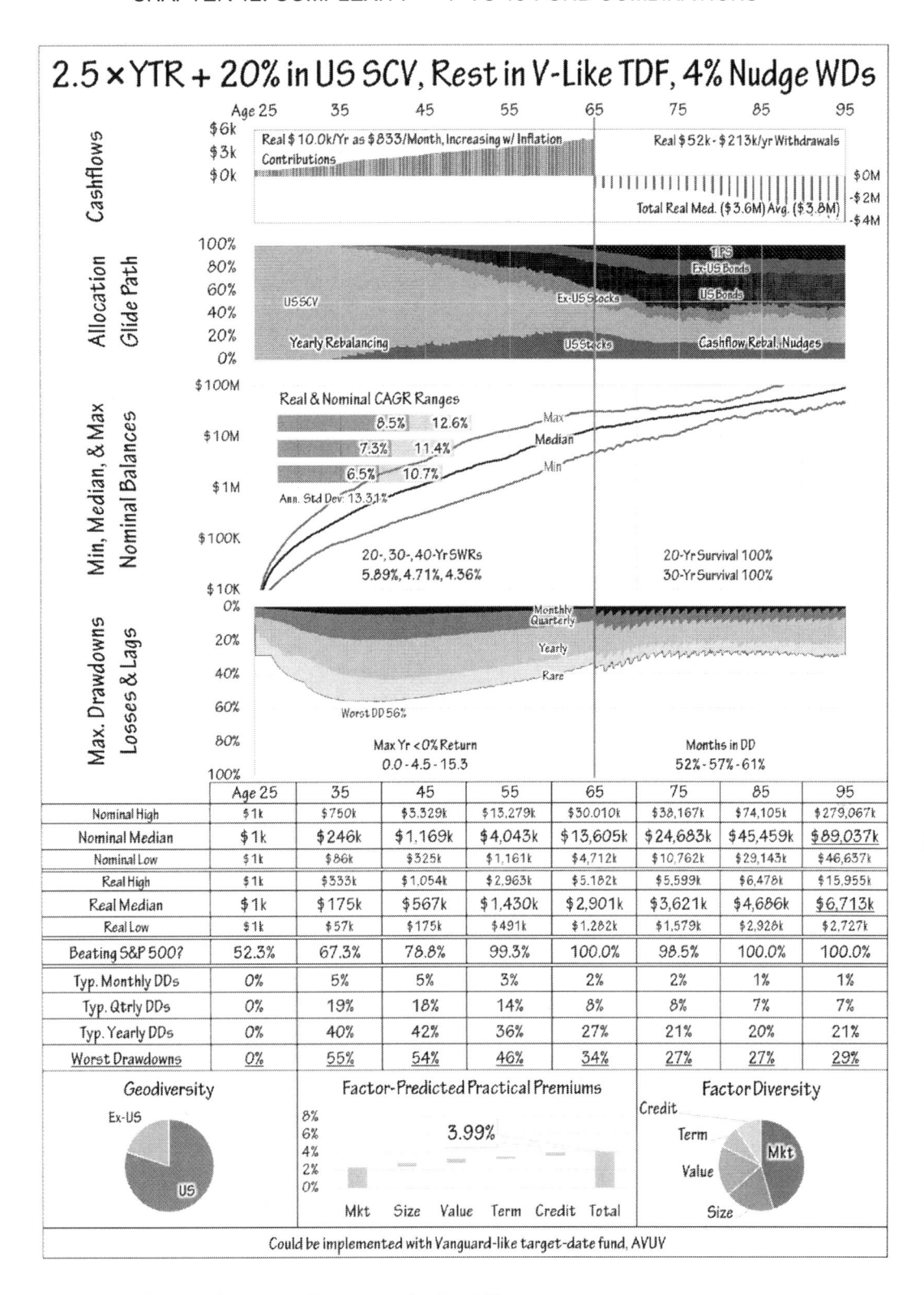

2.5 × YTR + 20% in US SCV, Rest in V-Like TDF, 4% Nudge WDs

	Age 25	35	45	55	65	75	85	95
Nominal High	$1k	$750k	$3,329k	$13,279k	$30,010k	$38,167k	$74,105k	$279,067k
Nominal Median	$1k	$246k	$1,169k	$4,043k	$13,605k	$24,683k	$45,459k	$89,037k
Nominal Low	$1k	$86k	$325k	$1,161k	$4,712k	$10,762k	$29,143k	$46,637k
Real High	$1k	$333k	$1,054k	$2,963k	$5,182k	$5,599k	$6,478k	$15,955k
Real Median	$1k	$175k	$567k	$1,430k	$2,901k	$3,621k	$4,686k	$6,713k
Real Low	$1k	$57k	$175k	$491k	$1,282k	$1,579k	$2,928k	$2,727k
Beating S&P 500?	52.3%	67.3%	78.8%	99.3%	100.0%	98.5%	100.0%	100.0%
Typ. Monthly DDs	0%	5%	5%	3%	2%	2%	1%	1%
Typ. Qtrly DDs	0%	19%	18%	14%	8%	8%	7%	7%
Typ. Yearly DDs	0%	40%	42%	36%	27%	21%	20%	21%
Worst Drawdowns	0%	55%	54%	46%	34%	27%	27%	29%

Could be implemented with Vanguard-like target-date fund, AVUV

Figure 57. Backtest of Aggressive 2 Funds for Life strategy

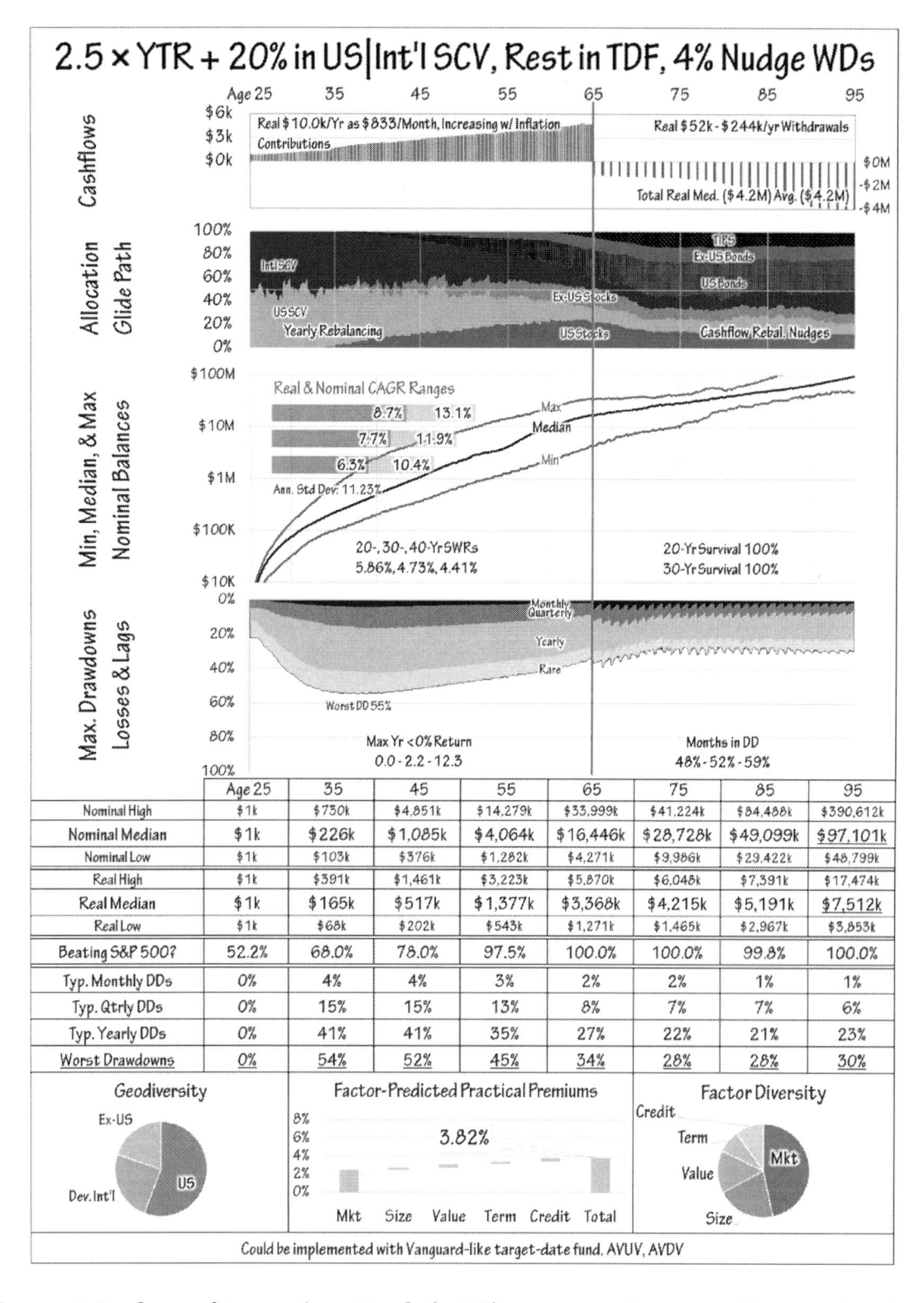

Figure 58. Backtest of Aggressive 2 Funds for Life strategy using US and international small-cap value

The headline is that these three approaches performed quite similarly in the past, but a couple of differences that stand out. First, the level of geographic diversification varies significantly across the three options. The 2 Funds for Life solution is more heavily tilted toward the US, so it doesn't have as much geographic diversification. The 3-Fund solution has the highest geographic diversification and looks to have delivered higher returns over this timeframe. Second, the Merriman Aggressive Target-Date Glide Path was designed as a "to retirement," not "through retirement," glide path, so it gets to its most conservative asset allocation at age 65. The 2 Funds for Life and 3-Fund approaches align with the Vanguard "through" glide path and don't reach their most conservative allocation until age 72. That means the drawdown risk is a little higher right at retirement for the simpler solutions but lower by age 75.

Are these differences enough to justify the higher complexity of the Merriman Aggressive Target-Date Glide Path? I think most investors would say no, especially since the 2-Fund solution only requires rebalancing two funds once a year until retirement and nudge withdrawals thereafter.

The reason for the more complex portfolios isn't performance. It's fine control at a level many investors can do without.

If complexity is not required to get a good return per unit of risk, why do we hear about so many complex portfolios and investment strategies? One reason is regret avoidance. If you hold a little of a lot of different asset classes, you won't feel as bad when you hear which one performed the best in the prior year because you'll have held some of it. Another reason is that it's hard to sell simplicity. Who is going to pay an advisor or robo-advisor to manage two funds? Professional money managers and others in the financial services industry need to justify their fees and costs. One of the simplest ways to do that is to explain how complex it is to manage our investments. In fact, a complex portfolio is easier for them to manage because they can put every investor in the same portfolio and use all the independent knobs to adjust it for each client. If every portfolio holds the same 13 investments in various target percentages, it's much easier for them to automate the management of hundreds of portfolios.

Simple 2- or 3-Fund portfolios delivered returns per unit of risk that were just as good or better than complex portfolios. And since they were easier to follow, DIY investors were more likely to get those returns.

Whether simple or complex, almost all the strategies we've looked at so far have survived all the way to the end of the 70 years tested. That's because our assumptions have been somewhat ideal. What happens when things don't go as planned? We'll look at that next.

Chapter 13
Resilience — Surviving the Unexpected

Milnesium tardigradum — *Tardigrades are so resilient that some have survived the radiation, near-vacuum, and frigid temperatures of outer space.*

Many long-lived animals have defensive attributes that are rarely needed but are lifesaving under threatening conditions. Tortoise shells, elephant tusks, jellyfish stinging cells (nematocysts) help each species survive infrequent but life-threatening attacks.

What would you say if I told you the "risky" small-cap value funds we added to the "conservative" target-date funds in the 2 Funds for Life strategies actually make them more resilient?

So far, the scenarios we've run assume a uniform (some might say best case) way of saving for 40 years, then withdrawing 4% increasing with inflation until age 95. But what if things don't go as planned? What if our first 10 years of savings go toward a down payment on a house or establishing a business? What if we lose our job unexpectedly and are forced to retire early? What if we have the good luck of living longer in retirement? What if we need to withdraw more than 4% to meet our living expenses? And what if we freak out along the way and don't stick with the plan?

We can't test all the possibilities, but one extreme example might be telling.

Here's a set of assumptions for a surprise early retirement scenario:

- For some unknown reason, after working only 30 years, we're forced to retire at age 55.
- Through age 55, we invest in a TDF or 2 Funds for Life strategy as if we'll retire at age 65.
- At age 55, we switch to the TDF or 2 Funds for Life target allocation that fits a new retiree.
- For approaches that use annual rebalancing in retirement, the modeled allocation will also change at age 55.
- For approaches that use nudge withdrawals in retirement, the target-date fund allocation will change at age 55 along with the target second fund allocation. Still, it may take some years for the second fund to reach its target through nudge withdrawals.
- For the Aggressive 2 Funds for Life strategy, we'll also model it without the age 55 rebalance to see what difference it makes.

- Because we retire early, we'll likely need a higher withdrawal rate from a smaller nest egg. Since our savings rate was $10k/year (15% of our income), if we need 75% of our preretirement income to live on in retirement, we need a real withdrawal rate of $50k/year.
- Finally, since we retire early, we'll have more years of retirement, say, 40 instead of 30.

Can any of the approaches we've looked at survive this combination of stresses? How much lower will the total withdrawals and end balances be? Let's see. Table 13 summarizes the backtest results for these assumptions:

	Results for Surprise Early (Age 55) Retirement w/ 5% WD's to Age 95 (Assumes target asset allocations adjust to retirement allocations at age 55)						
	Real End Balance Range	Average Real WDs	Worst Peak DD & Age	Worst DD @ 55, 95	40-Year SWR	40-Year, Survival %	% of Times > S&P 500
"Buffet Strategy" Fixed 90 | 10 S&P 500 | ST Bonds	$2.71M $1.05M $0k	$1.7M $43k/yr	100% @ 67	45% 100%	2.40%	63%	0%
Vanguard-Like Target-date Fund	$1.87M $0k $0k	$1.6M $40k/yr	100% @ 68	33% 100%	2.91%	46%	0%
Easy 2FFL Fixed 90 | 10 TDF | US SCV	$4.55M $1.03M $0k	$1.8M $45k/yr	100% @ 73	37% 100%	NA	63%	25%
Moderate 2FFL 1.5 X YTR in US SCV, Rest in V-Like TDF	$5.06M $1.26M $0k	$1.8M $45k/yr	100% @ 70	36% 100%	3.52%	75%	29%
Aggressive 2FFL 2.5 X YTR + 20% in US SCV, Rest in V-Like TDF One Rebalance at Age 55 Followed by Nudge WD's	$17.6M $5.72M $208k	$2.0M $50k/yr	60% @ 94	44% 57%	4.37%	100%	100%
Aggressive 2FFL 2.5 X YTR + 20% in US SCV, Rest in V-Like TDF No Rebalance at Age 55 Followed by Nudge WD's	$34.9M $13.2M $4.32M	$2.0M $50k/yr	60% @ 89	44% 48%	4.59%	100%	100%

Table 13. Surprise early retirement comparison of Buffett strategy, Vanguard-like target-date fund, and 2 Funds for Life strategies with and without at-retirement rebalancing

As expected, these difficult "surprise" assumptions lowered survival rates for the more conservative approaches. The Buffett approach, Vanguard-like target-date fund, and Easy 2 Funds for Life scenarios all had survival rates under 65% instead of the 98% to 100% we saw with the more ideal scenarios at the end of chapter 10. The moderate 2 Funds for Life strategy pulled that up to 75%, but that means it still failed 25% of the time.

The big surprise is that the Aggressive 2 Funds for Life approaches had 100% 40-year survival rates regardless of the rebalancing approach. We might have expected a lower survival rate for the scenario in which we do a single rebalance to the 20% allocation before starting the nudge withdrawals, but that's not the case. It still survived 100% of the time and managed to deliver a median real end balance of $5.72M, albeit with 44% to 57% drawdowns in retirement and a worst-case real end balance of $208k. For the Aggressive 2 Funds for Life strategy that used only nudge-withdrawal rebalancing, the allocation to US small-cap value at age 55 is 45%, and the withdrawals aren't enough to pull it down. That kept portfolio volatility high in retirement, but it also delivered the highest median real end balance of $13.2M.

Of all the stops on our journey, this may be one of the most surprising and instructive. At the start of our quest, many of us probably thought bonds were safe and stocks were risky. Once we learned about more-volatile small and value stocks, we might have seen them as having higher returns but also being riskier. These stress tests are telling us something entirely different.

> **In the long-run, target-date fund investors who hold some small-cap value equities are likely safer and more resilient than investors who don't.**

The detailed backtests are included in the following pages. You'll notice some gaps and omissions due to many portfolios not surviving to the end.

We're nearing the end of our quest, but before we head home, we need to reflect on the fuzziness of our crystal ball.

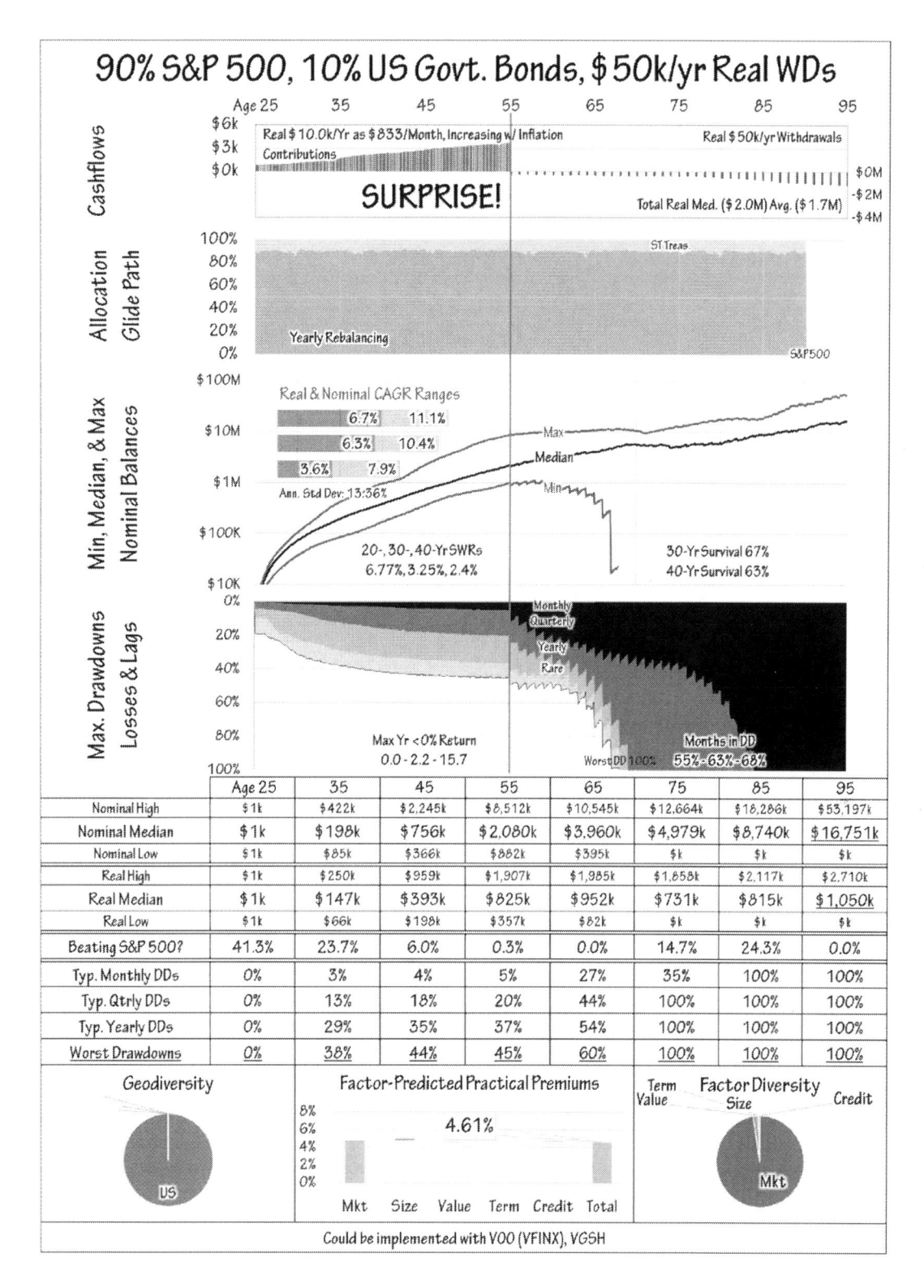

CHAPTER 13: RESILIENCE — SURVIVING THE UNEXPECTED

Figure 59. Backtest of Buffett strategy with a surprise, early, age 55 retirement

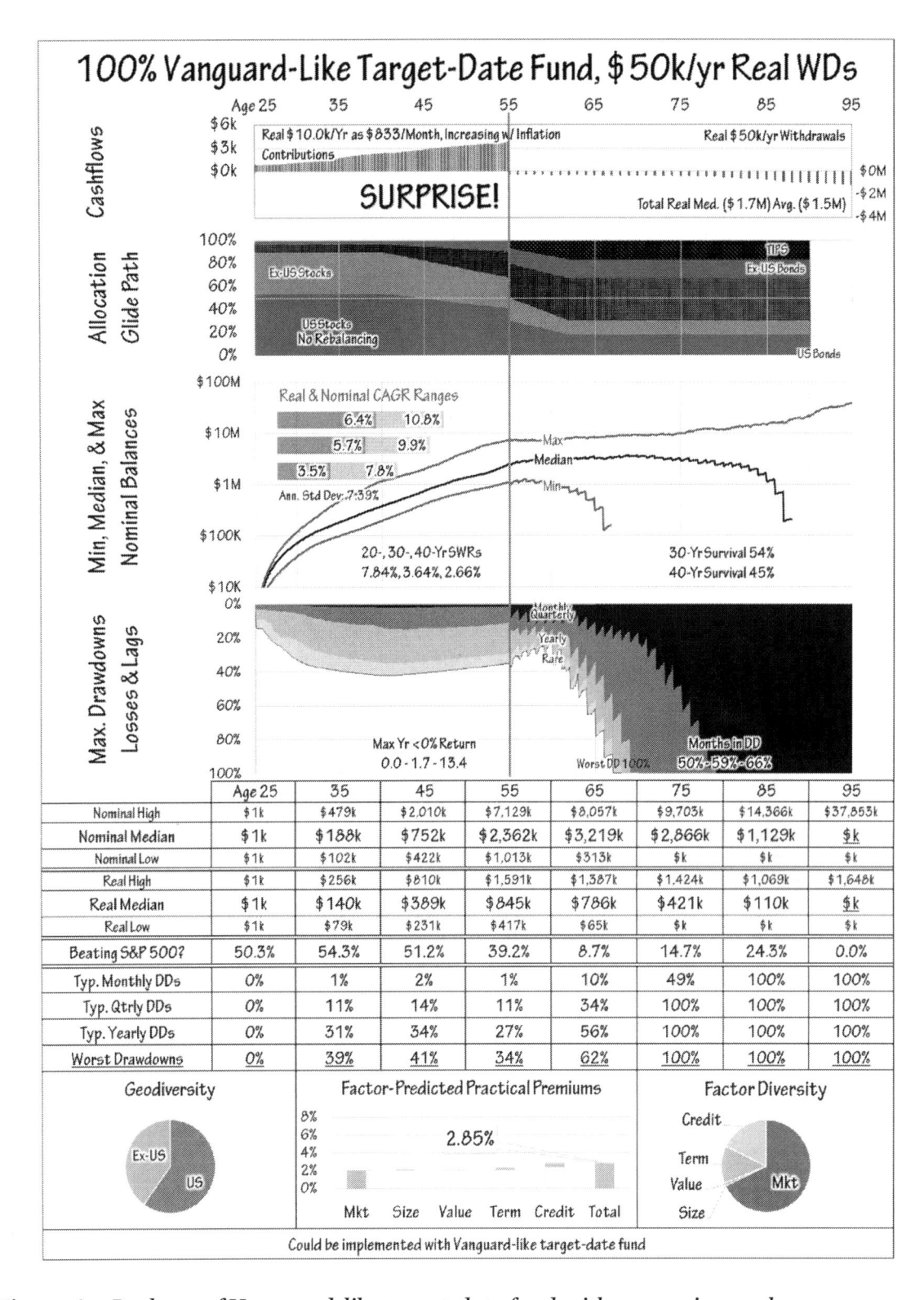

Figure 60. Backtest of Vanguard-like target-date fund with a surprise, early, age 55 retirement

CHAPTER 13: RESILIENCE — SURVIVING THE UNEXPECTED

90% V-Like TDF, 10% US SCV, $50k/yr Real WDs

	Age 25	35	45	55	65	75	85	95
Nominal High	$1k	$482k	$2,147k	$7,777k	$11,825k	$15,343k	$28,076k	$94,237k
Nominal Median	$1k	$190k	$818k	$2,559k	$4,572k	$6,310k	$8,422k	$11,090k
Nominal Low	$1k	$101k	$418k	$990k	$1,006k	-$253k	-$314k	$k
Real High	$1k	$257k	$813k	$1,735k	$2,042k	$2,251k	$2,298k	$4,129k
Real Median	$1k	$145k	$395k	$919k	$995k	$926k	$845k	$761k
Real Low	$1k	$78k	$225k	$419k	$210k	-$37k	-$36k	$k
Beating S&P 500?	52.0%	60.5%	60.3%	67.0%	61.2%	43.0%	46.2%	17.2%
Typ. Monthly DDs	0%	2%	2%	2%	5%	16%	93%	100%
Typ. Qtrly DDs	0%	10%	12%	10%	13%	76%	100%	100%
Typ. Yearly DDs	0%	31%	35%	30%	25%	100%	100%	100%
Worst Drawdowns	0%	40%	43%	38%	33%	100%	100%	100%

Could be implemented with Vanguard-like target-date fund, AVUV

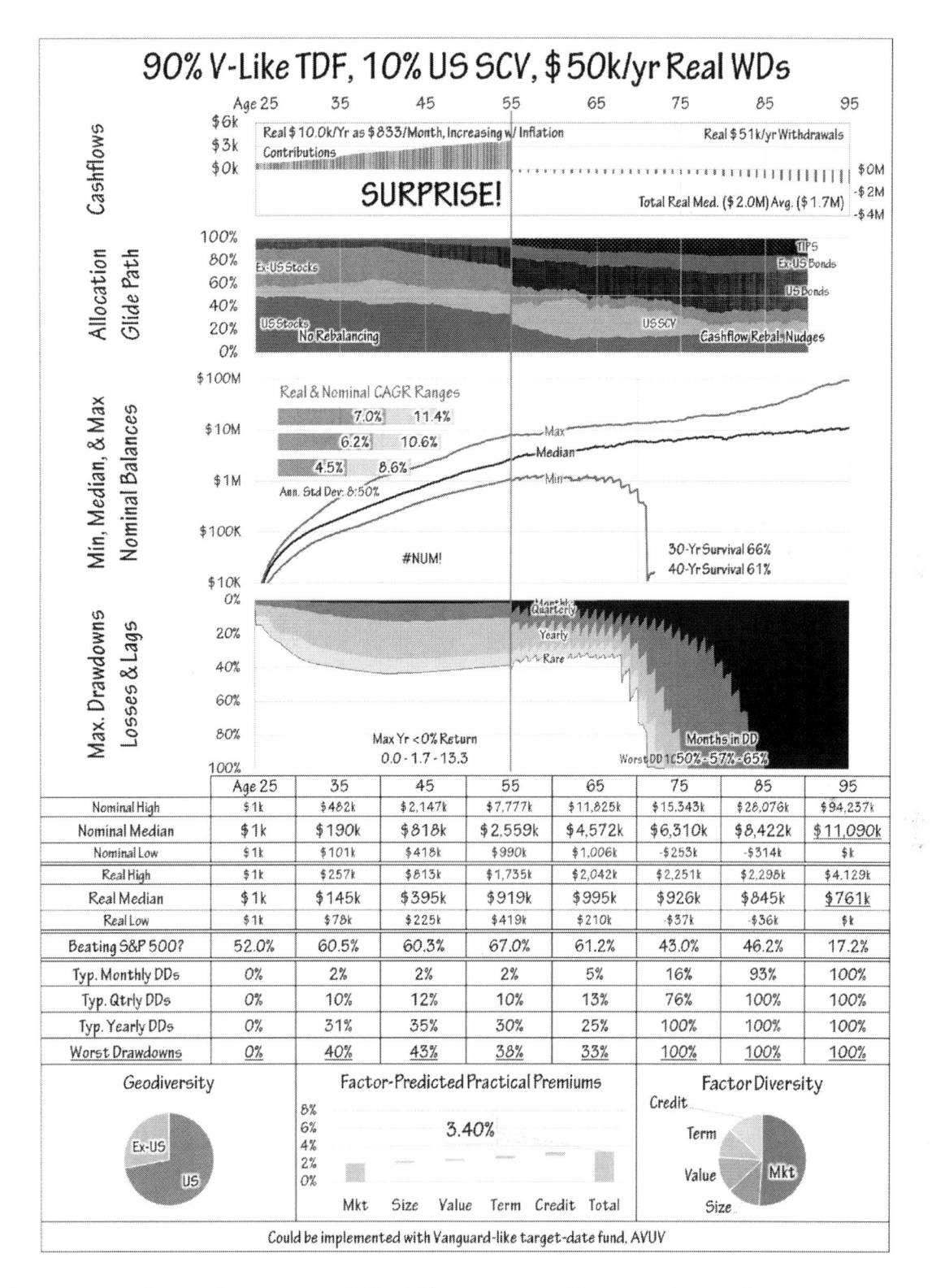

Figure 61. Backtest of Easy 2 Funds for Life strategy with a surprise, early, age 55 retirement

1.5 × YTR in US SCV, Rest in V-Like TDF, $50k/yr Real WDs

	Age 25	35	45	55	65	75	85	95
Nominal High	$1k	$512k	$2,625k	$9,582k	$12,562k	$17,097k	$31,132k	$96,327k
Nominal Median	$1k	$218k	$943k	$2,950k	$5,179k	$6,817k	$10,423k	$15,552k
Nominal Low	$1k	$101k	$386k	$1,092k	$564k	$k	$k	$k
Real High	$1k	$274k	$892k	$2,138k	$2,176k	$2,508k	$2,381k	$4,504k
Real Median	$1k	$158k	$446k	$1,067k	$1,145k	$1,000k	$1,051k	$1,078k
Real Low	$1k	$69k	$208k	$462k	$117k	$k	$k	$k
Beating S&P 500?	52.8%	60.8%	74.0%	89.0%	76.2%	67.8%	56.2%	15.2%
Typ. Monthly DDs	0%	2%	2%	2%	3%	4%	15%	100%
Typ. Qtrly DDs	0%	11%	12%	10%	15%	100%	100%	100%
Typ. Yearly DDs	0%	33%	36%	29%	38%	100%	100%	100%
Worst Drawdowns	0%	46%	45%	37%	49%	100%	100%	100%

Could be implemented with Vanguard-like target-date fund, AVUV

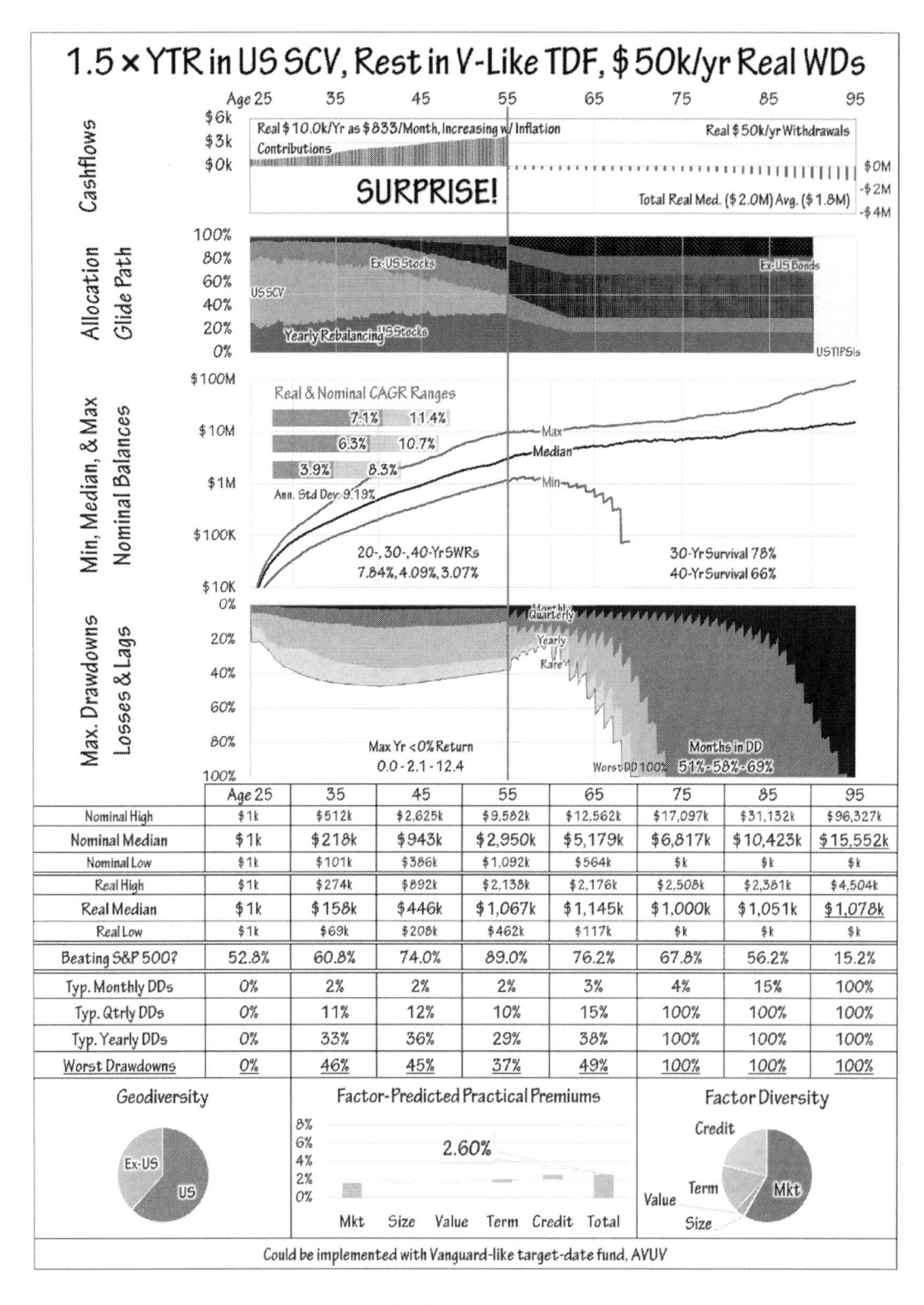

Figure 62. Backtest of Moderate 2 Funds for Life strategy with a surprise, early, age 55 retirement

CHAPTER 13: RESILIENCE — SURVIVING THE UNEXPECTED

2.5 × YTR + 20% in US SCV, Rest in TDF, $50k/yr Real WDs

Cashflows: Real $10.0k/Yr as $833/Month, Increasing w/ Inflation Contributions; Real $50k/yr Withdrawals; SURPRISE!; Total Real Med. ($2.0M) Avg. ($2.0M)

Allocation Glide Path: US SCV, Ex-US Stocks, US Stocks, Bonds, TIPS; Yearly Rebalancing; Cashflow Rebal. Nudges

Min, Median, & Max Nominal Balances: Real & Nominal CAGR Ranges: 9.3% / 13.9% (Max), 8.1% / 12.2% (Median), 7.0% / 11.1% (Min); Ann. Std Dev: 15.77%; 20-, 30-, 40-Yr SWRs: 8.97%, 4.82%, 4.57%; 30-Yr Survival 100%; 40-Yr Survival 100%

Max. Drawdowns, Losses & Lags: Monthly, Quarterly, Yearly, Rare; Worst DD 61%; Max Yr < 0% Return 0.0 - 4.5 - 15.3; Months in DD 54% - 61% - 66%

	Age 25	35	45	55	65	75	85	95
Nominal High	$1k	$750k	$3,329k	$13,022k	$29,326k	$47,736k	$188,124k	$775,043k
Nominal Median	$1k	$246k	$1,169k	$3,894k	$9,036k	$19,848k	$59,378k	$172,605k
Nominal Low	$1k	$86k	$325k	$1,040k	$2,876k	$10,038k	$23,014k	$51,536k
Real High	$1k	$333k	$1,054k	$2,906k	$5,063k	$7,003k	$12,503k	$34,265k
Real Median	$1k	$175k	$567k	$1,379k	$1,993k	$2,912k	$6,420k	$12,883k
Real Low	$1k	$57k	$175k	$440k	$709k	$1,473k	$2,617k	$4,114k
Beating S&P 500?	52.3%	67.3%	78.8%	99.2%	100.0%	100.0%	100.0%	100.0%
Typ. Monthly DDs	0%	5%	5%	3%	5%	5%	5%	6%
Typ. Qtrly DDs	0%	19%	18%	14%	17%	17%	19%	19%
Typ. Yearly DDs	0%	40%	42%	35%	34%	38%	42%	37%
Worst Drawdowns	0%	55%	54%	45%	44%	49%	54%	48%

Geodiversity: Ex-US, US

Factor-Predicted Practical Premiums: Mkt, Size, Value, Term, Credit, Total = 7.15%

Factor Diversity: Term, Value, Mkt, Size, Credit

Could be implemented with Vanguard-like target-date fund, AVUV

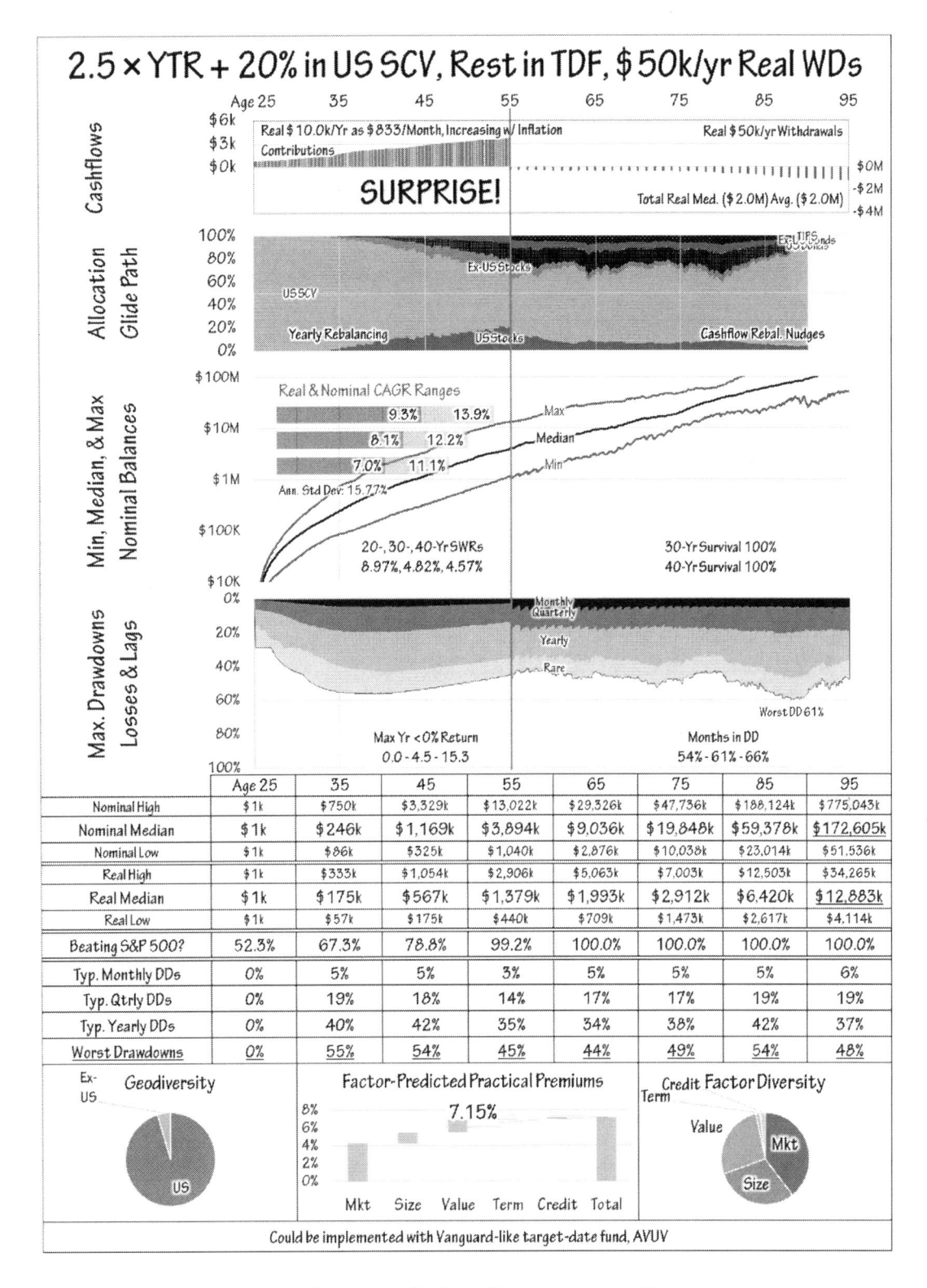

Figure 63. Backtest of Aggressive 2 Funds for Life strategy with a surprise, early, age 55 retirement and only nudge rebalancing

2.5 × YTR + 20% in US SCV, Rest in TDF, $50k/yr Real WDs

	Age 25	35	45	55	65	75	85	95
Nominal High	$1k	$750k	$3,329k	$13,113k	$23,321k	$36,370k	$101,789k	$354,157k
Nominal Median	$1k	$246k	$1,169k	$3,887k	$8,725k	$15,445k	$34,072k	$70,583k
Nominal Low	$1k	$86k	$325k	$1,067k	$2,526k	$3,418k	$3,527k	$542k
Real High	$1k	$333k	$1,054k	$2,926k	$4,039k	$5,336k	$6,917k	$16,561k
Real Median	$1k	$175k	$567k	$1,385k	$1,781k	$2,266k	$3,692k	$5,329k
Real Low	$1k	$57k	$175k	$451k	$527k	$502k	$406k	$50k
Beating S&P 500?	52.3%	67.3%	78.8%	99.2%	100.0%	100.0%	100.0%	100.0%
Typ. Monthly DDs	0%	5%	5%	3%	2%	1%	1%	2%
Typ. Qtrly DDs	0%	19%	18%	14%	9%	7%	7%	10%
Typ. Yearly DDs	0%	40%	42%	35%	24%	21%	19%	56%
Worst Drawdowns	0%	55%	54%	44%	32%	29%	25%	88%

Could be implemented with Vanguard-like target-date fund, AVUV

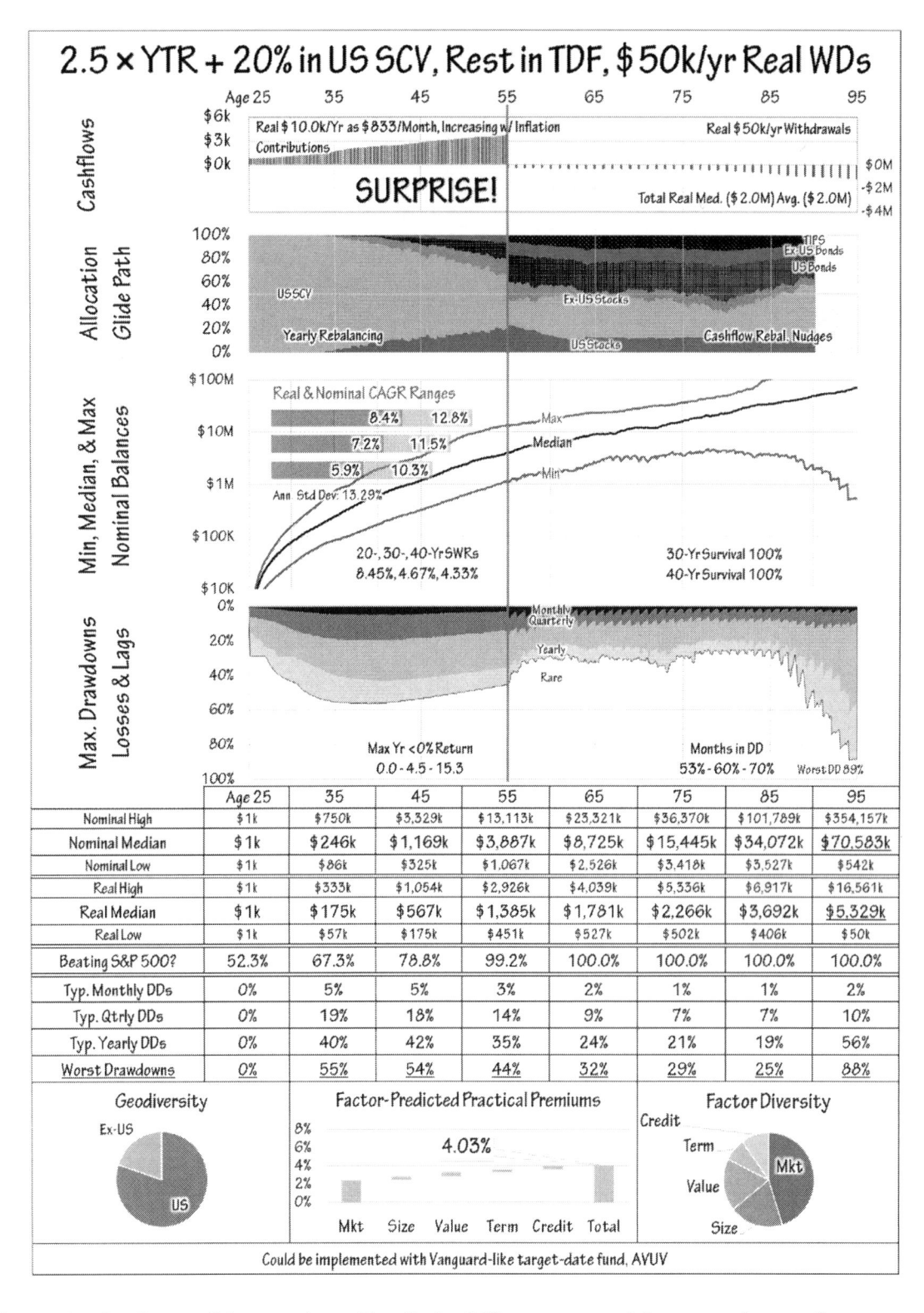

Figure 64. Backtest of Aggressive 2 Funds for Life strategy with a surprise, early, age 55 retirement, one rebalance at 55, then nudge withdrawals thereafter

Chapter 14
Contrarian Views — A Dose of Humility

Proteus anguinus — *The olm, the longest-lived amphibian, is blind and patient, able to survive without food for up to 10 years and to live more than 100 years.*

Life is a balance of confidence and humility. Too much confidence leads to rash behavior. Too much humility leads to paralysis. This chapter aims to balance things out.

As much as I've tried to show the uncertainty of past results, I fear that the clarity of black and white numbers, charts, and graphs may make us overconfident in our ability to choose winning strategies. The truth is that many of the strategies we've looked at have significant overlap in their likely outcomes. You can see this in Figure 65, which shows the relative likelihood of different total financial benefits from the Vanguard-like target-date fund and 2 Funds for Life strategies:

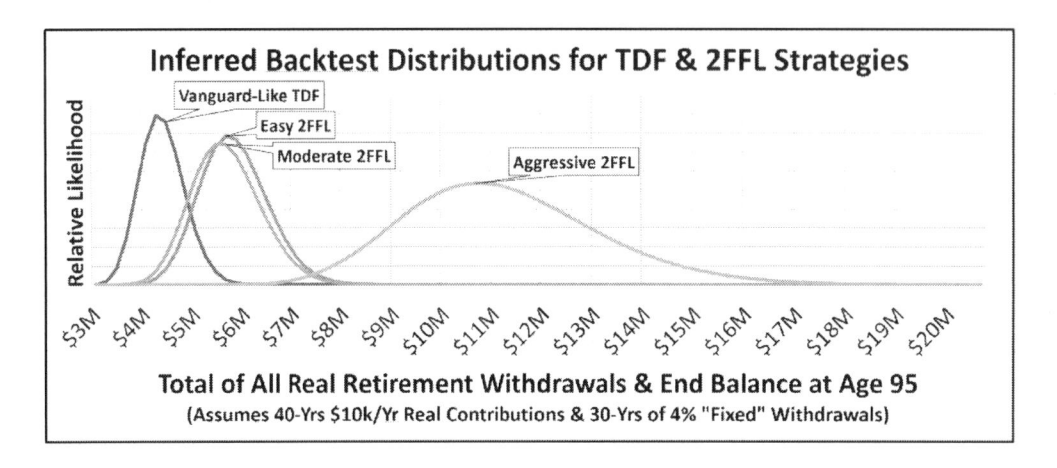

Figure 65. Inferred distributions of total real withdrawals and end balances for Vanguard-like target-date fund and Easy, Moderate, and Aggressive 2 Funds for Life strategies

The Easy and Moderate 2 Funds for Life strategies have practically the same expected total of withdrawals and end balances and differ primarily in implementation and risk-benefit timing. Both overlap the Vanguard-like target-date fund expected outcomes as well. Though it's still reasonable to choose an approach because it had a better past median outcome, it might still underperform an approach with a worse median historical outcome for decades or even a lifetime.

All backtesting gets us is an educated guess about what's more or less likely to happen in the future. That educated guess is still valuable. Without it, we're flying blind.

There are many reasons to be skeptical of any backtesting. I'll list a few here. The point isn't to ignore them but to consider them as indicative at best and misleading at worst.

CHAPTER 14: CONTRARIAN VIEWS — A DOSE OF HUMILITY

1. The future may not be like the past. There is no guarantee that stocks will outperform bonds or that small and value will outperform large and growth. History suggests that they have over the long term, but the future can be different.

2. Historical return sequences are imperfect. There aren't fund return sequences for all the different asset classes we've modeled going back to 1970. We've had to fill some of those in with the best data we could find.

3. Since the advantages of investing in a wider range of assets like small and value are more widely understood and available through ETFs and mutual funds today than in the past, they may produce smaller premiums in the future.

4. Today's high market valuations and low bond interest rates may reduce returns for the next decade or longer.

5. If we'd been able to backtest further back in time, say to 1928 and the Great Depression, drawdowns would have been substantially worse. We may have to endure more volatility than what's reflected in the backtests to get the returns they've delivered. (See Appendix 7 for a deeper exploration of the impact of the 1928 returns.)

6. The circular bootstrapping method I've used, where the 2019 returns are followed by 1970, could produce substantially better or worse scenarios than the straight historical sequence.

7. The circular bootstrapping method also understates the amount of variation 45 to 55 years into the lifetime scenarios (ages 70-80). That's because there is really only one independent 50-year return sequence compared to 600 different return sequences for every other duration of time.

8. The circular bootstrapping method often encompasses the 1970s period of high inflation twice, resulting in a greater difference between real and nominal returns than we would expect given our recent history of relatively

low inflation. Will high inflation return? We don't know. Is it more realistic to look at the real returns rather than the nominal returns? Yes, and we did.

9. No one is likely to execute any strategy as perfectly as the backtests assume. We're all human and likely to be inconsistent. We might skip rebalancing for a year or a decade. We might freak out and sell at the wrong time. We might flit from one winning strategy to another. There's no way to backtest all of these variations, but they happen and will be part of most of our experiences.

10. The backtests use monthly returns data, but many investors watch their portfolios daily. Daily volatility and drawdowns are greater, so again, you may have to tolerate more risk than you think to get the return you expect. The moral of the story is "Don't peek!"

11. The backtests don't include taxes. Taxes will either reduce what you invest or what you can spend if you're taxed on your withdrawals.

12. The backtests don't include the cost of an advisor. If you need an advisor to stay the course with one of these strategies and that costs you between 0.3% and 1.0% of your portfolio per year, it will dramatically lower your end balance. I prefer to think you can learn enough to do it on your own, but you'll be better off paying for the help if you really need an advisor.

Don't get me wrong. I think we can learn a lot from the backtesting simulations we've seen on our quest. It's also good to realize they aren't as precise or conclusive as the tables, charts, and graphs might make them look.

Another objection I expect will be that by combining assets with the target-date fund, we're violating the sanctity of their glide path design. It's true, but we should probably consider a mass-market target-date fund glide path designer's task and objectives before deciding to accept it. We can get some insight from a quote from Vanguard's 2015 document, "Vanguard's approach to target-date funds." I've underlined the key phrase:

If we expect the risk-reward relationships of the past to prevail in the future, it makes sense that simulation output would conclude that higher allocations to riskier asset classes will overall lead to greater wealth accumulation and retirement income over an investor's life cycle. <u>If maximization of wealth is the primary goal, then a higher equity allocation would be an appropriate strategy.</u> However, this does not account for the downside risk that investors would need to withstand (as just mentioned) on a short-term basis. Conversely, if minimization of risk is the goal, simulation results would lean toward much more conservative allocations.

Vanguard, and other target-date fund providers, are designing one-size-fits-all funds for any given retirement date. They know nothing about how knowledgeable, patient, risk-averse, or disciplined their customers will be. If they choose a strategy that requires unusual patience, they could be doing their customers of average or less-than-average patience a great disservice, triggering them to panic sell after a period when the strategy lags the market. (For a look at whether differences between target-date funds might impact a 2 Funds for Life strategy, see Appendix 5.)

My job in writing this book is much easier. I don't have to recommend something for you to use. I just describe options from which you can choose.

Finally, I think it's important to refute the idea that small-cap value is some invincible super asset class. After having shown so many examples where it would have helped produce dramatically better results in the past, some of you may be thinking, "Why invest in anything else?" There were many points along this journey where I wondered that myself. Let's revisit the chart we started with showing the effect of mixing bonds with the S&P 500 and US small-cap value but with returns going back to 1928. Though we don't have returns going back that far for all of the asset classes in the target-date fund, we do have them for these three:

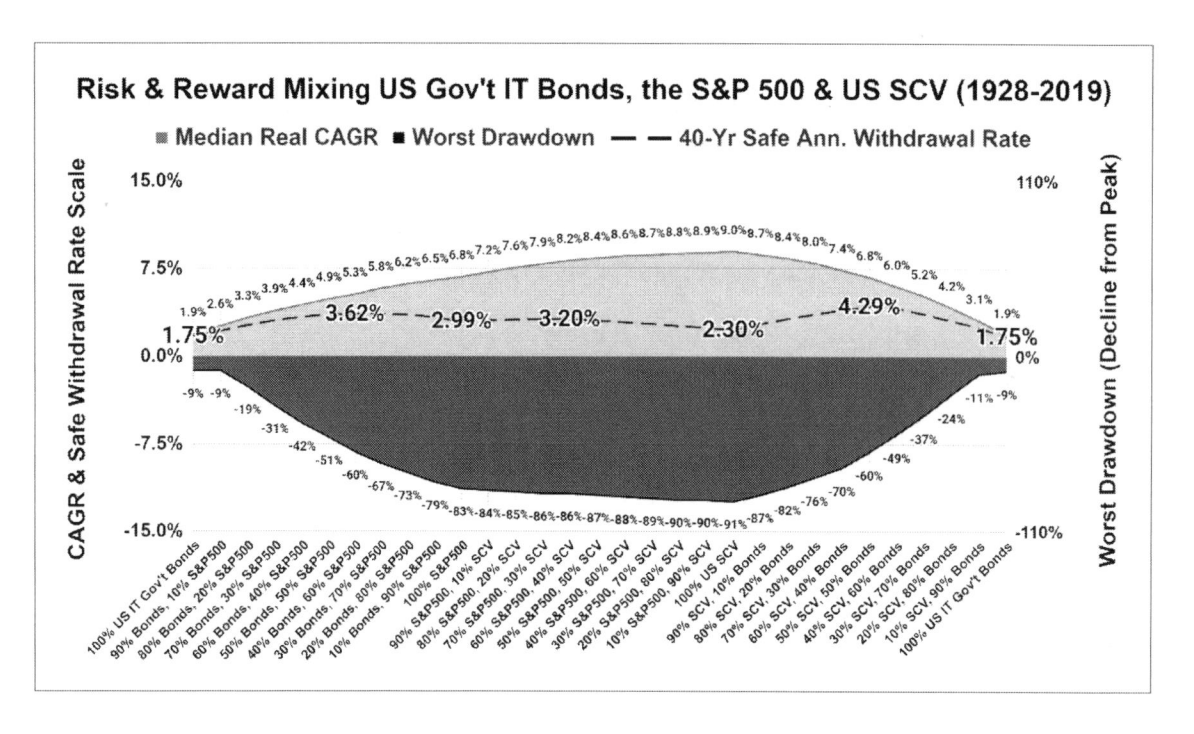

Figure 66. Risk and reward versus a mix of intermediate-term US government bonds, S&P 500, and US small-cap-value using 1928-2019 historical returns

If this doesn't provide the dose of humility I'm hoping for, I'm not sure what will. When we run our backtests back to 1928 we see much deeper drawdowns and lower safe withdrawal rates because they include the market crash of 1929 and the economic turmoil of the Great Depression. The All-Small-Cap-Value portfolio was particularly bad with a safe withdrawal rate of 2.30% and a worst-case drawdown of 91%! Some might say that was an extraordinarily bad time for US markets and that we now have mechanisms in place to avoid such disasters. Others would point out that the longer we live, the more likely we are to see extreme events. Whichever perspective resonates with you, it's best to remember that we can never really know what the future holds.

Chapter 15
Bringing it Home — Conclusions

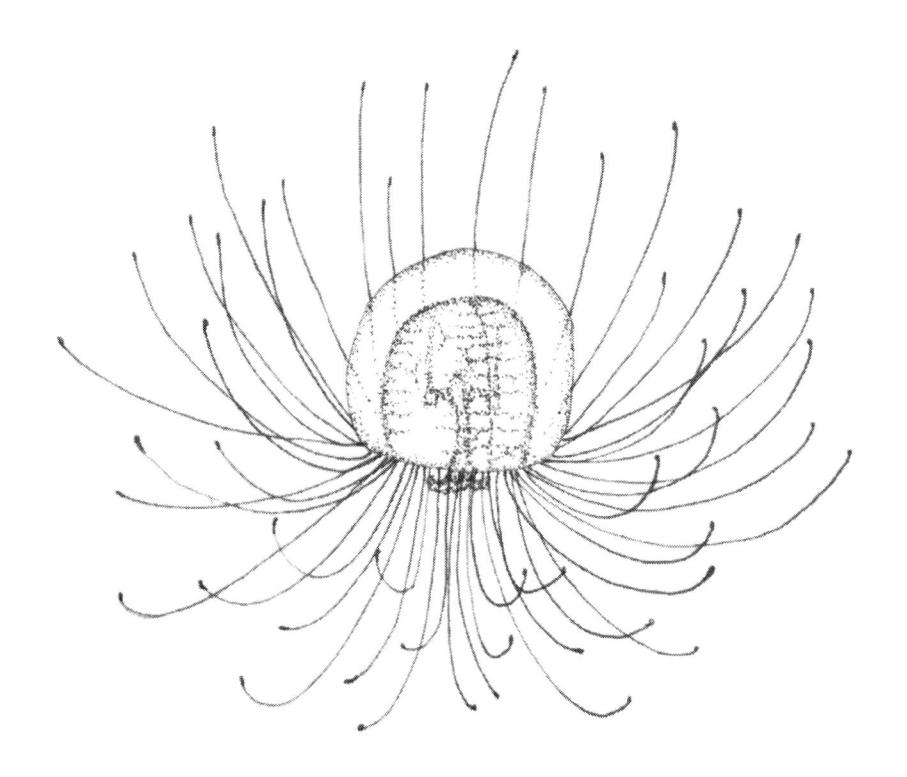

Turritopsis dohrnii — *The immortal jellyfish can revert from a mature adult to a juvenile form, allowing it to live indefinitely.*

Though Charles Darwin's quest on the HMS Beagle was only five years, he would write in his biography, "The voyage of the Beagle has been by far the most important event in my life and has determined my whole career."

Our quest has been much shorter, but it might still be life-changing.

We set out to find some simple and effective, long-lived investing strategies and succeeded. We found Easy, Moderate, and Aggressive 2 Funds for Life strategies. We also found 3-Fund barbell portfolios that could surpass complex fixed allocation portfolios in returns per unit of risk. So, what's next? Putting them to work. We've touched on this throughout the book, but here are the steps if you haven't already started:

> **1. Saving.** If most of us start by saving what we can and increase it as quickly as practical until we're saving 10% to 20% of our salary per year, we should have enough money to invest wisely and retire at a reasonable age. If we can put it on autopilot with monthly contributions taken from our paychecks, that's all the better. As we learned, those monthly contributions will smooth the ride in the early years and ensure we buy more when the market is down and cheap, and less when it's up and expensive.
>
> **2. Investing.** As we've seen, investing strategies don't have to be complex to be effective or long-lived. A 2 Funds for Life strategy is likely to perform every bit as well as a more complex portfolio. Combining a target-date fund and a small-cap value fund gives you broad and meaningful diversification across bonds, stocks, and small-cap value stocks. If you want greater geographic diversification, you can split the small-cap value allocation across US and international funds. You should know enough now to decide which of the Easy, Moderate, or Aggressive 2 Funds for Life strategies is best for you. You can also consider the variations described in Chapter 12 and Appendix 1. Remember, the key differences between them are:
>
> - Rebalancing, which provides more control over the timing of drawdowns but reduces expected returns.

- Age-scaling, or years-to-retirement multiplier, helps put more volatility in the early years and less in the later years. It increases the expected balance at retirement and the withdrawals we can live on during retirement.
- The minimum small-cap value allocation floor tends to increase risk, reward, and resilience throughout our lives, but at the cost of higher expected drawdowns at all ages.

The important thing is to pick one and get started.

3. Persisting. Whichever strategy you choose, it's critical to stay the course. Better investing results come through dogged persistence. Few things will lower the expected returns of an investing strategy more than panic selling, panic buying, and performance chasing by selling what's done poorly and buying what's hot. This is where I hope some of the charts, data, and lessons of this book can help you to choose an approach and stick with it. A written plan can greatly improve your chances of following through and staying invested when times get tough, even if it's just a few sentences on a piece of paper.

4. Retiring. Deciding when to retire is a complex life decision, but knowing when you can afford to retire is a relatively straightforward financial calculation. The key question is whether or not the required withdrawal rate is safe. To find out, we need to know:

- How much will we need to live on, including taxes?
- How much will come from Social Security or other sources outside of our investments?
- How much will need to come from our investments?
- How long do we think our retirement will last?
- What is a safe withdrawal rate for our investments over that timeframe?
- What age restrictions, if any, are there on accessing our retirement funds?

As long as the required withdrawals from the retirement investments are at or under the safe withdrawal rate for our investment strategy and the number of years in retirement, retirement should be affordable. That doesn't necessarily mean we should retire, just that we could. There are many good reasons to keep working past the time when we can first afford to retire, but there can also be worthwhile reasons to retire and move on.

Whether you retire early or late, it's a good time to speak with a financial planner, or at the very least, to write your own financial plan. This is the time to determine what your "salary" will be in retirement. Remember, the fixed withdrawal strategies used throughout this book are based on calculating a percentage of the total retirement savings investment at retirement, then scaling it by inflation over time. Calculating the first year's withdrawal and writing it down, along with a few words about how you will calculate inflation in the future, are good first steps. Adding details about your overall investing strategy, the frequency of withdrawals, and plans to rebalance periodically or with nudge withdrawals should also be part of the plan.

5. Taking comfort in the plan. As my good friend Paul Merriman likes to say, "There will always be the good news in column A and the bad news in column B." If you adopt a plan, write it down, and stick with it, you'll be better equipped to ignore the news and noise that surrounds us. Nothing can protect us from feeling stressed or anxious about finances entirely, but if we have a sound plan that we've committed to, it can provide some added comfort and stability. Sometimes it makes sense to update a plan. The fact that it's written down will force us to take time before changing course, and that time will help us pause, think, and avoid rash emotional decisions.

Taking comfort in the plan could also extend your life. Numerous studies have shown that stress in general, and financial stress in particular, contribute to shortened life expectancy. If you can get started early, choose a plan that you can stick with, and then set up automatic paycheck withdrawals and investing so it's all on autopilot, you'll be in a much better position to relax. The same is true in retirement. Having a plan that you have confidence in and can manage easily will free you to do more enjoyable and more important things in life.

And what makes it all work? Two things.

First, we're placing a bet that humanity continues to thrive, innovate, and grow the worldwide economy. The bet is in the form of ownership and loans, or stocks and bonds. It's not magic, but it takes hope and optimism. If you fundamentally believe that the world is doomed and headed for catastrophic failure, you wouldn't place this bet. History would not be on your side though. Although individual companies fail every day, countries fail from time to time, and the world economy has gone through ups and downs, the long-term trend is clear. Those on the optimistic side of this bet have won overwhelmingly.

Second, we're betting on ourselves. We're betting that we can stay the course. If you absolutely need to keep up with your neighbors when the S&P 500 is crushing it, then you should invest in the S&P 500. If you do, though, you will need to be dispassionate when your returns are as bad as theirs during market downturns. If, on the other hand, you want a different return and are willing to tolerate decades of lag to get it, you're a good candidate to diversify further. The simple 2 Funds for Life strategies laid out in this book aren't complicated, but they require patient persistence. The backtesting provides strong evidence that investing something in a diversifying fund is likely to help, but only if you stick with it. If you bail out after 10 years of underperformance, then buy back in after a run-up in price, you'll likely never reap the rewards the backtests have shown. Backtests can't show what will happen in the future and how you'll behave. That's why you must figure out how much "different" you can stomach. I think most people could easily tolerate having 10% of their portfolio underperform for decades in hopes that it will eventually outperform. I think far fewer could tolerate the same underperformance for 30% or more of their portfolio. In the end, you need to decide what your risk tolerance is — not just for drawdowns, but also for underperformance relative to the broader market.

We live in amazing times. Investing has never been easier or cheaper. Automation abounds in the form of retirement account paycheck withdrawals, automatic investing, and self-adjusting target-date funds. Even for those without employer programs, companies like M1 Finance can automate the process with monthly bank account transfers and automatic investing. I hope this book inspires people, young and old, to choose a simple, effective, long-lived investing strategy and put it on autopilot so when the time comes to retire, they are pleasantly surprised at how ready they are. And for those who are already in retirement, I hope this book provides good reason to accept a little more volatility in exchange for reduced long-term risk. History suggests that we will likely be rewarded if we do.

Appendix
Detours & Details

Heterocephalus glaber — *The naked mole-rat is the longest-lived rodent, with an estimated maximum lifespan of 32 years.*

Since first introducing the 2 Funds for Life strategies with Paul Merriman in October 2018, I've received many questions from whom my teachers used to call "interested students." I'm sure some of you have lingering questions too. The appendices of this book address many of them. The topics of interest they cover appear in parentheses.

Appendices:

1. Alternative 2-Fund Recipes (2 Funds for Life)
2. Alternative Second Funds (2 Funds for Life)
3. Early Retirement, or FIRE (2 Funds for Life)
4. Recommended Funds (2 Funds for Life)
5. Target-Date Funds Other Than Vanguard
6. Target-Date Funds with Early or Late Dates
7. Backtesting to 1928 (deeper history)
8. Backtesting Return Sources & Methods (deeper history)
9. Contribution Frequency & Drawdowns (portfolio management)
10. Nudge Withdrawals vs. Rebalancing (portfolio management)
11. Changing an Existing Portfolio (portfolio management)
12. 2 Funds for Life Yearly Allocation Tables (portfolio management)

Appendix 1
Alternative 2 Fund Recipes

Curious readers will certainly have wondered by now about alternatives to the three 2 Funds for Life examples used in the book. What if we combined the YTR 1.5× multiplier with a 10% minimum allocation to the second fund? What about a 3× multiplier? Though the possible combinations are endless, we can learn a lot by looking at the 20 possible combinations of four minimum 2nd fund allocations (0%, 10%, 20%, 30%) and five year-to-retirement multipliers (0, 1.5, 2.0, 2.5, 3.0). Here's a description of the space we'll explore in this appendix.

- The 0%|0× case is the base-case Vanguard-like target-date fund. It appears in the top left corner of the heatmaps in Figure 67.

- The 10%|0× case is the Easy 2 Funds for Life strategy that has no rebalancing except for nudge withdrawals in retirement. It appears in the second-from-left box on the top row of the heatmaps in Figure 67.

- The other 0× cases, which have 20% and 30% allocations to US small-cap value, are also assumed to use no rebalancing except for the nudge withdrawals in retirement. They appear under the 20% and 30% labels in the top row of the heatmaps in Figure 67. We don't include annually rebalanced versions of the fixed allocations because most people willing to do annual rebalancing will likely also want to get the benefits of the age-scaled approaches. As a reminder, those benefits include higher safe withdrawal rates, total retirement withdrawals, median end balances, and lower drawdowns in retirement. The one drawback of the age-scaled approaches is higher worst-case drawdowns in the earlier years.

- The 0%|1.5× case is the Moderate 2 Funds for Life strategy that assumes annual rebalancing during accumulation and nudge withdrawals during retirement. It appears in the far left column of the second row of the heatmaps in Figure 67.

- The rest of the 1.5×, 2.0×, 2.5×, and 3.0× YTR multiplier cases also use annual rebalancing during accumulation and nudge withdrawals in retirement.
- The other scenario assumptions ($10k/year contributions increasing with inflation, 4% fixed withdrawals increasing with inflation) are the same as we've used throughout the book.

Figure 67 is a visualization of the "good news" (safe withdrawal rates, median total withdrawals, and end balances) and the "bad news" (maximum drawdowns at age 40, 65, and 95) for all 20 scenarios. Hopefully, this will help you find your "ultimate" 2 Funds for Life strategy.

APPENDIX 1: ALTERNATIVE 2 FUND RECIPES

The "Good News"

40-yr Retirement SWR

2nd Fund YTR Multiplier	Ending US SCV Ramp Value			
	0%	10%	20%	30%
0	3.84%	3.95%	4.02%	4.15%
1.5	3.84%	4.11%	4.33%	4.52%
2.0	3.84%	4.14%	4.34%	4.51%
2.5	3.84%	4.15%	4.36%	4.51%
3.0	3.84%	4.18%	4.36%	4.51%

Median Total Retirement WDs, Real Dollars ($M)

2nd Fund YTR Multiplier	Ending US SCV Ramp Value			
	0%	10%	20%	30%
0	$2.2	$2.4	$2.7	$3.0
1.5	$2.7	$3.0	$3.3	$3.5
2.0	$2.9	$3.2	$3.4	$3.7
2.5	$3.1	$3.3	$3.6	$3.9
3.0	$3.3	$3.6	$3.8	$4.1

Median Age 95 Ending Balance, Real Dollars ($M)

2nd Fund YTR Multiplier	Ending US SCV Ramp Value			
	0%	10%	20%	30%
0	$2.2	$3.2	$4.7	$7.1
1.5	$2.8	$4.1	$5.9	$8.0
2.0	$3.0	$4.4	$6.3	$8.6
2.5	$3.3	$4.8	$6.7	$9.2
3.0	$3.5	$5.1	$7.1	$9.6

The "Bad News"

Maximum Drawdown, Near Age 40 (Age 66)

2nd Fund YTR Multiplier	Ending US SCV Ramp Value			
	0%	10%	20%	30%
0	42%	44%	(47%)	(52%)
1.5	47%	49%	51%	53%
2.0	50%	52%	54%	56%
2.5	52%	54%	56%	58%
3.0	55%	57%	59%	59%

Maximum Drawdown @ Age 65

2nd Fund YTR Multiplier	Ending US SCV Ramp Value			
	0%	10%	20%	30%
0	27%	35%	42%	47%
1.5	28%	30%	33%	37%
2.0	28%	31%	34%	37%
2.5	28%	31%	34%	37%
3.0	28%	31%	34%	38%

Maximum Drawdown @ Age 95

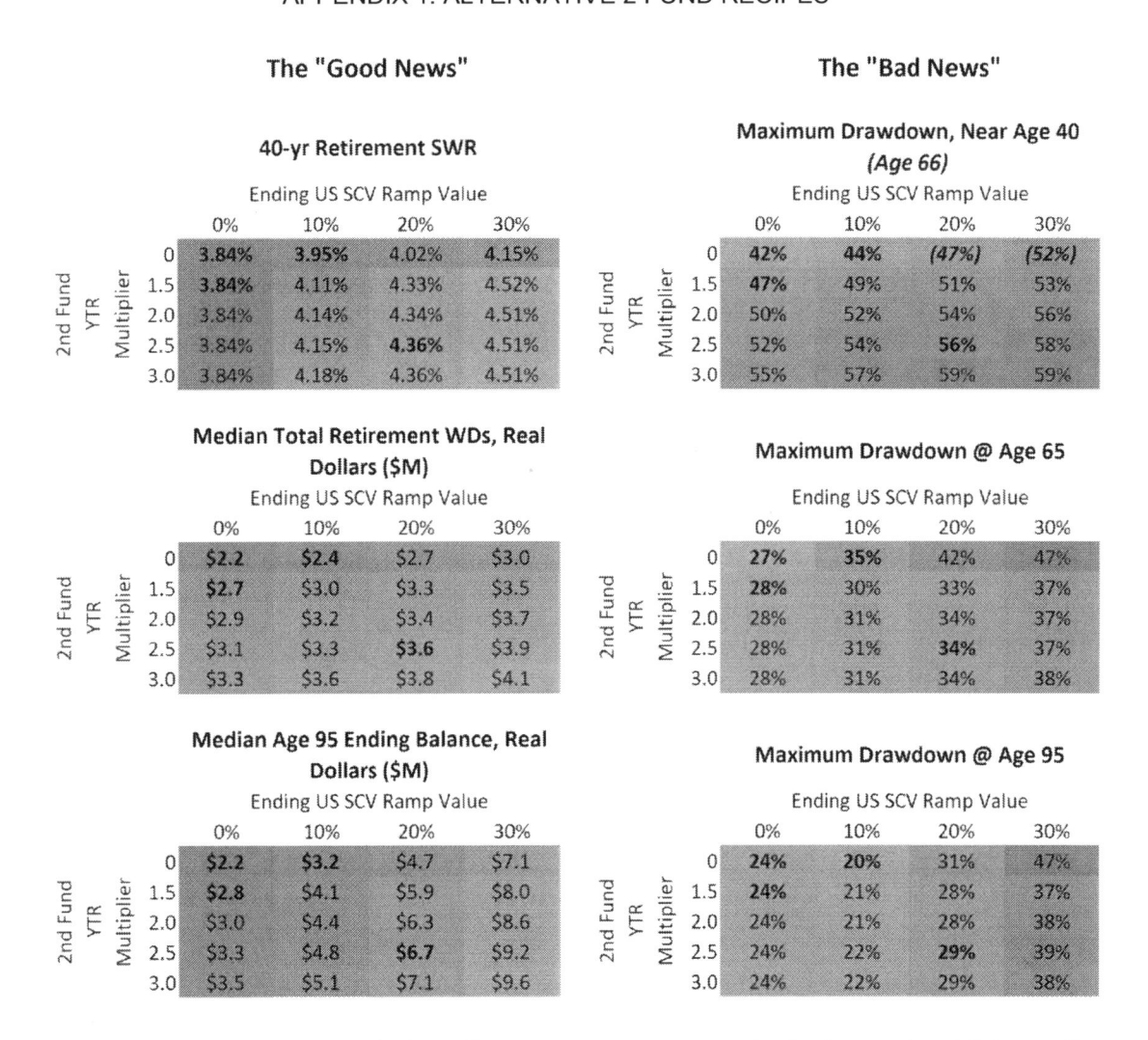

2nd Fund YTR Multiplier	Ending US SCV Ramp Value			
	0%	10%	20%	30%
0	24%	20%	31%	47%
1.5	24%	21%	28%	37%
2.0	24%	21%	28%	38%
2.5	24%	22%	29%	39%
3.0	24%	22%	29%	38%

Figure 67. Alternative 2 Funds for Life strategies summary including safe withdrawal rates, total withdrawals, end balances, and maximum drawdowns at age 40, 65, and 95

Not surprisingly, withdrawals and end balances increased in concert with the allocation to small-cap value. Drawdowns increased too, but all the scenarios survived, and safe withdrawal rates generally increased with higher small-cap value allocations. A few other points stand out.

First, the fixed allocations of 20% and 30% resulted in worst-case drawdowns right around retirement. Forty years of accumulation without rebalancing is just too long to wait and not have the small-cap value fund outgrow the target-date fund. With a large allocation to small-cap value at the beginning of retirement, the 4% nudge withdrawals aren't enough to bring it down. Though both allocations produced higher withdrawals and end balances than the target-date fund or 90|10 allocation, they did so with much higher drawdowns. Furthermore, they didn't produce total withdrawals or end balances that were as good as the YTR-scaled approaches. If you're forced to access small-cap value in a second fund and rebalancing between funds isn't possible, these are viable options. If you can rebalance between the target-date fund and small-cap value fund, the YTR-scaled options are much better.

Second, higher YTR multipliers always led to higher median total retirement withdrawals, end balances, and age 40 drawdowns. You can see this by scanning the charts from top to bottom. This isn't surprising, but it's interesting to see how much difference it made.

Third, the higher the minimum small-cap value allocation, the higher the median total retirement withdrawals, end balances, drawdown depths, and safe withdrawal rates throughout. You can see this by scanning the charts from left to right. This isn't surprising either, but once again, it's interesting to see how much difference it can make.

Between these summary charts and the backtests that follow, you should have enough information to pick a strategy that fits your risk profile.

The detailed backtests for all 20 of these approaches are in the pages that follow.

APPENDIX 1: ALTERNATIVE 2 FUND RECIPES

100% Vanguard-Like Target-Date Fund, 4% Fixed Withdrawals

	Age 25	35	45	55	65	75	85	95
Nominal High	$1k	$479k	$2,010k	$7,379k	$12,900k	$15,480k	$23,900k	$64,532k
Nominal Median	$1k	$188k	$752k	$2,516k	$8,004k	$12,276k	$18,479k	$29,241k
Nominal Low	$1k	$102k	$422k	$1,120k	$3,360k	$5,421k	$10,435k	$10,142k
Real High	$1k	$256k	$810k	$1,646k	$2,393k	$2,271k	$2,655k	$3,569k
Real Median	$1k	$140k	$389k	$896k	$1,737k	$1,801k	$1,812k	$2,180k
Real Low	$1k	$79k	$231k	$461k	$748k	$795k	$1,050k	$588k
Beating S&P 500?	50.3%	54.3%	51.2%	39.8%	14.7%	2.8%	0.0%	0.0%
Typ. Monthly DDs	0%	1%	2%	2%	1%	1%	1%	1%
Typ. Qtrly DDs	0%	11%	14%	11%	7%	5%	5%	6%
Typ. Yearly DDs	0%	31%	34%	29%	22%	16%	14%	18%
Worst Drawdowns	0%	39%	41%	35%	27%	20%	19%	24%

Could be implemented with Vanguard-like target-date fund

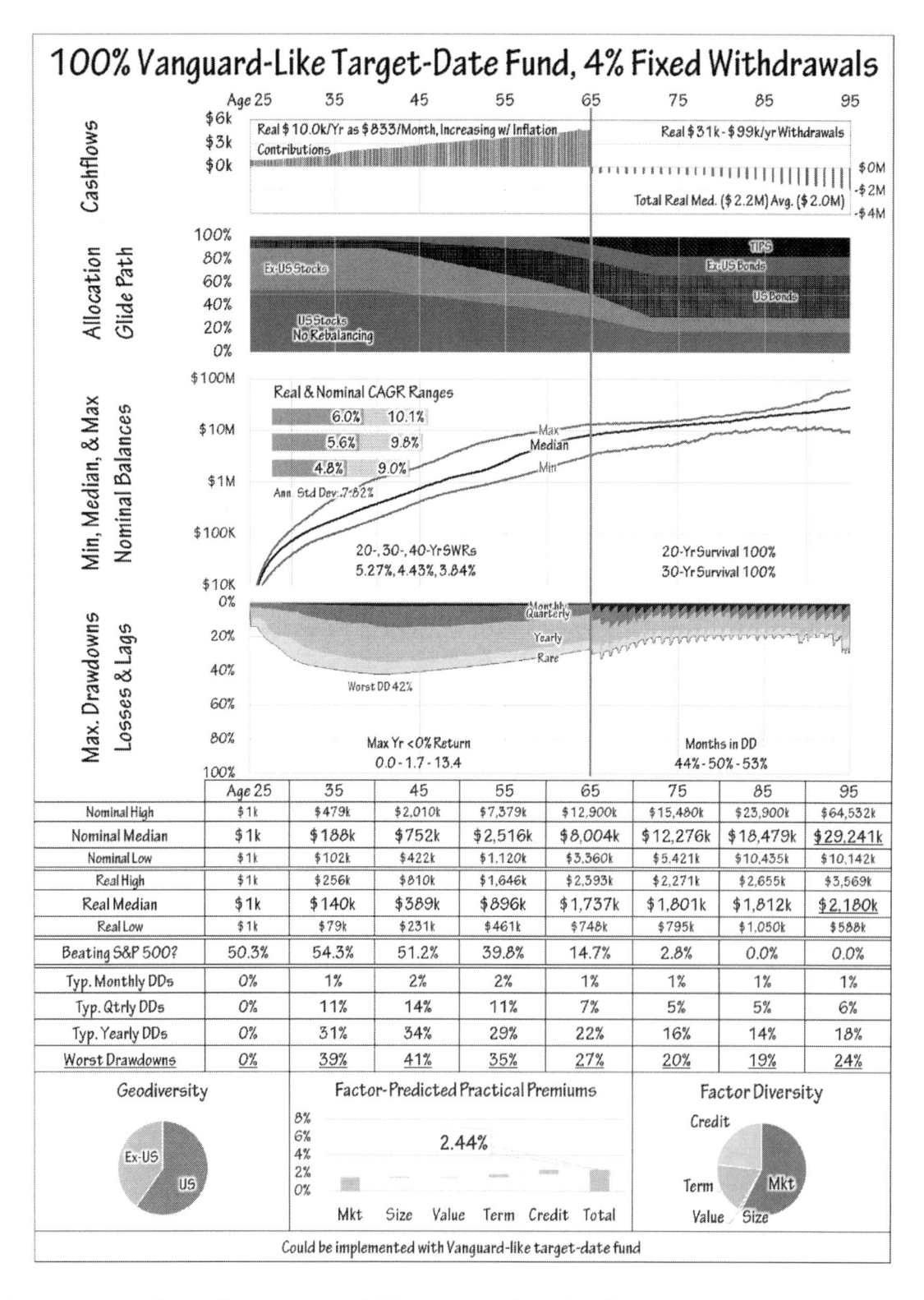

Figure 68. Backtest for Vanguard-like target-date fund

APPENDIX 1: ALTERNATIVE 2 FUND RECIPES

90% V-Like TDF, 10% US Small-Cap Value, 4% Nudge WDs

Cashflows: Real $10.0k/Yr as $833/Month, Increasing w/ Inflation Contributions; Real $36k – $120k/yr Withdrawals; Total Real Med. ($2.4M) Avg. ($2.4M)

Allocation Glide Path: Ex-US Stocks, US Stocks, US SCV, TIPS, Ex-US Bonds, US Bonds; No Rebalancing / Cashflow Rebal. Nudges

Min, Median, & Max Nominal Balances:
Real & Nominal CAGR Ranges: 6.7% – 10.8%; 6.2% – 10.3%; 5.4% – 9.5%
Ann. Std Dev: 8.66%
20-, 30-, 40-Yr SWRs: 5.51%, 4.34%, 3.95%
20-Yr Survival 100%; 30-Yr Survival 100%

Max. Drawdowns Losses & Lags: Monthly, Quarterly, Yearly, Rare
Worst DD 44%
Max Yr < 0% Return: 0.0 - 1.7 - 13.3
Months in DD: 46% - 51% - 55%

	Age 25	35	45	55	65	75	85	95
Nominal High	$1k	$482k	$2,147k	$8,025k	$16,776k	$19,889k	$34,528k	$112,272k
Nominal Median	$1k	$190k	$818k	$2,740k	$9,170k	$15,285k	$24,839k	$43,142k
Nominal Low	$1k	$101k	$418k	$1,103k	$3,374k	$6,264k	$13,824k	$18,301k
Real High	$1k	$257k	$813k	$1,791k	$2,897k	$2,918k	$3,761k	$5,228k
Real Median	$1k	$145k	$395k	$971k	$1,945k	$2,242k	$2,430k	$3,160k
Real Low	$1k	$78k	$225k	$467k	$877k	$919k	$1,363k	$850k
Beating S&P 500?	52.0%	60.5%	60.3%	67.0%	62.0%	32.2%	18.5%	15.3%
Typ. Monthly DDs	0%	2%	2%	2%	2%	1%	1%	1%
Typ. Qtrly DDs	0%	10%	12%	10%	8%	7%	5%	4%
Typ. Yearly DDs	0%	31%	35%	31%	28%	17%	16%	15%
Worst Drawdowns	0%	40%	43%	39%	35%	22%	21%	20%

Geodiversity: Ex-US, US

Factor-Predicted Practical Premiums: 3.06% (Mkt, Size, Value, Term, Credit, Total)

Factor Diversity: Credit, Term, Value, Size, Mkt

Could be implemented with Vanguard-like target-date fund, AVUV

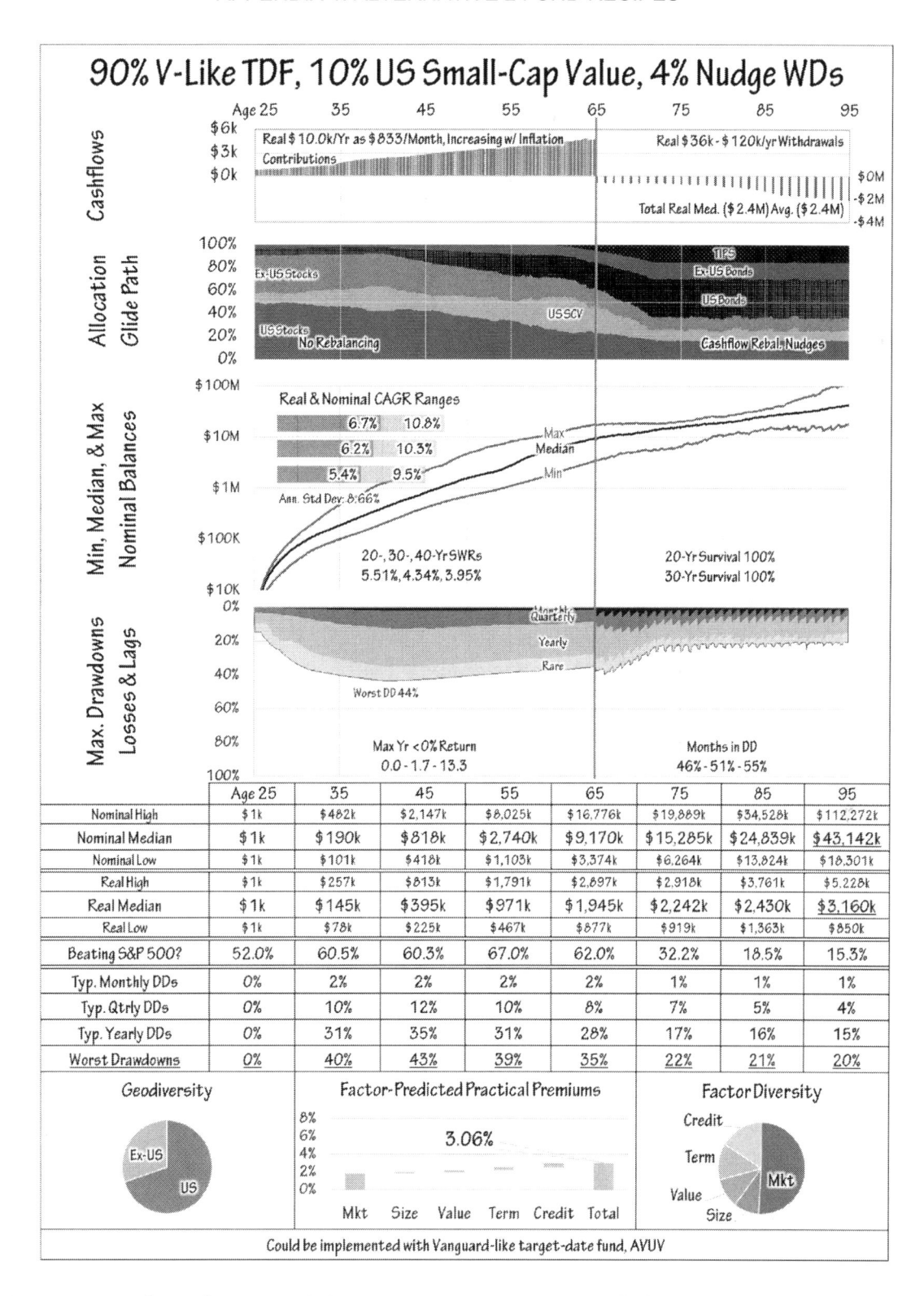

Figure 69. Backtest for 10% minimum, 0 × YTR, Easy 2 Funds for Life strategy

80% V-Like TDF, 20% US Small-Cap Value, 4% Nudge WDs

	Age 25	35	45	55	65	75	85	95
Nominal High	$1k	$484k	$2,284k	$8,670k	$21,048k	$27,971k	$51,214k	$197,648k
Nominal Median	$1k	$194k	$873k	$3,010k	$10,377k	$18,801k	$34,952k	$66,219k
Nominal Low	$1k	$100k	$404k	$1,080k	$3,388k	$7,337k	$18,569k	$27,194k
Real High	$1k	$259k	$827k	$1,935k	$3,634k	$4,104k	$5,828k	$8,905k
Real Median	$1k	$147k	$411k	$1,049k	$2,173k	$2,758k	$3,477k	$4,702k
Real Low	$1k	$77k	$217k	$457k	$1,007k	$1,076k	$1,647k	$1,278k
Beating S&P 500?	51.7%	60.5%	67.8%	75.3%	74.0%	89.5%	88.7%	71.2%
Typ. Monthly DDs	0%	2%	3%	3%	2%	3%	1%	1%
Typ. Qtrly DDs	0%	9%	12%	12%	12%	11%	7%	7%
Typ. Yearly DDs	0%	31%	36%	34%	33%	25%	20%	24%
Worst Drawdowns	0%	42%	45%	42%	42%	31%	26%	31%

Could be implemented with Vanguard-like target-date fund, AVUV

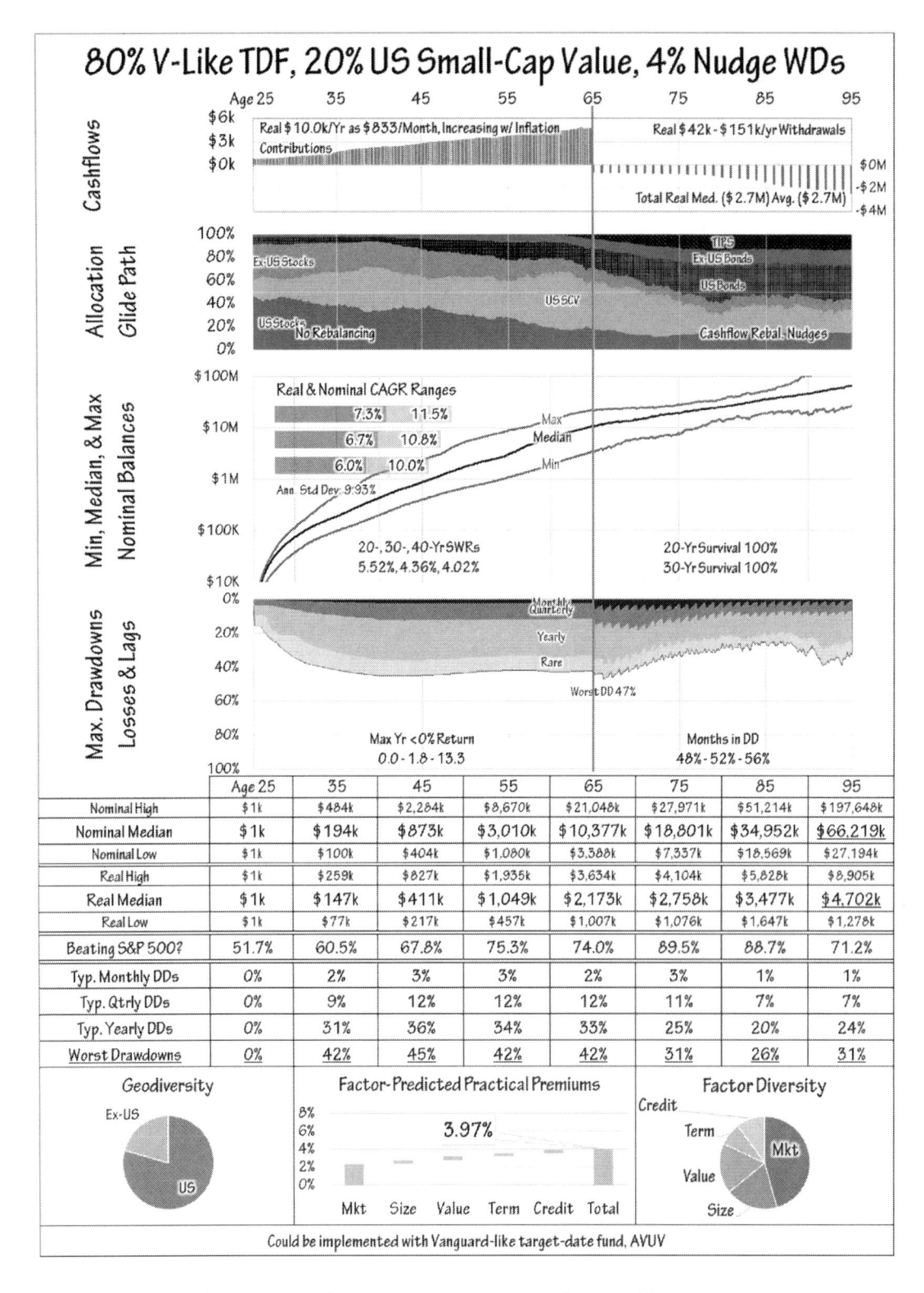

Figure 70. Backtest for 20% minimum, 0 × YTR, 2 Funds for Life strategy

APPENDIX 1: ALTERNATIVE 2 FUND RECIPES

70% V-Like TDF, 30% US Small-Cap Value, 4% Nudge WDs

	Age 25	35	45	55	65	75	85	95
Nominal High	$1k	$487k	$2,422k	$9,331k	$25,319k	$37,301k	$74,188k	$357,237k
Nominal Median	$1k	$203k	$923k	$3,257k	$11,459k	$22,826k	$48,181k	$101,224k
Nominal Low	$1k	$99k	$389k	$1,058k	$3,402k	$8,881k	$22,964k	$45,396k
Real High	$1k	$260k	$863k	$2,111k	$4,371k	$5,472k	$8,196k	$16,670k
Real Median	$1k	$151k	$429k	$1,132k	$2,401k	$3,349k	$4,806k	$7,082k
Real Low	$1k	$74k	$209k	$448k	$1,013k	$1,303k	$2,039k	$2,133k
Beating S&P 500?	52.5%	60.2%	71.3%	81.5%	81.5%	95.7%	100.0%	98.0%
Typ. Monthly DDs	0%	2%	3%	3%	3%	5%	3%	3%
Typ. Qtrly DDs	0%	10%	13%	14%	15%	15%	12%	12%
Typ. Yearly DDs	0%	32%	37%	36%	37%	33%	30%	37%
Worst Drawdowns	0%	43%	47%	46%	47%	41%	39%	47%

Could be implemented with Vanguard-like target-date fund, AVUV

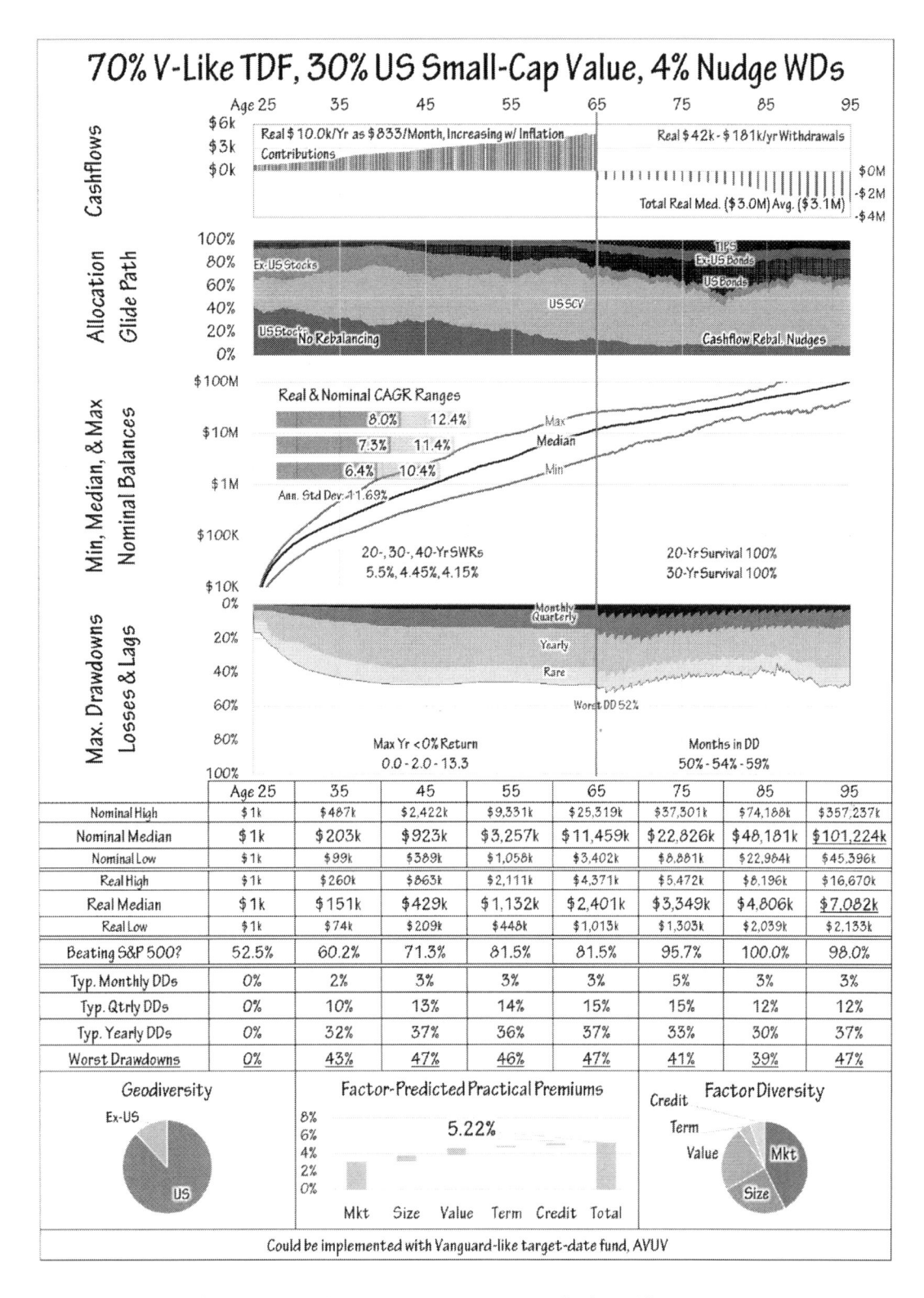

Figure 71. Backtest for 30% minimum, 0 × YTR, 2 Funds for Life strategy

2 FUNDS FOR LIFE

1.5 × YTR in US SCV, Rest in V-Like TDF, 4% Fixed WDs

	Age 25	35	45	55	65	75	85	95
Nominal High	$1k	$512k	$2,625k	$9,798k	$17,990k	$21,793k	$33,456k	$93,104k
Nominal Median	$1k	$218k	$943k	$3,150k	$10,206k	$15,624k	$23,519k	$36,744k
Nominal Low	$1k	$101k	$386k	$1,192k	$4,079k	$6,627k	$12,717k	$13,010k
Real High	$1k	$274k	$892k	$2,186k	$3,104k	$3,197k	$3,308k	$4,344k
Real Median	$1k	$158k	$446k	$1,120k	$2,186k	$2,292k	$2,330k	$2,828k
Real Low	$1k	$69k	$208k	$504k	$916k	$972k	$1,280k	$754k
Beating S&P 500?	52.8%	60.8%	74.0%	89.2%	77.0%	58.5%	29.7%	25.5%
Typ. Monthly DDs	0%	2%	2%	2%	1%	1%	1%	1%
Typ. Qtrly DDs	0%	11%	12%	10%	6%	5%	5%	6%
Typ. Yearly DDs	0%	33%	36%	30%	22%	16%	14%	18%
Worst Drawdowns	0%	46%	45%	38%	28%	20%	19%	24%

Could be implemented with Vanguard-like target-date fund, AVUV

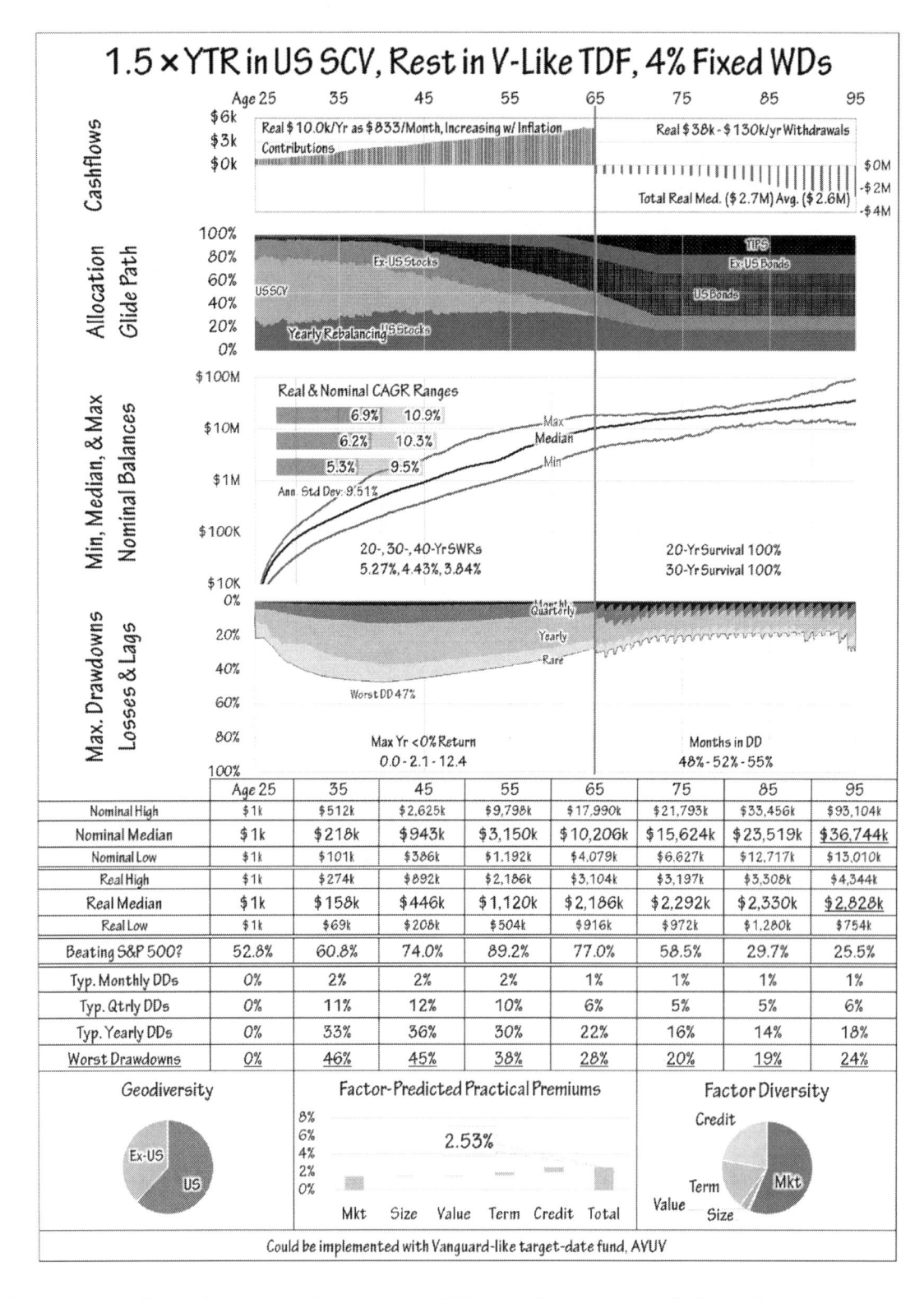

Figure 72. Backtest for 0% minimum, 1.5 × YTR, Moderate 2 Funds for Life strategy

168

APPENDIX 1: ALTERNATIVE 2 FUND RECIPES

1.5 × YTR + 10% in US SCV, Rest in V-Like TDF, 4% Nudge WDs

Cashflows: Real $10.0k/Yr as $833/Month, Increasing w/ Inflation Contributions; Real $42k - $149k/yr Withdrawals; Total Real Med. ($3.0M) Avg. ($2.9M)

Allocation Glide Path: US SCV, Ex-US Stocks, TIPS, Ex-US Bonds, US Bonds; Yearly Rebalancing 9 Stocks; Cashflow Rebal. Nudges

Min, Median, & Max Nominal Balances: Real & Nominal CAGR Ranges: 7.4%–11.4%, 6.6%–10.8%, 5.8%–9.9%; Ann. Std Dev: 10.45%; 20-, 30-, 40-Yr SWRs 5.61%, 4.51%, 4.11%; 20-Yr Survival 100%, 30-Yr Survival 100%

Max. Drawdowns Losses & Lags: Monthly, Quarterly, Yearly, Rare; Worst DD 49%; Max Yr < 0% Return 0.0 - 2.4 - 13.1; Months in DD 50% - 53% - 57%

	Age 25	35	45	55	65	75	85	95
Nominal High	$1k	$536k	$2,773k	$10,497k	$20,713k	$25,710k	$44,653k	$141,965k
Nominal Median	$1k	$226k	$996k	$3,366k	$11,210k	$18,586k	$30,881k	$53,269k
Nominal Low	$1k	$100k	$371k	$1,171k	$4,170k	$7,985k	$17,800k	$23,615k
Real High	$1k	$277k	$928k	$2,342k	$3,586k	$3,772k	$4,321k	$6,484k
Real Median	$1k	$162k	$468k	$1,198k	$2,389k	$2,727k	$3,073k	$4,084k
Real Low	$1k	$66k	$200k	$496k	$1,030k	$1,171k	$1,809k	$1,368k
Beating S&P 500?	52.3%	62.7%	76.0%	96.0%	85.7%	89.8%	87.0%	62.8%
Typ. Monthly DDs	0%	3%	3%	2%	1%	1%	1%	1%
Typ. Qtrly DDs	0%	12%	14%	11%	7%	5%	5%	4%
Typ. Yearly DDs	0%	33%	37%	32%	24%	17%	17%	16%
Worst Drawdowns	0%	47%	47%	40%	30%	23%	21%	21%

Geodiversity: Ex-US, US

Factor-Predicted Practical Premiums: 3.15% (Mkt, Size, Value, Term, Credit, Total)

Factor Diversity: Credit, Term, Value, Size, Mkt

Could be implemented with Vanguard-like target-date fund, AVUV

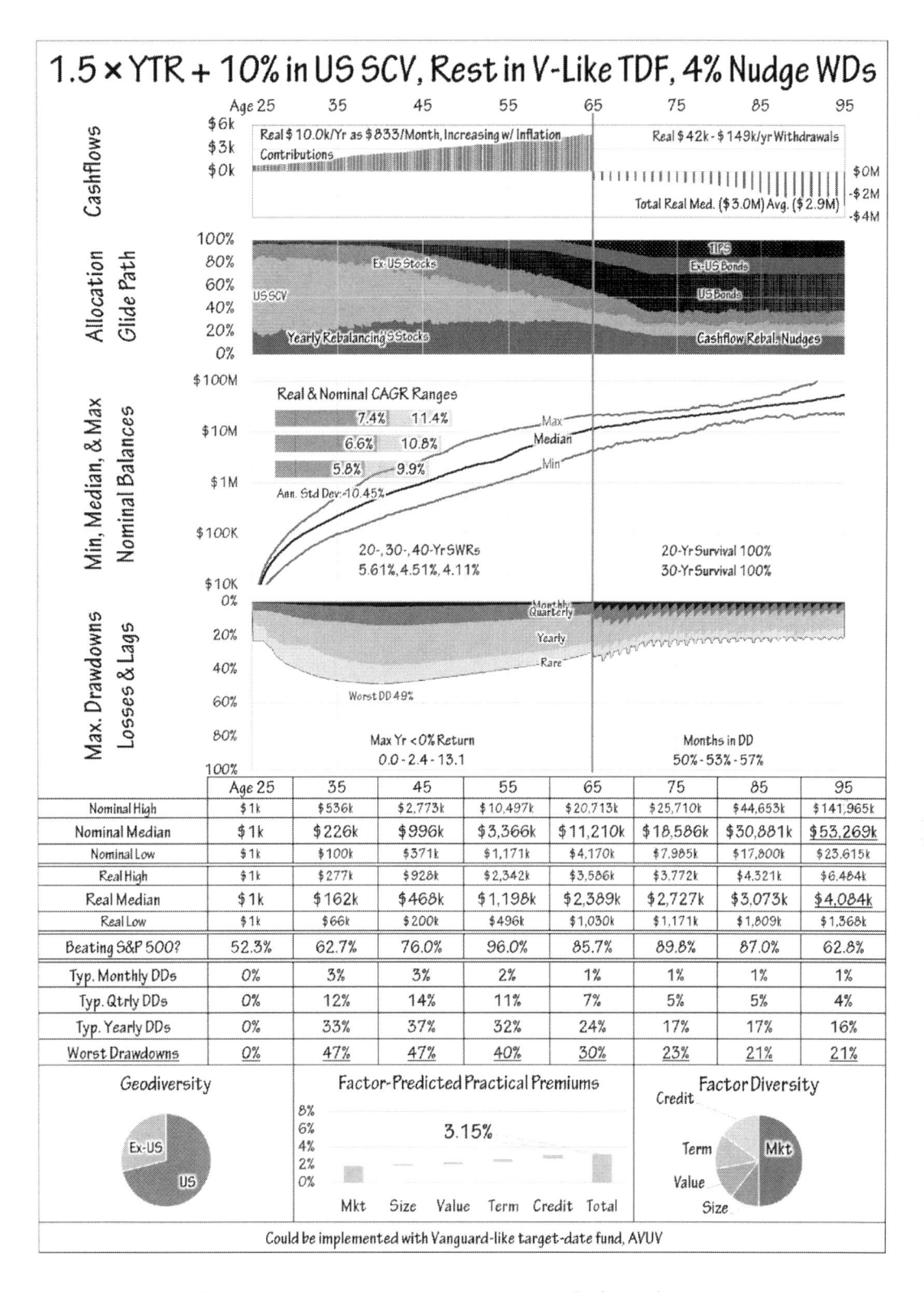

Figure 73. Backtest for 10% minimum, 1.5 × YTR, 2 Funds for Life strategy

1.5 × YTR + 20% in US SCV, Rest in V-Like TDF, 4% Nudge WDs

	Age 25	35	45	55	65	75	85	95
Nominal High	$1k	$588k	$2,930k	$11,258k	$24,755k	$30,981k	$59,637k	$220,895k
Nominal Median	$1k	$233k	$1,044k	$3,617k	$12,527k	$22,396k	$40,612k	$78,528k
Nominal Low	$1k	$96k	$356k	$1,147k	$4,266k	$9,502k	$25,649k	$40,430k
Real High	$1k	$279k	$965k	$2,512k	$4,274k	$4,545k	$5,755k	$13,762k
Real Median	$1k	$165k	$499k	$1,281k	$2,653k	$3,286k	$4,142k	$5,894k
Real Low	$1k	$64k	$191k	$485k	$1,170k	$1,394k	$2,497k	$2,364k
Beating S&P 500?	50.8%	63.7%	76.8%	97.2%	95.2%	95.5%	98.7%	100.0%
Typ. Monthly DDs	0%	3%	3%	3%	2%	2%	1%	1%
Typ. Qtrly DDs	0%	14%	15%	13%	8%	8%	7%	6%
Typ. Yearly DDs	0%	35%	38%	33%	26%	20%	20%	21%
Worst Drawdowns	0%	49%	49%	43%	33%	26%	26%	28%

Could be implemented with Vanguard-like target-date fund, AVUV

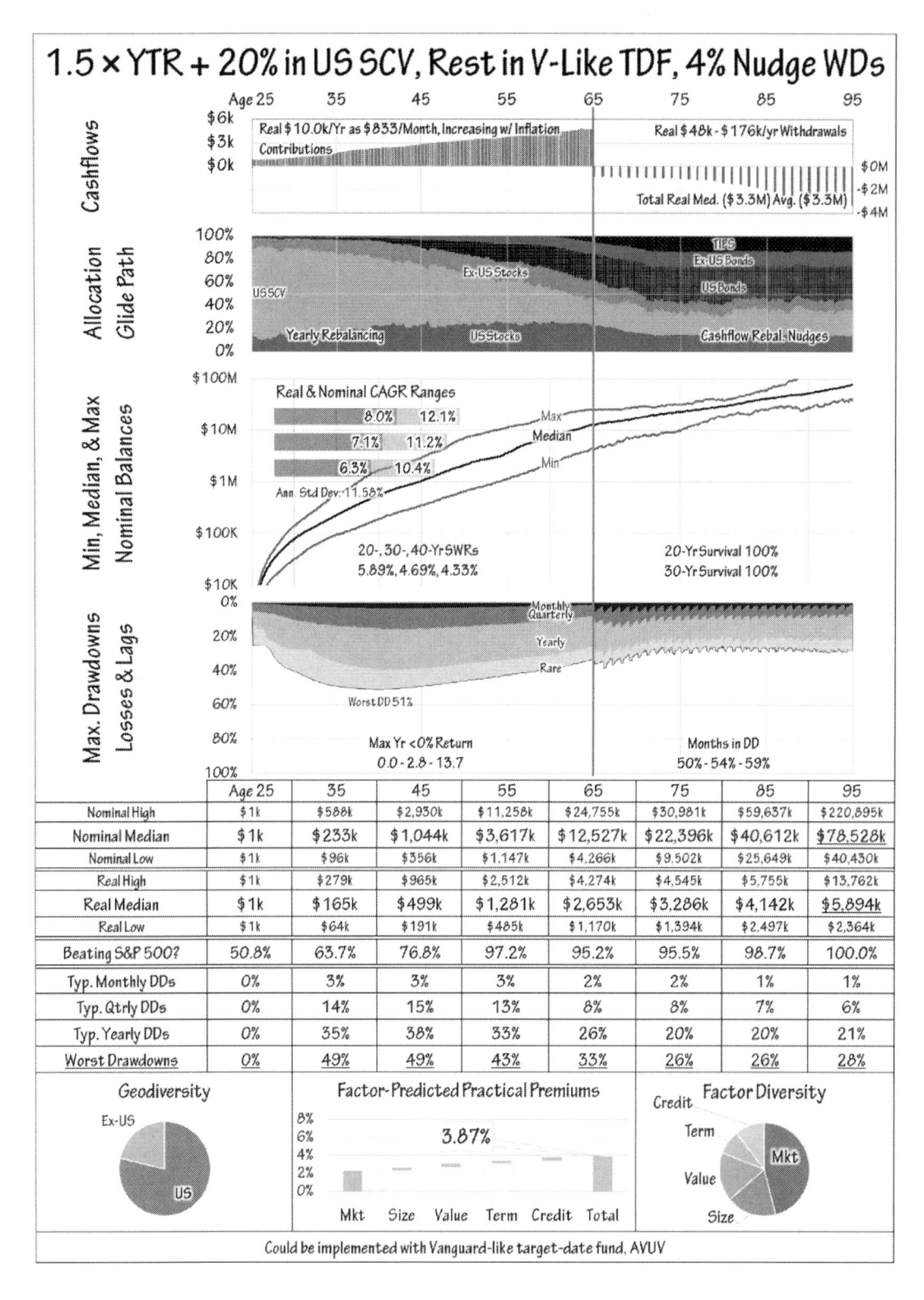

Figure 74. Backtest for 20% minimum, 1.5 × YTR, 2 Funds for Life strategy

APPENDIX 1: ALTERNATIVE 2 FUND RECIPES

1.5 × YTR + 30% in US SCV, Rest in V-Like TDF, 4% Nudge WDs

	Age 25	35	45	55	65	75	85	95
Nominal High	$1k	$640k	$3,076k	$11,966k	$28,293k	$36,255k	$79,479k	$311,247k
Nominal Median	$1k	$238k	$1,092k	$3,885k	$13,449k	$25,541k	$51,473k	$106,414k
Nominal Low	$1k	$93k	$341k	$1,122k	$4,235k	$11,291k	$28,476k	$59,751k
Real High	$1k	$284k	$999k	$2,670k	$4,885k	$5,319k	$7,915k	$23,419k
Real Median	$1k	$168k	$528k	$1,357k	$2,818k	$3,747k	$5,228k	$8,046k
Real Low	$1k	$62k	$184k	$475k	$1,261k	$1,657k	$2,773k	$3,656k
Beating S&P 500?	51.8%	65.5%	78.5%	97.5%	99.0%	99.8%	100.0%	100.0%
Typ. Monthly DDs	0%	3%	4%	3%	2%	2%	2%	2%
Typ. Qtrly DDs	0%	15%	17%	14%	10%	10%	10%	10%
Typ. Yearly DDs	0%	37%	40%	36%	28%	25%	25%	28%
Worst Drawdowns	0%	51%	51%	46%	37%	32%	34%	37%

Could be implemented with Vanguard-like target-date fund, AVUV

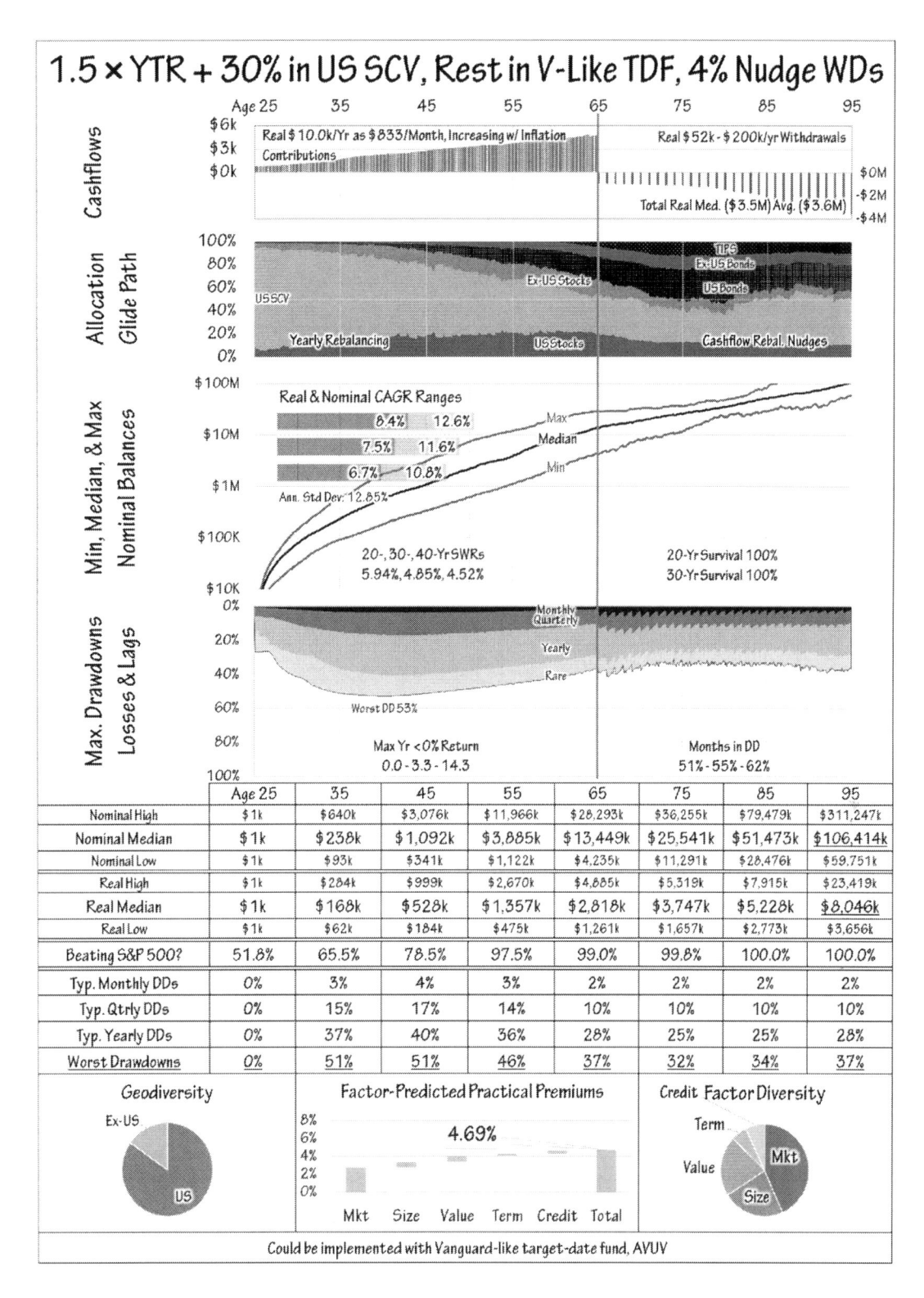

Figure 75. Backtest for 30% minimum, 1.5 × YTR, 2 Funds for Life strategy

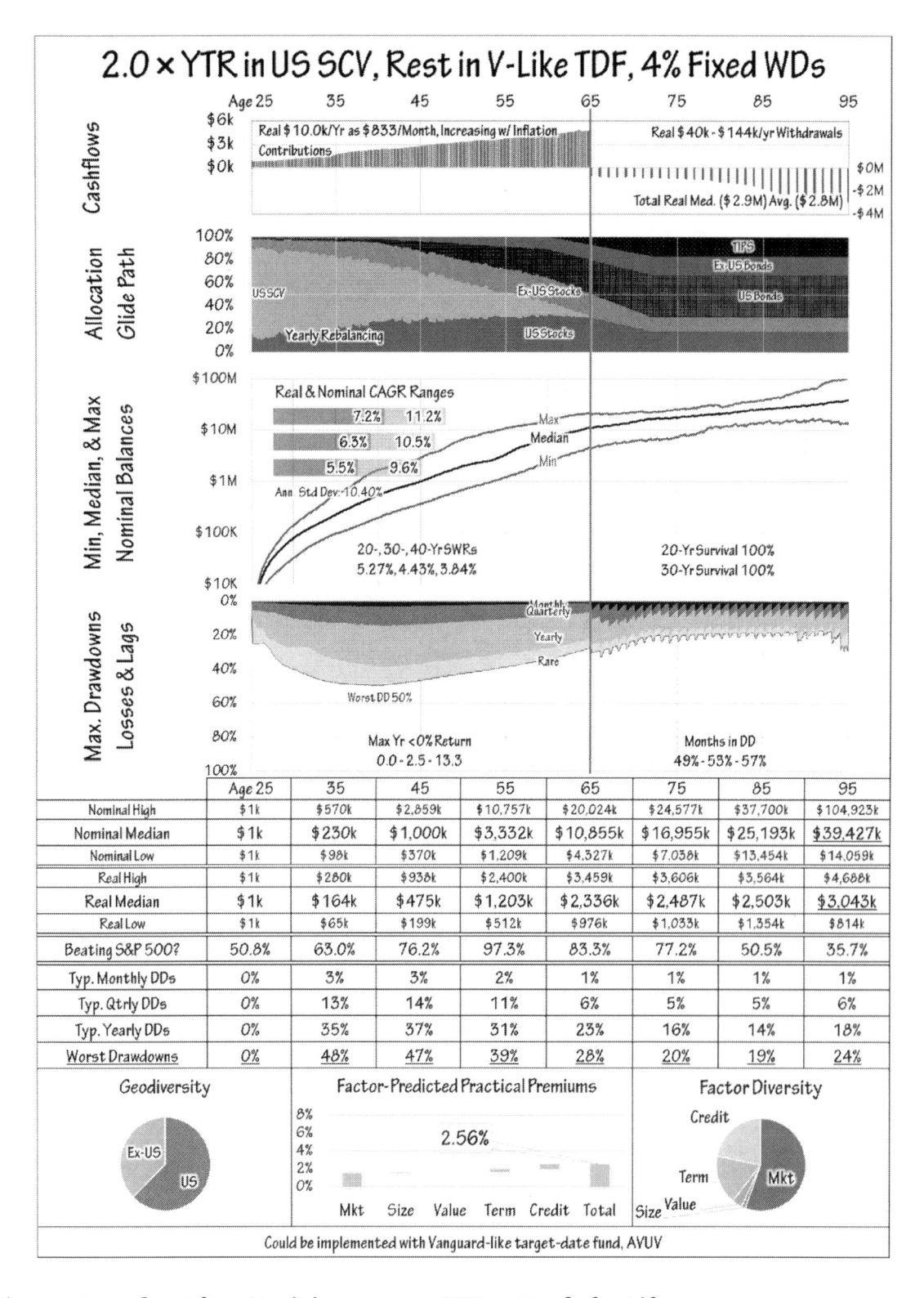

Figure 76. Backtest for 0% minimum, 2.0 × YTR, 2 Funds for Life strategy

APPENDIX 1: ALTERNATIVE 2 FUND RECIPES

2.0 × YTR + 10% in US SCV, Rest in V-Like TDF, 4% Nudge WDs

	Age 25	35	45	55	65	75	85	95
Nominal High	$1k	$622k	$3,014k	$11,505k	$23,030k	$29,230k	$50,171k	$160,599k
Nominal Median	$1k	$237k	$1,046k	$3,595k	$11,925k	$19,991k	$33,194k	$59,118k
Nominal Low	$1k	$94k	$355k	$1,185k	$4,408k	$8,543k	$19,027k	$26,162k
Real High	$1k	$282k	$973k	$2,567k	$3,984k	$4,288k	$4,681k	$7,185k
Real Median	$1k	$167k	$505k	$1,272k	$2,544k	$2,933k	$3,354k	$4,449k
Real Low	$1k	$62k	$191k	$501k	$1,093k	$1,253k	$1,926k	$1,526k
Beating S&P 500?	51.8%	64.2%	77.3%	98.2%	93.2%	92.0%	91.3%	87.2%
Typ. Monthly DDs	0%	3%	3%	2%	1%	1%	1%	1%
Typ. Qtrly DDs	0%	14%	15%	12%	7%	5%	5%	4%
Typ. Yearly DDs	0%	36%	38%	32%	24%	18%	17%	16%
Worst Drawdowns	0%	50%	49%	41%	31%	23%	21%	21%

Could be implemented with Vanguard-like target-date fund, AVUV

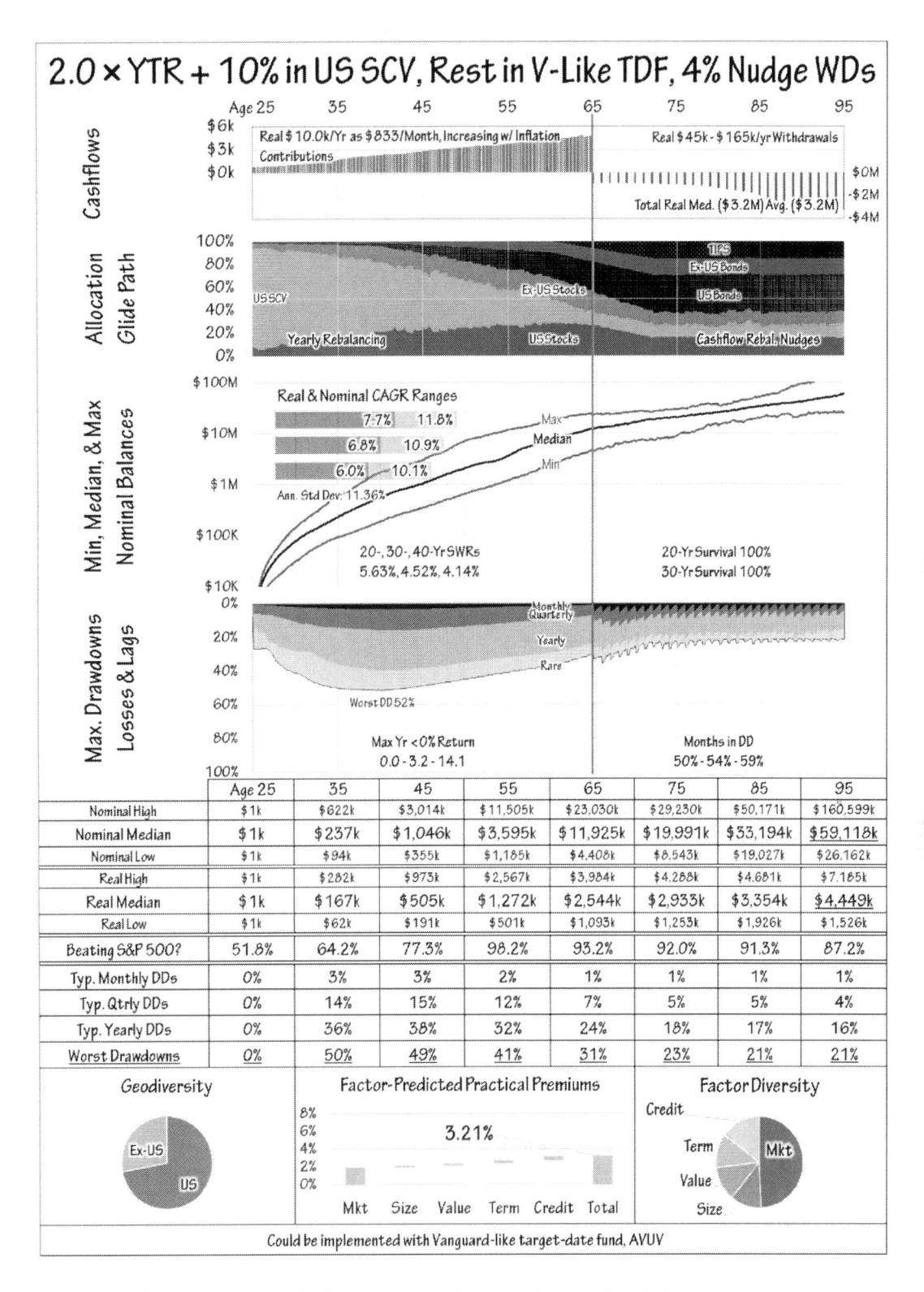

Figure 77. Backtest for 10% minimum, 2.0 × YTR, 2 Funds for Life strategy

2.0 × YTR + 20% in US SCV, Rest in V-Like TDF, 4% Nudge WDs

	Age 25	35	45	55	65	75	85	95
Nominal High	$1k	$679k	$3,180k	$12,275k	$26,903k	$34,430k	$65,732k	$243,862k
Nominal Median	$1k	$240k	$1,099k	$3,828k	$13,046k	$23,482k	$42,600k	$82,958k
Nominal Low	$1k	$90k	$340k	$1,158k	$4,433k	$10,025k	$27,102k	$42,869k
Real High	$1k	$302k	$1,010k	$2,739k	$4,645k	$5,051k	$6,064k	$14,410k
Real Median	$1k	$171k	$538k	$1,354k	$2,766k	$3,445k	$4,388k	$6,272k
Real Low	$1k	$60k	$183k	$490k	$1,217k	$1,471k	$2,718k	$2,507k
Beating S&P 500?	52.3%	65.5%	78.5%	97.8%	98.3%	97.0%	100.0%	100.0%
Typ. Monthly DDs	0%	4%	4%	3%	2%	2%	1%	1%
Typ. Qtrly DDs	0%	16%	17%	14%	8%	8%	7%	6%
Typ. Yearly DDs	0%	38%	40%	34%	26%	20%	20%	21%
Worst Drawdowns	0%	52%	51%	44%	34%	26%	26%	28%

Could be implemented with Vanguard-like target-date fund, AVUV

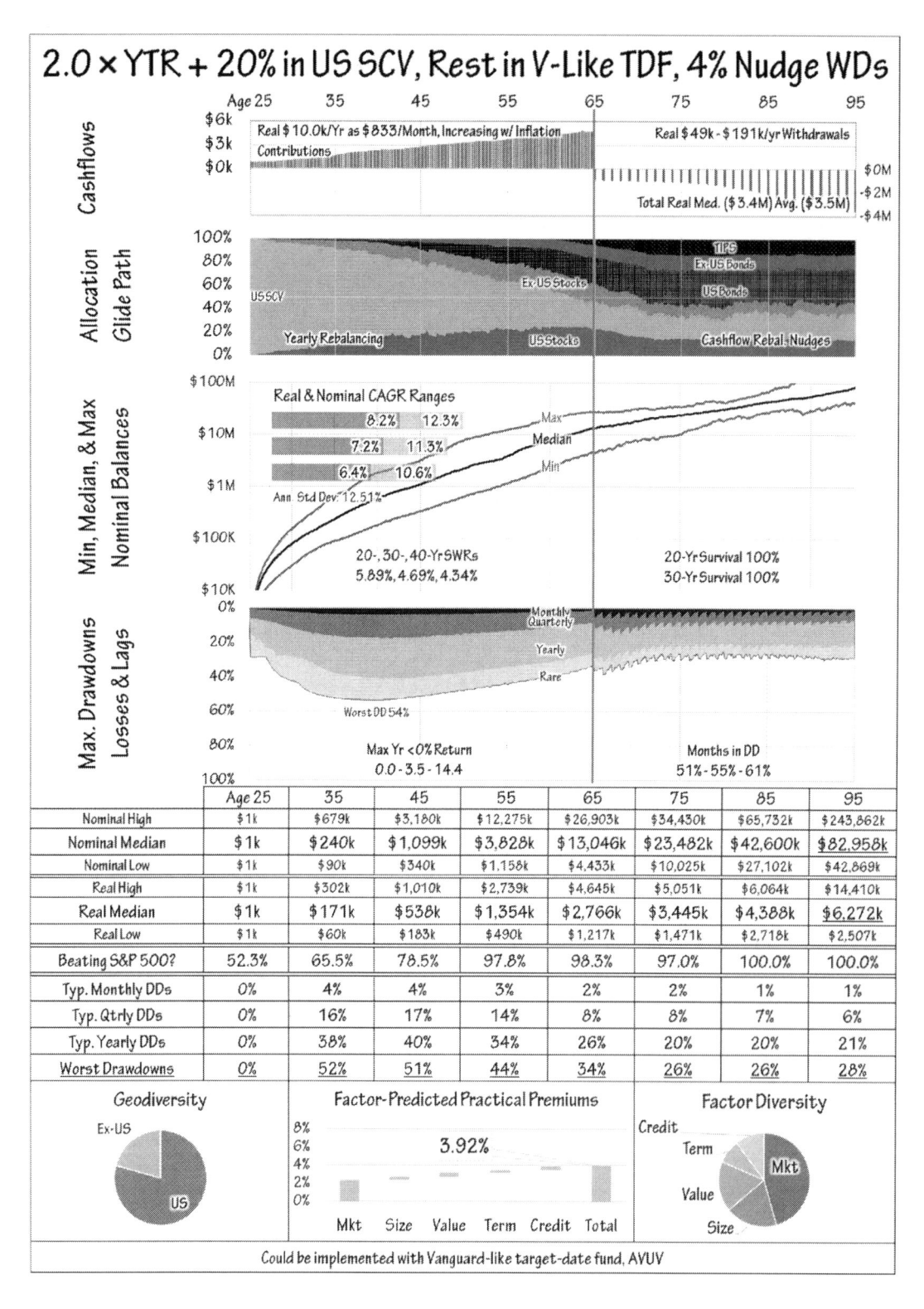

Figure 78. Backtest for 20% minimum, 2.0 × YTR, 2 Funds for Life strategy

APPENDIX 1: ALTERNATIVE 2 FUND RECIPES

2.0 × YTR + 30% in US SCV, Rest in V-Like TDF, 4% Nudge WDs

	Age 25	35	45	55	65	75	85	95
Nominal High	$1k	$730k	$3,309k	$13,092k	$31,282k	$40,756k	$89,085k	$355,755k
Nominal Median	$1k	$243k	$1,158k	$4,033k	$14,231k	$27,275k	$54,693k	$114,113k
Nominal Low	$1k	$87k	$326k	$1,131k	$4,462k	$11,997k	$30,609k	$63,302k
Real High	$1k	$324k	$1,049k	$2,929k	$5,401k	$5,979k	$8,540k	$25,337k
Real Median	$1k	$173k	$560k	$1,427k	$2,956k	$4,001k	$5,610k	$8,649k
Real Low	$1k	$58k	$175k	$478k	$1,328k	$1,760k	$2,981k	$3,944k
Beating S&P 500?	52.3%	66.8%	78.7%	98.0%	100.0%	100.0%	100.0%	100.0%
Typ. Monthly DDs	0%	4%	5%	3%	2%	3%	2%	2%
Typ. Qtrly DDs	0%	18%	18%	15%	11%	10%	10%	10%
Typ. Yearly DDs	0%	39%	42%	37%	29%	25%	26%	29%
Worst Drawdowns	0%	54%	54%	47%	37%	33%	34%	38%

Could be implemented with Vanguard-like target-date fund, AVUV

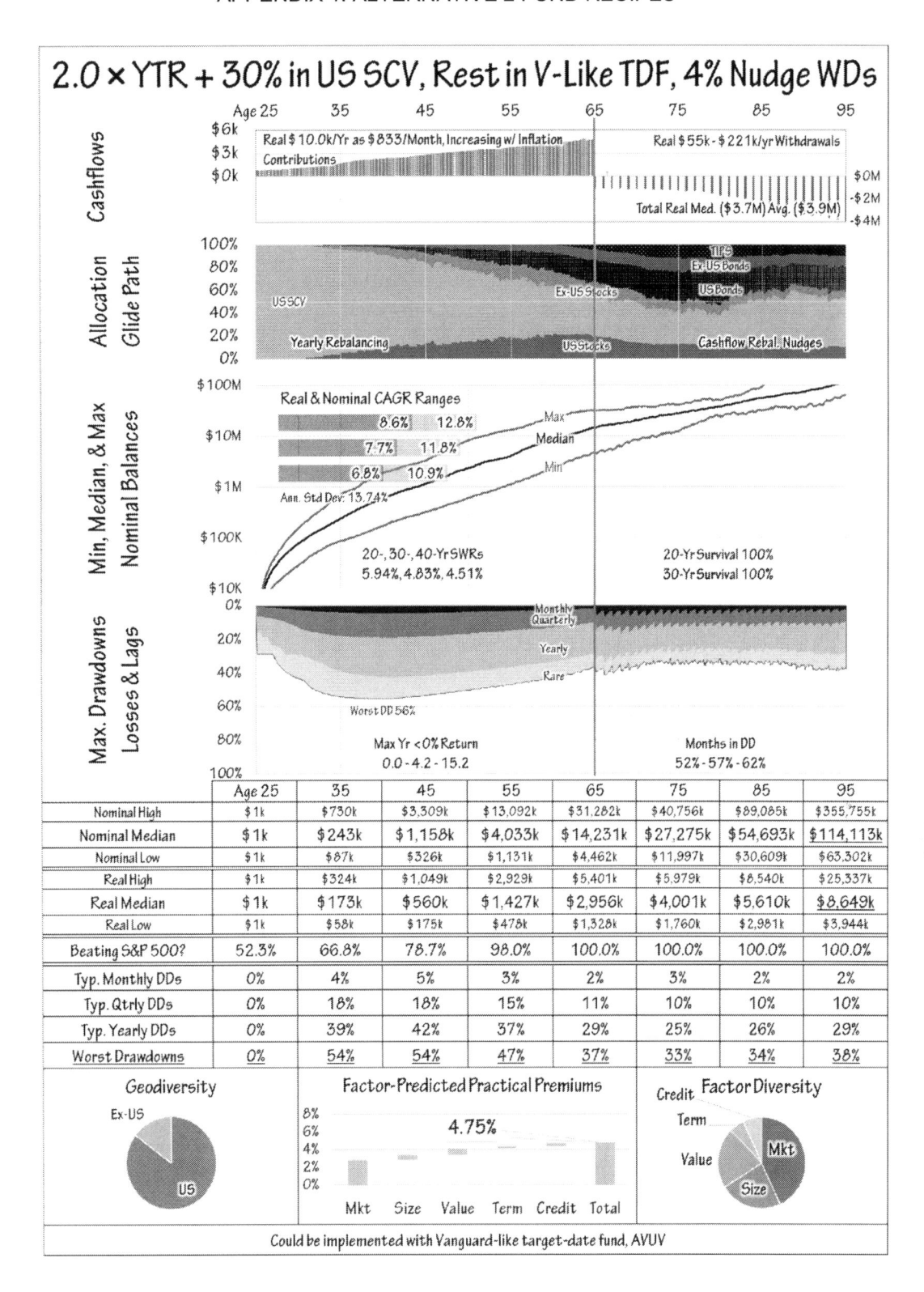

Figure 79. Backtest for 30% minimum, 2.0 × YTR, 2 Funds for Life strategy

2.5 × YTR in US SCV, Rest in V-Like TDF, 4% Fixed WDs

	Age 25	35	45	55	65	75	85	95
Nominal High	$1k	$661k	$3,117k	$11,794k	$22,230k	$27,904k	$42,385k	$117,974k
Nominal Median	$1k	$239k	$1,051k	$3,548k	$11,523k	$18,200k	$26,834k	$42,422k
Nominal Low	$1k	$92k	$354k	$1,223k	$4,575k	$7,450k	$14,163k	$15,146k
Real High	$1k	$294k	$990k	$2,632k	$3,854k	$4,094k	$3,824k	$5,271k
Real Median	$1k	$169k	$515k	$1,274k	$2,486k	$2,670k	$2,686k	$3,258k
Real Low	$1k	$61k	$190k	$517k	$1,036k	$1,093k	$1,425k	$877k
Beating S&P 500?	52.3%	65.0%	77.8%	99.5%	91.3%	87.5%	66.3%	49.2%
Typ. Monthly DDs	0%	3%	3%	2%	1%	1%	1%	1%
Typ. Qtrly DDs	0%	15%	15%	11%	7%	5%	5%	6%
Typ. Yearly DDs	0%	37%	38%	32%	23%	16%	14%	18%
Worst Drawdowns	0%	52%	49%	40%	28%	20%	19%	24%

Could be implemented with Vanguard-like target-date fund, AVUV

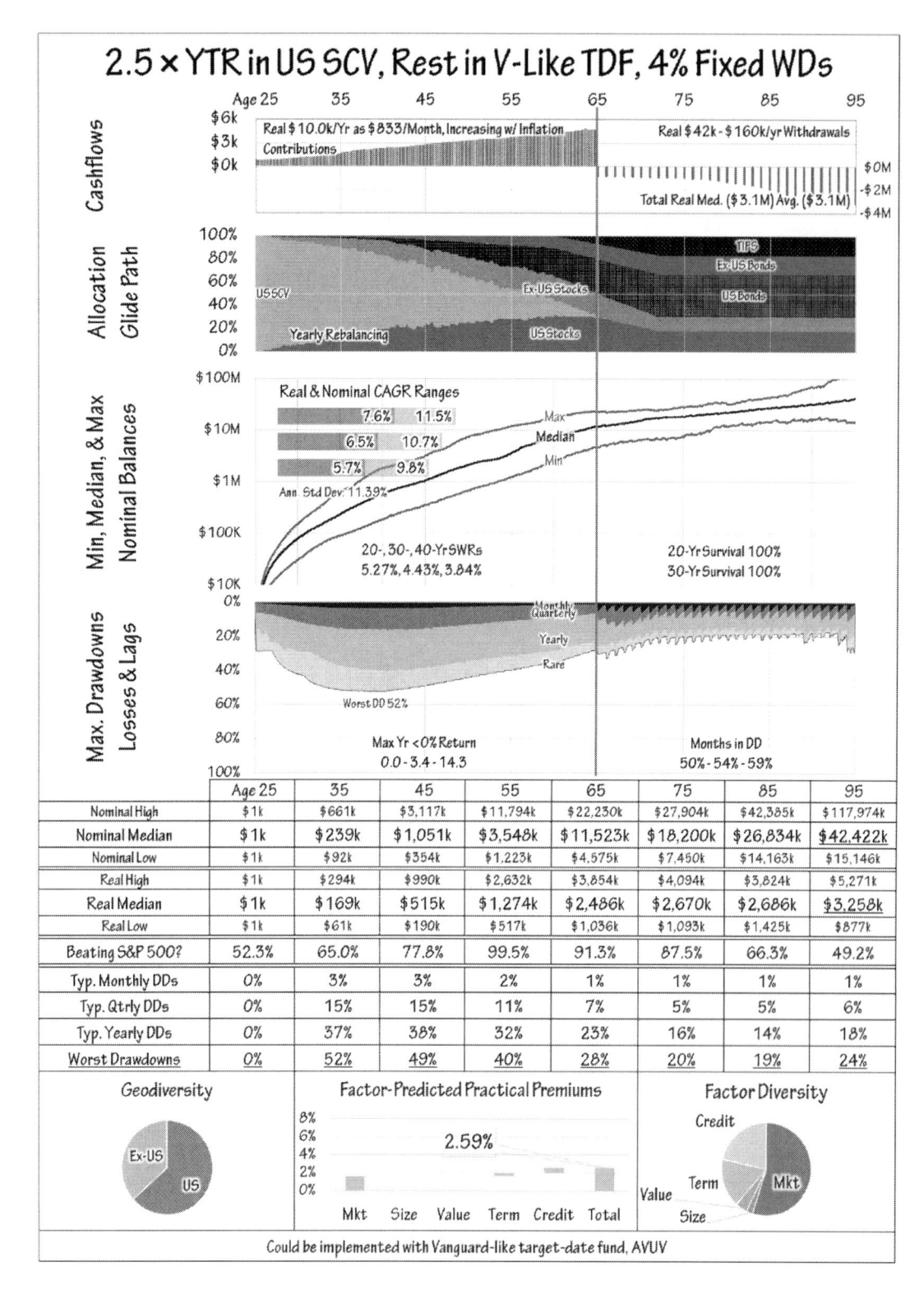

Figure 80. Backtest for 0% minimum, 2.5 × YTR, 2 Funds for Life strategy

APPENDIX 1: ALTERNATIVE 2 FUND RECIPES

2.5 × YTR + 10% in US SCV, Rest in V-Like TDF, 4% Nudge WDs

	Age 25	35	45	55	65	75	85	95
Nominal High	$1k	$715k	$3,263k	$12,621k	$25,532k	$33,087k	$57,062k	$185,069k
Nominal Median	$1k	$241k	$1,108k	$3,791k	$12,618k	$21,385k	$35,404k	**$64,104k**
Nominal Low	$1k	$88k	$339k	$1,195k	$4,655k	$9,103k	$20,900k	$29,699k
Real High	$1k	$317k	$1,033k	$2,816k	$4,420k	$4,854k	$5,027k	$8,269k
Real Median	$1k	$173k	$544k	$1,354k	$2,695k	$3,137k	$3,627k	**$4,836k**
Real Low	$1k	$59k	$183k	$506k	$1,156k	$1,335k	$2,116k	$1,724k
Beating S&P 500?	52.3%	66.3%	78.5%	99.3%	97.0%	94.3%	95.5%	93.7%
Typ. Monthly DDs	0%	4%	4%	3%	1%	1%	1%	1%
Typ. Qtrly DDs	0%	17%	17%	13%	7%	6%	5%	5%
Typ. Yearly DDs	0%	39%	40%	33%	24%	18%	17%	16%
Worst Drawdowns	0%	54%	51%	43%	31%	23%	22%	22%

Could be implemented with Vanguard-like target-date fund, AVUV

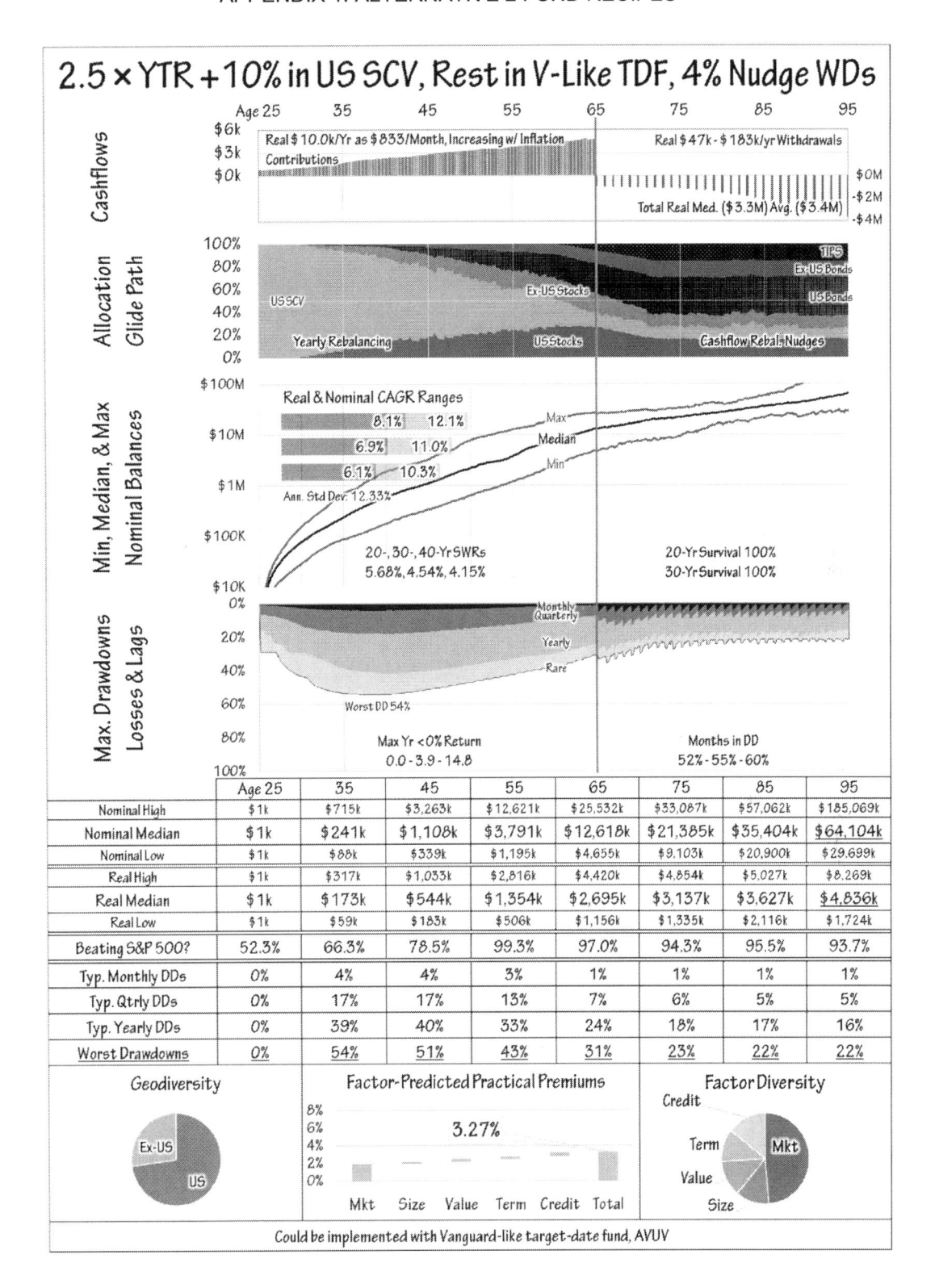

Figure 81. Backtest for 10% minimum, 2.5 × YTR, 2 Funds for Life strategy

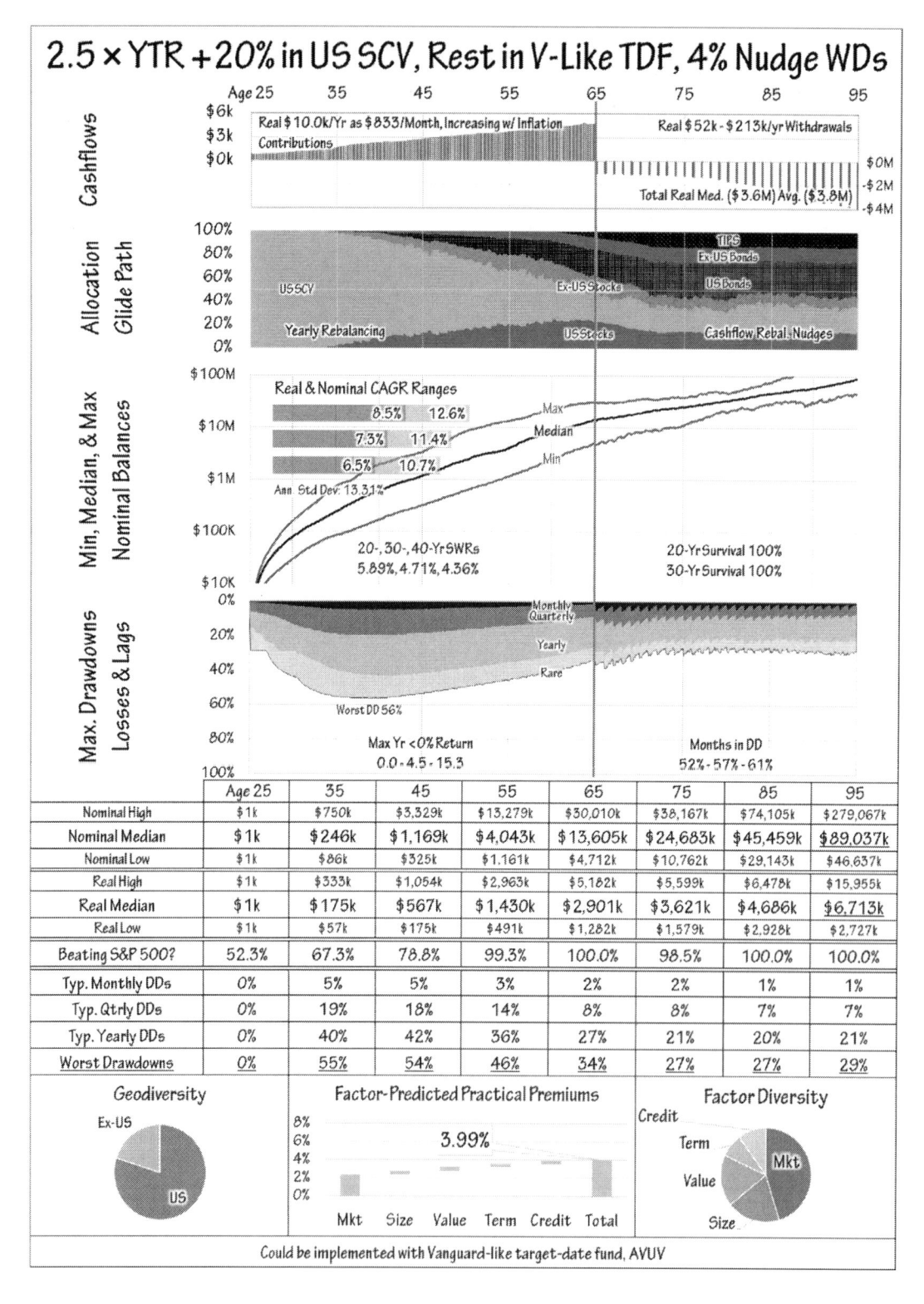

Figure 82. Backtest for 20% minimum, 2.5 × YTR, 2 Funds for Life strategy

APPENDIX 1: ALTERNATIVE 2 FUND RECIPES

2.5 × YTR +30% in US SCV, Rest in V-Like TDF, 4% Nudge WDs

	Age 25	35	45	55	65	75	85	95
Nominal High	$1k	$755k	$3,359k	$13,934k	$34,153k	$44,013k	$93,517k	$391,627k
Nominal Median	$1k	$246k	$1,227k	$4,258k	$14,797k	$28,268k	$57,327k	$122,547k
Nominal Low	$1k	$86k	$308k	$1,099k	$4,682k	$12,822k	$34,031k	$67,276k
Real High	$1k	$335k	$1,063k	$3,152k	$5,897k	$6,457k	$9,025k	$27,193k
Real Median	$1k	$175k	$582k	$1,514k	$3,133k	$4,147k	$5,944k	$9,157k
Real Low	$1k	$57k	$166k	$465k	$1,383k	$1,881k	$3,314k	$4,212k
Beating S&P 500?	52.3%	67.5%	79.2%	98.0%	100.0%	100.0%	100.0%	100.0%
Typ. Monthly DDs	0%	5%	5%	4%	2%	3%	2%	2%
Typ. Qtrly DDs	0%	19%	20%	16%	11%	10%	10%	10%
Typ. Yearly DDs	0%	40%	44%	38%	29%	25%	25%	28%
Worst Drawdowns	0%	56%	56%	49%	37%	33%	34%	39%

Could be implemented with Vanguard-like target-date fund, AVUV

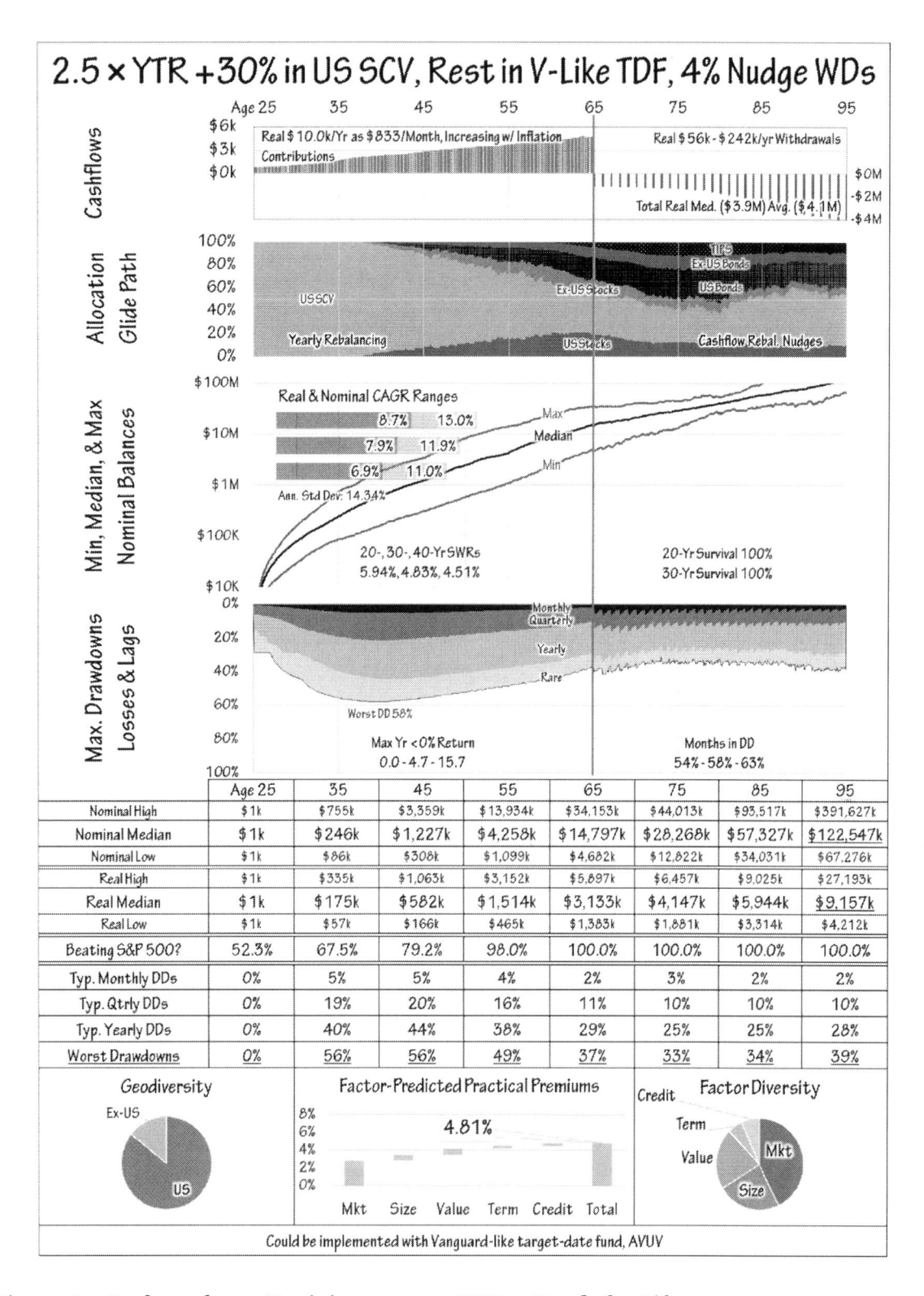

Figure 83. Backtest for 30% minimum, 2.5 × YTR, 2 Funds for Life strategy

2 FUNDS FOR LIFE

3.0 × YTR in US SCV, Rest in V-Like TDF, 4% Fixed WDs

	Age 25	35	45	55	65	75	85	95
Nominal High	$1k	$736k	$3,294k	$12,880k	$24,819k	$30,949k	$47,684k	$132,737k
Nominal Median	$1k	$245k	$1,117k	$3,758k	$12,094k	$19,293k	$28,405k	$45,418k
Nominal Low	$1k	$87k	$339k	$1,234k	$4,887k	$7,913k	$15,020k	$16,188k
Real High	$1k	$327k	$1,043k	$2,874k	$4,299k	$4,540k	$4,029k	$5,931k
Real Median	$1k	$174k	$553k	$1,356k	$2,635k	$2,830k	$2,867k	$3,470k
Real Low	$1k	$57k	$182k	$522k	$1,093k	$1,161k	$1,514k	$938k
Beating S&P 500?	52.3%	66.8%	78.5%	100.0%	95.8%	90.7%	86.3%	66.0%
Typ. Monthly DDs	0%	4%	4%	2%	1%	1%	1%	1%
Typ. Qtrly DDs	0%	18%	17%	12%	6%	5%	5%	6%
Typ. Yearly DDs	0%	40%	40%	32%	23%	16%	14%	18%
Worst Drawdowns	0%	55%	51%	41%	28%	20%	19%	24%

Could be implemented with Vanguard-like target-date fund, AVUV

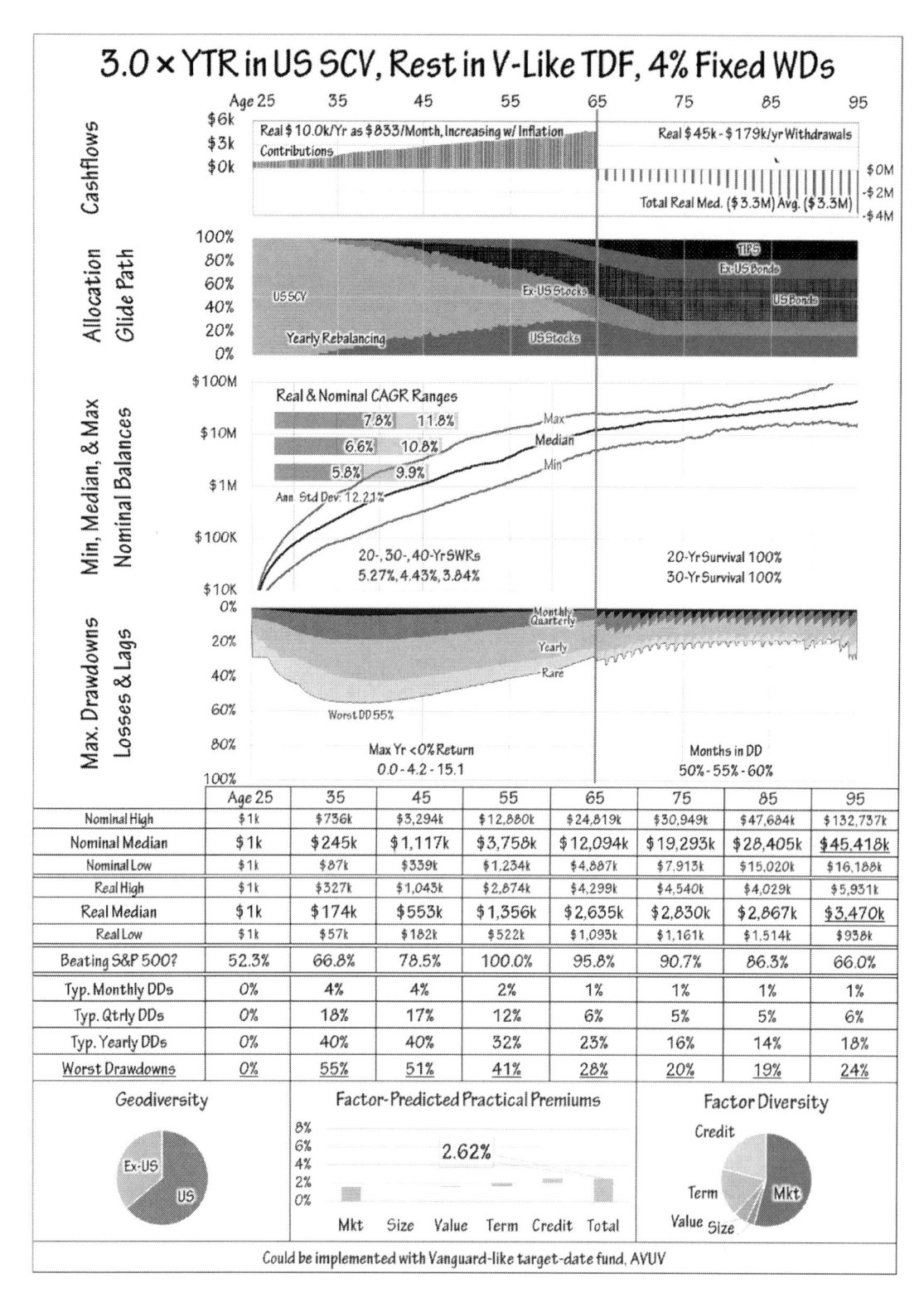

Figure 84. Backtest for 0% minimum, 3.0 × YTR, 2 Funds for Life strategy

APPENDIX 1: ALTERNATIVE 2 FUND RECIPES

3.0 × YTR + 10% in US SCV, Rest in V-Like TDF, 4% Nudge WDs

	Age 25	35	45	55	65	75	85	95
Nominal High	$1k	$755k	$3,360k	$13,346k	$28,386k	$35,480k	$62,917k	$206,465k
Nominal Median	$1k	$246k	$1,180k	$4,002k	$13,166k	$22,506k	$37,366k	$69,221k
Nominal Low	$1k	$86k	$323k	$1,178k	$4,933k	$9,773k	$22,270k	$32,659k
Real High	$1k	$335k	$1,039k	$2,978k	$4,901k	$5,205k	$5,314k	$9,225k
Real Median	$1k	$175k	$576k	$1,436k	$2,871k	$3,302k	$3,822k	$5,132k
Real Low	$1k	$57k	$174k	$498k	$1,205k	$1,434k	$2,263k	$1,901k
Beating S&P 500?	52.3%	67.5%	78.8%	99.8%	99.8%	95.5%	99.0%	99.5%
Typ. Monthly DDs	0%	5%	5%	3%	1%	1%	1%	1%
Typ. Qtrly DDs	0%	19%	18%	14%	8%	6%	5%	5%
Typ. Yearly DDs	0%	40%	42%	34%	25%	18%	17%	16%
Worst Drawdowns	0%	56%	54%	44%	31%	24%	22%	22%

Could be implemented with Vanguard-like target-date fund, AVUV

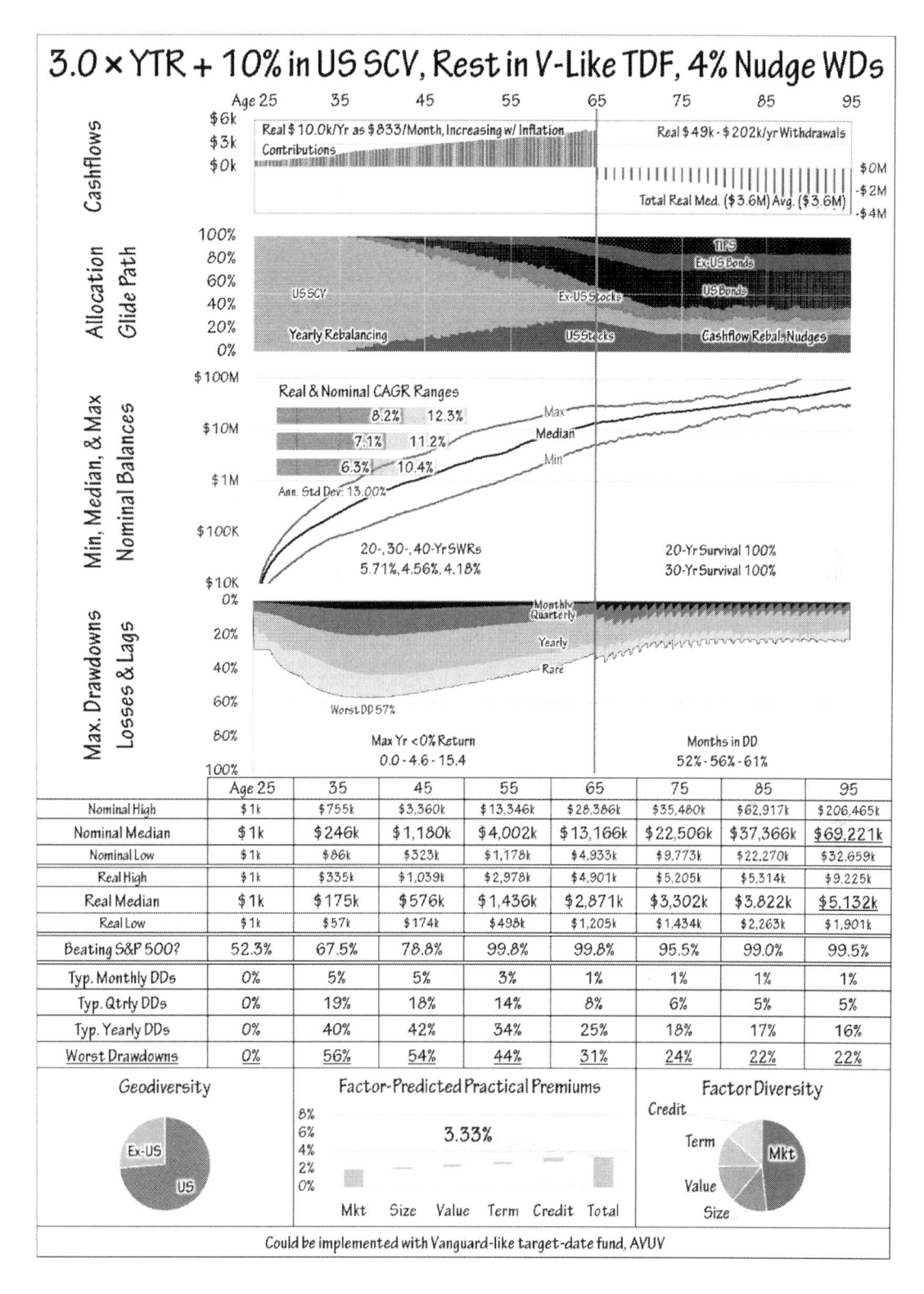

Figure 85. Backtest for 10% minimum, 3.0 × YTR, 2 Funds for Life strategy

3.0 × YTR + 20% in US SCV, Rest in V-Like TDF, 4% Nudge WDs

	Age 25	35	45	55	65	75	85	95
Nominal High	$1k	$755k	$3,353k	$13,762k	$32,074k	$40,352k	$78,526k	$298,884k
Nominal Median	$1k	$246k	$1,238k	$4,276k	$14,434k	$25,862k	$48,030k	$93,459k
Nominal Low	$1k	$86k	$305k	$1,124k	$4,886k	$11,489k	$31,028k	$50,578k
Real High	$1k	$335k	$1,074k	$3,113k	$5,538k	$5,920k	$6,868k	$17,194k
Real Median	$1k	$175k	$587k	$1,509k	$3,059k	$3,794k	$4,980k	$7,122k
Real Low	$1k	$57k	$164k	$475k	$1,295k	$1,685k	$3,152k	$2,958k
Beating S&P 500?	52.3%	67.5%	79.2%	98.2%	100.0%	100.0%	100.0%	100.0%
Typ. Monthly DDs	0%	5%	5%	4%	2%	2%	1%	1%
Typ. Qtrly DDs	0%	19%	20%	15%	8%	8%	7%	7%
Typ. Yearly DDs	0%	40%	44%	37%	27%	21%	20%	22%
Worst Drawdowns	0%	56%	56%	47%	34%	27%	27%	29%

Could be implemented with Vanguard-like target-date fund, AVUV

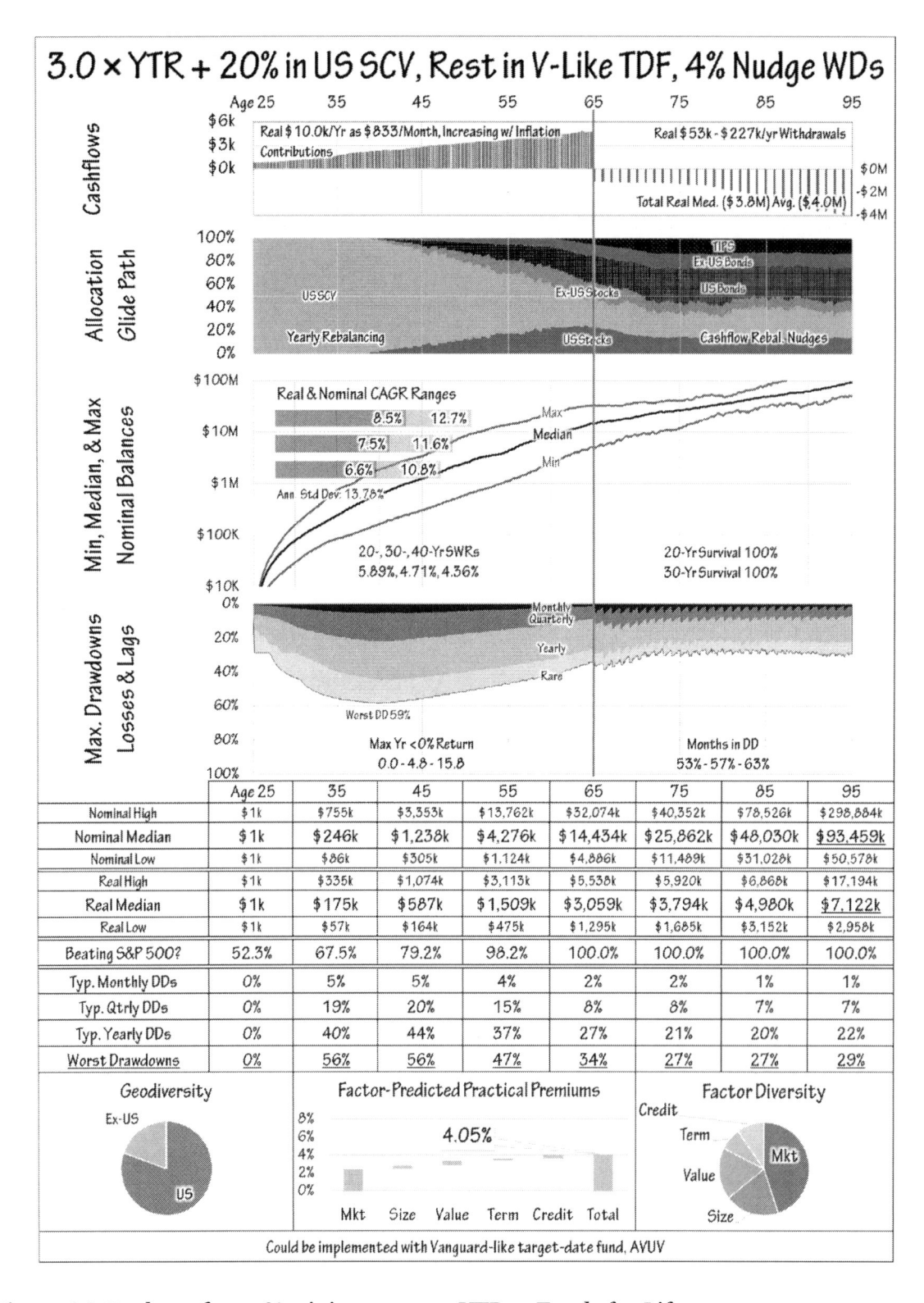

Figure 86. Backtest for 20% minimum, 3.0 × YTR, 2 Funds for Life strategy

APPENDIX 1: ALTERNATIVE 2 FUND RECIPES

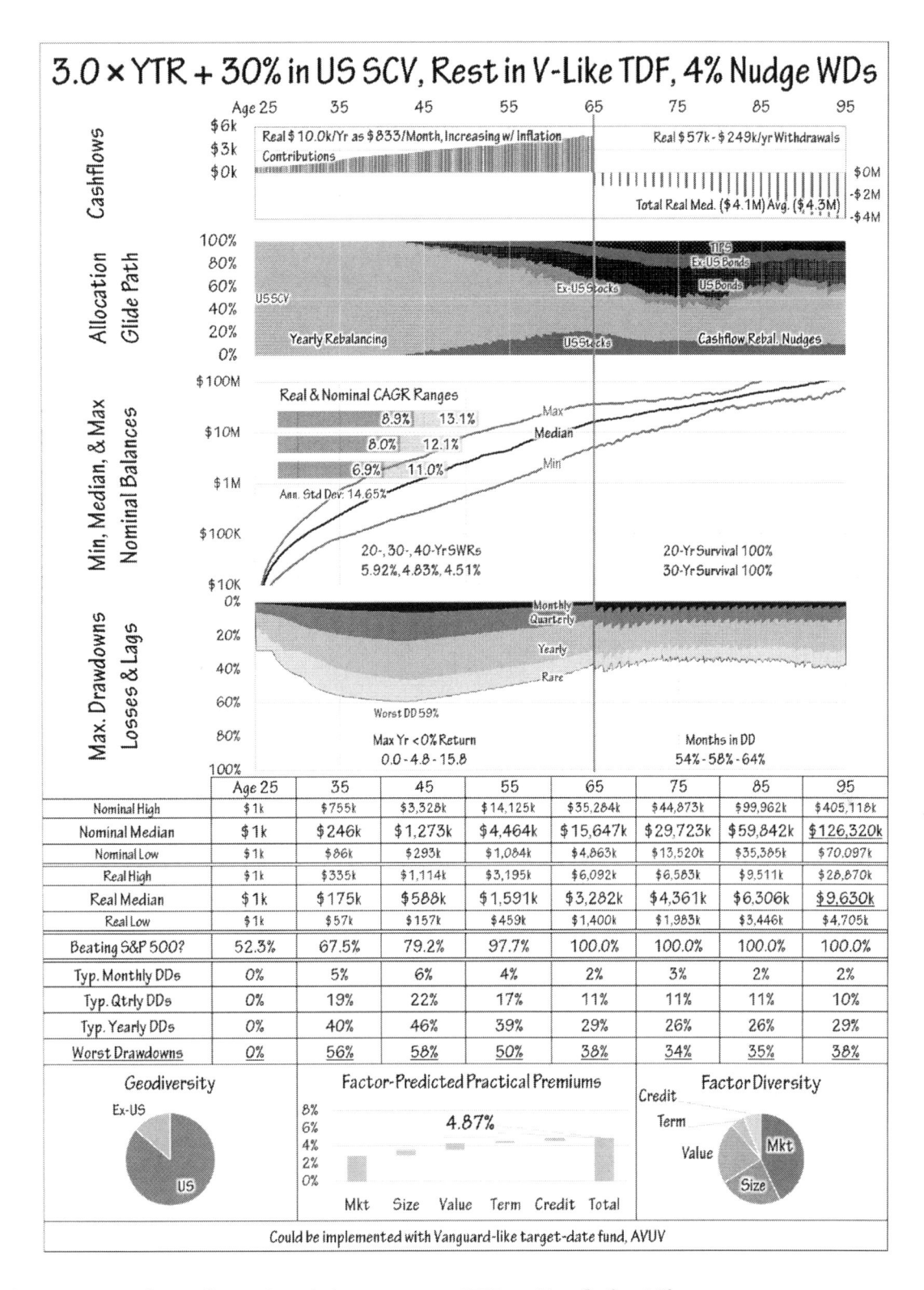

Figure 87. Backtest for 30% minimum, 3.0 × YTR, 2 Funds for Life strategy

Appendix 2
Alternative Second Funds

Many retirement accounts will not provide access to a small-cap value fund. Most, though, will have access to either a small-cap blend or large-cap value fund. What happens to the 2 Funds for Life strategies if we use one of those funds instead of small-cap value? Based on what we know from history, we would expect them to help, but not as much. In a sense, they're "weaker sauces" to spice our mix. Instead of getting two positive diversifying attributes in a single fund, we're only getting one. For investors, this creates a choice. Is it better to use one of the weaker sauce alternatives in our retirement account to keep everything together? Or is it better to invest some of our retirement savings in a second account where we can access a "stronger sauce" fund and deal with the added complexity? Or should we choose one of the more aggressive allocations to compensate for the lower risk and return of these options?

To help decide, we'll evaluate the 2 Funds for Life strategies we presented earlier using small blend and large value for the second funds. The scenario assumptions are the same as before. We assume $10k/year contributed on a monthly basis, increasing with inflation from age 25 to age 65. For consistency and to accommodate situations where rebalancing might be costly or impossible, the fixed 90|10 allocation still assumes no rebalancing before retirement. The others assume annual rebalancing before retirement. At age 65, annual withdrawals are set at 4% of the balance and occur annually, increasing with inflation through age 95. Rebalancing in retirement is only through nudge withdrawals, meaning the entire annual withdrawal is taken from the fund that's above its target allocation.

Let's see how these weaker sauce options did. We'll look at small-cap blend first, then large-cap value. Table 14 shows the comparison results for US small-cap blend

(SCB) and US small-cap value (SCV) for the 2nd fund. The results for using US small-cap value are shown in ~~strikethrough font~~.

2FFL Using Small-Cap Blend as 2nd Fund	Median Real End Balances	Median Real WDs	Worst Peak DD	Worst DD @ 65	40-Year SWR	30-Year, Survival %	% of Times > S&P 500
Easy 2FFL Fixed 90 | 10 TDF | US ~~SCV~~ SCB	$2.55M ~~$3.16M~~	$2.2M ~~$2.4M~~	43% ~~44%~~	30% ~~35%~~	4.00% ~~3.95%~~	100% ~~100%~~	0% ~~15%~~
Moderate 2FFL 1.5 X YTR in US ~~SCV~~ SCB, Rest in V-Like TDF	$2.40M ~~$2.82M~~	$2.3M ~~$2.7M~~	46% ~~47%~~	27% ~~28%~~	3.84% ~~3.84%~~	100% ~~100%~~	0% ~~26%~~
Aggressive 2FFL 2.5 X YTR + 20% in US ~~SCV~~ SCB, Rest in V-Like TDF	$3.65M ~~$6.71M~~	$2.5M ~~$3.6M~~	50% ~~56%~~	33% ~~34%~~	4.18% ~~4.36%~~	100% ~~100%~~	37% ~~100%~~

Table 14. Comparison of 2 Funds for Life strategies using US small-cap blend instead of US small-cap value

Using small-cap blend instead of small-cap value reduced peak drawdowns, end balances, total withdrawals, and the chance of beating the S&P 500.

It also reduced safe withdrawal rates for the Moderate and Aggressive 2 Funds for Life strategies.

One way to compensate for these effects would be to take a more aggressive approach. For example, if you thought the 1.5 × YTR in TDF plus SCV approach with a small-cap value second fund was right for you, you could use the 1.5 × YTR in TDF, but ramp to 10% in US SCB (instead of 0% in SCV), as described in Appendix 1.

For easy comparison, the next pages include the detailed backtests for the 2 Funds for Life approaches using US small-cap blend and US small-cap value. After that, we'll take a look at 2 Funds for Life with large-cap value.

APPENDIX 2: ALTERNATIVE SECOND FUNDS

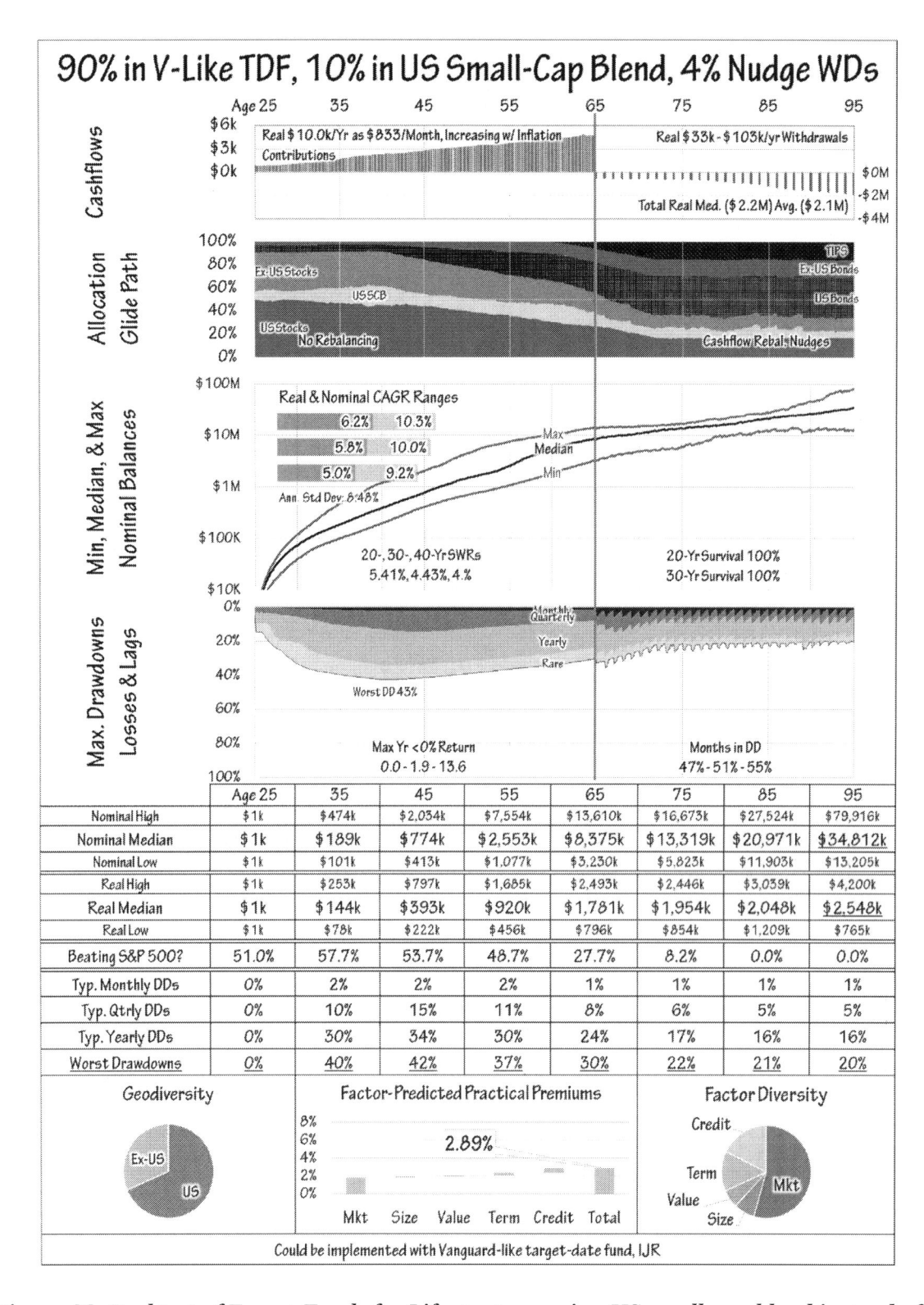

90% in V-Like TDF, 10% in US Small-Cap Blend, 4% Nudge WDs

	Age 25	35	45	55	65	75	85	95
Nominal High	$1k	$474k	$2,034k	$7,554k	$13,610k	$16,673k	$27,524k	$79,916k
Nominal Median	$1k	$189k	$774k	$2,553k	$8,375k	$13,319k	$20,971k	$34,812k
Nominal Low	$1k	$101k	$413k	$1,077k	$3,230k	$5,823k	$11,903k	$13,205k
Real High	$1k	$253k	$797k	$1,685k	$2,493k	$2,446k	$3,039k	$4,200k
Real Median	$1k	$144k	$393k	$920k	$1,781k	$1,954k	$2,048k	$2,548k
Real Low	$1k	$78k	$222k	$456k	$796k	$854k	$1,209k	$765k
Beating S&P 500?	51.0%	57.7%	53.7%	48.7%	27.7%	8.2%	0.0%	0.0%
Typ. Monthly DDs	0%	2%	2%	2%	1%	1%	1%	1%
Typ. Qtrly DDs	0%	10%	15%	11%	8%	6%	5%	5%
Typ. Yearly DDs	0%	30%	34%	30%	24%	17%	16%	16%
Worst Drawdowns	0%	40%	42%	37%	30%	22%	21%	20%

Could be implemented with Vanguard-like target-date fund, IJR

Figure 88. Backtest of Easy 2 Funds for Life strategy using US small-cap blend instead of US small-cap value

APPENDIX 2: ALTERNATIVE SECOND FUNDS

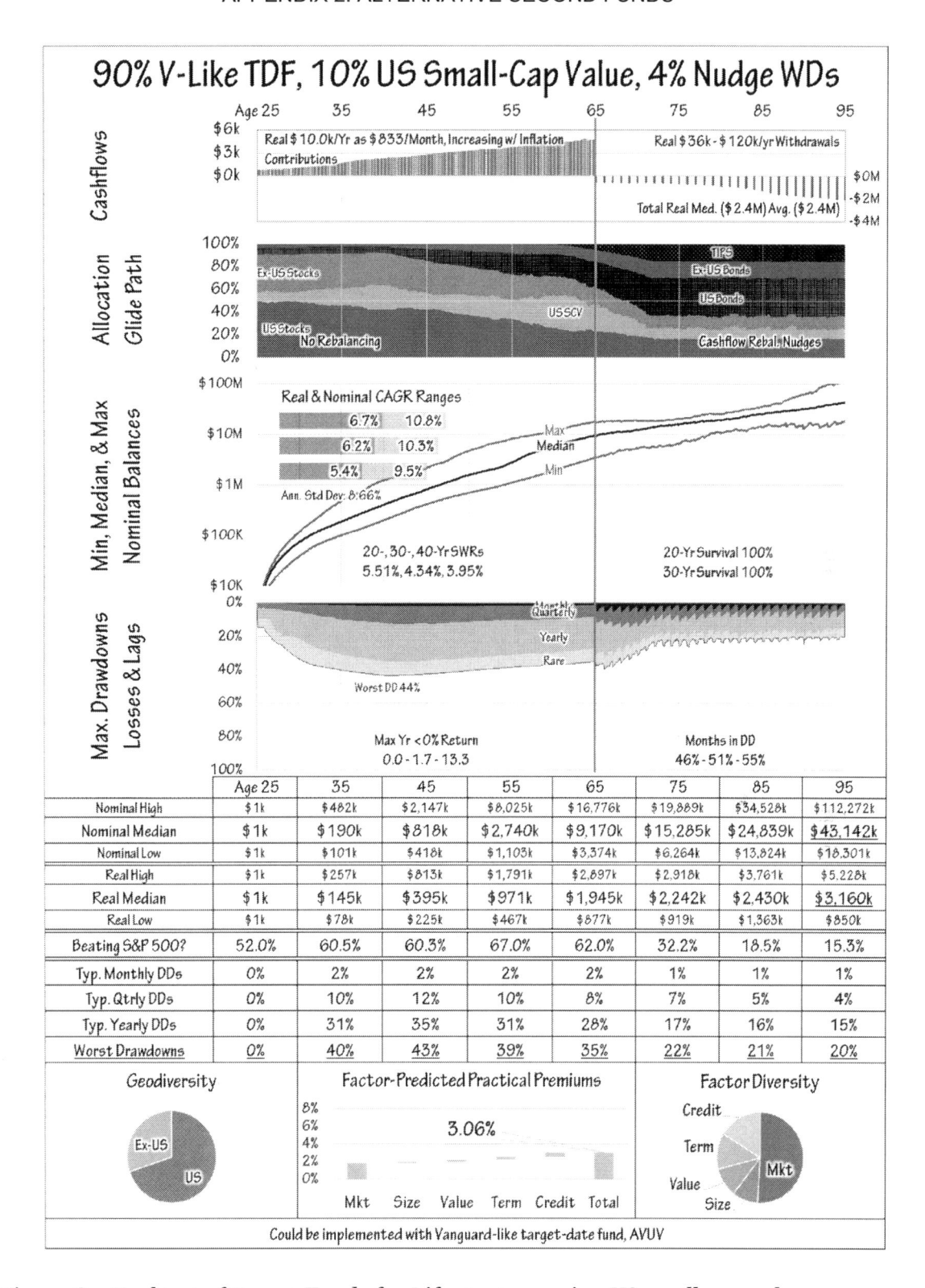

90% V-Like TDF, 10% US Small-Cap Value, 4% Nudge WDs

	Age 25	35	45	55	65	75	85	95
Nominal High	$1k	$482k	$2,147k	$8,025k	$16,776k	$19,889k	$34,528k	$112,272k
Nominal Median	$1k	$190k	$818k	$2,740k	$9,170k	$15,285k	$24,839k	$43,142k
Nominal Low	$1k	$101k	$418k	$1,103k	$3,374k	$6,264k	$13,824k	$18,301k
Real High	$1k	$257k	$813k	$1,791k	$2,897k	$2,918k	$3,761k	$5,228k
Real Median	$1k	$145k	$395k	$971k	$1,945k	$2,242k	$2,430k	$3,160k
Real Low	$1k	$78k	$225k	$467k	$877k	$919k	$1,363k	$850k
Beating S&P 500?	52.0%	60.5%	60.3%	67.0%	62.0%	32.2%	18.5%	15.3%
Typ. Monthly DDs	0%	2%	2%	2%	2%	1%	1%	1%
Typ. Qtrly DDs	0%	10%	12%	10%	8%	7%	5%	4%
Typ. Yearly DDs	0%	31%	35%	31%	28%	17%	16%	15%
Worst Drawdowns	0%	40%	43%	39%	35%	22%	21%	20%

Could be implemented with Vanguard-like target-date fund, AVUV

Figure 89. Backtest of Easy 2 Funds for Life strategy using US small-cap value

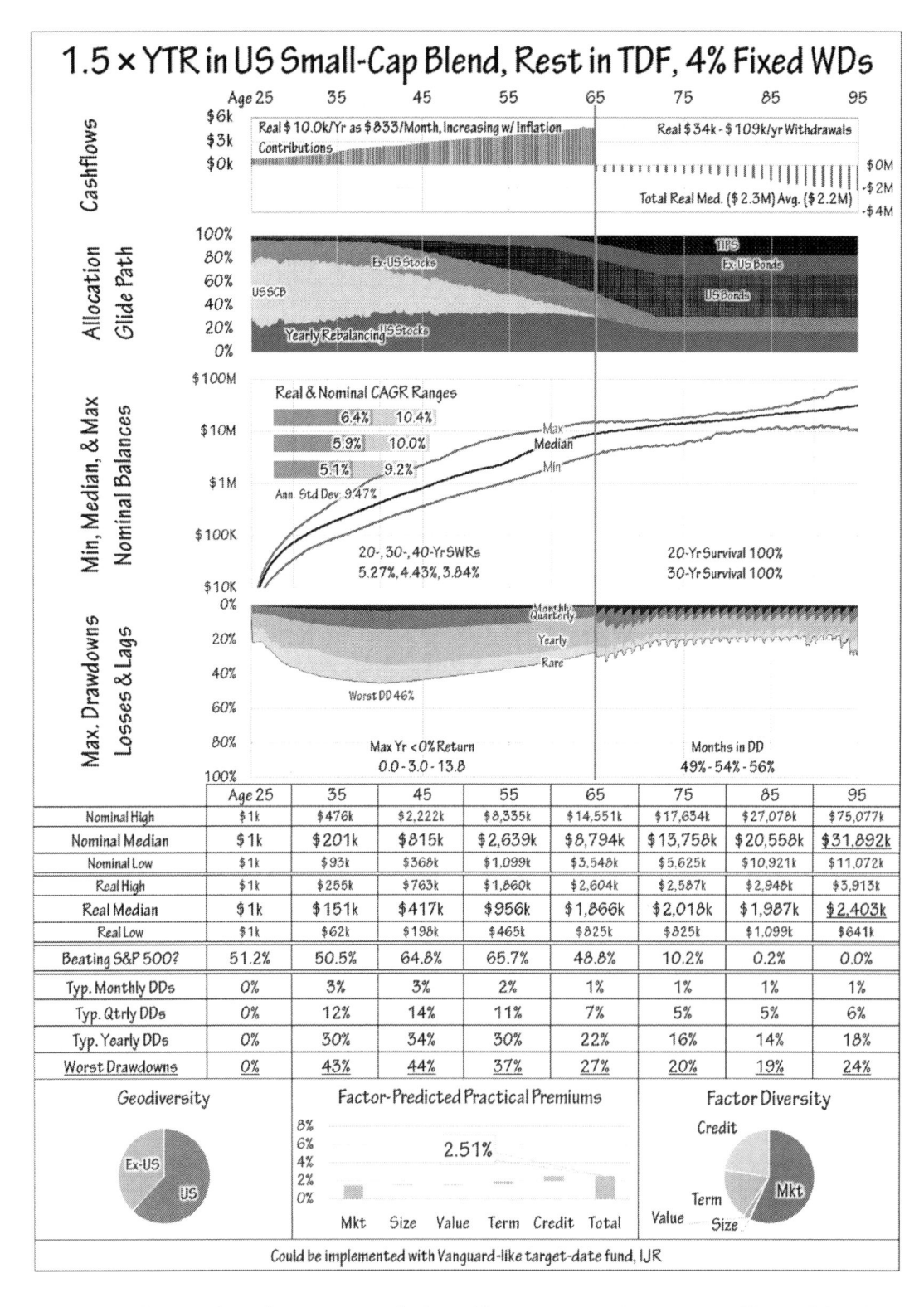

Figure 90. Backtest of Moderate 2 Funds for Life strategy using US small-cap blend instead of US small-cap value

APPENDIX 2: ALTERNATIVE SECOND FUNDS

1.5 × YTR in US SCV, Rest in V-Like TDF, 4% Fixed WDs

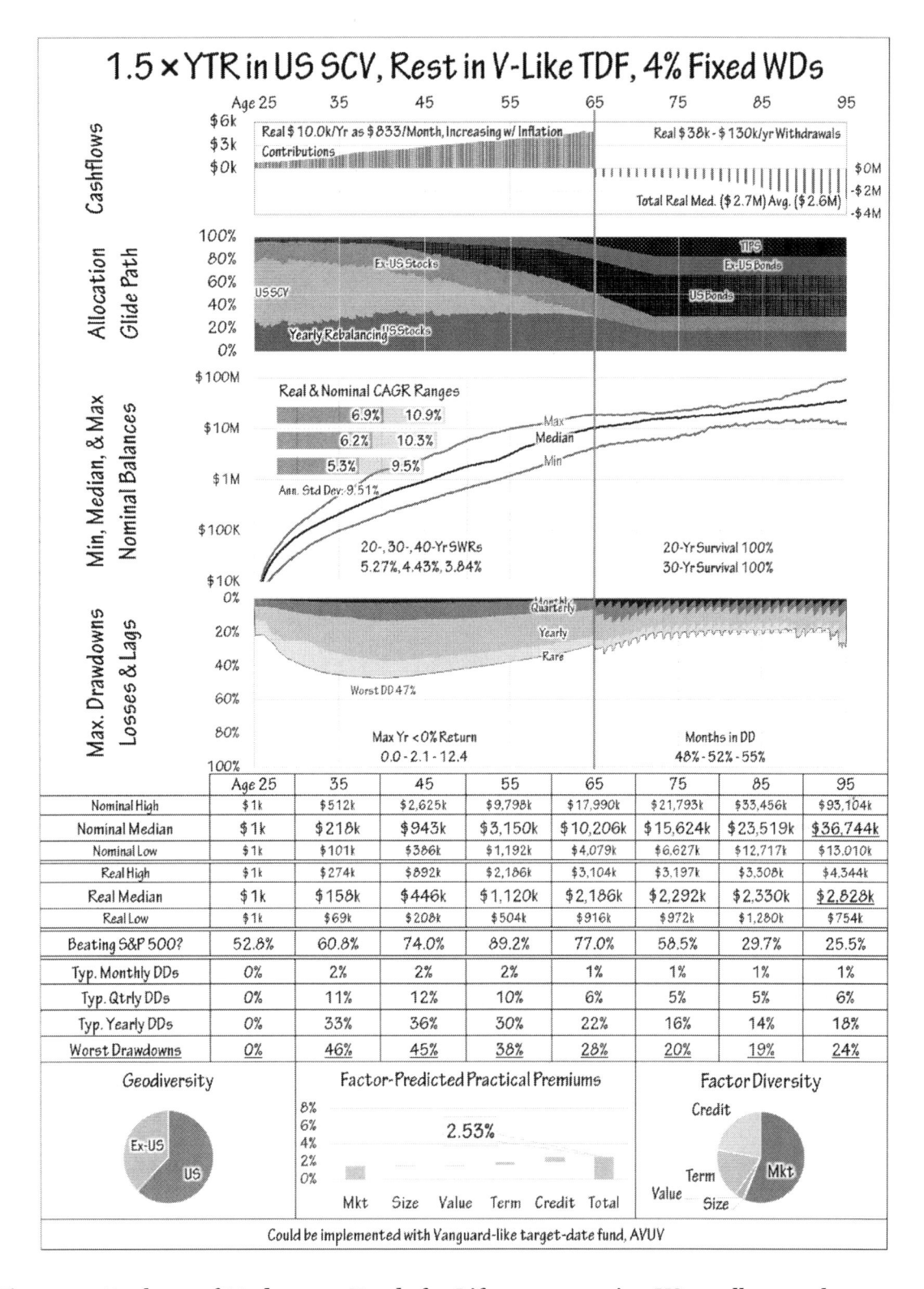

	Age 25	35	45	55	65	75	85	95
Nominal High	$1k	$512k	$2,625k	$9,798k	$17,990k	$21,793k	$33,456k	$93,104k
Nominal Median	$1k	$218k	$943k	$3,150k	$10,206k	$15,624k	$23,519k	$36,744k
Nominal Low	$1k	$101k	$386k	$1,192k	$4,079k	$6,627k	$12,717k	$13,010k
Real High	$1k	$274k	$892k	$2,186k	$3,104k	$3,197k	$3,308k	$4,344k
Real Median	$1k	$158k	$446k	$1,120k	$2,186k	$2,292k	$2,330k	$2,828k
Real Low	$1k	$69k	$208k	$504k	$916k	$972k	$1,280k	$754k
Beating S&P 500?	52.8%	60.8%	74.0%	89.2%	77.0%	58.5%	29.7%	25.5%
Typ. Monthly DDs	0%	2%	2%	2%	1%	1%	1%	1%
Typ. Qtrly DDs	0%	11%	12%	10%	6%	5%	5%	6%
Typ. Yearly DDs	0%	33%	36%	30%	22%	16%	14%	18%
Worst Drawdowns	0%	46%	45%	38%	28%	20%	19%	24%

Could be implemented with Vanguard-like target-date fund, AVUV

Figure 91. Backtest of Moderate 2 Funds for Life strategy using US small-cap value

2 FUNDS FOR LIFE

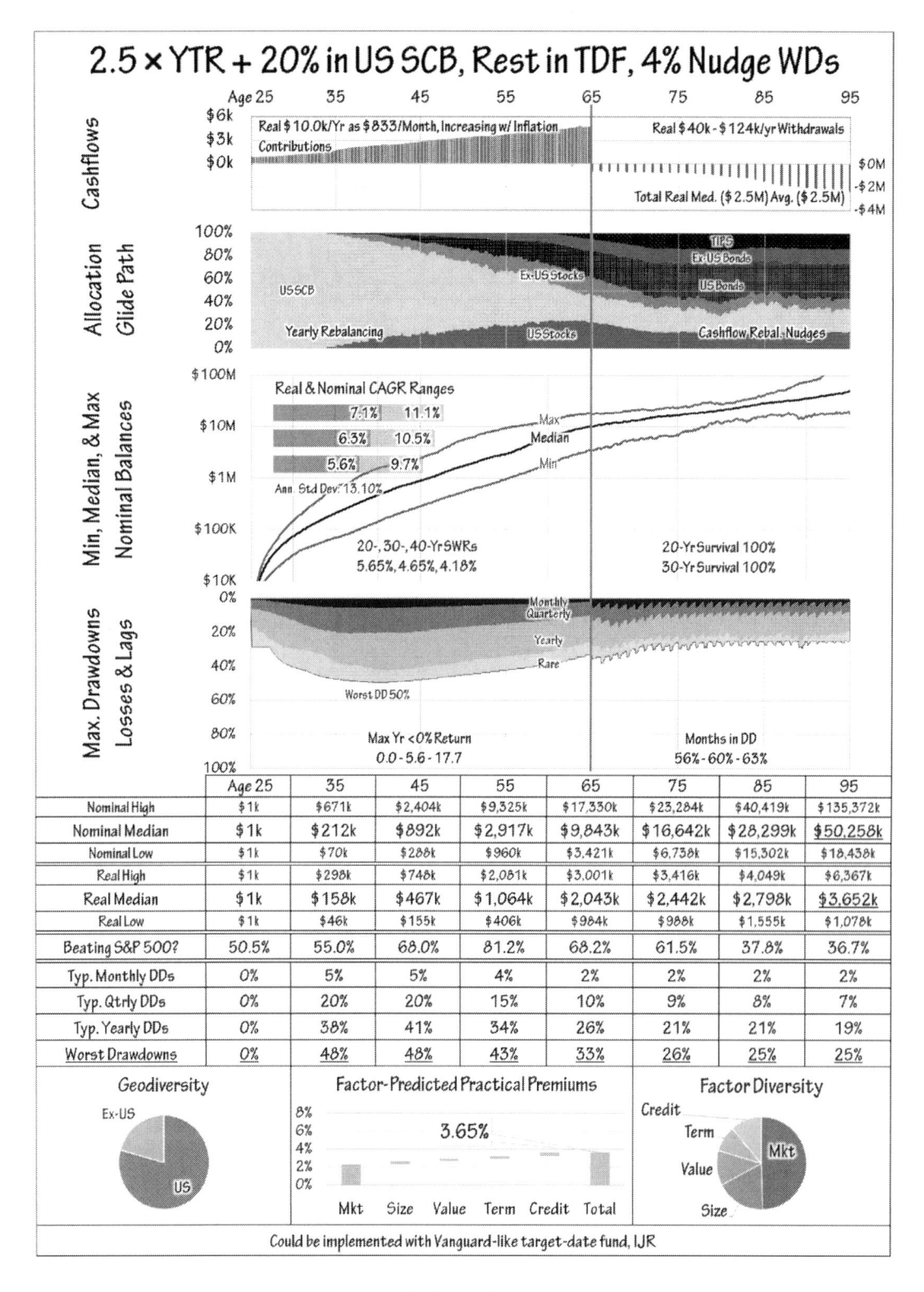

2.5 × YTR + 20% in US SCB, Rest in TDF, 4% Nudge WDs

	Age 25	35	45	55	65	75	85	95
Nominal High	$1k	$671k	$2,404k	$9,325k	$17,330k	$23,284k	$40,419k	$135,372k
Nominal Median	$1k	$212k	$892k	$2,917k	$9,843k	$16,642k	$28,299k	$50,258k
Nominal Low	$1k	$70k	$288k	$960k	$3,421k	$6,738k	$15,302k	$18,438k
Real High	$1k	$298k	$748k	$2,081k	$3,001k	$3,416k	$4,049k	$6,367k
Real Median	$1k	$158k	$467k	$1,064k	$2,043k	$2,442k	$2,798k	$3,652k
Real Low	$1k	$46k	$155k	$406k	$984k	$988k	$1,555k	$1,078k
Beating S&P 500?	50.5%	55.0%	68.0%	81.2%	68.2%	61.5%	37.8%	36.7%
Typ. Monthly DDs	0%	5%	5%	4%	2%	2%	2%	2%
Typ. Qtrly DDs	0%	20%	20%	15%	10%	9%	8%	7%
Typ. Yearly DDs	0%	38%	41%	34%	26%	21%	21%	19%
Worst Drawdowns	0%	48%	48%	43%	33%	26%	25%	25%

Could be implemented with Vanguard-like target-date fund, IJR

Figure 92. Backtest of Aggressive 2 Funds for Life strategy using US small-cap blend instead of US small-cap value

APPENDIX 2: ALTERNATIVE SECOND FUNDS

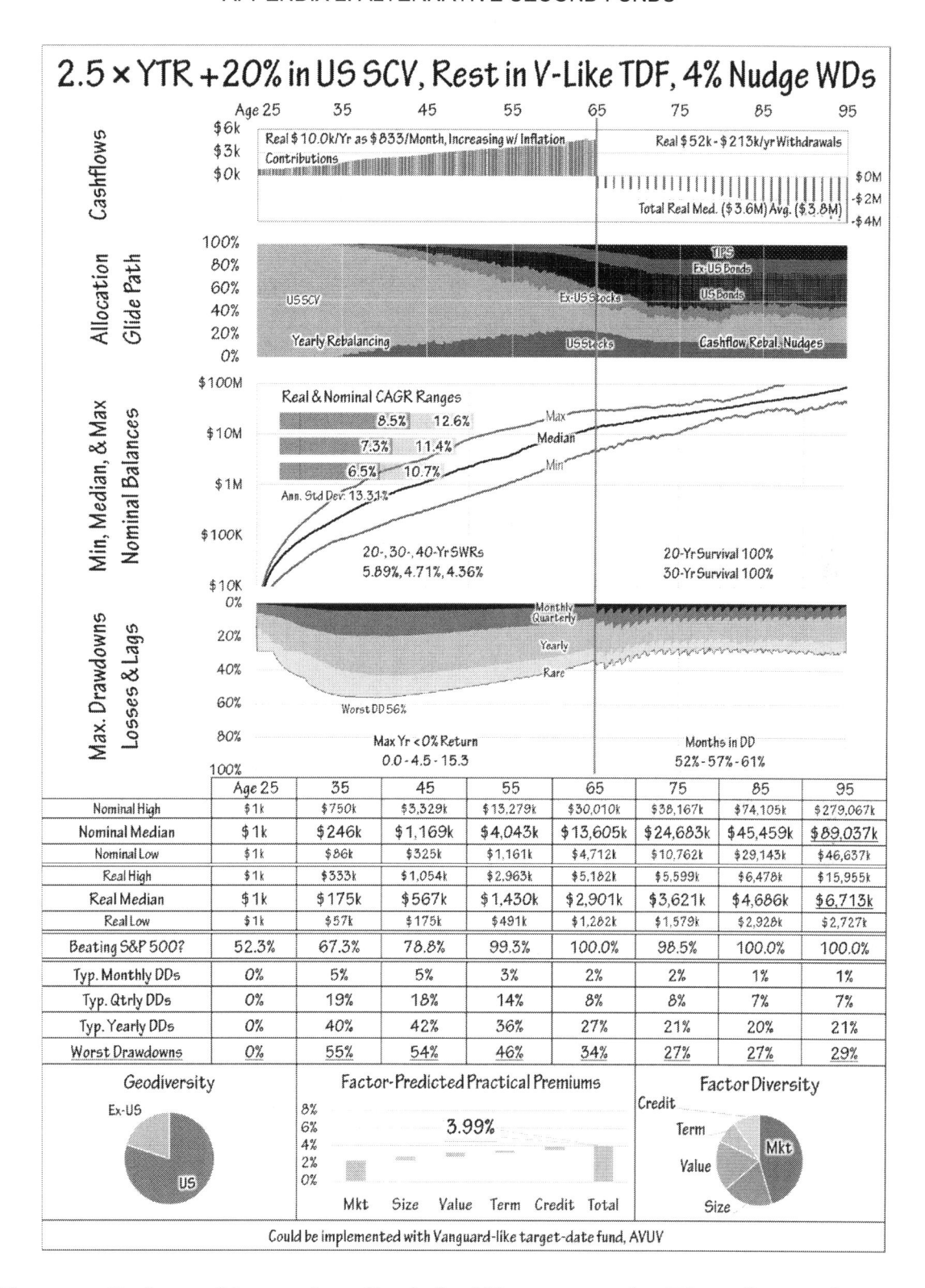

2.5 × YTR +20% in US SCV, Rest in V-Like TDF, 4% Nudge WDs

	Age 25	35	45	55	65	75	85	95
Nominal High	$1k	$750k	$3,329k	$13,279k	$30,010k	$38,167k	$74,105k	$279,067k
Nominal Median	$1k	$246k	$1,169k	$4,043k	$13,605k	$24,683k	$45,459k	$89,037k
Nominal Low	$1k	$86k	$325k	$1,161k	$4,712k	$10,762k	$29,143k	$46,637k
Real High	$1k	$333k	$1,054k	$2,963k	$5,182k	$5,599k	$6,478k	$15,955k
Real Median	$1k	$175k	$567k	$1,430k	$2,901k	$3,621k	$4,686k	$6,713k
Real Low	$1k	$57k	$175k	$491k	$1,282k	$1,579k	$2,928k	$2,727k
Beating S&P 500?	52.3%	67.3%	78.8%	99.3%	100.0%	98.5%	100.0%	100.0%
Typ. Monthly DDs	0%	5%	5%	3%	2%	2%	1%	1%
Typ. Qtrly DDs	0%	19%	18%	14%	8%	8%	7%	7%
Typ. Yearly DDs	0%	40%	42%	36%	27%	21%	20%	21%
Worst Drawdowns	0%	55%	54%	46%	34%	27%	27%	29%

Could be implemented with Vanguard-like target-date fund, AVUV

Figure 93. Backtest of Aggressive 2 Funds for Life strategy using US small-cap value

How do 2 Funds for Life strategies work with US large-cap value for the 2nd fund compared to using US small-cap value? (SCV 2nd fund results shown in ~~strikethrough~~ font in the table.)

2FFL Using Large-Cap Value as 2nd Fund	Median Real End Balances	Median Real WDs	Worst Peak DD	Worst DD @ 65	40-Year SWR	30-Year, Survival %	% of Times > S&P 500
Easy 2FFL Fixed 90 | 10 TDF | US ~~SCV~~ LCV	$2..80M ~~$3.16M~~	$2.3M ~~$2.4M~~	43% ~~44%~~	32% ~~35%~~	4.04% ~~3.95%~~	100% ~~100%~~	0% ~~15%~~
Moderate 2FFL 1.5 X YTR in US ~~SCV~~ LCV, Rest in V-Like TDF	$2.49M ~~$2.82M~~	$2.5M ~~$2.7M~~	47% ~~47%~~	27% ~~28%~~	3.84% ~~3.84%~~	100% ~~100%~~	0% ~~26%~~
Aggressive 2FFL 2.5 X YTR + 20% in US ~~SCV~~ LCV, Rest in V-Like TDF	$4.53M ~~$6.74M~~	$2.9M ~~$3.6M~~	55% ~~56%~~	34% ~~34%~~	4.30% ~~4.36%~~	100% ~~100%~~	81% ~~100%~~

Table 15. Comparison of 2 Funds for Life strategies using US large-cap value instead of US small-cap value

Large-cap value appears to have retained more of the risk and diversifying benefits than small-cap blend did, but it's still not as concentrated as small-cap value.

Using large-cap value instead of small-cap value had little effect on peak drawdowns or safe withdrawal rates, but it substantially reduced median end balances, withdrawals, and chances of beating the S&P 500 at age 95.

Once again, you can compensate for this by taking a more aggressive approach, but you may not need to be quite as aggressive.

For easy comparison, the next pages include the detailed backtests for the 2 Funds for Life approaches using large-cap value and small-cap value.

APPENDIX 2: ALTERNATIVE SECOND FUNDS

2 FUNDS FOR LIFE

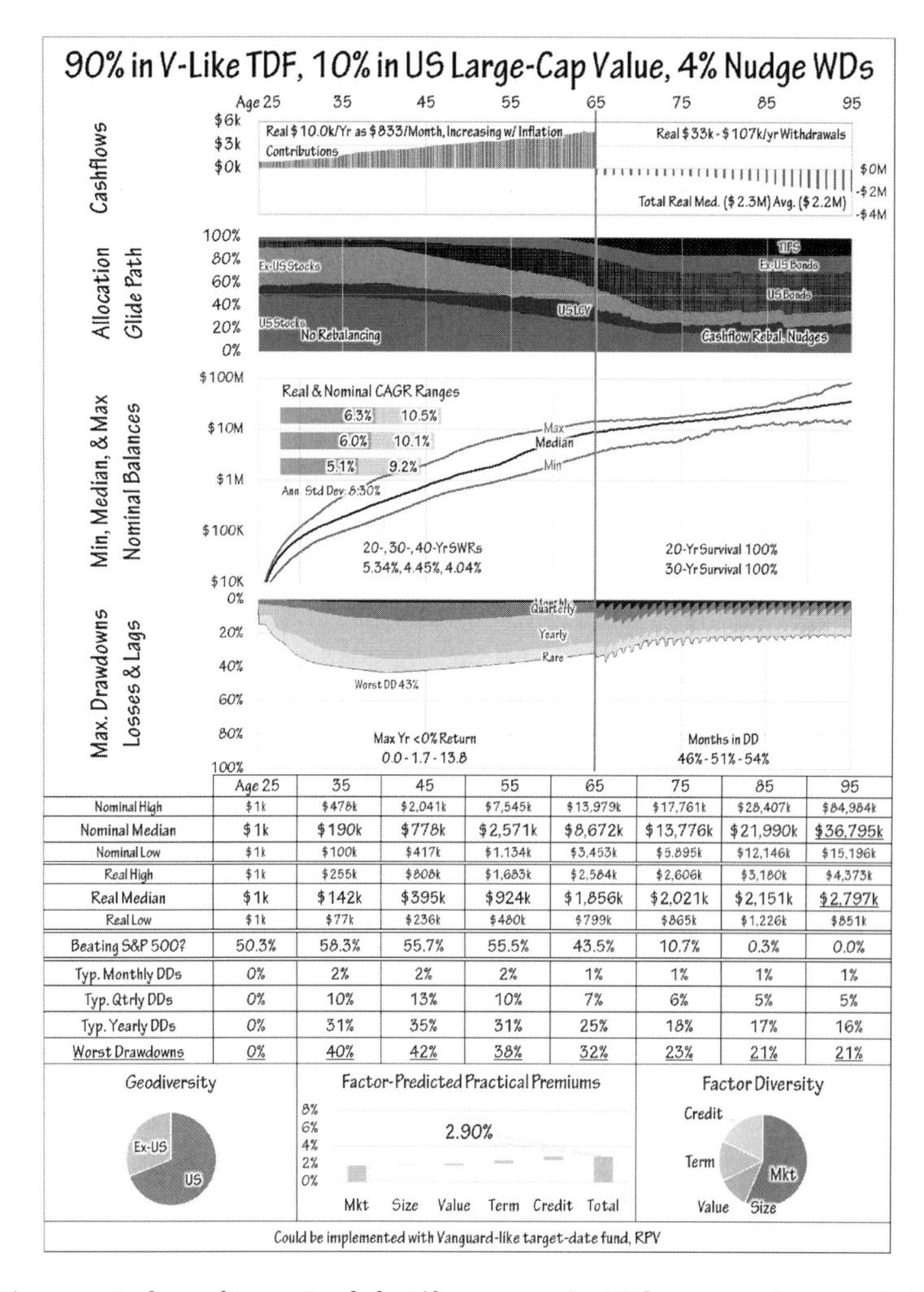

90% in V-Like TDF, 10% in US Large-Cap Value, 4% Nudge WDs

	Age 25	35	45	55	65	75	85	95
Nominal High	$1k	$478k	$2,041k	$7,545k	$13,979k	$17,761k	$28,407k	$84,984k
Nominal Median	$1k	$190k	$778k	$2,571k	$8,672k	$13,776k	$21,990k	$36,795k
Nominal Low	$1k	$100k	$417k	$1,134k	$3,453k	$5,895k	$12,146k	$15,196k
Real High	$1k	$255k	$808k	$1,683k	$2,584k	$2,606k	$3,180k	$4,373k
Real Median	$1k	$142k	$395k	$924k	$1,856k	$2,021k	$2,151k	$2,797k
Real Low	$1k	$77k	$236k	$480k	$799k	$865k	$1,226k	$851k
Beating S&P 500?	50.3%	58.3%	55.7%	55.5%	43.5%	10.7%	0.3%	0.0%
Typ. Monthly DDs	0%	2%	2%	2%	1%	1%	1%	1%
Typ. Qtrly DDs	0%	10%	13%	10%	7%	6%	5%	5%
Typ. Yearly DDs	0%	31%	35%	31%	25%	18%	17%	16%
Worst Drawdowns	0%	40%	42%	38%	32%	23%	21%	21%

Could be implemented with Vanguard-like target-date fund, RPV

Figure 94. Backtest of Easy 2 Funds for Life strategy using US large-cap value instead of US small-cap value

APPENDIX 2: ALTERNATIVE SECOND FUNDS

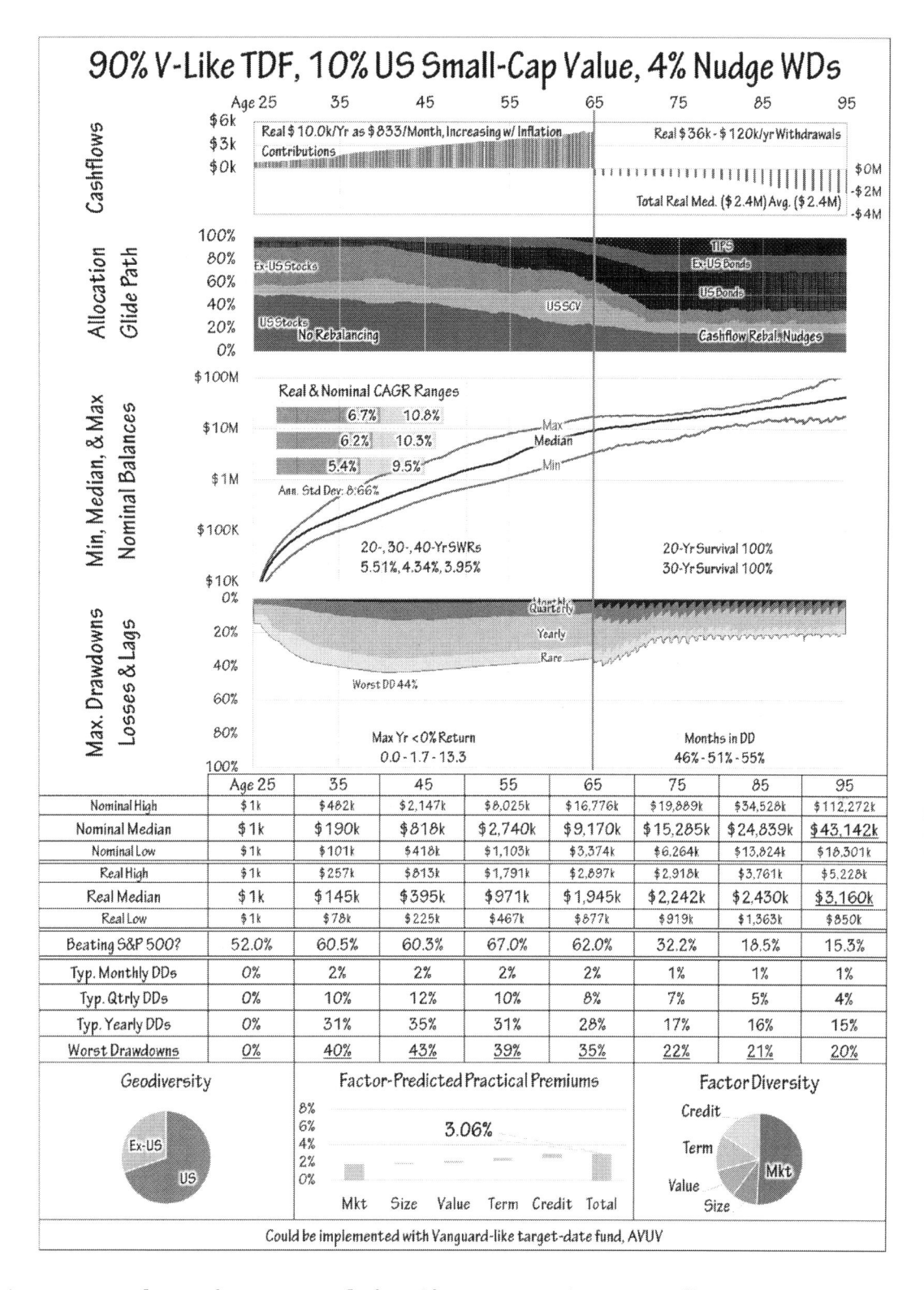

90% V-Like TDF, 10% US Small-Cap Value, 4% Nudge WDs

	Age 25	35	45	55	65	75	85	95
Nominal High	$1k	$482k	$2,147k	$8,025k	$16,776k	$19,889k	$34,528k	$112,272k
Nominal Median	$1k	$190k	$818k	$2,740k	$9,170k	$15,285k	$24,839k	$43,142k
Nominal Low	$1k	$101k	$418k	$1,103k	$3,374k	$6,264k	$13,824k	$18,301k
Real High	$1k	$257k	$813k	$1,791k	$2,897k	$2,918k	$3,761k	$5,228k
Real Median	$1k	$145k	$395k	$971k	$1,945k	$2,242k	$2,430k	$3,160k
Real Low	$1k	$78k	$225k	$467k	$877k	$919k	$1,363k	$850k
Beating S&P 500?	52.0%	60.5%	60.3%	67.0%	62.0%	32.2%	18.5%	15.3%
Typ. Monthly DDs	0%	2%	2%	2%	2%	1%	1%	1%
Typ. Qtrly DDs	0%	10%	12%	10%	8%	7%	5%	4%
Typ. Yearly DDs	0%	31%	35%	31%	28%	17%	16%	15%
Worst Drawdowns	0%	40%	43%	39%	35%	22%	21%	20%

Could be implemented with Vanguard-like target-date fund, AVUV

Figure 95. Backtest of Easy 2 Funds for Life strategy using US small-cap value

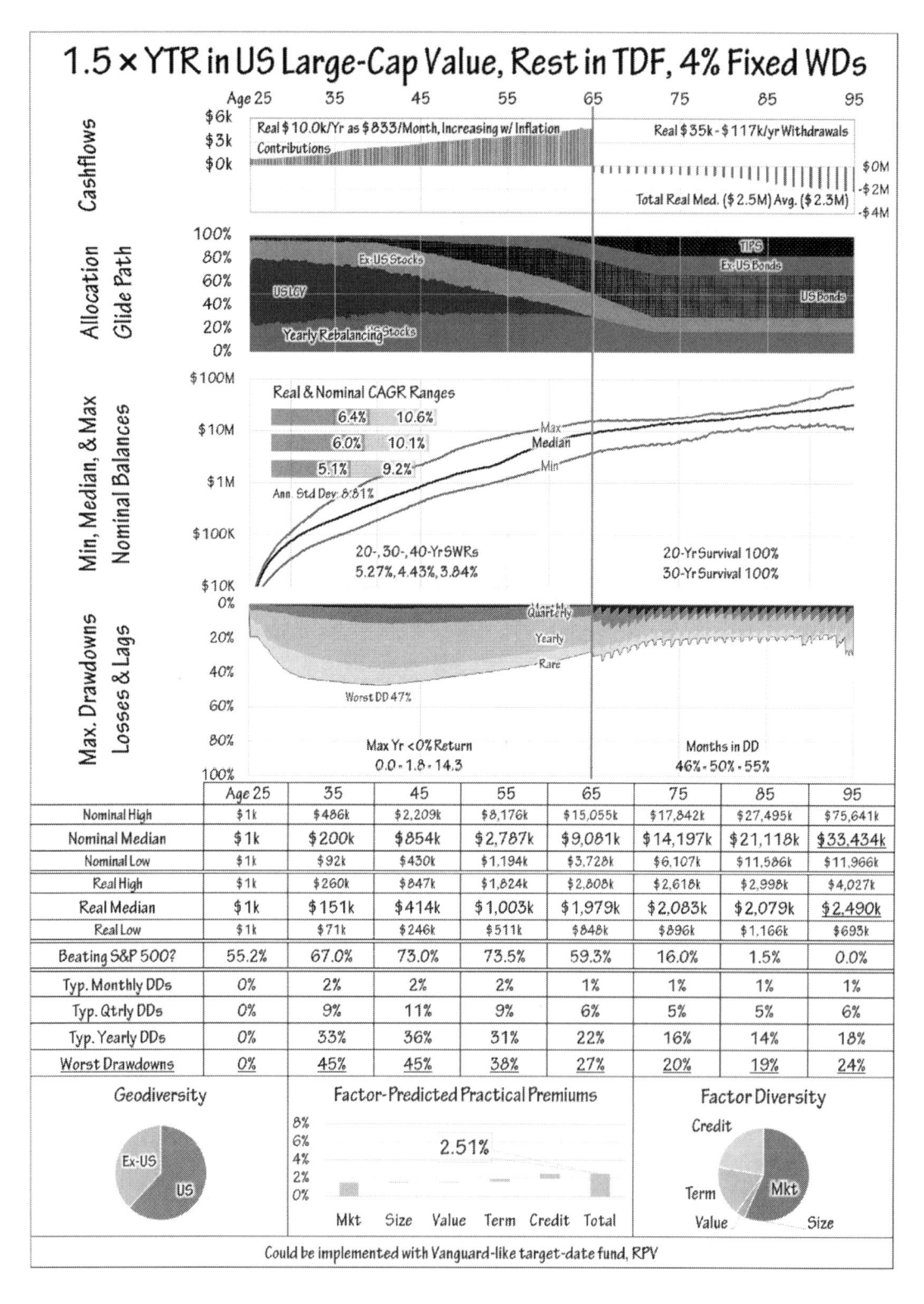

1.5 × YTR in US Large-Cap Value, Rest in TDF, 4% Fixed WDs

	Age 25	35	45	55	65	75	85	95
Nominal High	$1k	$486k	$2,209k	$8,176k	$15,055k	$17,842k	$27,495k	$75,641k
Nominal Median	$1k	$200k	$854k	$2,787k	$9,081k	$14,197k	$21,118k	$33,434k
Nominal Low	$1k	$92k	$430k	$1,194k	$3,728k	$6,107k	$11,586k	$11,966k
Real High	$1k	$260k	$847k	$1,824k	$2,808k	$2,618k	$2,998k	$4,027k
Real Median	$1k	$151k	$414k	$1,003k	$1,979k	$2,083k	$2,079k	$2,490k
Real Low	$1k	$71k	$246k	$511k	$848k	$896k	$1,166k	$693k
Beating S&P 500?	55.2%	67.0%	73.0%	73.5%	59.3%	16.0%	1.5%	0.0%
Typ. Monthly DDs	0%	2%	2%	2%	1%	1%	1%	1%
Typ. Qtrly DDs	0%	9%	11%	9%	6%	5%	5%	6%
Typ. Yearly DDs	0%	33%	36%	31%	22%	16%	14%	18%
Worst Drawdowns	0%	45%	45%	38%	27%	20%	19%	24%

Could be implemented with Vanguard-like target-date fund, RPV

Figure 96. Backtest of Moderate 2 Funds for Life strategy using US large-cap value instead of US small-cap value

APPENDIX 2: ALTERNATIVE SECOND FUNDS

1.5 × YTR in US SCV, Rest in V-Like TDF, 4% Fixed WDs

	Age 25	35	45	55	65	75	85	95
Nominal High	$1k	$512k	$2,625k	$9,798k	$17,990k	$21,793k	$33,456k	$93,104k
Nominal Median	$1k	$218k	$943k	$3,150k	$10,206k	$15,624k	$23,519k	$36,744k
Nominal Low	$1k	$101k	$386k	$1,192k	$4,079k	$6,627k	$12,717k	$13,010k
Real High	$1k	$274k	$892k	$2,186k	$3,104k	$3,197k	$3,308k	$4,344k
Real Median	$1k	$158k	$446k	$1,120k	$2,186k	$2,292k	$2,330k	$2,828k
Real Low	$1k	$69k	$208k	$504k	$916k	$972k	$1,280k	$754k
Beating S&P 500?	52.8%	60.8%	74.0%	89.2%	77.0%	58.5%	29.7%	25.5%
Typ. Monthly DDs	0%	2%	2%	2%	1%	1%	1%	1%
Typ. Qtrly DDs	0%	11%	12%	10%	6%	5%	5%	6%
Typ. Yearly DDs	0%	33%	36%	30%	22%	16%	14%	18%
Worst Drawdowns	0%	46%	45%	38%	28%	20%	19%	24%

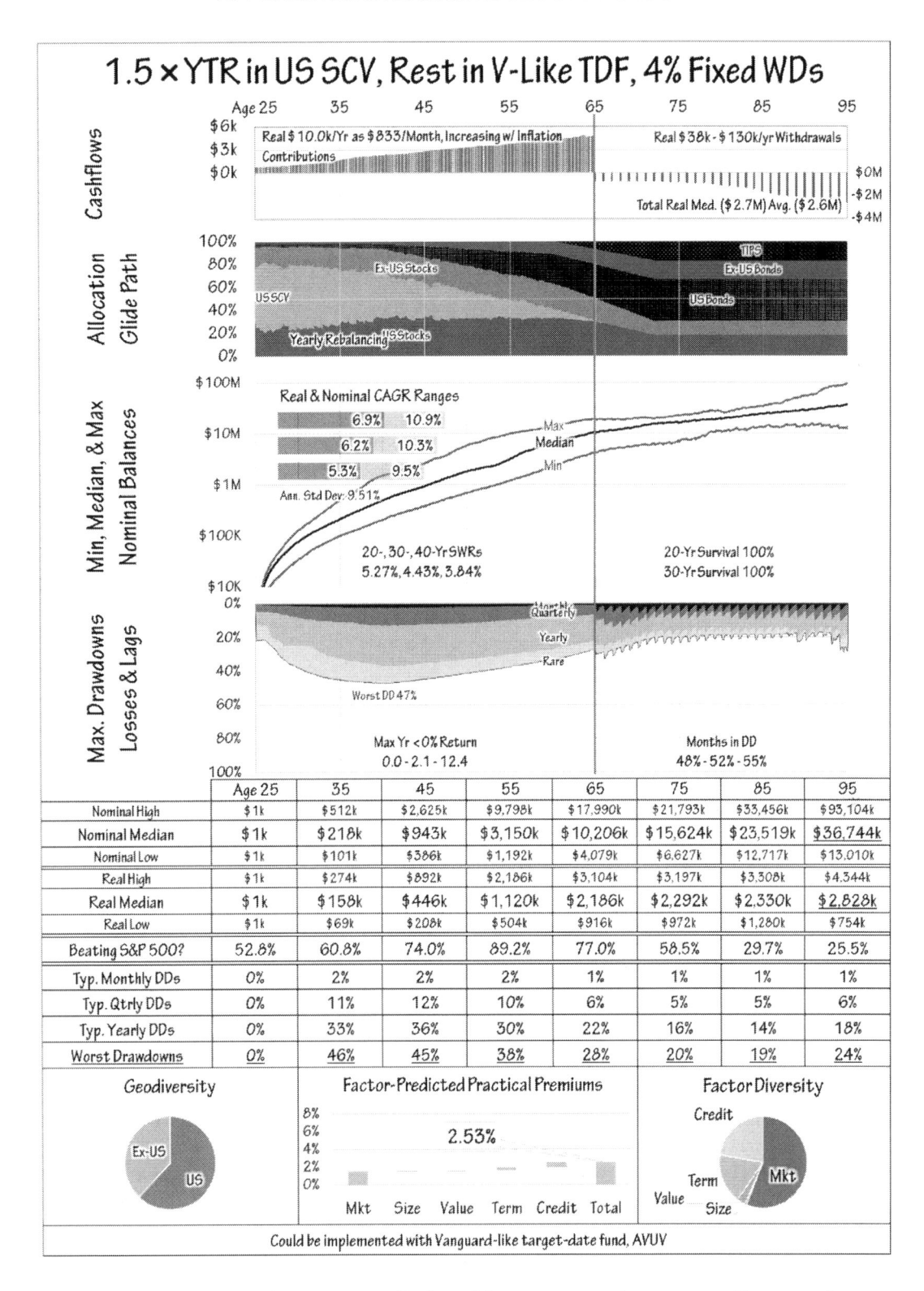

Could be implemented with Vanguard-like target-date fund, AVUV

Figure 97. Backtest of Moderate 2 Funds for Life strategy using US small-cap value

2.5 × YTR + 20% in US LCV, Rest in TDF, 4% Nudge WDs

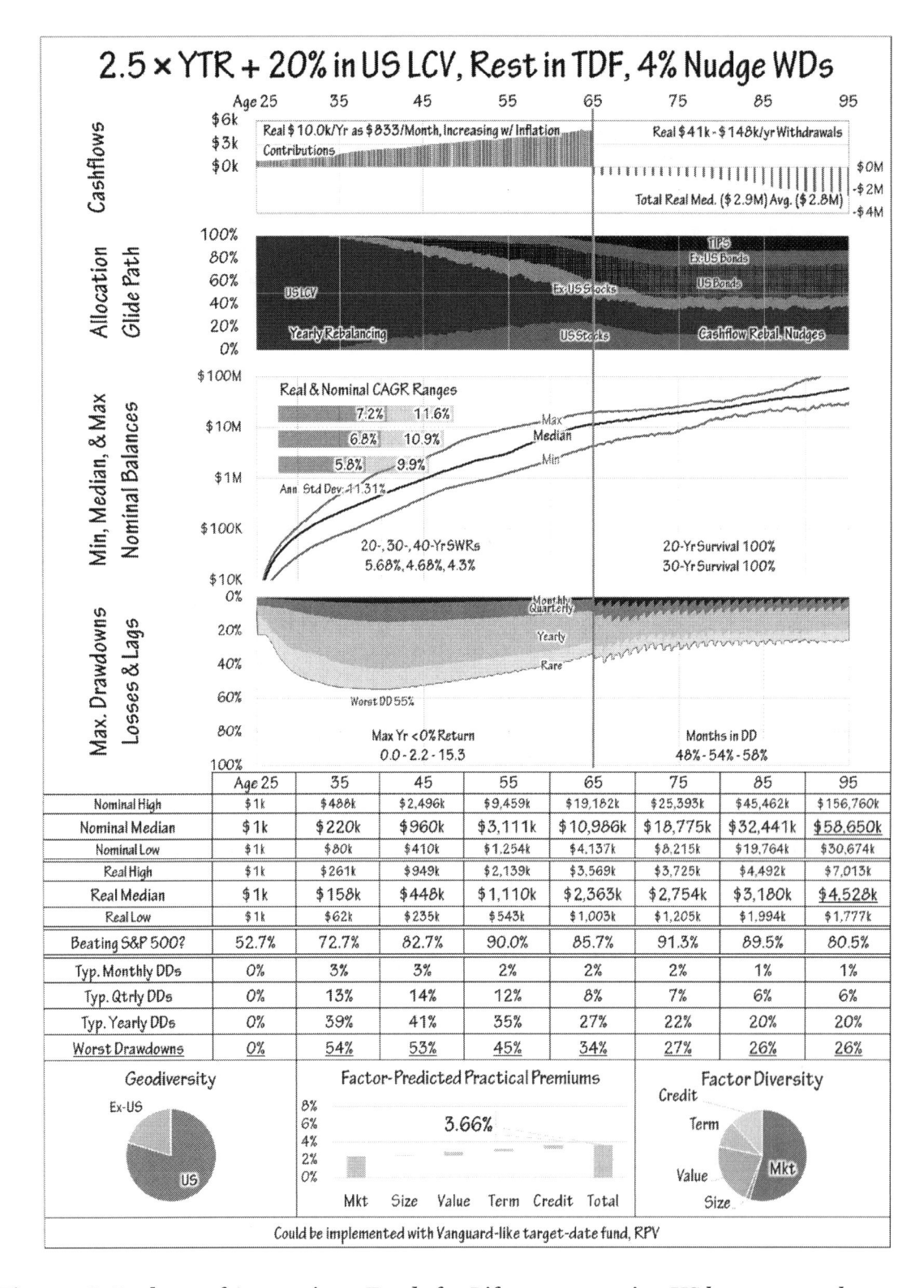

	Age 25	35	45	55	65	75	85	95
Nominal High	$1k	$488k	$2,496k	$9,459k	$19,182k	$25,393k	$45,462k	$156,760k
Nominal Median	$1k	$220k	$960k	$3,111k	$10,986k	$18,775k	$32,441k	$58,650k
Nominal Low	$1k	$80k	$410k	$1,254k	$4,137k	$8,215k	$19,764k	$30,674k
Real High	$1k	$261k	$949k	$2,139k	$3,569k	$3,725k	$4,492k	$7,013k
Real Median	$1k	$158k	$448k	$1,110k	$2,363k	$2,754k	$3,180k	$4,528k
Real Low	$1k	$62k	$235k	$543k	$1,003k	$1,205k	$1,994k	$1,777k
Beating S&P 500?	52.7%	72.7%	82.7%	90.0%	85.7%	91.3%	89.5%	80.5%
Typ. Monthly DDs	0%	3%	3%	2%	2%	2%	1%	1%
Typ. Qtrly DDs	0%	13%	14%	12%	8%	7%	6%	6%
Typ. Yearly DDs	0%	39%	41%	35%	27%	22%	20%	20%
Worst Drawdowns	0%	54%	53%	45%	34%	27%	26%	26%

Could be implemented with Vanguard-like target-date fund, RPV

Figure 98. Backtest of Aggressive 2 Funds for Life strategy using US large-cap value instead of US small-cap value

APPENDIX 2: ALTERNATIVE SECOND FUNDS

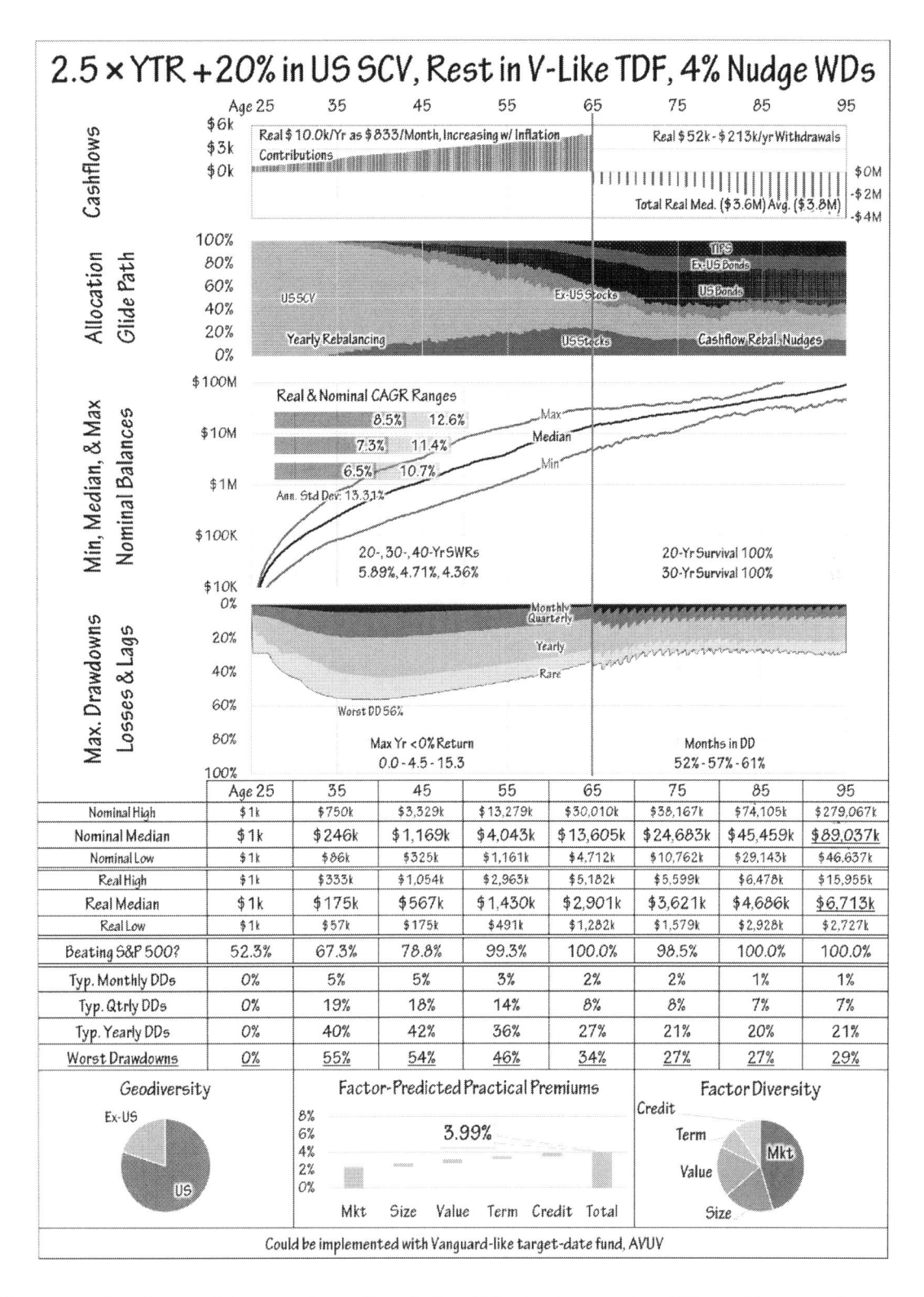

2.5 × YTR + 20% in US SCV, Rest in V-Like TDF, 4% Nudge WDs

	Age 25	35	45	55	65	75	85	95
Nominal High	$1k	$750k	$3,329k	$13,279k	$30,010k	$38,167k	$74,105k	$279,067k
Nominal Median	$1k	$246k	$1,169k	$4,043k	$13,605k	$24,683k	$45,459k	$89,037k
Nominal Low	$1k	$86k	$325k	$1,161k	$4,712k	$10,762k	$29,143k	$46,637k
Real High	$1k	$333k	$1,054k	$2,963k	$5,182k	$5,599k	$6,478k	$15,955k
Real Median	$1k	$175k	$567k	$1,430k	$2,901k	$3,621k	$4,686k	$6,713k
Real Low	$1k	$57k	$175k	$491k	$1,282k	$1,579k	$2,928k	$2,727k
Beating S&P 500?	52.3%	67.3%	78.8%	99.3%	100.0%	98.5%	100.0%	100.0%
Typ. Monthly DDs	0%	5%	5%	3%	2%	2%	1%	1%
Typ. Qtrly DDs	0%	19%	18%	14%	8%	8%	7%	7%
Typ. Yearly DDs	0%	40%	42%	36%	27%	21%	20%	21%
Worst Drawdowns	0%	55%	54%	46%	34%	27%	27%	29%

Could be implemented with Vanguard-like target-date fund, AVUV

Figure 99. Backtest of Aggressive 2 Funds for Life strategy using US small-cap value

Appendix 3
Early Retirement, or FIRE, with 2 Funds for Life

Followers of the FIRE (financial independence, retire early) movement tend to save more, retire earlier, and stay retired longer. Even though their scenarios are different, the backtests in this book can help.

The backtests can be adapted to other starting balances, savings rates, and timelines by analyzing the intermediate results numbers.

For example, let's imagine an investor who's 45 years old, has $100k saved, is planning to retire in 20 years at age 65, and is considering the moderate 2 Funds for Life approach. First, they would look at the backtest data table (shown here) for that approach:

	Age 25	35	45	55	65	75	85	95
Nominal High	$1k	$512k	$2,625k	$9,798k	$17,990k	$21,793k	$33,456k	$93,104k
Nominal Median	$1k	$218k	$943k	$3,150k	$10,206k	$15,624k	$23,519k	$36,744k
Nominal Low	$1k	$101k	$386k	$1,192k	$4,079k	$6,627k	$12,717k	$13,010k
Real High	$1k	$274k	$892k	$2,186k	$3,104k	$3,197k	$3,308k	$4,344k
Real Median	$1k	$158k	$446k	$1,120k	$2,186k	$2,292k	$2,330k	$2,828k
Real Low	$1k	$69k	$208k	$504k	$916k	$972k	$1,280k	$754k
Beating S&P 500?	52.8%	60.8%	74.0%	89.2%	77.0%	58.5%	29.7%	25.5%
Typ. Monthly DDs	0%	2%	2%	2%	1%	1%	1%	1%
Typ. Qtrly DDs	0%	11%	12%	10%	6%	5%	5%	6%
Typ. Yearly DDs	0%	33%	36%	30%	22%	16%	14%	18%
Worst Drawdowns	0%	46%	45%	38%	28%	20%	19%	24%

Table 16. Moderate 2 Funds for Life data table from the backtest

They could normalize to either the real or nominal numbers, but the real numbers are more relatable, so let's use them. At age 45, the real median balance in the test scenario was $446k. Since the investor has $100k, we'll divide the numbers in the table by 4.46 ($446k/$100k) to scale them to their current savings. Assuming they start saving at $10k/year increasing with inflation now (age 45) and invest 1.5 × YTR in a US small-cap value fund with the rest in a Vanguard-like target-date fund, the table suggests they might have about $500k ($2,186k/4.46 = $490.1k) in their account at age 65. They can also look at the range. The worst case was $916k/4.46, or $205.4k, and the best case was $3,104k/4.46, or $696.0k. Assuming a 4% safe withdrawal rate and assuming the future resembles the past, they might be able to safely withdraw $8.2k to $27.8k per year to live on. If those numbers sound too small, they might consider using one of the more aggressive strategies, saving at a higher rate, or retiring later.

Due to licensing constraints and usability issues, I can't give investors our backtesting tool, but there are publicly available websites to help you do your own analysis. My personal favorite is Portfolio Visualizer. The capabilities available for free are quite extensive. You can even analyze simple glide paths using the "Financial Goals" option of "Monte Carlo Simulation."

The Merriman Financial Education Foundation website is also a wealth of information, including portfolio and fund recommendations, fine-tuning tables, educational articles, videos, and podcasts.

Here are some other resources for even greater knowledge:

The Dimensional Fund Advisors historical perspectives on asset class returns are available in their annual DFA matrix book. You can usually find a copy online by googling "DFA Matrix book pdf."

If you're interested in current valuations, and expected gross and net returns for differentiating fund strategies, the RAFI Smart Beta Interactive website is a great resource.

For more information on how international returns have varied through the years, I recommend the Credit Suisse Yearbook Summary pdfs, which are also available online. Every year they touch on different topics. If you read them all, you'll learn a lot and be much more grounded in your understanding of global versus single country risk.

If you want to build your own backtester or study historical returns, the Kenneth French factor return data available at his Dartmouth website might also be of interest.

Appendix 4
Recommended Funds

Once you've decided on your basic investing philosophy, you'll need to choose specific funds to implement it. Fund choice is not nearly as important as the choice of stocks versus bonds or how much to put into a second diversifying fund such as small-cap value, but it still matters. Funds with unnecessarily high expenses can be a huge drain on an investor's long-term performance. Funds that claim to deliver diversifying attributes such as size and value but only provide a little exposure are also likely to underperform expectations. Every couple of years, I screen thousands of funds and do an extensive evaluation of hundreds to try to find the ones that deliver the best bang for the buck in the categories that fit the portfolios we recommend at the Merriman Financial Education Foundation.

For our latest detailed recommendations, I suggest visiting the Merriman Financial Education Foundation website. We have podcasts and articles that dive deeper into the methodology used to prioritize and select our recommended funds. The foundation is a nonprofit organization with no financial incentives to favor one fund, broker, or company. In the spirit of full disclosure and transparency, I acknowledge that I own some, if not all, of the Best-in-Class funds and several of the alternative recommendations.

Here are the 2021 Best in Class ETF recommendations and alternative recommendations:

	Best-in-Class	Alternative Recommendations
US Large Cap Blend	Avantis U.S. Equity (AVUS)	Vanguard S&P 500 (VOO), Vanguard Total US Market (VTI), iShares Core S&P 500 (IVV), SPDR Large Cap (SPLG), Schwab Large-Cap (SCHX)
US Large Cap Value	Invesco S&P 500 Pure Value (RPV)	Vanguard Russell 1000 Value Index (VONV), iShares Core US Value (IUSV), Schwab U.S. Large-Cap Value (SCHV), S&P 500 Value (SPYV)
US Small Cap Blend	iShares Core S&P Small-Cap (IJR)	Vanguard S&P Small-Cap 600 Index (VIOO), Russell Micro-Cap (IWC), Schwab U.S. Small-Cap (SCHA), SPDR Small Cap (SPSM)
US Small Cap Value	Avantis U.S. Small Cap Value (AVUV)	Vanguard S&P Small-Cap 600 Value (VIOV), SPDR Small Cap Value (SLYV), iShares S&P; SmCp 600 Value (US), Invesco S&P SmallCap 600 Pure Value ETF (RZV)
US REIT	Vanguard Real Estate Index (VNQ)	Fidelity MSCI Real Estate (FREL), iShares U.S. REIT (USRT), Schwab U.S. REIT (SCHH)
Int'l Large Cap Blend	Avantis International Equity (AVDE)	Vanguard FTSE Developed Markets (VEA), iShares Core MSCI EAFE (IEFA), SPDR World Ex-US (SPDW), Schwab Intl Equity (SCHF)
Int'l Large Cap Value	iShares MSCI EAFE Value (EFV)	Vanguard International High Dividend (VYMI), Fidelity International Value Factor ETF (FIVA), SPDR S&P Intl Dividend (DWX)
Int'l Small Cap Blend	Schwab Fundamental International Small Company Index (FNDC)	Vanguard FTSE All-World ex-US Small-Cap Index (VSS), iShares MSCI EAFE SmCap (SCZ), SPDR S&P Intl. Small Cap (GWX), Schwab Intl Sm-Cp Equity (SCHC)
Int'l Small Cap Value	Avantis International Small Cap Value (AVDV)	WisdomTree Intl. S. Cap Div (DLS)
Emerging Markets	Avantis Emerging Markets Equity (AVEM)	Vanguard FTSE Emerging Markets (VWO), iShares Core MSCI EmMkts. (IEMG), SPDR Emerging Markets (SPEM), Schwab Emerging Mkt Eq (SCHE)
Em. Mkts. Small Cap	---	WisdomTree Emerging Markets SmCp Div ETF (DGS), iShares MSCI Em. Mkts. Sm.-Cap (EEMS), SPDR Emerging Mkts. S. Cap (EWX)
Int'l REITs	---	Vanguard Global ex-US Real Estate (VNQI), iShares FTSE Real Estate ex-US (IFGL),
Short-Term Bonds	Vanguard Short-Term Government Bond (VGSH)	iShares Barclays S-T Treasury (SHY), SPDR Short Term Treasury (SPTS), Schwab S-T U.S. Treasury (SCHO)
Int.-Term Bonds	SPDR Inter. Term Treasury (SPTI)	iShares Barclays 7-10 Yr Treasury (IEF), Vanguard Intermediate-Term Government Bond (VGIT), Schwab I-T U.S. Treasury (SCHR)
Infl.-Prot. Bonds	Vanguard Short-Term Infl. Prot. Securities (VTIP)	iShares Barclays 0-5 TIPS (STIP), Schwab U.S. TIPS (SCHP)

Figure 100. Recommended 2021 Best-in-Class ETFs and alternatives

We rarely recommend the lowest-cost funds.

Cheap funds with weak exposure to the factors that drive returns are like diluted hot sauce. Even if you use double the amount, you don't get the same kick!

Some investors will have more limited choices in their retirement savings accounts. What then?

If your choices are limited, you might consider using the free portfolio "Match Factor Exposures" tool at Portfolio Visualizer. If you select "Portfolio" as the type of "Match Target," you can enter the funds you have available as "Clone Assets" and the "Target Portfolio" of assets you don't have access to, then click "Create Clone." The website creates two different types of clones: a factor-exposure clone and a returns-based clone. One or the other may do a better job of matching the target portfolio. The "Returns Regression R^2" is an indication of the quality of the match. The higher the number, the better. Depending on how limited your choices are, the match can be great with an R^2 of 99% or better, or not so great with an R^2 of 95% or less. When considering whether to use one of the clones, you should look beyond the match to see how well the clone portfolio preserves geographic and factor diversification. The exposure to the market, size, and value factors will likely make a bigger difference for long-term returns. Still, geographic diversification could matter more when the US leads or lags international markets for a time.

Astute readers may have noticed that the Avantis funds in our best-in-class ETF recommendations are classified as "active" funds. Aren't low-cost, passively-managed index funds supposed to outperform actively managed funds? Although that's generally true, in recent years, the lines have become blurred. Today, there are many "passive" indexes that include "active" qualities such as market timing and alternative weighting schemes. There are also many "active" funds that systematically track different parts of the market but are "active" primarily to avoid the downsides of rigidly following a public index. These systematic, active funds can, for example, make changes to their holdings without the risk of other traders anticipating their trades and profiting from them. In our analysis, the Avantis funds appear to be highly systematic in their portfolio management, with over 97% of their performance attributable to movements of the market segments they claim to invest in, leaving only 3% to discretion. That, combined with their expected returns from the exposures they provide to the market, size, and value factors minus their reasonable expenses, earned them their best-in-class recommendations.

My final thought on fund choice is that Perfect is the enemy of Good Enough. People who invest quickly in good-enough funds will likely do better over the long term than people who hold off investing while they are perfecting the fund choices they'll use.

Appendix 5
Target-Date Funds
Other Than Vanguard

For many investors, the concept of choice in target-date funds is academic. Often there is only one provider of target-date funds available in their employer-offered 401(k). Since Vanguard had over 37% market share in 2020, they are the most likely provider investors will see. That's why I've used their glide path as the reference for all the backtesting in this book. There are other providers, though, and some investors may wonder whether the 2 Funds for Life strategies will work for them too.

A great reference for understanding the broader target-date fund market is Morningstar. In recent years they have published an annual report surveying the target-date fund landscape. In 2020, the title was "2020 Target-Date Strategy Landscape." One of the most relevant pieces of information in that report for this question was a summary chart showing the full range of factor exposures across all target-date funds. We can draw this picture if we combine that information with similar information from their website regarding small-cap value funds:

Overlap of Target Date & Small Cap Value Funds

Source: Morningstar "2020 Target-Date Strategy Landscape" data as of 12/31/2019 and Morningstar category small value as of Nov 30, 2020

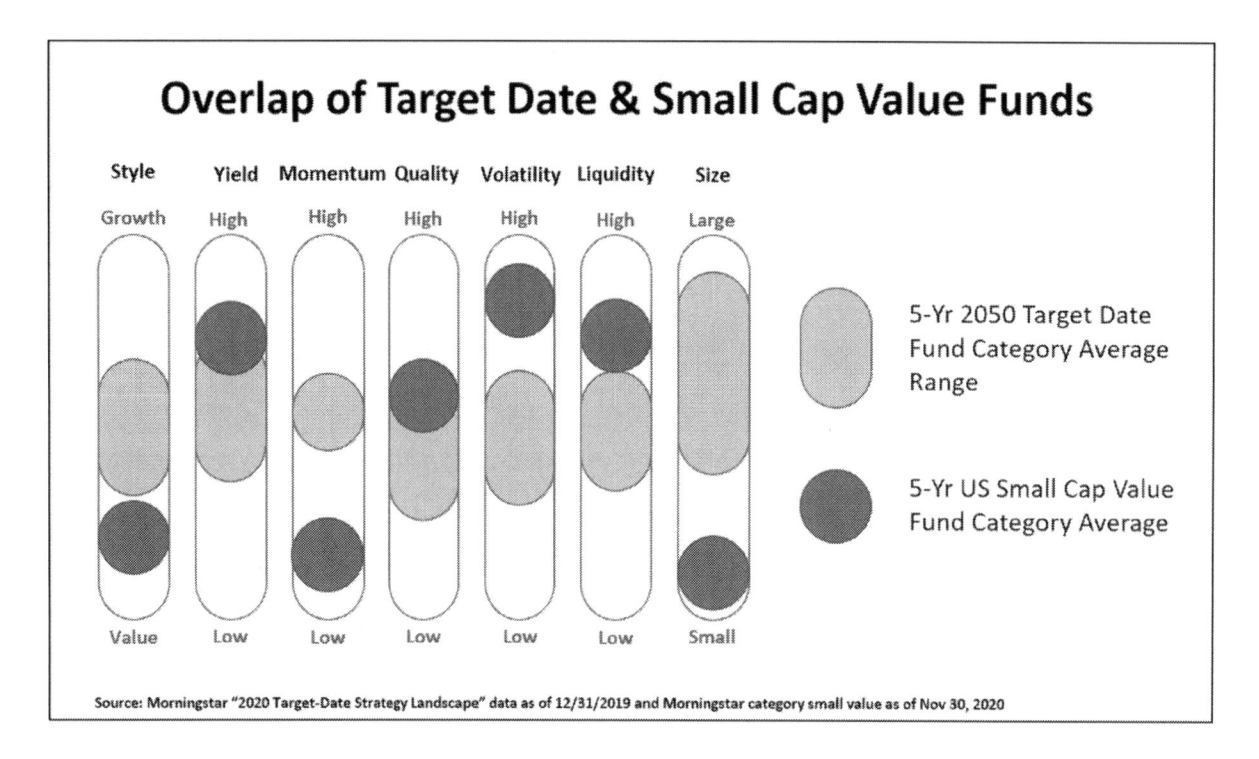

Figure 101. Overlap of target-date and small-cap value funds

If you focus on the style bar on the left and the size bar on the right, it becomes clear that the average small-cap value fund will not overlap with any of the target-date funds in either value or size.

A small-cap value fund should provide meaningful diversification for practically any target-date fund.

Will the difference be greater for some than others? Yes. Will the difference help all target-date funds at least a little over the long-term? Probably. We don't know the future, but if it's anything like the past, the market should reward patient target-date fund investors who put at least part of their portfolio in a small-cap value fund.

Appendix 6
Target-Date Funds with Early or Late Dates

Since target-date funds are only available in five- or 10-year increments, most investors will need to select a date that's a little sooner or later than their actual expected retirement date.

Choosing an earlier target date nudges risk and returns lower.

Choosing a later target date nudges them higher.

To see this in action, let's look at the results of using a target date that's five years early, just right, and five years late. Let's also look at the impact of the same changes using the Aggressive 2 Funds for Life strategy:

Effects of Early, On-Time, or Late TDF Date Selection	Median Real End Balance Range	Median Real Total WD's	Worst Drawdown	Age Where Worst DD Occurs	Worst Drawdown at Age 65	40-Year Safe Withdraw Rate
Vanguard-Like Target-date Fund 5 Years Early Date	$3.26M $1.89M $771k	$2.0M	40%	36 years	20%	4.11%
Vanguard-Like Target-date Fund On-Time Date	$3.57M $2.18M $588k	$2.2M	42%	40 years	27%	3.84%
Vanguard-Like Target-date Fund 5 Years Late Date	$4.04M $2.46M $473k	$2.2M	49%	95 years	32%	3.60%
2.5 X YTR + 20% in US SCV, Rest in TDF 5 Years Early Date	$11.4M $5.24M $2.50M	$3.2M	53%	35 years	27%	4.43%
2.5 X YTR + 20% in US SCV, Rest in TDF On-Time Date	$16.0M $6.71M $2.73M	$3.6M	56%	40 years	34%	4.36%
2.5 X YTR + 20% in US SCV, Rest in TDF 5 Years Late Date	$30.7M $10.35M $4.68M	$4.0M	58%	40 years	41%	4.54%

Table 17. Comparison of early, on time, and late target-date fund backtest results

For the target-date fund alone, choosing an earlier date lowered drawdown risks, but it also reduced median end balances and withdrawals. Safe withdrawal rates increased, but they were based on a lower initial balance. Going from early to later dates increased drawdown risks and ages where they occurred, but it also increased median end balances by about 30% and total withdrawals by about 10%. Total withdrawals increased because the median initial balance at age 65 was higher.

The story for the 2 Funds for Life scenarios is similar but more extreme. Instead of a 28% increase, the median end balance for the Aggressive 2 Funds for Life strategy went up by more than 90%, and worst age 65 drawdowns increased by 14%. Interestingly, the age where the worst drawdowns occurred didn't shift significantly from the on-time to five years late Aggressive 2 Funds for Life scenarios. The 40-year safe withdrawal rate also didn't decline with later dates as it did for the 100% target-date fund scenarios. In fact, the highest safe withdrawal rate was for the 5 year late Aggressive 2 Funds for Life approach.

So, what should we do?

Since the target-date fund and 2 Funds for Life approaches are developed and tested around the target dates lining up, picking the one closest to your expected retirement makes sense. If you're right in the middle between two dates, though, the choice will depend on what you want and whether you're using a target-date fund on its own or a 2 Funds for Life approach.

If you're using a target-date fund on its own, picking a later date will increase your expected end balance range and withdrawals slightly but also increase risk. Picking an earlier date does the opposite.

If you're using a 2 Funds for Life approach, picking an earlier date will lower drawdown risk around retirement and lower expected end balances, total withdrawals, and safe withdrawal rates. If you're relatively comfortable staying the course through market drawdowns, you might choose the later date. If you're more skittish, you might be better off with the earlier date.

Here are the time-shifted and on-time backtests for comparison:

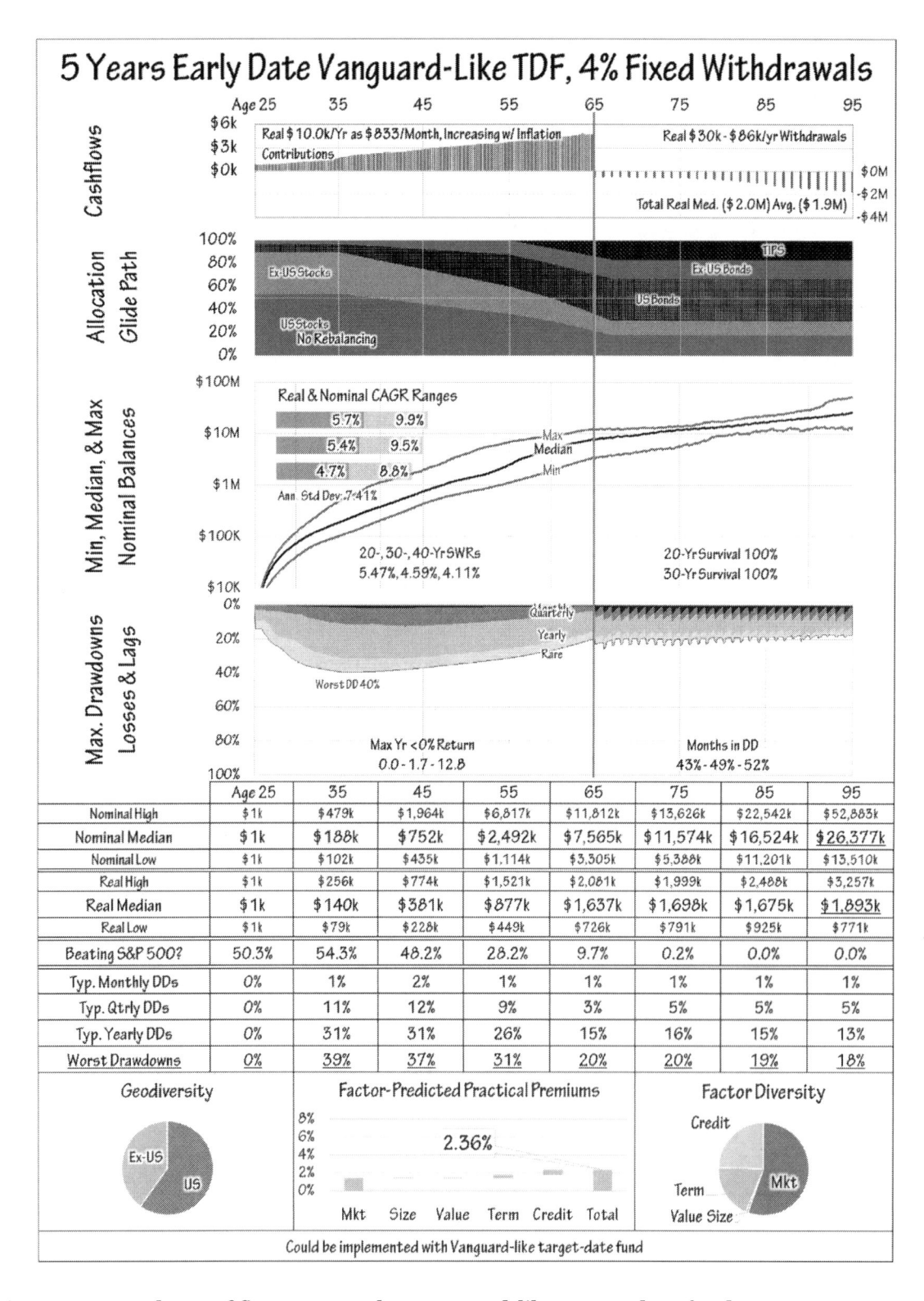

Figure 102. Backtest of five years early Vanguard-like target-date fund

APPENDIX 6: TARGET-DATE FUNDS WITH EARLY OR LATE DATES

100% Vanguard-Like Target-Date Fund, 4% Fixed Withdrawals

Cashflows: Real $10.0k/Yr as $833/Month, Increasing w/ Inflation Contributions; Real $31k - $99k/yr Withdrawals; Total Real Med. ($2.2M) Avg. ($2.0M)

Allocation Glide Path: Ex-US Stocks, US Stocks, No Rebalancing, TIPS, Ex-US Bonds, US Bonds

Min, Median, & Max Nominal Balances:
Real & Nominal CAGR Ranges: 6.0% / 10.1% (Max), 5.6% / 9.8% (Median), 4.8% / 9.0% (Min)
Ann. Std Dev: 7.82%
20-, 30-, 40-Yr SWRs: 5.27%, 4.43%, 3.84%
20-Yr Survival 100%; 30-Yr Survival 100%

Max. Drawdowns Losses & Lags: Worst DD 42%; Max Yr <0% Return 0.0 - 1.7 - 13.4; Months in DD 44% - 50% - 53%

	Age 25	35	45	55	65	75	85	95
Nominal High	$1k	$479k	$2,010k	$7,379k	$12,900k	$15,480k	$23,900k	$64,532k
Nominal Median	$1k	$188k	$752k	$2,516k	$8,004k	$12,276k	$18,479k	$29,241k
Nominal Low	$1k	$102k	$422k	$1,120k	$3,360k	$5,421k	$10,435k	$10,142k
Real High	$1k	$256k	$810k	$1,646k	$2,393k	$2,271k	$2,655k	$3,569k
Real Median	$1k	$140k	$389k	$896k	$1,737k	$1,801k	$1,812k	$2,180k
Real Low	$1k	$79k	$231k	$461k	$748k	$795k	$1,050k	$588k
Beating S&P 500?	50.3%	54.3%	51.2%	39.8%	14.7%	2.8%	0.0%	0.0%
Typ. Monthly DDs	0%	1%	2%	2%	1%	1%	1%	1%
Typ. Qtrly DDs	0%	11%	14%	11%	7%	5%	5%	6%
Typ. Yearly DDs	0%	31%	34%	29%	22%	16%	14%	18%
Worst Drawdowns	0%	39%	41%	35%	27%	20%	19%	24%

Geodiversity: Ex-US, US

Factor-Predicted Practical Premiums: 2.44% (Mkt, Size, Value, Term, Credit, Total)

Factor Diversity: Credit, Mkt, Term, Value, Size

Could be implemented with Vanguard-like target-date fund

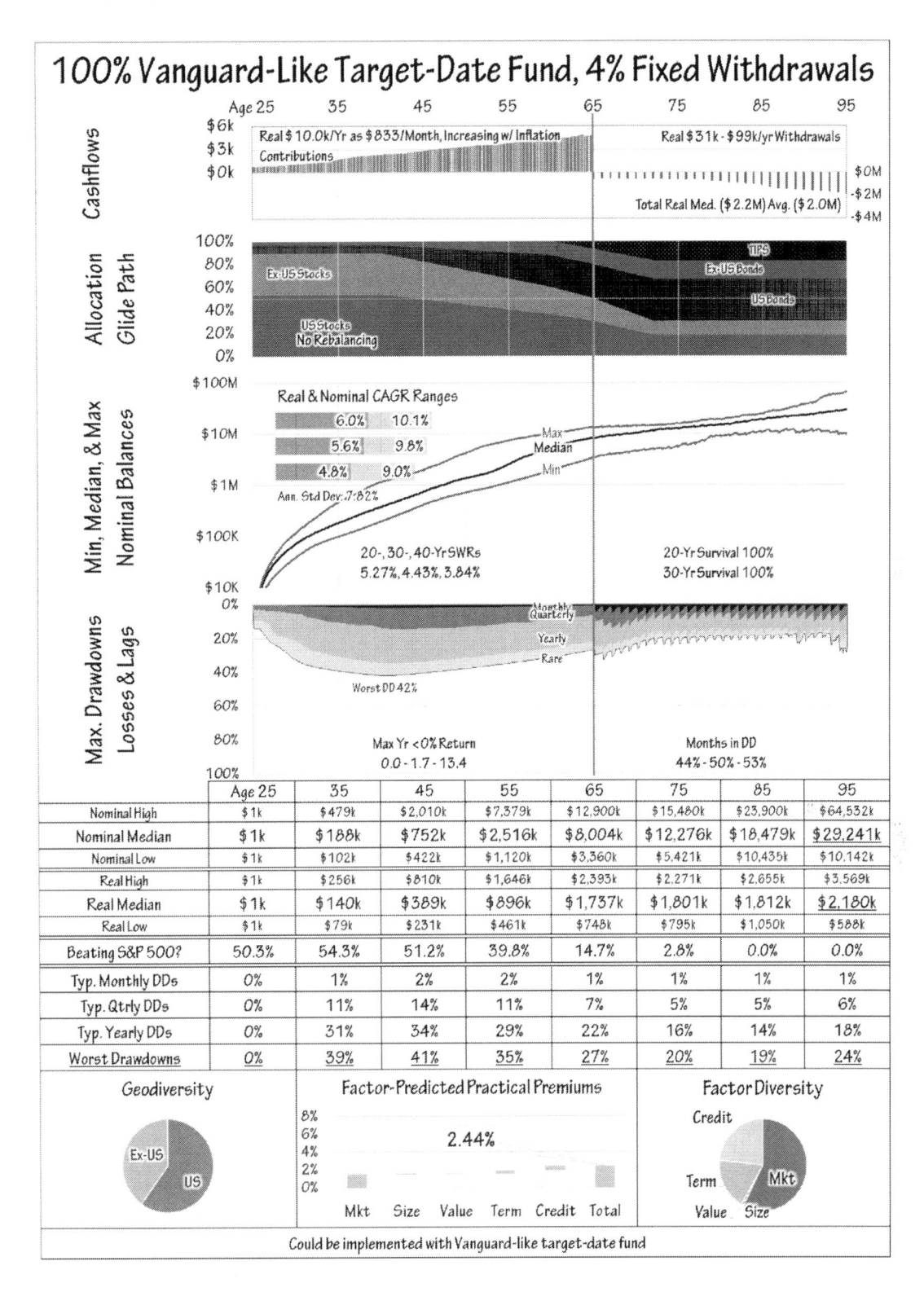

Figure 103. Backtest of on-time Vanguard-like target-date fund

2 FUNDS FOR LIFE

5 Years Late Date Vanguard-Like TDF, 4% Fixed Withdrawals

	Age 25	35	45	55	65	75	85	95
Nominal High	$1k	$479k	$2,023k	$7,814k	$14,348k	$17,546k	$27,623k	$80,536k
Nominal Median	$1k	$188k	$756k	$2,513k	$8,450k	$13,528k	$20,494k	$32,980k
Nominal Low	$1k	$102k	$406k	$1,123k	$3,354k	$5,575k	$10,565k	$8,164k
Real High	$1k	$256k	$830k	$1,744k	$2,676k	$2,574k	$2,992k	$4,041k
Real Median	$1k	$140k	$391k	$911k	$1,801k	$1,985k	$1,974k	$2,463k
Real Low	$1k	$79k	$227k	$468k	$772k	$818k	$1,063k	$473k
Beating S&P 500?	50.3%	54.3%	52.5%	45.0%	24.0%	9.0%	0.3%	0.0%
Typ. Monthly DDs	0%	1%	2%	2%	1%	2%	1%	1%
Typ. Qtrly DDs	0%	11%	16%	14%	10%	8%	5%	7%
Typ. Yearly DDs	0%	31%	37%	32%	26%	19%	17%	33%
Worst Drawdowns	0%	39%	44%	39%	32%	24%	21%	45%

Could be implemented with Vanguard-like target-date fund

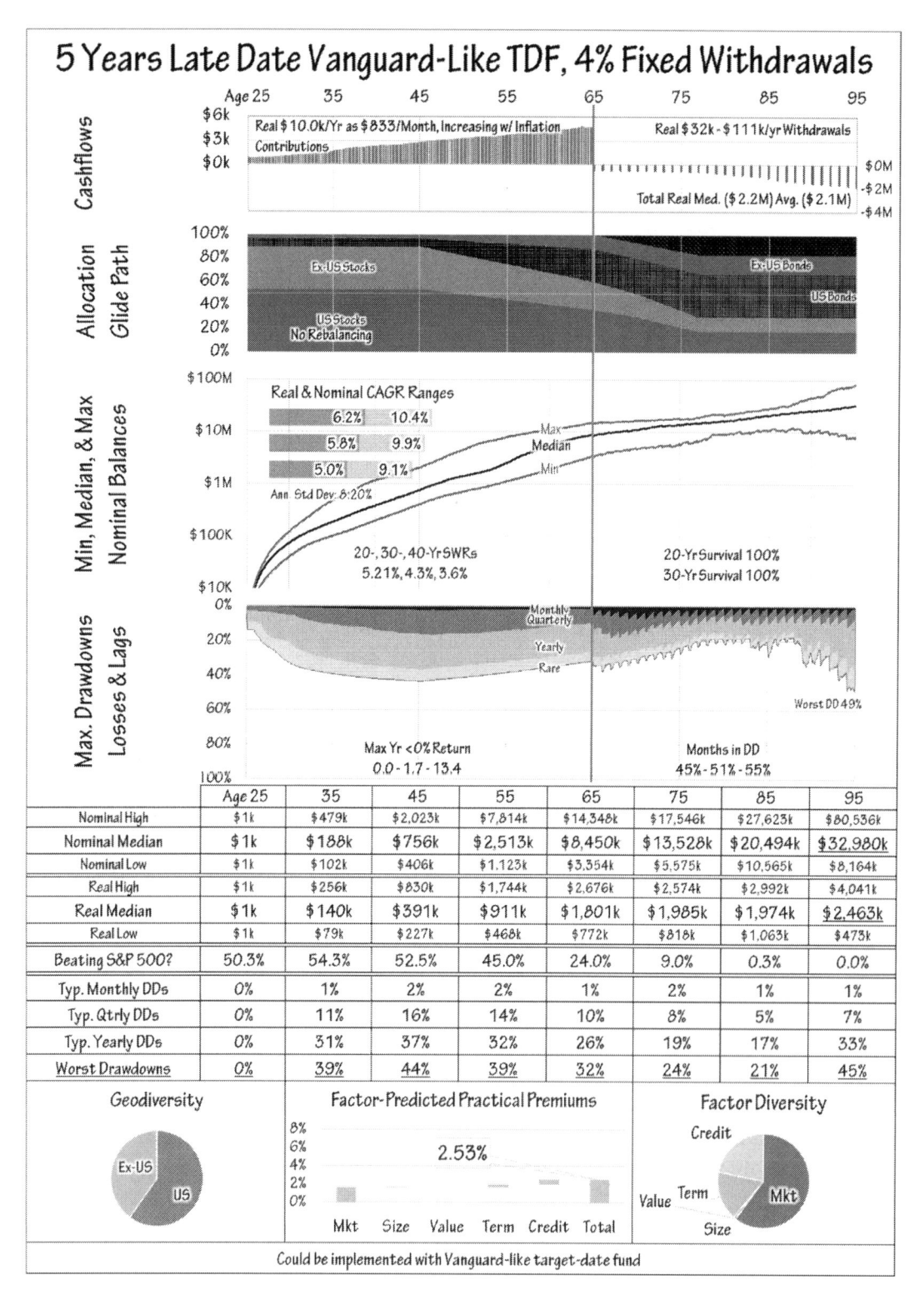

Figure 104. Backtest of five years late Vanguard-like target-date fund

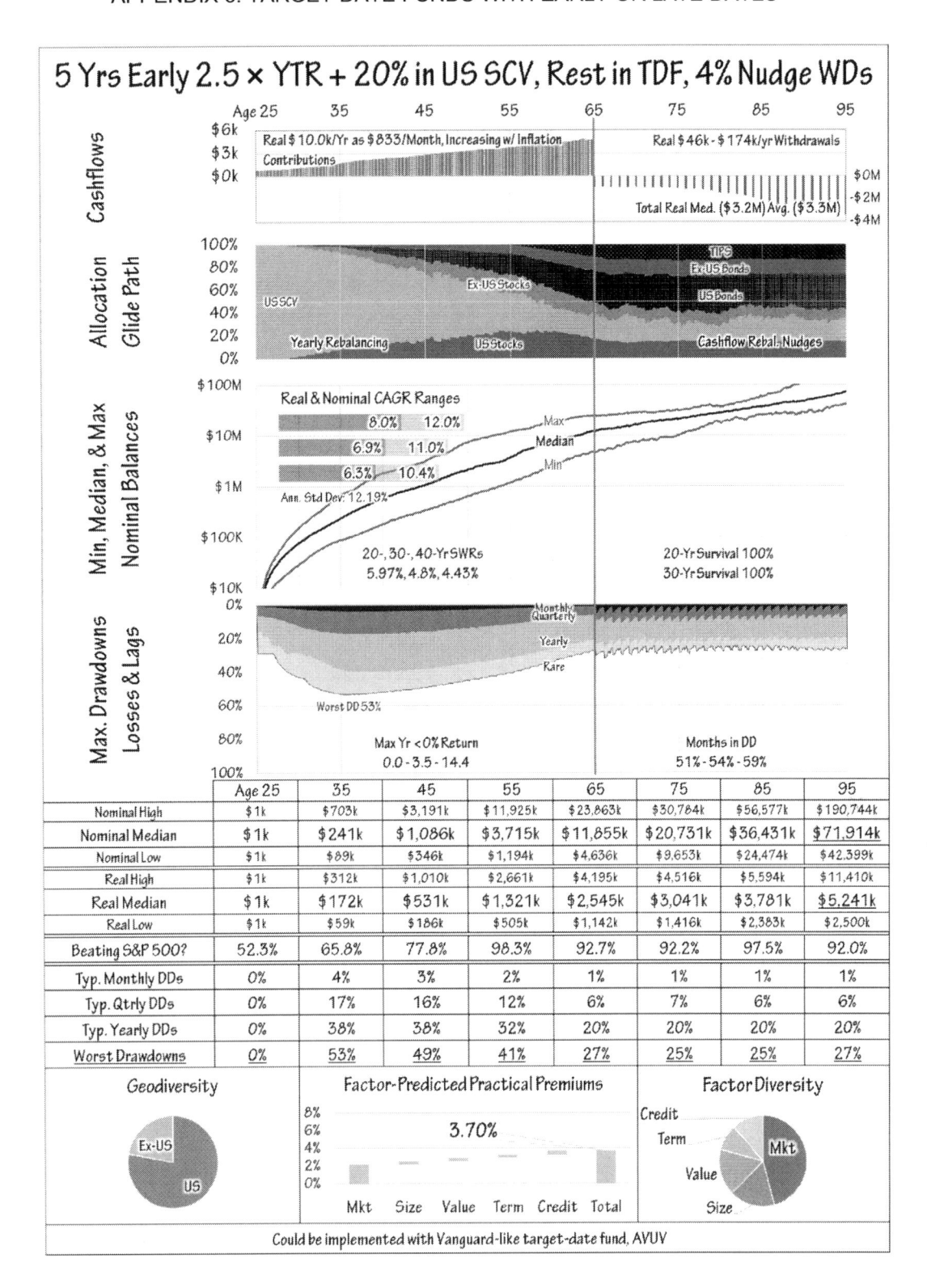

APPENDIX 6: TARGET-DATE FUNDS WITH EARLY OR LATE DATES

Figure 105. Backtest of five years early Aggressive 2 Funds for Life strategy

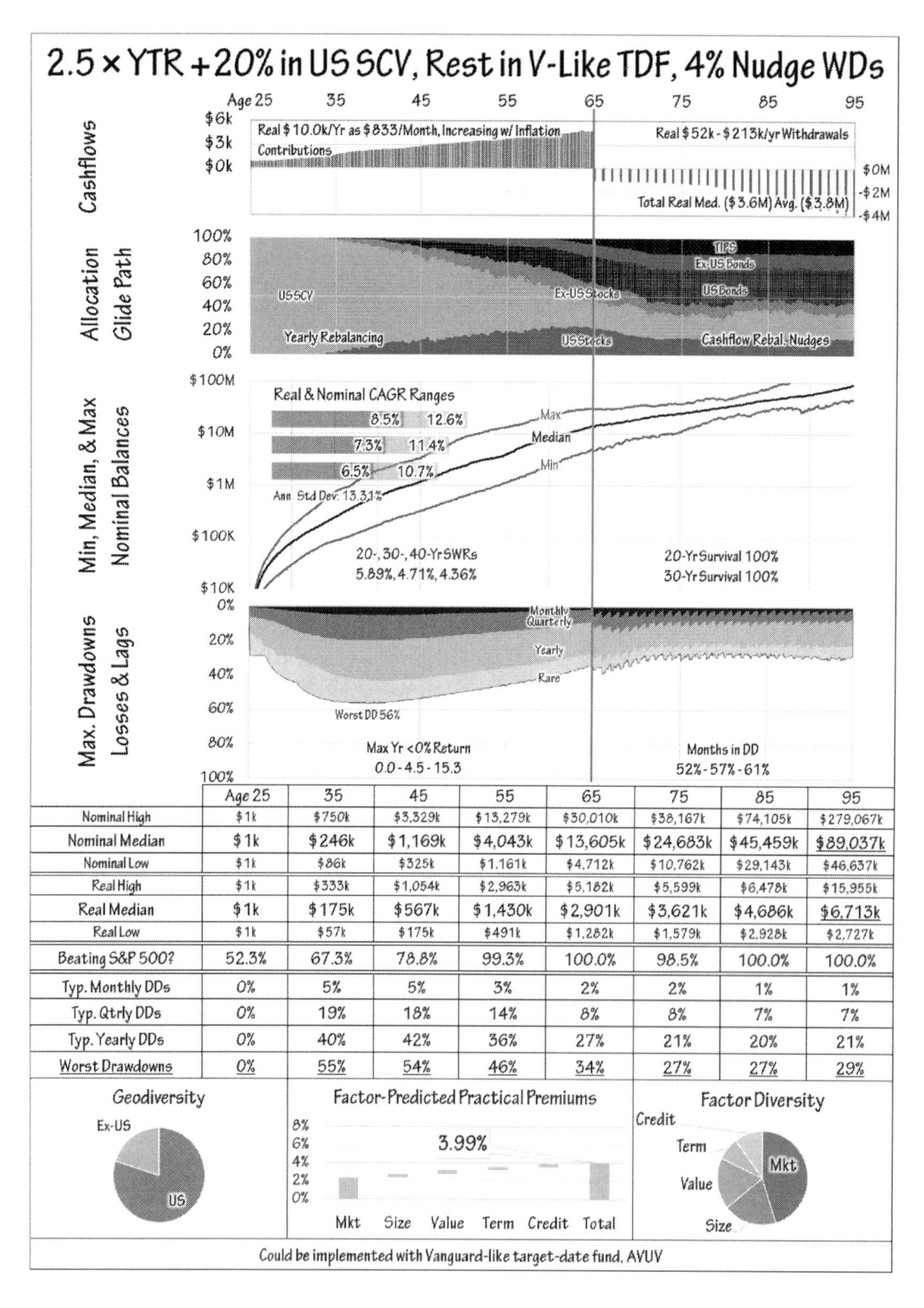

Figure 106. Backtest of on-time Aggressive 2 Funds for Life strategy

APPENDIX 6: TARGET-DATE FUNDS WITH EARLY OR LATE DATES

	Age 25	35	45	55	65	75	85	95
Nominal High	$1k	$755k	$3,389k	$14,427k	$36,807k	$48,542k	$107,872k	$471,267k
Nominal Median	$1k	$246k	$1,242k	$4,318k	$15,493k	$30,595k	$63,632k	$139,323k
Nominal Low	$1k	$86k	$300k	$1,093k	$4,584k	$13,011k	$35,812k	$71,656k
Real High	$1k	$335k	$1,087k	$3,263k	$6,355k	$7,121k	$9,854k	$30,678k
Real Median	$1k	$175k	$582k	$1,541k	$3,224k	$4,488k	$6,593k	$10,354k
Real Low	$1k	$57k	$161k	$463k	$1,365k	$1,909k	$3,487k	$4,681k
Beating S&P 500?	52.3%	67.5%	79.2%	98.7%	100.0%	100.0%	100.0%	100.0%
Typ. Monthly DDs	0%	5%	6%	4%	2%	3%	3%	3%
Typ. Qtrly DDs	0%	19%	21%	17%	12%	12%	11%	11%
Typ. Yearly DDs	0%	40%	45%	39%	32%	29%	27%	31%
Worst Drawdowns	0%	56%	58%	50%	41%	36%	36%	40%

Could be implemented with Vanguard-like target-date fund, AVUV

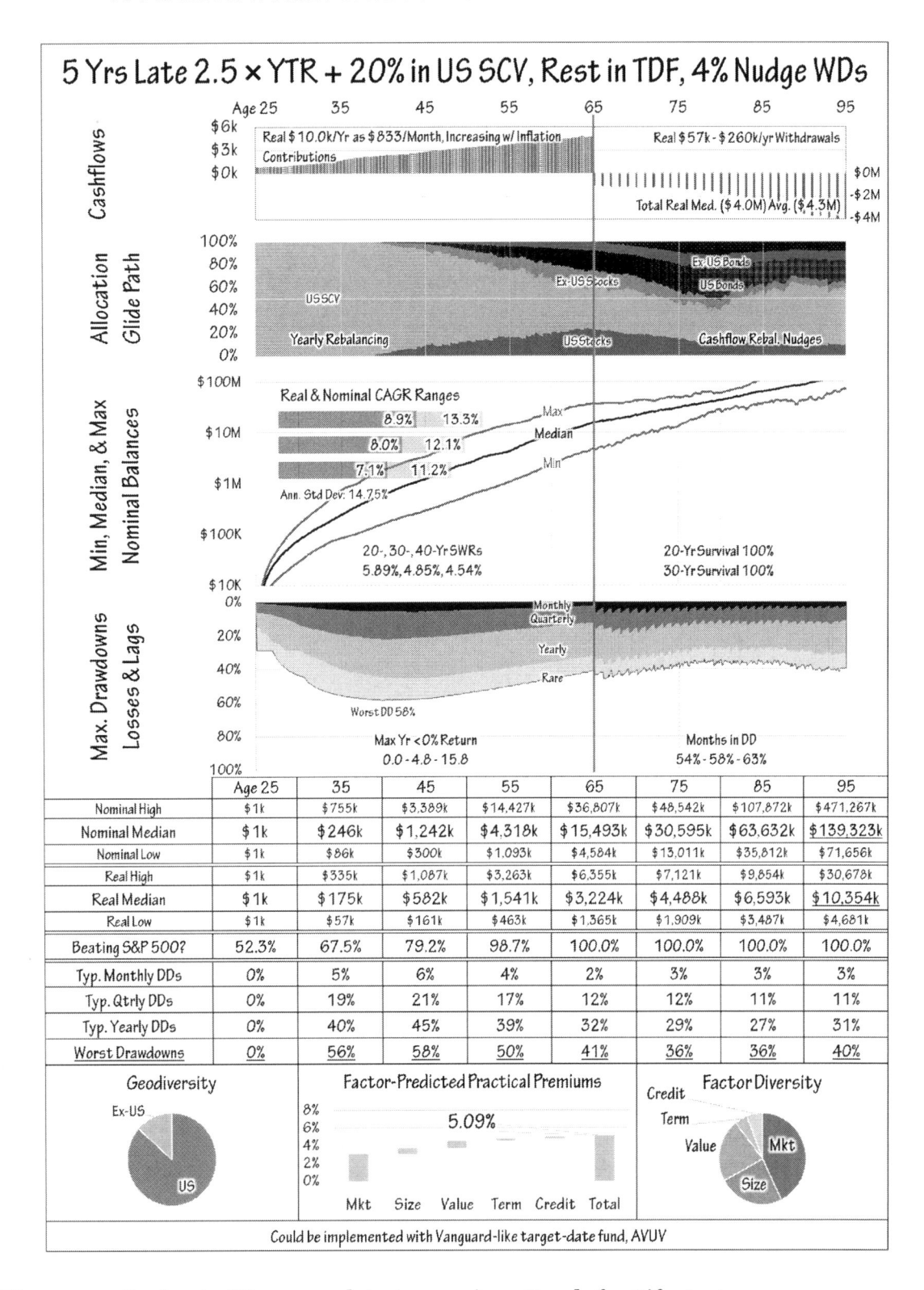

Figure 107. Backtest of five years late Aggressive 2 Funds for Life strategy

2 FUNDS FOR LIFE

Appendix 7
Backtesting to 1928

If we use estimates to fill the return gaps going back to 1928, we see much deeper drawdowns for all the scenarios tested.

The Great Depression was a horrible time for stocks, and it's not included in the 1970-2019 return history used in backtests throughout this book. How much worse would they look if we included it? We can't know exactly because there aren't return histories back that far for all assets. We can get an idea, though, by using the rhyme and regress substitute return sequences we've generated for the missing asset classes (see Appendix 8 for details). Here's what we find:

		Comparison of 1970-2019 (Top) and 1928-2019 (Bottom) Backtest Results						
		Median Real End Balances	Median Real WDs	Worst Peak DD	Worst DD @ 65	40-Year SWR	30-Year, Survival %	% of Times > S&P 500
Buffett strategy Fixed 90 | 10 S&P 500 | ST Bonds	1970-2019	$6.61M $4.29M $0k	$2.1M $70k/yr	100% @ 90	46%	2.52%	98%	0%
	1928-2019	$12.3M $4.79M $0k	$2.1M $70k/yr	100% @85	79%	2.12%	96%	0%
Vanguard-Like Target-date Fund	1970-2019	$3.93M $2.18M $588k	$2.2M $73k/yr	42% @ 40	27%	3.84%	100%	0%
	1928-2019	$4.26M $1.70M $0k	$1.8M $60k/yr	100% @91	49%	2.76%	98%	0%
Easy 2FFL Fixed 90 | 10 TDF | US SCV	1970-2019	$5.23M $3.16M $850k	$2.4M $80k/yr	44% @ 40	35%	3.95%	100%	15%
	1928-2019	$15.5M $2.51M $0k	$2.3M $80k/yr	100% @90	55%	3.09%	99%	27%
Moderate 2FFL 1.5 X YTR in US SCV, Rest in V-Like TDF	1970-2019	$4.34M $2.82M $754k	$2.7M $90k/yr	47% @ 40	28%	3.84%	100%	26%
	1928-2019	$6.40M $2.40M $0k	$2.6M $87k/yr	100% @92	50%	2.76%	98%	22%
Aggressive 2FFL 2.5 X YTR + 20% in US SCV, Rest in V-Like TDF	1970-2019	$16.0M $6.71M $2.73M	$3.6M $120k/yr	56% @ 40	34%	4.36%	100%	100%
	1928-2019	$33.6M $5.58M $731k	$4.2M $140k/yr	86% @40	62%	3.93%	100%	69%

Table 18. Comparison of 1970-2019 and 1928-2019 backtests of Buffett strategy; Vanguard-like target-date fund; Easy, Moderate, and Aggressive 2 Funds for Life strategies

Almost everything gets worse when we test our scenarios back to 1928. Drawdowns were deeper, safe withdrawal rates were smaller, real end-balances were reduced, and portfolios that failed ran out of money sooner. For the Aggressive 2 Funds for Life approach, total real withdrawals increased, but for all other scenarios real withdrawals stayed the same or decreased. If there's a surprise, it's that the 30-year survival rates didn't decline substantially.

The 1929 market crash and the tough decade that followed the Great Depression are the reason for the increased drawdowns. If you retired on or around 1928 and were invested in the most Aggressive 2 Funds for Life strategy, you would have seen your portfolio decline to about 15% of its original value before starting the climb back up to previous highs. It was great news for young investors buying new shares, but for a retiree hoping to live off their savings, it would have been worrisome, to say the least.

Surprisingly, all these approaches, including the most Aggressive 2 Funds for Life strategies, had enough diversification to survive this extreme set of historical returns more than 96% of the time. How can that be? To start with, the 4% safe withdrawal rate is conservative. It's important to remember that it's based on surviving the single, absolute worst-case scenario tested. Even though it exceeds the safe withdrawal rate for some of these portfolios over this longer timeframe, it only exceeds them rarely and only in the absolute worst-case conditions. Add to that the fact that the withdrawals are adjusted for inflation, and you start to get a recipe for success. For some part of the 1920s, there was deflation instead of inflation, meaning retirees would have decreased withdrawals. It's this combination of a conservative, safe withdrawal rate and inflation-adjusted returns that helped ensure high success rates even through these turbulent times.

So, what do we take away from this?

I think it's a good reminder that the future is uncertain, and we may have to live through deeper drawdowns than we think. Had these target-date funds and 2 Funds for Life strategies been available to investors in the Great Depression, investors who

APPENDIX 7: BACKTESTING TO 1928

stayed the course would still have done well. Only a tiny percentage of the scenarios ran out of money. The vast majority still funded healthy withdrawals and left a sizable legacy at the end.

All the 2 Funds for Life strategies also still outperformed the pure Vanguard-like target-date fund. Significant increases in median end balances, withdrawals, survival rates, and safe withdrawal rates were possible, with only small drawdown risk increases. It's somewhat comforting to know that the deeper history still validates the same basic conclusion that adding a second diversifying fund is likely to help.

For easy comparison, here are the 1970-2019 and 1928-2019 detailed backtests:

2 FUNDS FOR LIFE

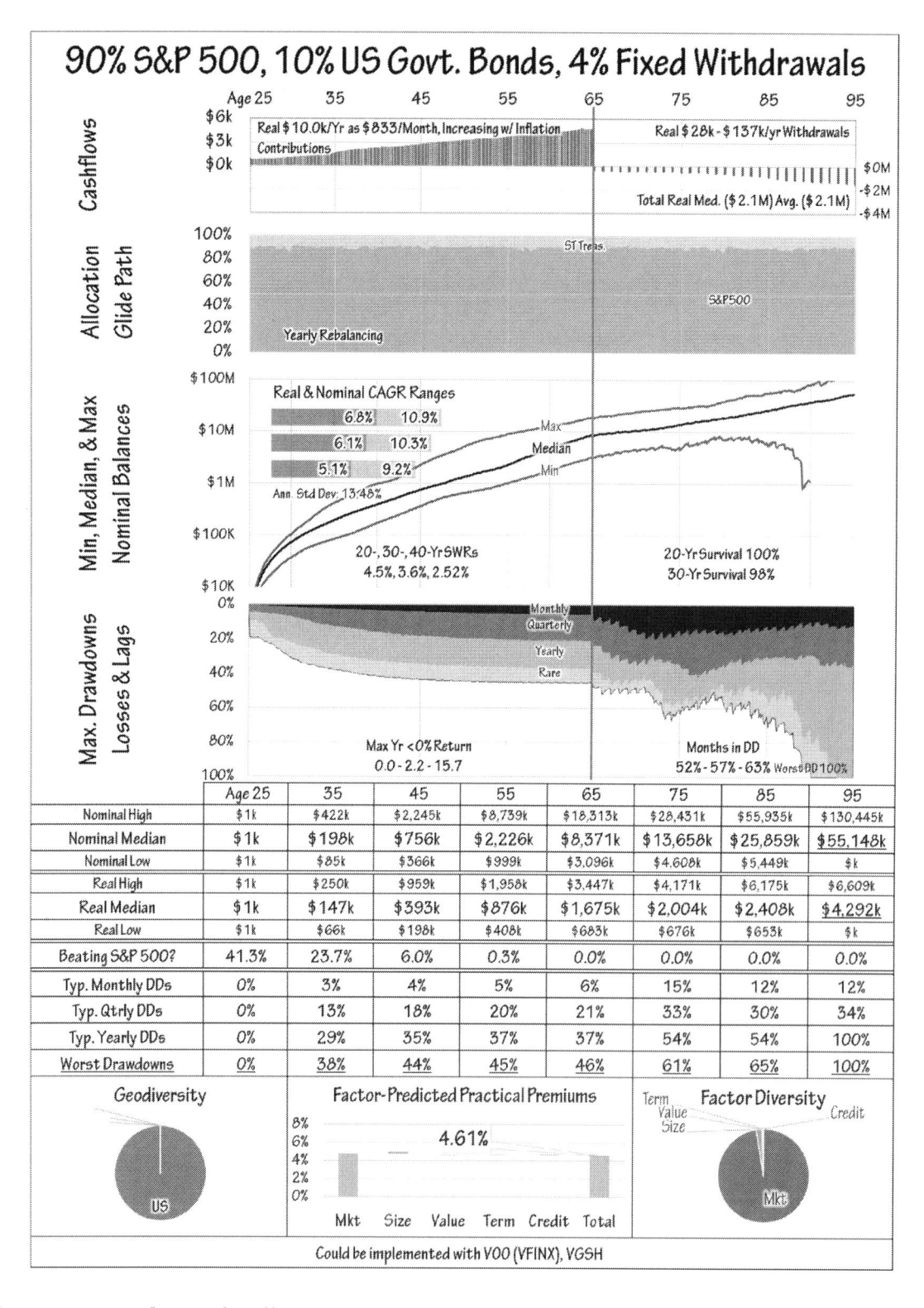

90% S&P 500, 10% US Govt. Bonds, 4% Fixed Withdrawals

	Age 25	35	45	55	65	75	85	95
Nominal High	$1k	$422k	$2,245k	$8,739k	$18,313k	$28,431k	$55,935k	$130,445k
Nominal Median	$1k	$198k	$756k	$2,226k	$8,371k	$13,658k	$25,859k	$55,148k
Nominal Low	$1k	$85k	$366k	$999k	$3,096k	$4,608k	$5,449k	$k
Real High	$1k	$250k	$959k	$1,958k	$3,447k	$4,171k	$6,175k	$6,609k
Real Median	$1k	$147k	$393k	$876k	$1,675k	$2,004k	$2,408k	$4,292k
Real Low	$1k	$66k	$198k	$408k	$683k	$676k	$653k	$k
Beating S&P 500?	41.3%	23.7%	6.0%	0.3%	0.0%	0.0%	0.0%	0.0%
Typ. Monthly DDs	0%	3%	4%	5%	6%	15%	12%	12%
Typ. Qtrly DDs	0%	13%	18%	20%	21%	33%	30%	34%
Typ. Yearly DDs	0%	29%	35%	37%	37%	54%	54%	100%
Worst Drawdowns	0%	38%	44%	45%	46%	61%	65%	100%

Could be implemented with VOO (VFINX), VGSH

Figure 108. Backtest of Buffett strategy using 1970-2019 returns

APPENDIX 7: BACKTESTING TO 1928

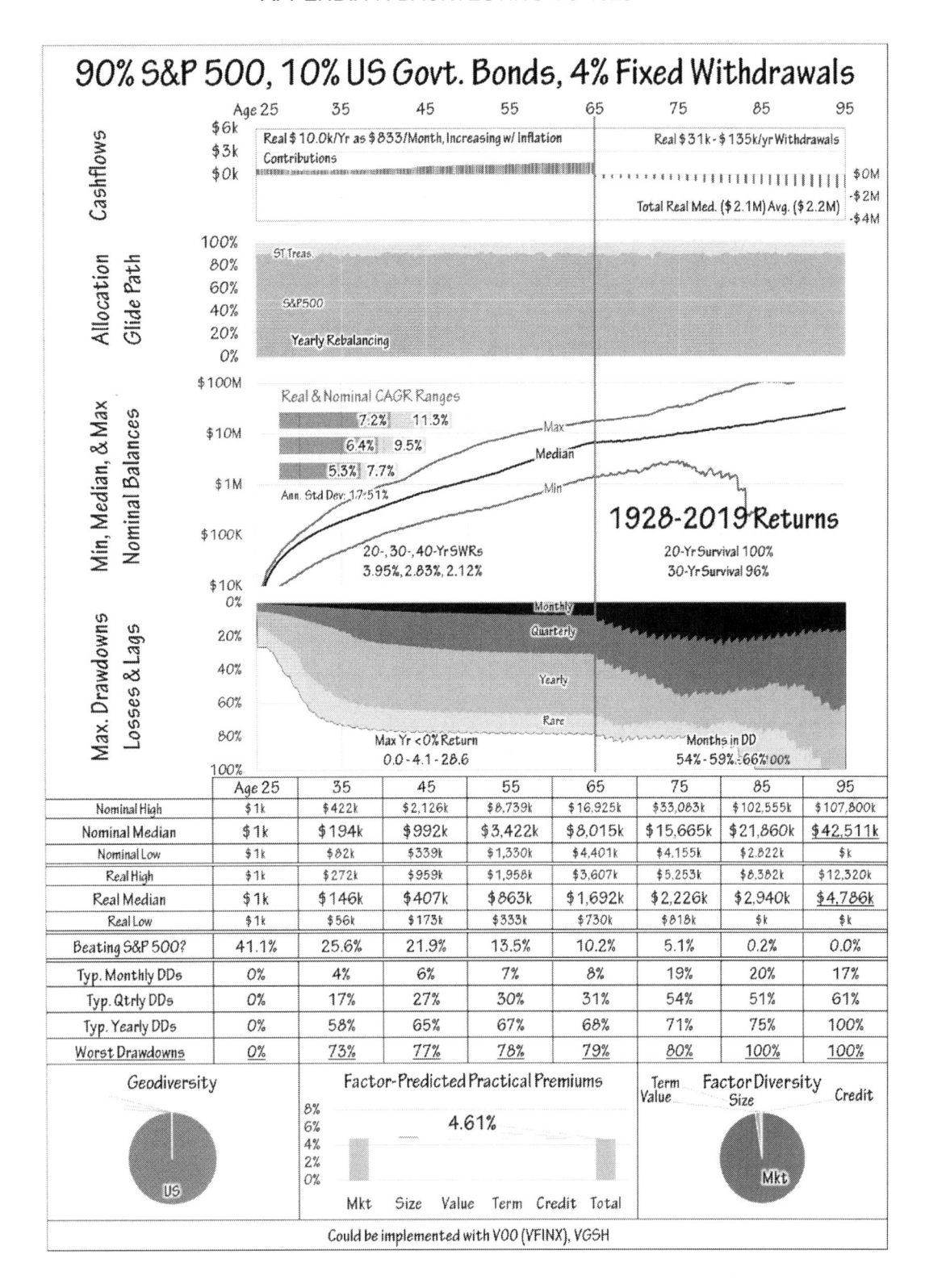

90% S&P 500, 10% US Govt. Bonds, 4% Fixed Withdrawals

	Age 25	35	45	55	65	75	85	95
Nominal High	$1k	$422k	$2,126k	$8,739k	$16,925k	$33,083k	$102,555k	$107,800k
Nominal Median	$1k	$194k	$992k	$3,422k	$8,015k	$15,665k	$21,860k	$42,511k
Nominal Low	$1k	$82k	$339k	$1,330k	$4,401k	$4,155k	$2,822k	$k
Real High	$1k	$272k	$959k	$1,958k	$3,607k	$5,253k	$8,382k	$12,320k
Real Median	$1k	$146k	$407k	$863k	$1,692k	$2,226k	$2,940k	$4,786k
Real Low	$1k	$56k	$173k	$333k	$730k	$818k	$k	$k
Beating S&P 500?	41.1%	25.6%	21.9%	13.5%	10.2%	5.1%	0.2%	0.0%
Typ. Monthly DDs	0%	4%	6%	7%	8%	19%	20%	17%
Typ. Qtrly DDs	0%	17%	27%	30%	31%	54%	51%	61%
Typ. Yearly DDs	0%	58%	65%	67%	68%	71%	75%	100%
Worst Drawdowns	0%	73%	77%	78%	79%	80%	100%	100%

Could be implemented with VOO (VFINX), VGSH

Figure 109. Backtest of Buffett strategy using 1928-2019 returns

100% Vanguard-Like Target-Date Fund, 4% Fixed Withdrawals

	Age 25	35	45	55	65	75	85	95
Nominal High	$1k	$479k	$2,010k	$7,379k	$12,900k	$15,480k	$23,900k	$64,532k
Nominal Median	$1k	$188k	$752k	$2,516k	$8,004k	$12,276k	$18,479k	$29,241k
Nominal Low	$1k	$102k	$422k	$1,120k	$3,360k	$5,421k	$10,435k	$10,142k
Real High	$1k	$256k	$810k	$1,646k	$2,393k	$2,271k	$2,655k	$3,569k
Real Median	$1k	$140k	$389k	$896k	$1,737k	$1,801k	$1,812k	$2,180k
Real Low	$1k	$79k	$231k	$461k	$748k	$795k	$1,050k	$588k
Beating S&P 500?	50.3%	54.3%	51.2%	39.8%	14.7%	2.8%	0.0%	0.0%
Typ. Monthly DDs	0%	1%	2%	2%	1%	1%	1%	1%
Typ. Qtrly DDs	0%	11%	14%	11%	7%	5%	5%	6%
Typ. Yearly DDs	0%	31%	34%	29%	22%	16%	14%	18%
Worst Drawdowns	0%	39%	41%	35%	27%	20%	19%	24%

Could be implemented with Vanguard-like target-date fund

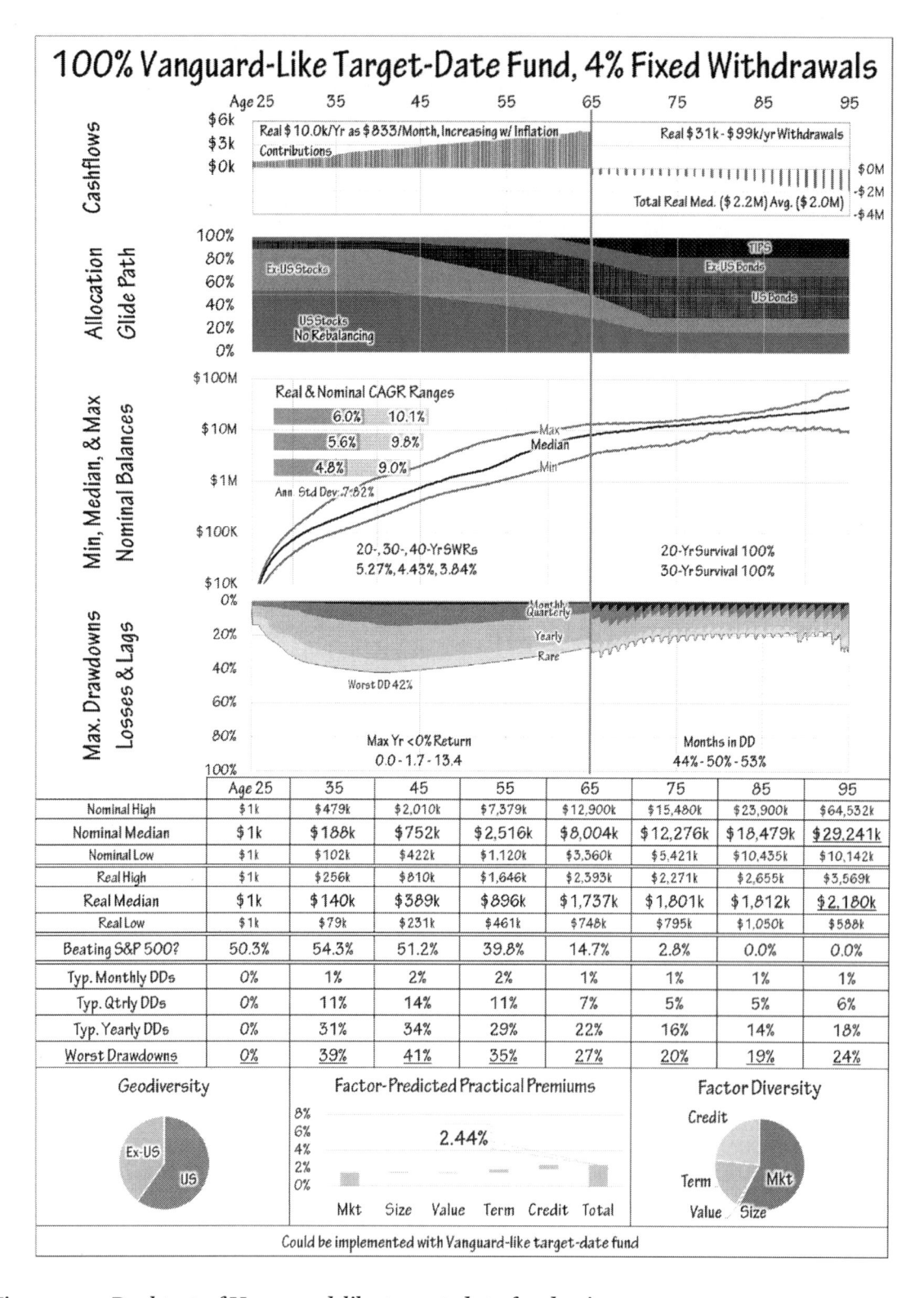

Figure 110. Backtest of Vanguard-like target-date fund using 1970-2019 returns

APPENDIX 7: BACKTESTING TO 1928

Vanguard-Like Target-Date Fund, 4% Fixed Withdrawals

	Age 25	35	45	55	65	75	85	95
Nominal High	$1k	$479k	$2,010k	$7,379k	$13,664k	$19,693k	$36,381k	$59,457k
Nominal Median	$1k	$185k	$832k	$2,486k	$8,550k	$13,618k	$16,175k	$18,865k
Nominal Low	$1k	$108k	$318k	$1,228k	$2,701k	$3,372k	$5,672k	$7,847k
Real High	$1k	$256k	$810k	$1,646k	$2,199k	$2,833k	$3,593k	$4,258k
Real Median	$1k	$139k	$404k	$861k	$1,453k	$1,566k	$1,410k	$1,696k
Real Low	$1k	$62k	$187k	$431k	$867k	$652k	$402k	$k
Beating S&P 500?	49.3%	48.8%	45.9%	40.0%	25.3%	11.7%	1.1%	0.3%
Typ. Monthly DDs	0%	2%	2%	2%	1%	4%	5%	5%
Typ. Qtrly DDs	0%	12%	17%	13%	8%	13%	22%	69%
Typ. Yearly DDs	0%	41%	50%	44%	36%	30%	39%	100%
Worst Drawdowns	0%	60%	65%	58%	49%	39%	52%	100%

Could be implemented with Vanguard-like target-date fund

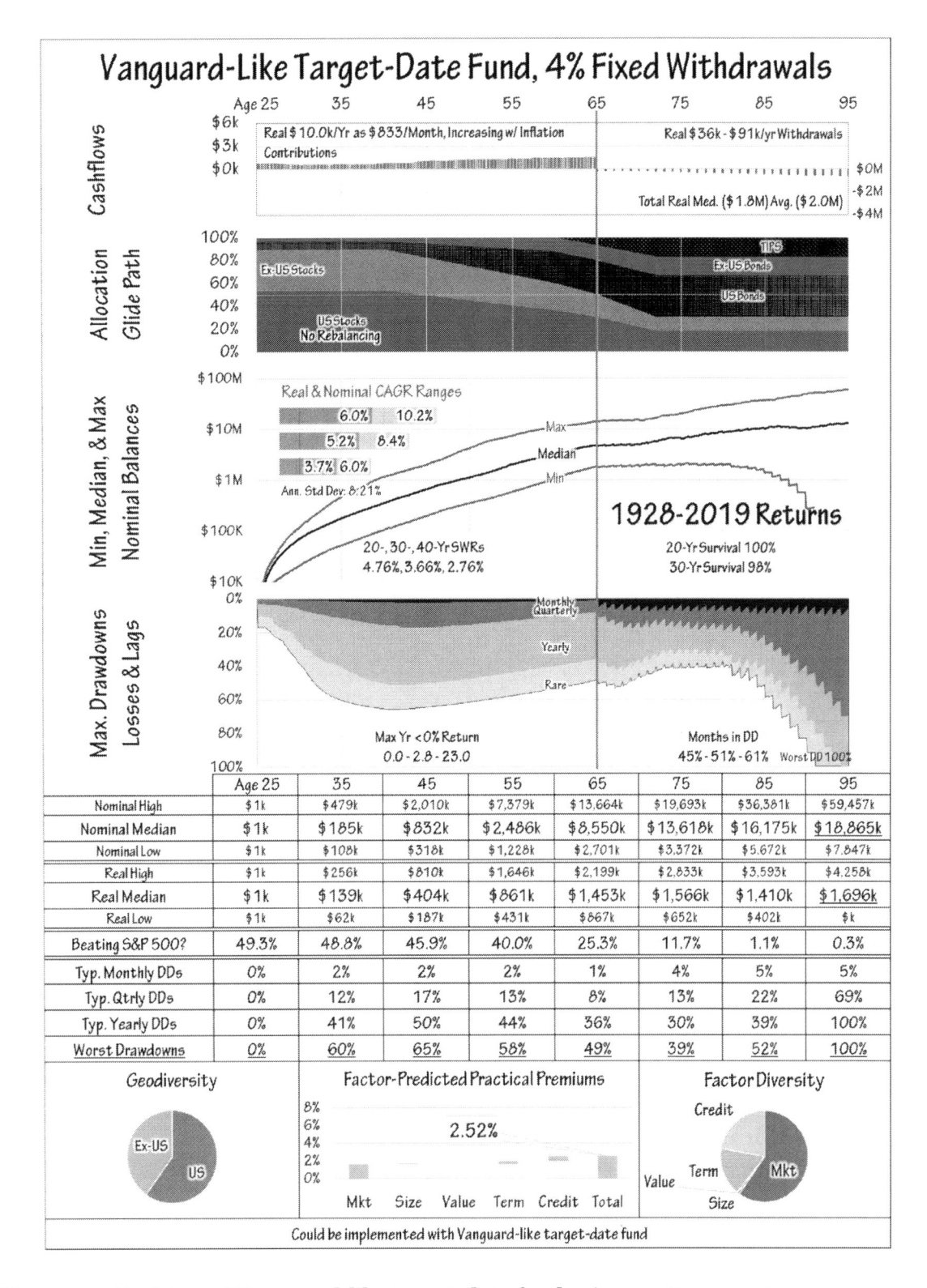

Figure 111. Backtest of Vanguard-like target-date fund using 1928-2019 returns

2 FUNDS FOR LIFE

90% V-Like TDF, 10% US Small-Cap Value, 4% Nudge WDs

	Age 25	35	45	55	65	75	85	95
Nominal High	$1k	$482k	$2,147k	$8,025k	$16,776k	$19,889k	$34,528k	$112,272k
Nominal Median	$1k	$190k	$818k	$2,740k	$9,170k	$15,285k	$24,839k	$43,142k
Nominal Low	$1k	$101k	$418k	$1,103k	$3,374k	$6,264k	$13,824k	$18,301k
Real High	$1k	$257k	$813k	$1,791k	$2,897k	$2,918k	$3,761k	$5,228k
Real Median	$1k	$145k	$395k	$971k	$1,945k	$2,242k	$2,430k	$3,160k
Real Low	$1k	$78k	$225k	$467k	$877k	$919k	$1,363k	$850k
Beating S&P 500?	52.0%	60.5%	60.3%	67.0%	62.0%	32.2%	18.5%	15.3%
Typ. Monthly DDs	0%	2%	2%	2%	2%	1%	1%	1%
Typ. Qtrly DDs	0%	10%	12%	10%	8%	7%	5%	4%
Typ. Yearly DDs	0%	31%	35%	31%	28%	17%	16%	15%
Worst Drawdowns	0%	40%	43%	39%	35%	22%	21%	20%

Could be implemented with Vanguard-like target-date fund, AVUV

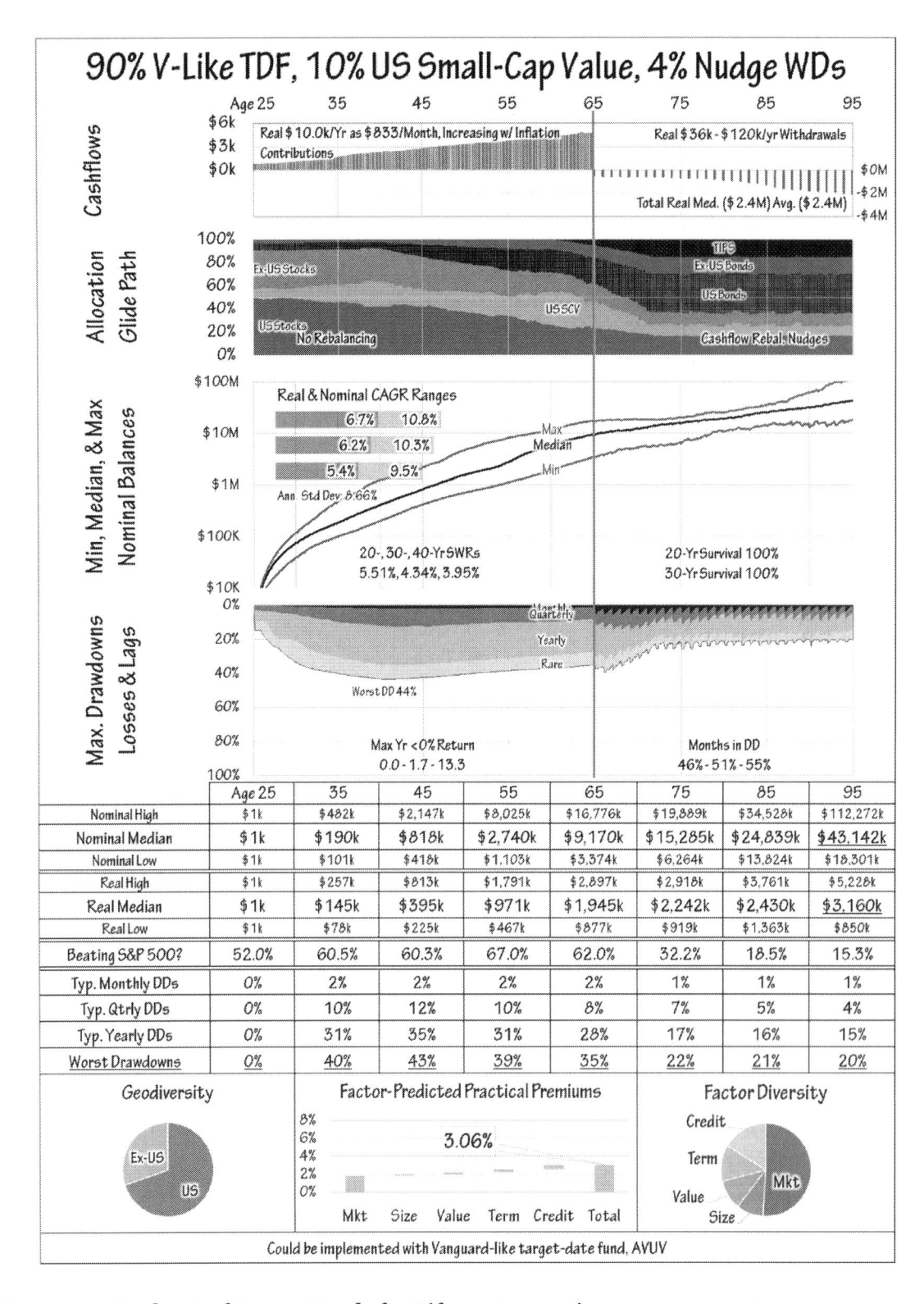

Figure 112. Backtest of Easy 2 Funds for Life strategy using 1970-2019 returns

APPENDIX 7: BACKTESTING TO 1928

90% V-Like TDF, 10% in US Small-Cap Value, 4% Nudge WDs

	Age 25	35	45	55	65	75	85	95
Nominal High	$1k	$482k	$2,147k	$8,025k	$17,849k	$32,969k	$94,335k	$217,152k
Nominal Median	$1k	$193k	$961k	$3,137k	$11,026k	$19,575k	$25,629k	$32,234k
Nominal Low	$1k	$104k	$364k	$1,426k	$4,171k	$4,296k	$2,980k	$k
Real High	$1k	$257k	$813k	$1,791k	$2,933k	$3,722k	$7,710k	$15,486k
Real Median	$1k	$146k	$413k	$945k	$1,829k	$2,137k	$2,207k	$2,513k
Real Low	$1k	$58k	$174k	$400k	$906k	$854k	$423k	$k
Beating S&P 500?	50.1%	55.2%	54.6%	48.6%	48.8%	40.9%	34.2%	26.8%
Typ. Monthly DDs	0%	2%	3%	3%	3%	4%	4%	5%
Typ. Qtrly DDs	0%	12%	16%	15%	14%	16%	15%	26%
Typ. Yearly DDs	0%	43%	53%	48%	43%	35%	36%	75%
Worst Drawdowns	0%	62%	66%	61%	55%	43%	44%	100%

Could be implemented with Vanguard-like target-date fund, AVUV

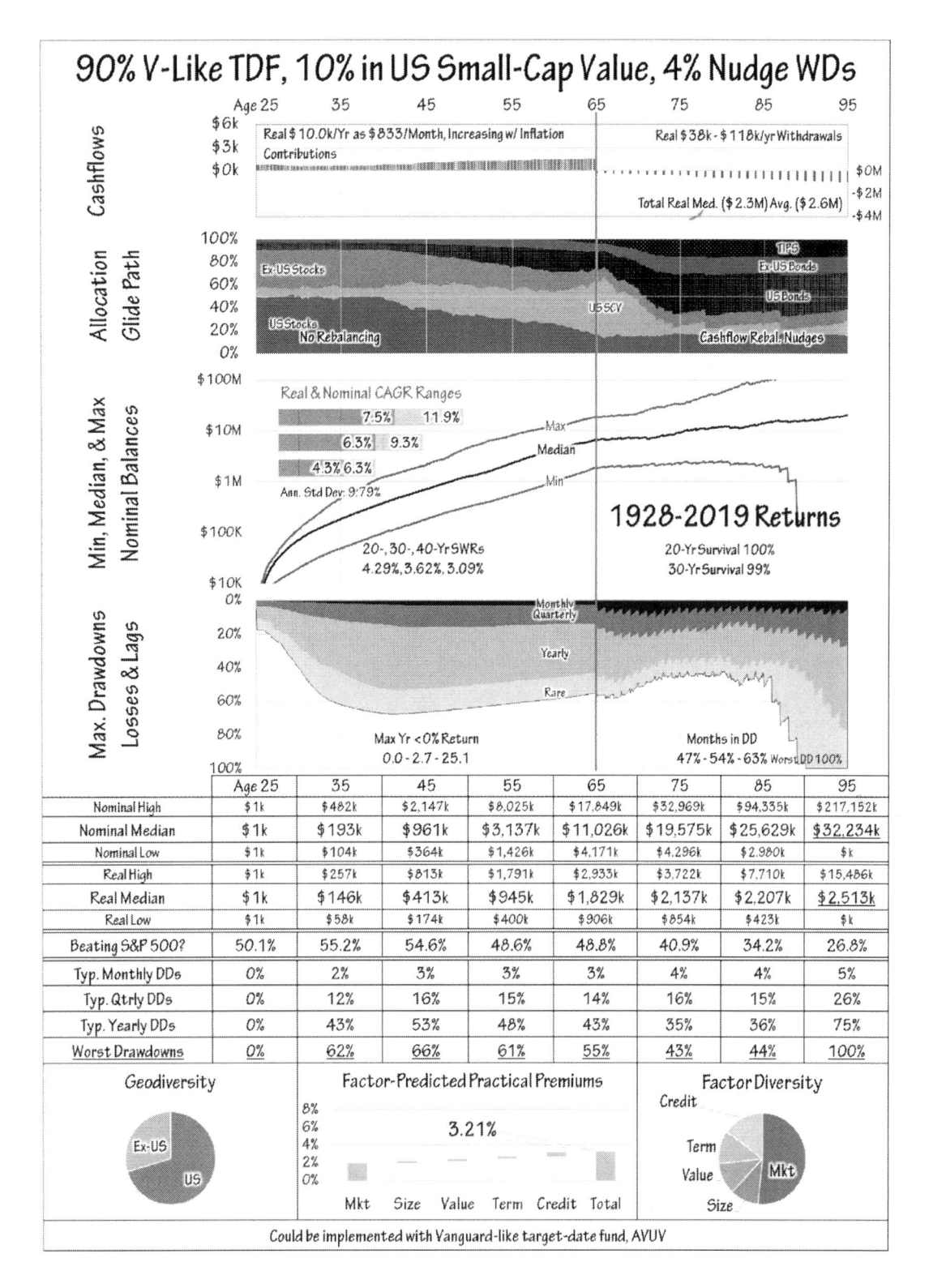

Figure 113. Backtest of Easy 2 Funds for Life strategy using 1928-2019 returns

1.5 × YTR in US SCV, Rest in V-Like TDF, 4% Fixed WDs

	Age 25	35	45	55	65	75	85	95
Nominal High	$1k	$512k	$2,625k	$9,798k	$17,990k	$21,793k	$33,456k	$93,104k
Nominal Median	$1k	$218k	$943k	$3,150k	$10,206k	$15,624k	$23,519k	$36,744k
Nominal Low	$1k	$101k	$386k	$1,192k	$4,079k	$6,627k	$12,717k	$13,010k
Real High	$1k	$274k	$892k	$2,186k	$3,104k	$3,197k	$3,308k	$4,344k
Real Median	$1k	$158k	$446k	$1,120k	$2,186k	$2,292k	$2,330k	$2,828k
Real Low	$1k	$69k	$208k	$504k	$916k	$972k	$1,280k	$754k
Beating S&P 500?	52.8%	60.8%	74.0%	89.2%	77.0%	58.5%	29.7%	25.5%
Typ. Monthly DDs	0%	2%	2%	2%	1%	1%	1%	1%
Typ. Qtrly DDs	0%	11%	12%	10%	6%	5%	5%	6%
Typ. Yearly DDs	0%	33%	36%	30%	22%	16%	14%	18%
Worst Drawdowns	0%	46%	45%	38%	28%	20%	19%	24%

Could be implemented with Vanguard-like target-date fund, AVUV

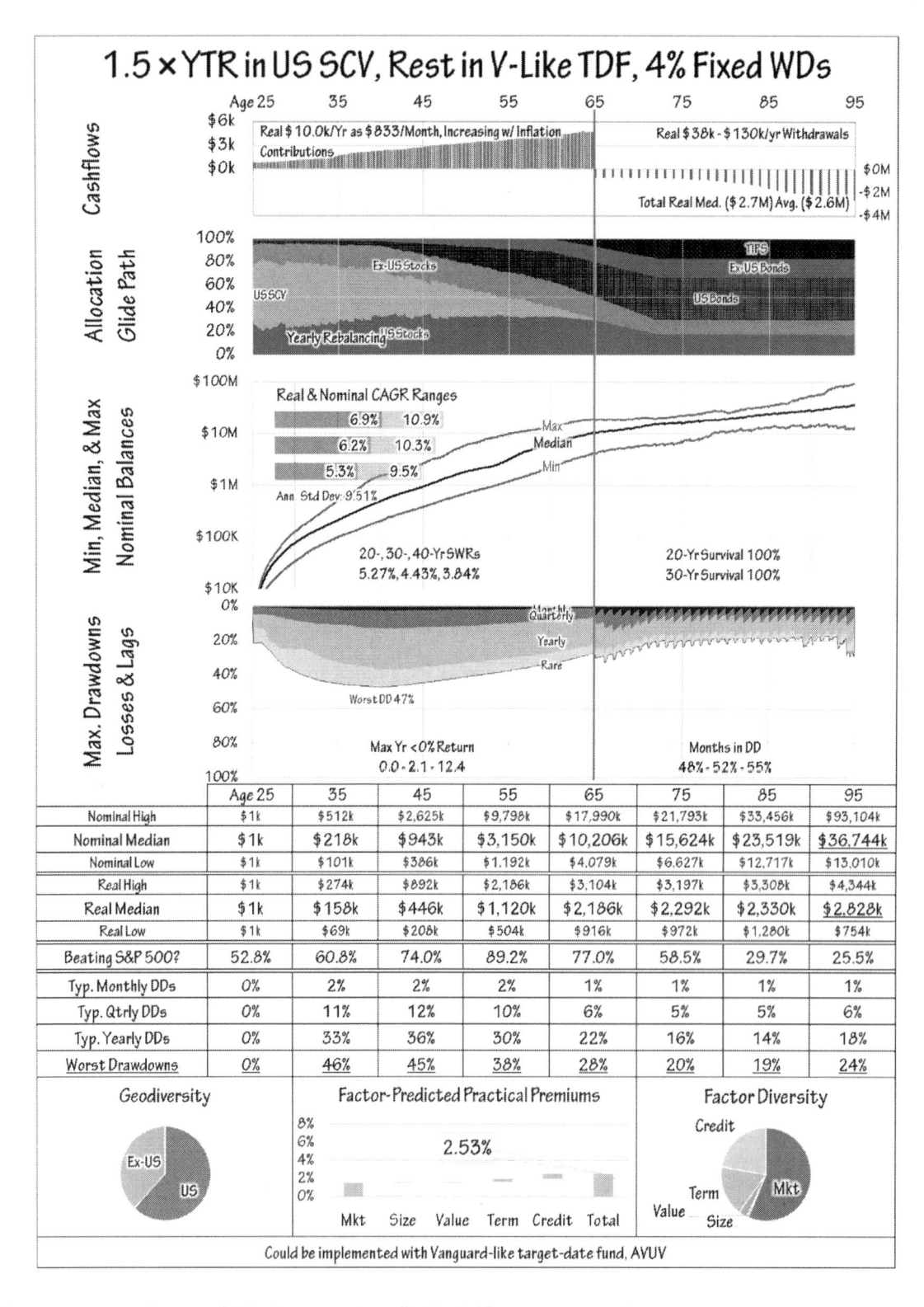

Figure 114. Backtest of Moderate 2 Funds for Life strategy using 1970-2019 returns

APPENDIX 7: BACKTESTING TO 1928

1.5 × YTR in US SCV, Rest in TDF, 4% Fixed WDs

	Age 25	35	45	55	65	75	85	95
Nominal High	$1k	$512k	$2,625k	$9,798k	$18,926k	$28,808k	$59,966k	$95,009k
Nominal Median	$1k	$236k	$1,196k	$3,939k	$12,490k	$19,716k	$23,322k	$28,063k
Nominal Low	$1k	$98k	$472k	$1,740k	$4,101k	$5,141k	$8,948k	$12,378k
Real High	$1k	$274k	$892k	$2,186k	$3,153k	$3,714k	$5,094k	$6,395k
Real Median	$1k	$163k	$478k	$1,103k	$2,086k	$2,336k	$2,039k	$2,400k
Real Low	$1k	$39k	$134k	$411k	$859k	$729k	$484k	$k
Beating S&P 500?	52.4%	66.3%	64.9%	63.4%	59.7%	48.5%	33.5%	21.5%
Typ. Monthly DDs	0%	3%	4%	3%	1%	4%	5%	6%
Typ. Qtrly DDs	0%	19%	21%	17%	9%	13%	21%	69%
Typ. Yearly DDs	0%	56%	62%	52%	38%	30%	39%	100%
Worst Drawdowns	0%	72%	73%	64%	50%	39%	52%	100%

Geodiversity — Factor-Predicted Practical Premiums 2.65% — Factor Diversity

Could be implemented with Vanguard-like target-date fund, AVUV

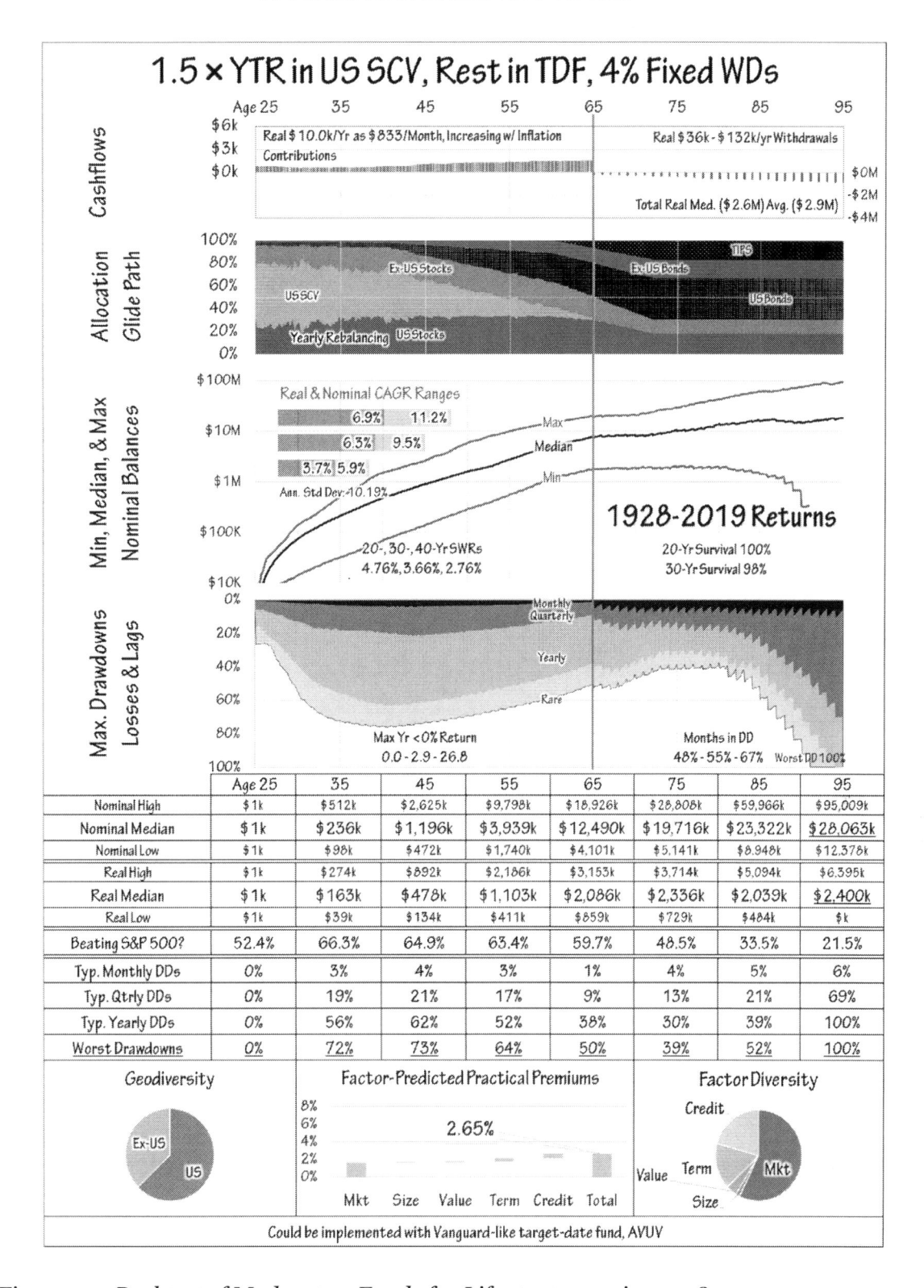

Figure 115. Backtest of Moderate 2 Funds for Life strategy using 1928-2019 returns

2 FUNDS FOR LIFE

2.5 × YTR +20% in US SCV, Rest in V-Like TDF, 4% Nudge WDs

	Age 25	35	45	55	65	75	85	95
Nominal High	$1k	$750k	$3,329k	$13,279k	$30,010k	$38,167k	$74,105k	$279,067k
Nominal Median	$1k	$246k	$1,169k	$4,043k	$13,605k	$24,683k	$45,459k	$89,037k
Nominal Low	$1k	$86k	$325k	$1,161k	$4,712k	$10,762k	$29,143k	$46,637k
Real High	$1k	$333k	$1,054k	$2,963k	$5,182k	$5,599k	$6,478k	$15,955k
Real Median	$1k	$175k	$567k	$1,430k	$2,901k	$3,621k	$4,686k	$6,713k
Real Low	$1k	$57k	$175k	$491k	$1,282k	$1,579k	$2,928k	$2,727k
Beating S&P 500?	52.3%	67.3%	78.8%	99.3%	100.0%	98.5%	100.0%	100.0%
Typ. Monthly DDs	0%	5%	5%	3%	2%	2%	1%	1%
Typ. Qtrly DDs	0%	19%	18%	14%	8%	8%	7%	7%
Typ. Yearly DDs	0%	40%	42%	36%	27%	21%	20%	21%
Worst Drawdowns	0%	55%	54%	46%	34%	27%	27%	29%

Could be implemented with Vanguard-like target-date fund, AVUV

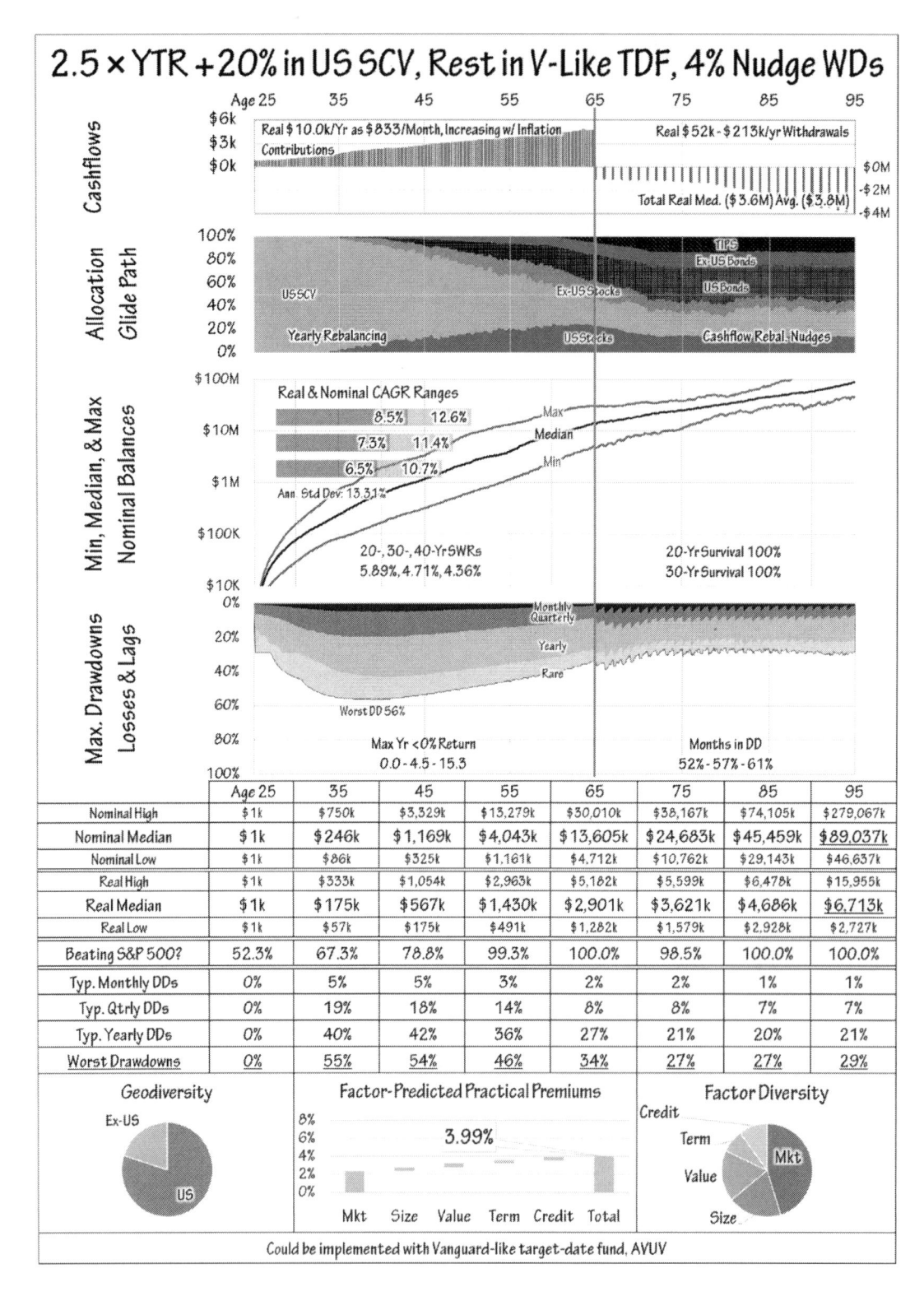

Figure 116. Backtest of Aggressive 2 Funds for Life strategy using 1970-2019 returns

APPENDIX 7: BACKTESTING TO 1928

2.5 × YTR + 20% in US SCV, Rest in TDF, 4% Nudge WDs

	Age 25	35	45	55	65	75	85	95
Nominal High	$1k	$750k	$3,369k	$13,611k	$31,703k	$63,550k	$168,449k	$470,489k
Nominal Median	$1k	$282k	$1,642k	$6,993k	$20,396k	$36,669k	$56,998k	$68,251k
Nominal Low	$1k	$68k	$505k	$2,587k	$8,302k	$10,912k	$18,675k	$28,720k
Real High	$1k	$414k	$1,266k	$3,912k	$5,468k	$7,061k	$13,767k	$33,553k
Real Median	$1k	$182k	$645k	$1,471k	$3,352k	$3,683k	$4,465k	$5,581k
Real Low	$1k	$20k	$78k	$310k	$905k	$1,128k	$1,134k	$731k
Beating S&P 500?	50.3%	66.1%	77.0%	84.5%	77.3%	76.5%	74.0%	68.8%
Typ. Monthly DDs	0%	7%	8%	6%	3%	4%	4%	5%
Typ. Qtrly DDs	0%	34%	34%	27%	17%	23%	18%	17%
Typ. Yearly DDs	0%	70%	74%	66%	51%	43%	42%	39%
Worst Drawdowns	0%	84%	84%	75%	62%	50%	51%	48%

Could be implemented with Vanguard-like target-date fund, AVUV

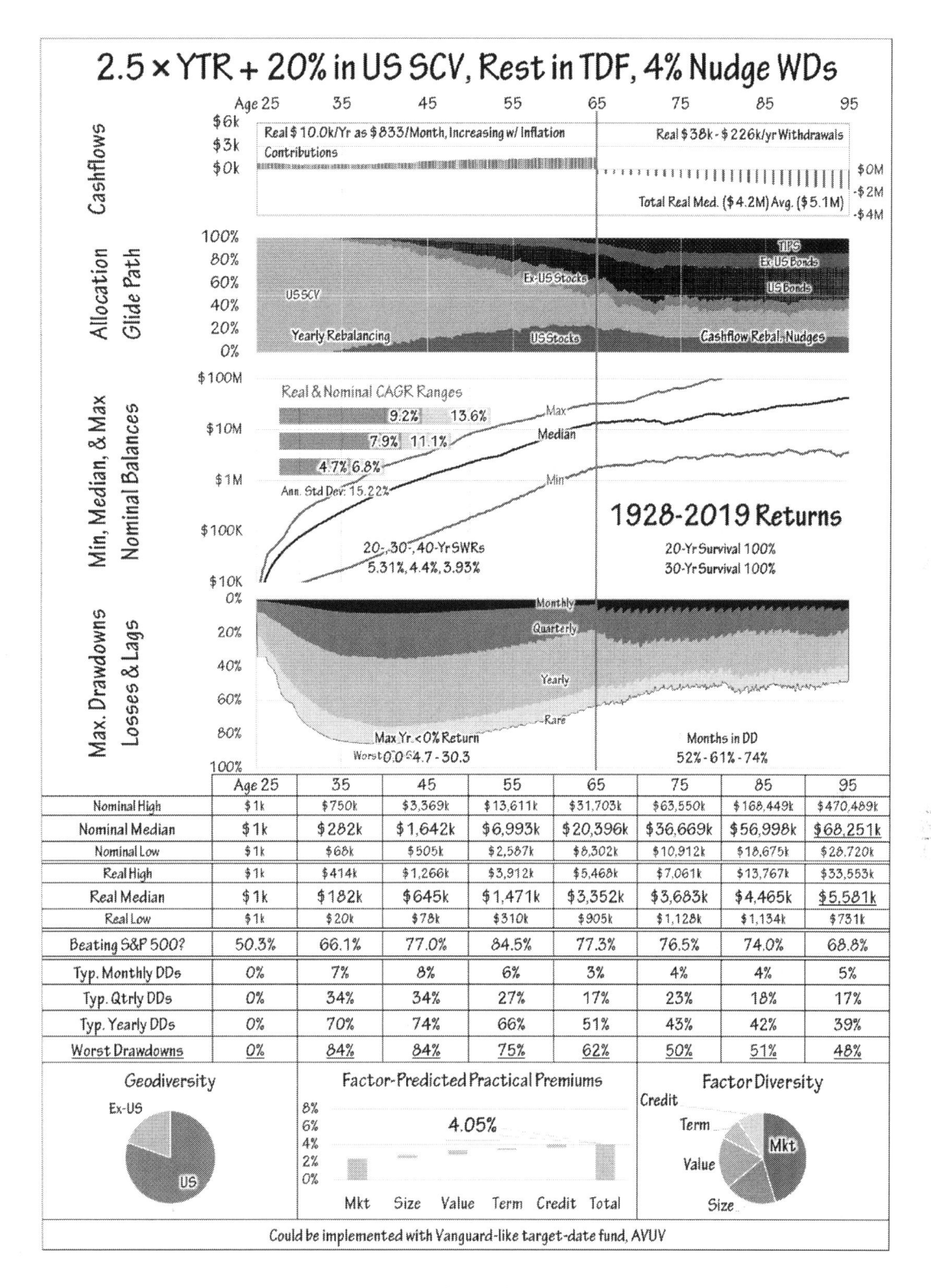

Figure 117. Backtest of Aggressive 2 Funds for Life strategy using 1928-2019 returns

Appendix 8
Backtesting Return Sources & Methods

We only have a complete asset class return history for the Ultimate Buy-and-Hold equities portfolio going back to 1989. In the past, we resorted to filling asset class return history gaps with the next-closest asset return available to us. Since there are older US return histories available, that meant the portfolio we based our backtests on became progressively less and less diversified internationally for the years between 1970 and 1989. Because the international markets outperformed the US over this timeframe, it understated returns and diversification effects. In 2020, we changed our approach to address these shortcomings. Here's what we did.

We start with a set of real-world fund and index returns for each of the desired asset classes. Where indexes are used, we subtract annual fund expense ratios to approximate what do-it-yourself investors could realize. Here are those funds, indexes, and expense ratios. Gaps are noted. We will discuss how we fill in those gaps next.

	ERs	Sources & Gaps (Not to Scale)			
US Total Stock Market	0.03%	1928-2019 CRSP Deciles 1-10 Index (Total US Market)			
US S&P 500	0.03%	1928-2019 US S&P 500 Index			
US Large-Cap Blend	0.03%	1/1928-12/1990: DFA US Large-Cap Index		1/1991-9/1999: DFA Large Company Portfolio Class 1	10/1999-12/2020: DFA Large Company Portfolio
US Large-Cap Value	0.35%	1/1928-2/1993: DFA US Large-Cap Value Index		3/1993-12/2019: DFA US Large-Cap Value Portfolio Class I	
US Small-cap Blend	0.06%	1/1928:3/1992: DFA US Small-cap Index		4/1992-12/2019: DFA US Small-cap Portfolio Class I	
US Small-cap Value	0.20%	1/1928-3/1993: Dimensional US Small-cap Value Index		4/1993:12/2019: DFA US Small-cap Value Portfolio Class 1	
US REITs	0.12%	1928-1971 GAP	1/1972-12/1977: NAREIT Tot. Return Index	1/1978-1/1993: Dow Jones US Select REIT Index	2/1993-12/2019: DFA Real Estate Securities Portfolio Class I
Int'l Large-Cap Blend	0.05%	1928-1969 GAP	1/1970-7/1991: MSCI EAFE Index (net div.)		8/1991-12/2019: DFA Large-Cap International Portfolio Class I
Int'l Large-Cap Value	0.39%	1928-1974 GAP	1/1975-2/1994: MSCI EAFE Value Index (net div.)		3/1994-12/2019: DFA International Value Portfolio Class I
Int'l Small-Cap Blend	0.39%	1928-1969 GAP	1/1970-9/1996: Dimensional Small-Cap Index		10/1996-12/2019: DFA International Small Company Portfolio Class I
Int'l Small-Cap Value	0.58%	1928-6/1981 GAP	7/1981-12/1994: Dimensional International Small-Cap Value Index		1/1995-12/2019: DFA International Small-Cap Value Portfolio Class I
Emerging Markets Large-Cap Blend	0.10%	1928-1988 GAP	1/1989-4/1994: Fama/French Emerging Markets Index		5/1994-12/2019: DFA Emerging Markets Portfolio Class I
EM Small-Cap Blend	0.63%	1928-1988 GAP	1/1989-3/1998: Dimensional Emerging Markets Small Index		4/1998-12/2019: DFA Emerging Markets Small-Cap Portfolio Class I
EM Value	0.63%	1928-1988 GAP	1/1989-4/1998: Dimensional Emerging Markets Value Index		5/1998-12/2019: DFA Emerging Markets Value Portfolio Class I
Ex-US REIT	0.12%	1928-6/1989 GAP	7/1989-12/2019: S&P Global ex-US REIT Index (gross div.)		
Commodities	0.59%	1928-1/1991 GAP	2/1989-12/2019: Bloomberg Commodity Total Return Index		
Gold	0.25%	1/1928-12/2019: Gold Prices from World Gold Council			
Intermediate-Term Gov't Bonds	0.06%	1928-1972: 5-Yr. US Treas. Notes	1/1973-10/1990: Bloomberg Barclays U.S. Treasury Bond Index		11/1990-12/2019: DFA Intermediate Gov't Fixed Income Portfolio Class I
Short-Term Gov't Bonds	0.05%	1928-1969 GAP	1/1970-6/1977: ICE BofA 1-Year US Treasury Note Index		7/1977-12/2019: ICE BofA 1-3 Year US Treasury Index
US TIPS Bonds	0.05%	1928-2/1997 GAP	3/1997-9/2006: Bloomberg Barclays U.S. TIPS Index		10/2006-12/2019: DFA Inflation Protected Securities Portfolio Class I
US Total Bond Market	0.04%	1928-1975 GAP	1/1976-12/2019: Bloomberg Barclays U.S. Aggregate Bond Index		
WW Total Bond Market	0.06%	1928-1989 GAP	1/1990-12/2019: Bloomberg Barclays Global Aggregate Bond Index (hedged to USD)		
Ex-US Total Bond Market	0.08%	1928-1989 GAP	1/1990-12/2019: Bloomberg Barclays Global Aggregate ex-US Bond Index (hedged to USD)		
WW Stock Mkt	Varies	Calculated from US, Int'l & EM returns & 1928 starting market sizes			

Table 19. Backtest return sources, gaps, and expense-ratio assumptions

APPENDIX 8: BACKTESTING RETURN SOURCES & METHODS

To fill in the gaps that begin as late as 1997 and as early as 1969, we use a rhyme, regress, and scale process.

We start by running a regression analysis for each of the asset classes with gaps. We run it against all the return sequences that go back as far as we need to fill in the gaps. This includes those listed (e.g., US large-cap blend) and approximations to the overall returns for the ex-US developed countries and emerging stock markets. The resulting equations let us approximate the missing returns based on the return histories. These are our regression-based returns.

The next step is to look for what we call "rhyming return matches" and choose whether to use them or the regression-based return. Here, the idea is to compare the known returns in a year with an asset-return gap to all the years in which the gap asset returns are known and pick the one that matches, or "rhymes," the best. If the match is good (error below threshold), we'll use the rhyming return. If the match is poor (error above threshold), we'll use the regression-based return. We determine the match's quality by calculating the root sum of squares of the differences of the returns divided by the square root of the number of returns in the calculation. The error threshold we use is 0.7%, resulting in 72.4% of the returns being rhyming returns and 27.6% being regression-based.

The last step is to scale the returns of the international and emerging markets so they roughly match the overall returns we've been able to extract from publicly available data. To do this, we apply a quarterly adjustment so the cumulative growth of the international large-cap blend and emerging markets blend returns aligns with the published chart data at quarterly intervals. We also apply the international large-cap blend corrections to all other international asset returns (e.g., large-cap value, small-cap blend, small-cap value). We apply the emerging markets correction to the emerging markets small and value returns too. This preserves the premiums for large and small or value and growth within the international and emerging markets return sequences as the corrections are applied.

We believe the result is a significant improvement over the previous approach of simply substituting the next best asset classes. It more accurately reflects the available return data for the US versus international markets and the differences between asset classes within those markets.

Appendix 9
Contribution Frequency & Drawdowns

Most of the analysis in this book assumes monthly contributions. What if contributions are made on a quarterly or yearly basis? The answer is that drawdowns increase in the earlier years of an investor's experience.

Less frequent contributions result in higher drawdowns because there's more time for the market to accumulate losses without being masked by new contributions. Here's a chart showing the difference between monthly, quarterly, yearly, and one-time or lump-sum investing in a Vanguard-like target-date fund. The darkest bands are the depths of drawdowns that are likely to be experienced monthly or quarterly. The lightest bands extend all the way to the worst-case drawdowns (rare) seen within the total 1970 through 2019 history tested.

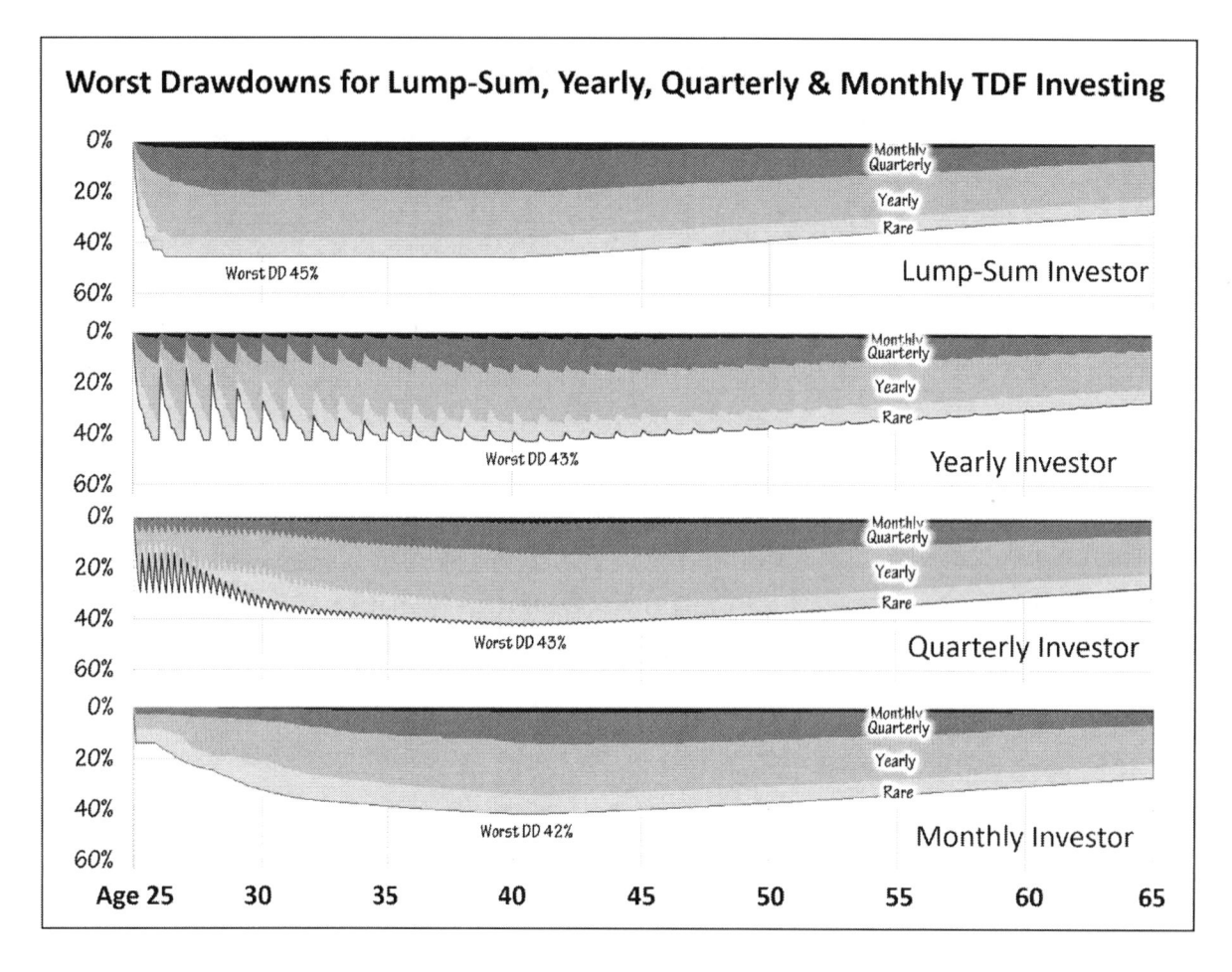

Figure 118. Worst drawdowns for lump-sum, yearly, quarterly, and monthly contributions to a Vanguard-like target-date fund

Since our highest capacity for risk is in the early years, the higher drawdowns in those years shouldn't be a concern for young investors as long as they stay invested.

Another way to reduce perceived drawdowns is to not look very often at your account. The longer you wait to look, the less likely you are to be disappointed. For a passive buy-and-hold investor who has put things on autopilot, this isn't a bad strategy. In fact, it's a great strategy.

Appendix 10
Nudge Withdrawals vs. Rebalancing

I recommended nudge withdrawals as part of the Easy and Aggressive 2 Funds for Life strategies because they're simpler, behaviorally more natural, and likely to produce good results. In this appendix, we'll look at the data to back that up.

The table below shows the summary results for the Easy and Aggressive 2 Funds for Life strategies with the recommended nudge withdrawals and annual rebalancing in retirement. For the Easy strategy, we also show the impact of rebalancing during accumulation and retirement. In the annual rebalancing scenarios, the assumption is that the portfolio will be rebalanced to the desired allocation annually, either through selectively applying some or all of the withdrawal and buying or selling the different funds as necessary. In the nudge rebalancing withdrawal scenarios, the assumption is that the annual withdrawal in retirement comes entirely from whichever fund exceeds its desired allocation.

	Post-Retirement *Nudge Rebalancing* Withdrawals Real Median End-Balances	Post-Retirement *Annual Rebalancing* Real Median End-Balances	Post-Retirement *Nudge Rebalancing* Withdrawals Worst Drawdowns @ 65, 85, 95	Post-Retirement *Annual Rebalancing* Worst Drawdowns @ 65, 85, 95
Easy 2FFL (Preretirement, No Rebalancing) Fixed 90 | 10 TDF | US SCV	$5.23M **$3.16M** $850k	$5.11M **$3.37M** $1.20M	35%, 21%, 20%	35%, 22%, 21%
Easy 2FFL Rebal. (Preretirement Ann. Rebalancing) Fixed 90 | 10 TDF | US SCV	$4.84M **$3.07M** $1.00M	$4.97M **$3.29M** $1.16M	30%, 21%, 21% (1-5% lower @ 40-65)	30%, 22%, 21% (1-5% lower @ 40-65)
Aggressive 2FFL (Preretirement Ann. Rebalancing) 2.5 X YTR + 20% in US SCV, Rest in V-Like TDF	$16.0M **$6.71M** $2.73M	$11.9M **$6.71M** $2.77M	34%, 27%, 29%	34%, 26%, 25%

Table 20. Comparison of nudge withdrawals versus annual rebalancing for 2 Funds for Life strategies

The headline finding is that the differences between nudge withdrawal rebalancing and annual rebalancing are small. The most meaningful difference comes from rebalancing the 90|10 Easy 2 Funds for Life scenario during accumulation. It lowered the age 65 worst drawdown by 5% — 30% instead of 35% for the unrebalanced Easy approach. Other than that, the differences were small enough that most investors wouldn't notice them. The average difference in the median total end balance was between 0 and 7 percentage points higher for annual rebalancing at the end of our 70-year scenarios. At age 85, the difference in drawdowns between the nudge withdrawals and annual rebalancing was within 1 percentage point across the board. This was also true at age 95 except for the Aggressive 2 Funds for Life scenario, where the nudge withdrawals couldn't keep the small-cap value allocation in check.

Since the annual rebalancing and nudge withdrawal rebalancing approaches produced such similar results, investors should choose the one they're most likely to do and not fret too much about doing it perfectly.

The detailed backtest results for the nudge withdrawal and partial or complete annually rebalanced scenarios follow. The rebalancing approaches are noted at the bottom of the Allocation Glidepath charts. Cashflow rebalance nudges are the same thing as nudge withdrawals.

APPENDIX 10: NUDGE WITHDRAWALS VS. REBALANCING

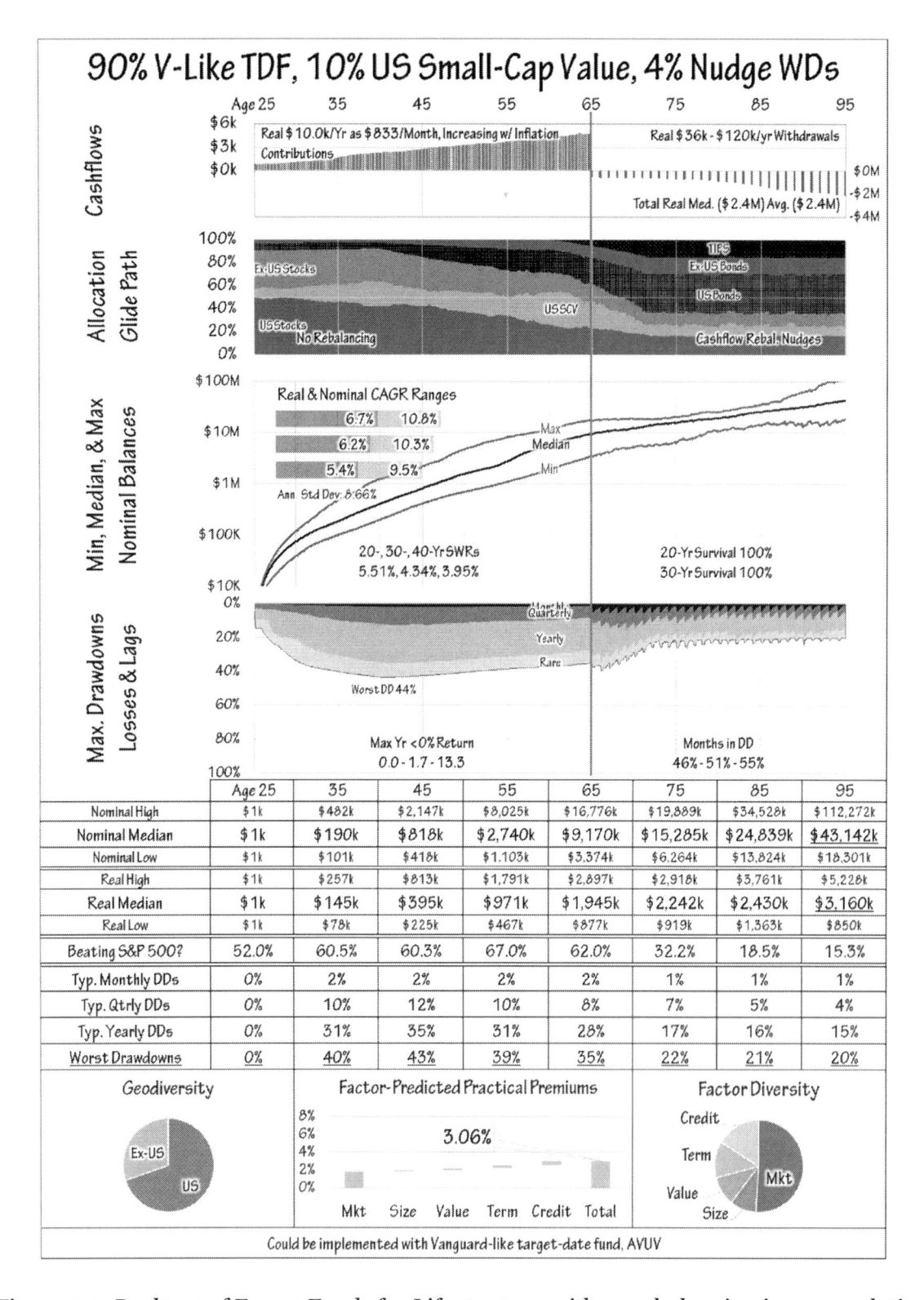

Figure 119. Backtest of Easy 2 Funds for Life strategy with no rebalancing in accumulation and nudge rebalancing in retirement

APPENDIX 10: NUDGE WITHDRAWALS VS. REBALANCING

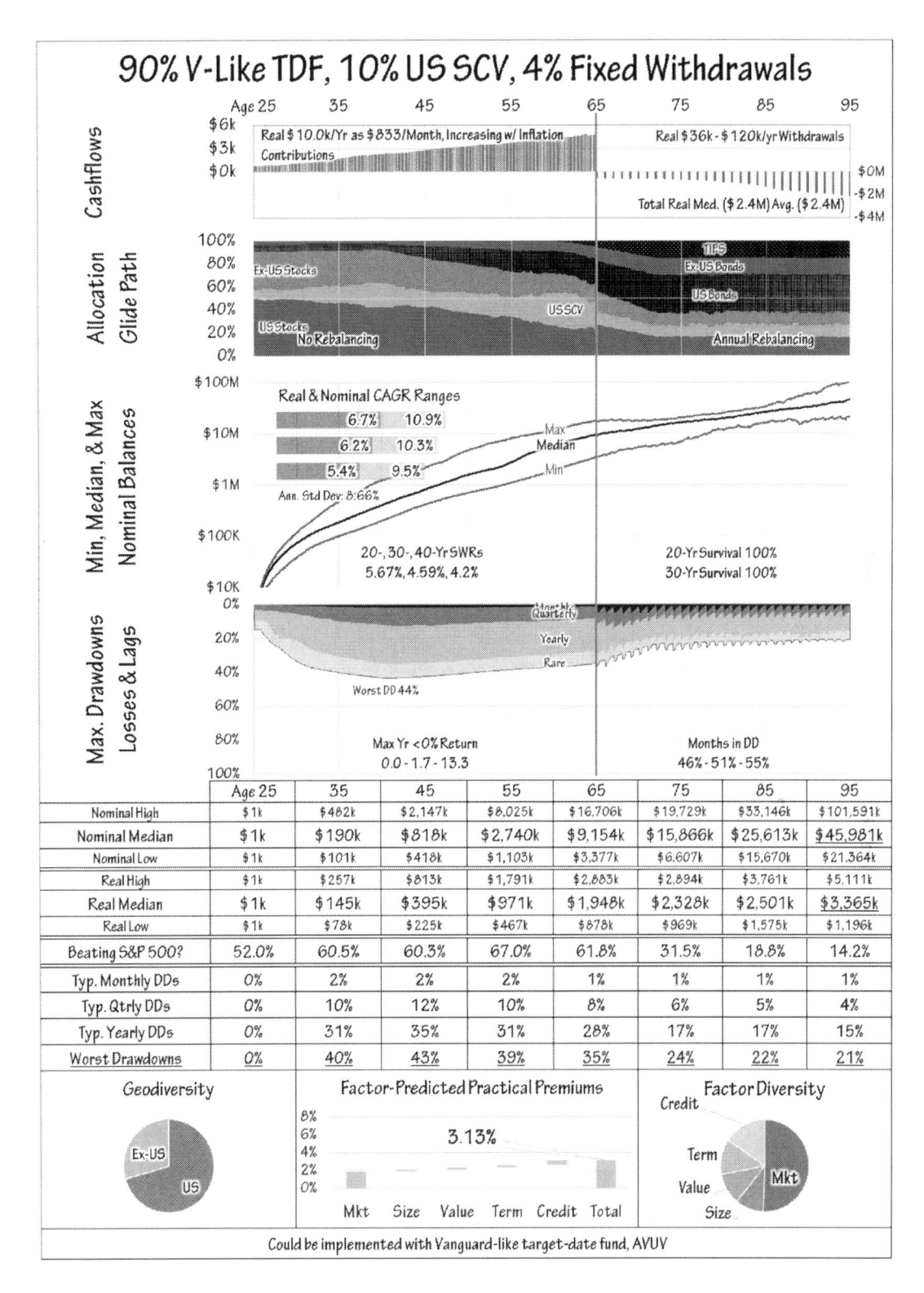

90% V-Like TDF, 10% US SCV, 4% Fixed Withdrawals

	Age 25	35	45	55	65	75	85	95
Nominal High	$1k	$482k	$2,147k	$8,025k	$16,706k	$19,729k	$33,146k	$101,591k
Nominal Median	$1k	$190k	$818k	$2,740k	$9,154k	$15,866k	$25,613k	$45,981k
Nominal Low	$1k	$101k	$418k	$1,103k	$3,377k	$6,607k	$15,670k	$21,364k
Real High	$1k	$257k	$813k	$1,791k	$2,883k	$2,894k	$3,761k	$5,111k
Real Median	$1k	$145k	$395k	$971k	$1,948k	$2,328k	$2,501k	$3,365k
Real Low	$1k	$78k	$225k	$467k	$878k	$969k	$1,575k	$1,196k
Beating S&P 500?	52.0%	60.5%	60.3%	67.0%	61.8%	31.5%	18.8%	14.2%
Typ. Monthly DDs	0%	2%	2%	2%	1%	1%	1%	1%
Typ. Qtrly DDs	0%	10%	12%	10%	8%	6%	5%	4%
Typ. Yearly DDs	0%	31%	35%	31%	28%	17%	17%	15%
Worst Drawdowns	0%	40%	43%	39%	35%	24%	22%	21%

Could be implemented with Vanguard-like target-date fund, AVUV

Figure 120. Backtest of Easy 2 Funds for Life strategy with no rebalancing in accumulation and annual rebalancing in retirement

90% TDF, 10% US SCV, Ann. Rebal. <65, 4% Nudge WDs >65

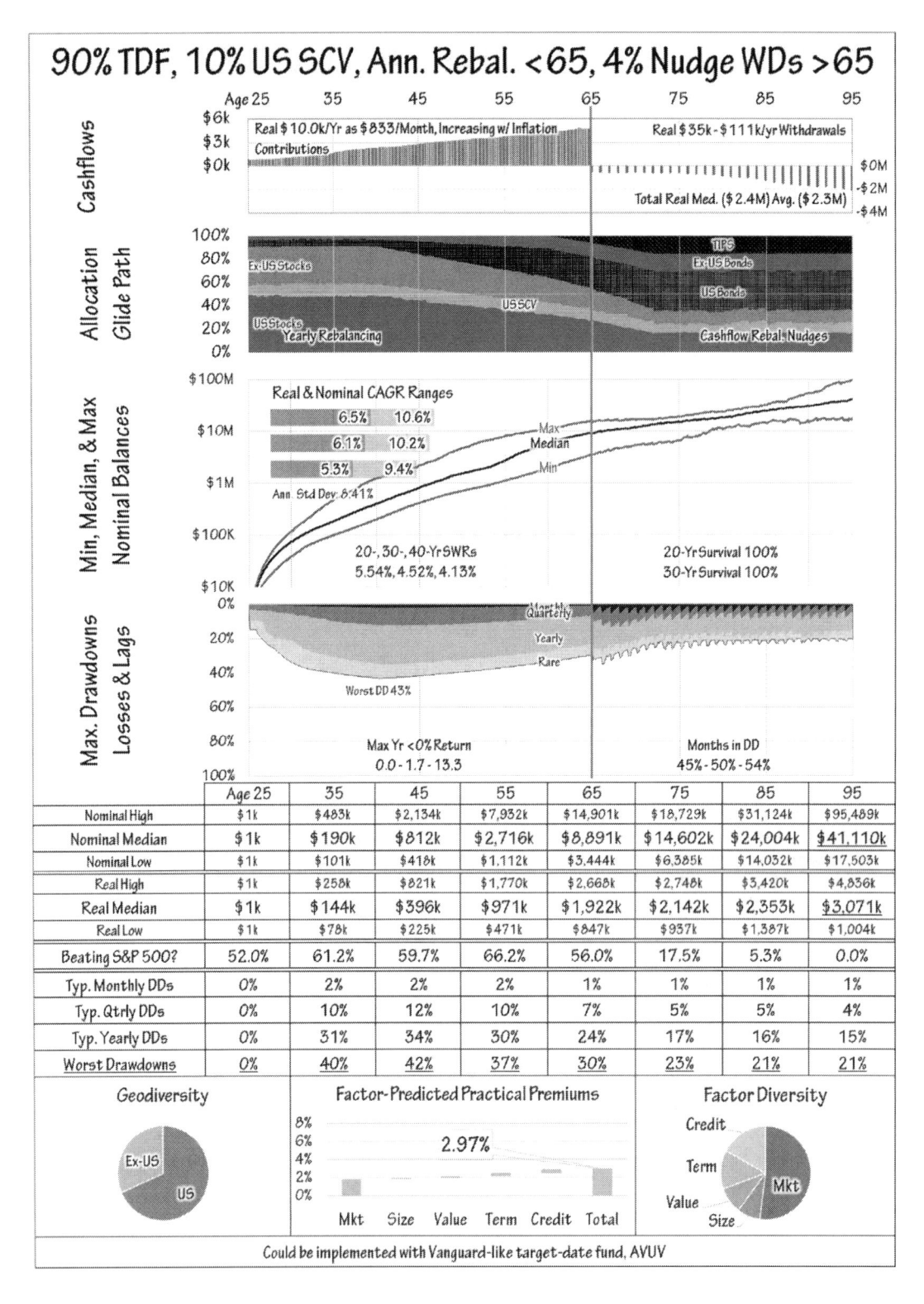

	Age 25	35	45	55	65	75	85	95
Nominal High	$1k	$483k	$2,134k	$7,932k	$14,901k	$18,729k	$31,124k	$95,489k
Nominal Median	$1k	$190k	$812k	$2,716k	$8,891k	$14,602k	$24,004k	$41,110k
Nominal Low	$1k	$101k	$418k	$1,112k	$3,444k	$6,385k	$14,032k	$17,503k
Real High	$1k	$258k	$821k	$1,770k	$2,668k	$2,748k	$3,420k	$4,836k
Real Median	$1k	$144k	$396k	$971k	$1,922k	$2,142k	$2,353k	$3,071k
Real Low	$1k	$78k	$225k	$471k	$847k	$937k	$1,387k	$1,004k
Beating S&P 500?	52.0%	61.2%	59.7%	66.2%	56.0%	17.5%	5.3%	0.0%
Typ. Monthly DDs	0%	2%	2%	2%	1%	1%	1%	1%
Typ. Qtrly DDs	0%	10%	12%	10%	7%	5%	5%	4%
Typ. Yearly DDs	0%	31%	34%	30%	24%	17%	16%	15%
Worst Drawdowns	0%	40%	42%	37%	30%	23%	21%	21%

Could be implemented with Vanguard-like target-date fund, AVUV

Figure 121. Backtest of Easy 2 Funds for Life strategy with annual rebalancing in accumulation and nudge rebalancing in retirement

APPENDIX 10: NUDGE WITHDRAWALS VS. REBALANCING

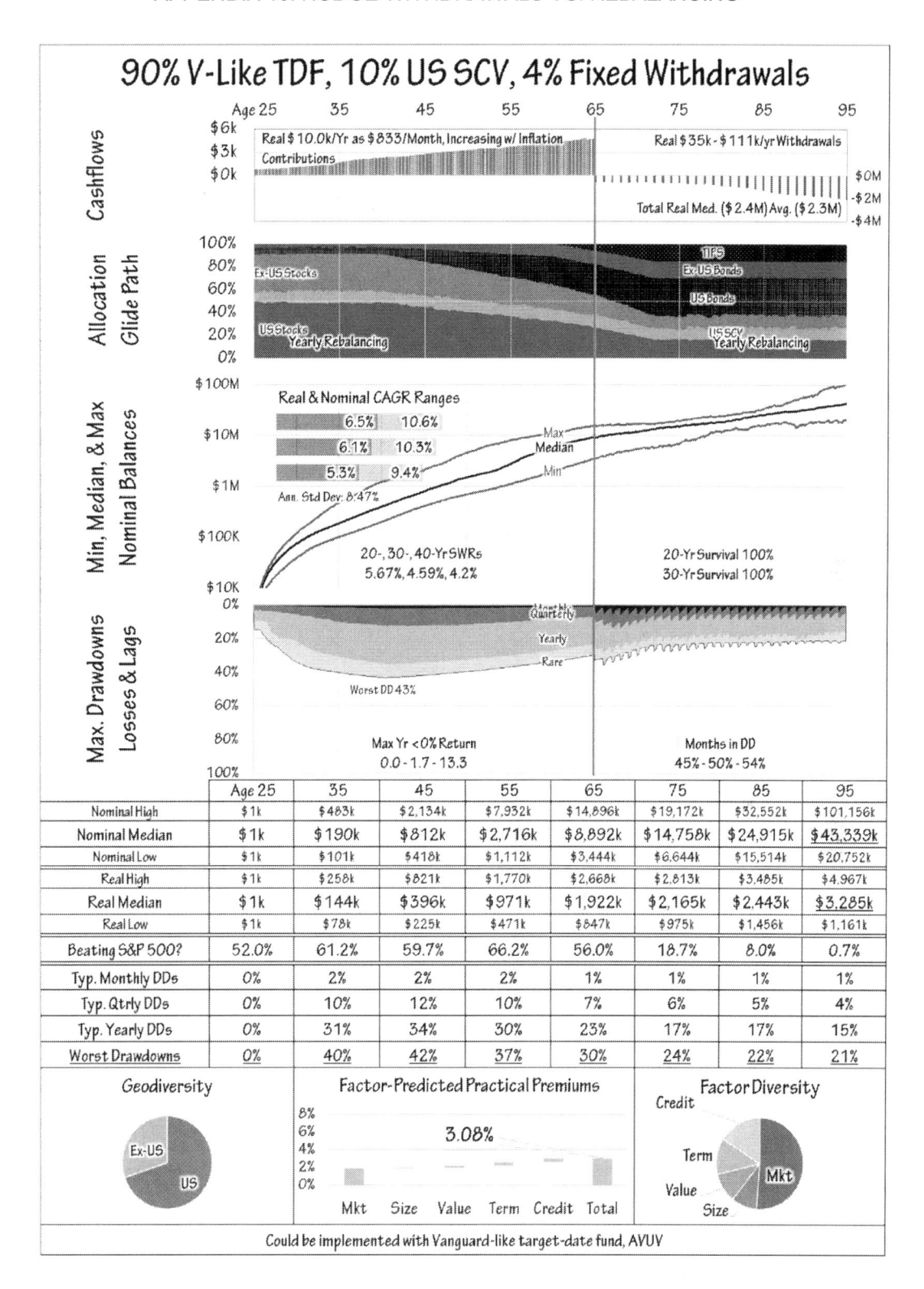

90% V-Like TDF, 10% US SCV, 4% Fixed Withdrawals

	Age 25	35	45	55	65	75	85	95
Nominal High	$1k	$483k	$2,134k	$7,932k	$14,896k	$19,172k	$32,552k	$101,156k
Nominal Median	$1k	$190k	$812k	$2,716k	$8,892k	$14,758k	$24,915k	$43,339k
Nominal Low	$1k	$101k	$418k	$1,112k	$3,444k	$6,644k	$15,514k	$20,752k
Real High	$1k	$258k	$821k	$1,770k	$2,668k	$2,813k	$3,485k	$4,967k
Real Median	$1k	$144k	$396k	$971k	$1,922k	$2,165k	$2,443k	$3,285k
Real Low	$1k	$78k	$225k	$471k	$847k	$975k	$1,456k	$1,161k
Beating S&P 500?	52.0%	61.2%	59.7%	66.2%	56.0%	18.7%	8.0%	0.7%
Typ. Monthly DDs	0%	2%	2%	2%	1%	1%	1%	1%
Typ. Qtrly DDs	0%	10%	12%	10%	7%	6%	5%	4%
Typ. Yearly DDs	0%	31%	34%	30%	23%	17%	17%	15%
Worst Drawdowns	0%	40%	42%	37%	30%	24%	22%	21%

Could be implemented with Vanguard-like target-date fund, AVUV

Figure 122. Backtest of Easy 2 Funds for Life strategy with annual rebalancing in accumulation and annual rebalancing in retirement

2.5 × YTR + 20% in US SCV, Rest in V-Like TDF, 4% Nudge WDs

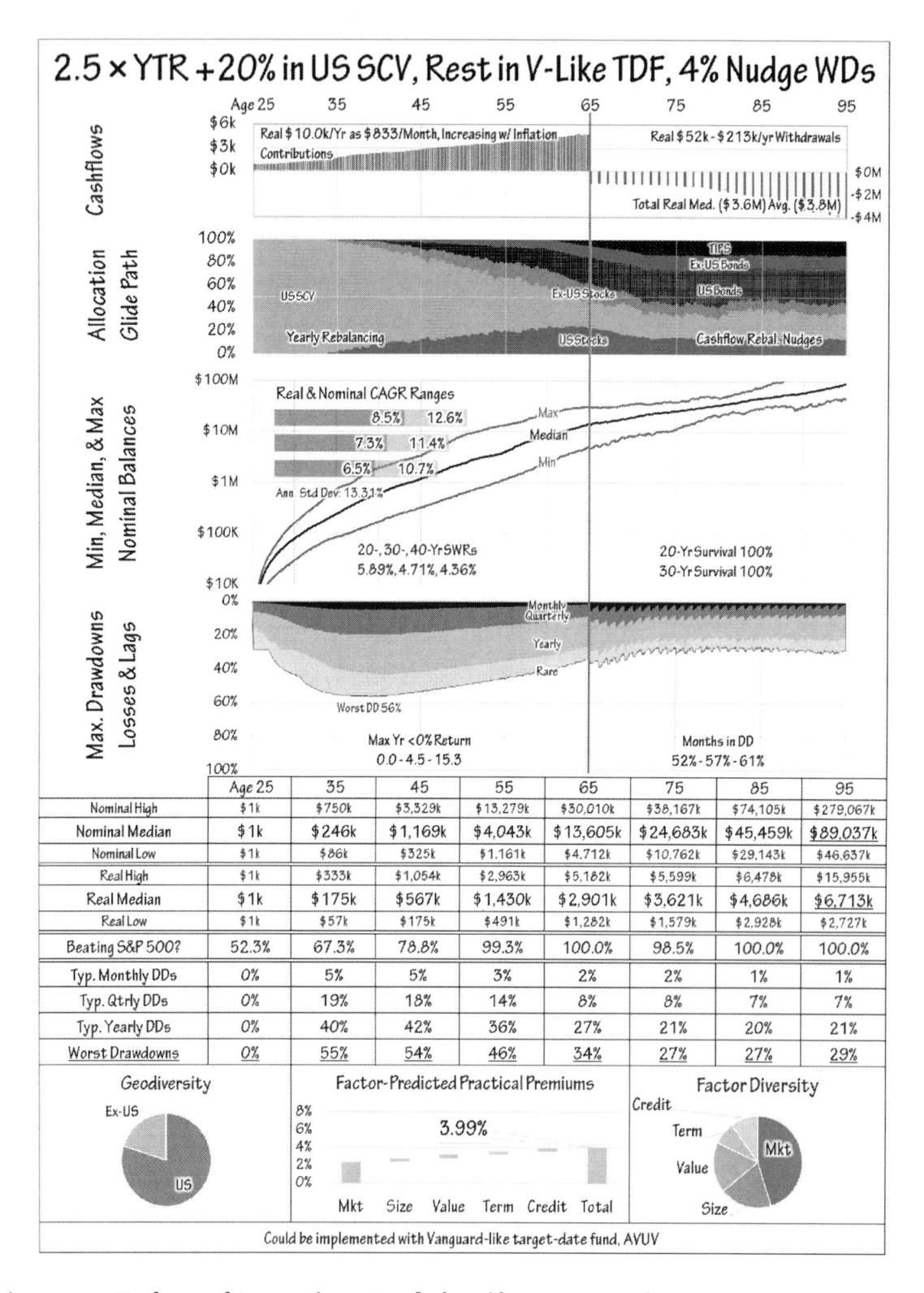

	Age 25	35	45	55	65	75	85	95
Nominal High	$1k	$750k	$3,329k	$13,279k	$30,010k	$38,167k	$74,105k	$279,067k
Nominal Median	$1k	$246k	$1,169k	$4,043k	$13,605k	$24,683k	$45,459k	$89,037k
Nominal Low	$1k	$86k	$325k	$1,161k	$4,712k	$10,762k	$29,143k	$46,637k
Real High	$1k	$333k	$1,054k	$2,963k	$5,182k	$5,599k	$6,478k	$15,955k
Real Median	$1k	$175k	$567k	$1,430k	$2,901k	$3,621k	$4,686k	$6,713k
Real Low	$1k	$57k	$175k	$491k	$1,282k	$1,579k	$2,928k	$2,727k
Beating S&P 500?	52.3%	67.3%	78.8%	99.3%	100.0%	98.5%	100.0%	100.0%
Typ. Monthly DDs	0%	5%	5%	3%	2%	2%	1%	1%
Typ. Qtrly DDs	0%	19%	18%	14%	8%	8%	7%	7%
Typ. Yearly DDs	0%	40%	42%	36%	27%	21%	20%	21%
Worst Drawdowns	0%	55%	54%	46%	34%	27%	27%	29%

Could be implemented with Vanguard-like target-date fund, AVUV

Figure 123. Backtest of Aggressive 2 Funds for Life strategy with annual rebalancing in accumulation and nudge rebalancing in retirement

APPENDIX 10: NUDGE WITHDRAWALS VS. REBALANCING

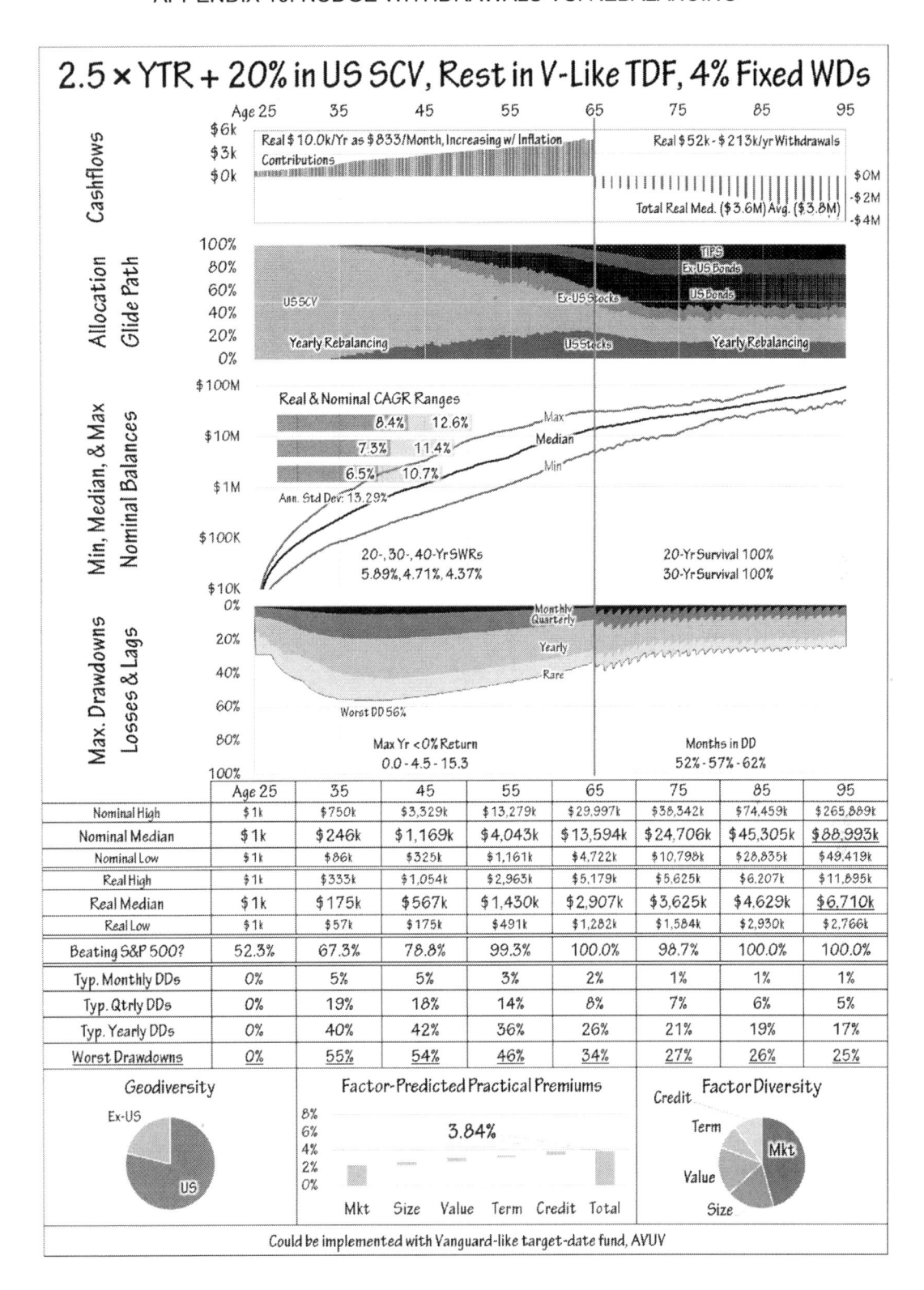

2.5 × YTR + 20% in US SCV, Rest in V-Like TDF, 4% Fixed WDs

	Age 25	35	45	55	65	75	85	95
Nominal High	$1k	$750k	$3,329k	$13,279k	$29,997k	$38,342k	$74,459k	$265,889k
Nominal Median	$1k	$246k	$1,169k	$4,043k	$13,594k	$24,706k	$45,305k	$88,993k
Nominal Low	$1k	$86k	$325k	$1,161k	$4,722k	$10,798k	$28,835k	$49,419k
Real High	$1k	$333k	$1,054k	$2,963k	$5,179k	$5,625k	$6,207k	$11,895k
Real Median	$1k	$175k	$567k	$1,430k	$2,907k	$3,625k	$4,629k	$6,710k
Real Low	$1k	$57k	$175k	$491k	$1,282k	$1,584k	$2,930k	$2,766k
Beating S&P 500?	52.3%	67.3%	78.8%	99.3%	100.0%	98.7%	100.0%	100.0%
Typ. Monthly DDs	0%	5%	5%	3%	2%	1%	1%	1%
Typ. Qtrly DDs	0%	19%	18%	14%	8%	7%	6%	5%
Typ. Yearly DDs	0%	40%	42%	36%	26%	21%	19%	17%
Worst Drawdowns	0%	55%	54%	46%	34%	27%	26%	25%

Could be implemented with Vanguard-like target-date fund, AVUV

Figure 124. Backtest of Aggressive 2 Funds for Life strategy with annual rebalancing in accumulation and annual rebalancing in retirement

Appendix 11
Changing an Existing Portfolio

What if you already have a hodgepodge portfolio? Maybe it's a collection of stocks. Maybe it's a collection of mutual funds or ETFs. If it's in a tax-deferred or tax-free account, there's no tax penalty for changing it to what you want. If it's in a taxable account, though, there could be tax consequences to selling. Before making a change, it's best to figure out how much the taxes will be and decide how long it will take to see the expected advantages of the change before you break even. If it's going to take a decade or more to see the new portfolio deliver enough of an advantage to pay for the cost of changing, just living with the existing portfolio might be the better option. Remember, even if there's an expected advantage, there's no guarantee you'll get it. Taxes are immediate and certain. Expected returns are delayed and uncertain.

Selling stocks or funds to change investing approaches in taxable accounts can trigger taxes, so investors should consider whether changes are worth the costs before proceeding.

There are no easy solutions to figuring this out, but there are two tools I've found useful in my own work: Morningstar's Instant X-Ray and Portfolio Visualizer's Monte Carlo Simulator.

If you set up a free account at Morningstar, you can enter your portfolio information and run an X-Ray to see how much of it is large, mid, small, value, blend, and growth. After running the analysis, you'll see how your portfolio is distributed on their 3×3 style boxes. (We described this framework in Chapter 5.) Ideally, you would do this analysis independently for the US, international developed, and emerging markets parts of your portfolio. You can then enter that information into a portfolio at Portfolio Visualizer as an asset allocation on their Monte Carlo Simulation page. You could also enter your holdings there. Either way, once you've entered the information at Portfolio Visualizer, you can run a Monte Carlo simulation to see a range of expected results over time and compare them to the tables in this book. If the result is a lot better than what you see here, you might want to stick with what you've got. If the result is a lot worse, then you have added motivation to change.

Everybody's circumstances are different, but our emotions and feelings are similar. It's easy to get excited about changing to a shiny new approach and to pursue it immediately. It's better to slow down a bit and consider the pros and cons in an unemotional data-driven way. If you do, I think you'll be more confident in the result and more willing to stick with it whether or not you decide to change.

Appendix 12
2 Funds for Life Yearly Allocation Tables

The following pages give the percentage allocations for the various 2 Funds for Life strategies described in this book. The left-hand Age column assumes that retirement will happen at age 65. If you plan to retire at a different age, the right-hand Years to-Retirement column may be more useful.

Age	1.5 X Years to Retirement		1.5 X YTR + 10%		1.5 X YTR + 20%		1.5 X YTR + 30%		Years to Ret.
	2nd Fund	TDF	2nd Fund	TDF	2nd Fund	TDF	2nd Fund	TDF	
20	67.5%	32.5%	77.5%	22.5%	87.5%	12.5%	97.5%	2.5%	45
21	66.0%	34.0%	76.0%	24.0%	86.0%	14.0%	96.0%	4.0%	44
22	64.5%	35.5%	74.5%	25.5%	84.5%	15.5%	94.5%	5.5%	43
23	63.0%	37.0%	73.0%	27.0%	83.0%	17.0%	93.0%	7.0%	42
24	61.5%	38.5%	71.5%	28.5%	81.5%	18.5%	91.5%	8.5%	41
25	60.0%	40.0%	70.0%	30.0%	80.0%	20.0%	90.0%	10.0%	40
26	58.5%	41.5%	68.5%	31.5%	78.5%	21.5%	88.5%	11.5%	39
27	57.0%	43.0%	67.0%	33.0%	77.0%	23.0%	87.0%	13.0%	38
28	55.5%	44.5%	65.5%	34.5%	75.5%	24.5%	85.5%	14.5%	37
29	54.0%	46.0%	64.0%	36.0%	74.0%	26.0%	84.0%	16.0%	36
30	52.5%	47.5%	62.5%	37.5%	72.5%	27.5%	82.5%	17.5%	35
31	51.0%	49.0%	61.0%	39.0%	71.0%	29.0%	81.0%	19.0%	34
32	49.5%	50.5%	59.5%	40.5%	69.5%	30.5%	79.5%	20.5%	33
33	48.0%	52.0%	58.0%	42.0%	68.0%	32.0%	78.0%	22.0%	32
34	46.5%	53.5%	56.5%	43.5%	66.5%	33.5%	76.5%	23.5%	31
35	45.0%	55.0%	55.0%	45.0%	65.0%	35.0%	75.0%	25.0%	30
36	43.5%	56.5%	53.5%	46.5%	63.5%	36.5%	73.5%	26.5%	29
37	42.0%	58.0%	52.0%	48.0%	62.0%	38.0%	72.0%	28.0%	28
38	40.5%	59.5%	50.5%	49.5%	60.5%	39.5%	70.5%	29.5%	27
39	39.0%	61.0%	49.0%	51.0%	59.0%	41.0%	69.0%	31.0%	26
40	37.5%	62.5%	47.5%	52.5%	57.5%	42.5%	67.5%	32.5%	25
41	36.0%	64.0%	46.0%	54.0%	56.0%	44.0%	66.0%	34.0%	24
42	34.5%	65.5%	44.5%	55.5%	54.5%	45.5%	64.5%	35.5%	23
43	33.0%	67.0%	43.0%	57.0%	53.0%	47.0%	63.0%	37.0%	22
44	31.5%	68.5%	41.5%	58.5%	51.5%	48.5%	61.5%	38.5%	21
45	30.0%	70.0%	40.0%	60.0%	50.0%	50.0%	60.0%	40.0%	20
46	28.5%	71.5%	38.5%	61.5%	48.5%	51.5%	58.5%	41.5%	19
47	27.0%	73.0%	37.0%	63.0%	47.0%	53.0%	57.0%	43.0%	18
48	25.5%	74.5%	35.5%	64.5%	45.5%	54.5%	55.5%	44.5%	17
49	24.0%	76.0%	34.0%	66.0%	44.0%	56.0%	54.0%	46.0%	16
50	22.5%	77.5%	32.5%	67.5%	42.5%	57.5%	52.5%	47.5%	15
51	21.0%	79.0%	31.0%	69.0%	41.0%	59.0%	51.0%	49.0%	14
52	19.5%	80.5%	29.5%	70.5%	39.5%	60.5%	49.5%	50.5%	13
53	18.0%	82.0%	28.0%	72.0%	38.0%	62.0%	48.0%	52.0%	12
54	16.5%	83.5%	26.5%	73.5%	36.5%	63.5%	46.5%	53.5%	11
55	15.0%	85.0%	25.0%	75.0%	35.0%	65.0%	45.0%	55.0%	10
56	13.5%	86.5%	23.5%	76.5%	33.5%	66.5%	43.5%	56.5%	9
57	12.0%	88.0%	22.0%	78.0%	32.0%	68.0%	42.0%	58.0%	8
58	10.5%	89.5%	20.5%	79.5%	30.5%	69.5%	40.5%	59.5%	7
59	9.0%	91.0%	19.0%	81.0%	29.0%	71.0%	39.0%	61.0%	6
60	7.5%	92.5%	17.5%	82.5%	27.5%	72.5%	37.5%	62.5%	5
61	6.0%	94.0%	16.0%	84.0%	26.0%	74.0%	36.0%	64.0%	4
62	4.5%	95.5%	14.5%	85.5%	24.5%	75.5%	34.5%	65.5%	3
63	3.0%	97.0%	13.0%	87.0%	23.0%	77.0%	33.0%	67.0%	2
64	1.5%	98.5%	11.5%	88.5%	21.5%	78.5%	31.5%	68.5%	1
65	0.0%	100.0%	10.0%	90.0%	20.0%	80.0%	30.0%	70.0%	0
66	0.0%	100.0%	10.0%	90.0%	20.0%	80.0%	30.0%	70.0%	-1
67	0.0%	100.0%	10.0%	90.0%	20.0%	80.0%	30.0%	70.0%	-2
68	0.0%	100.0%	10.0%	90.0%	20.0%	80.0%	30.0%	70.0%	-3
69	0.0%	100.0%	10.0%	90.0%	20.0%	80.0%	30.0%	70.0%	-4
70	0.0%	100.0%	10.0%	90.0%	20.0%	80.0%	30.0%	70.0%	-5

Table 21. 2 Funds for Life allocations for 1.5 × multiplier

APPENDIX 12: 2 FUNDS FOR LIFE YEARLY ALLOCATION TABLES

Age	2 X Years to Retirement		2 X YTR + 10%		2 X YTR + 20%		2 X YTR + 30%		Years to Ret.
	2nd Fund	TDF	2nd Fund	TDF	2nd Fund	TDF	2nd Fund	TDF	
20	90.0%	10.0%	100.0%	0.0%	100.0%	0.0%	100.0%	0.0%	45
21	88.0%	12.0%	98.0%	2.0%	100.0%	0.0%	100.0%	0.0%	44
22	86.0%	14.0%	96.0%	4.0%	100.0%	0.0%	100.0%	0.0%	43
23	84.0%	16.0%	94.0%	6.0%	100.0%	0.0%	100.0%	0.0%	42
24	82.0%	18.0%	92.0%	8.0%	100.0%	0.0%	100.0%	0.0%	41
25	80.0%	20.0%	90.0%	10.0%	100.0%	0.0%	100.0%	0.0%	40
26	78.0%	22.0%	88.0%	12.0%	98.0%	2.0%	100.0%	0.0%	39
27	76.0%	24.0%	86.0%	14.0%	96.0%	4.0%	100.0%	0.0%	38
28	74.0%	26.0%	84.0%	16.0%	94.0%	6.0%	100.0%	0.0%	37
29	72.0%	28.0%	82.0%	18.0%	92.0%	8.0%	100.0%	0.0%	36
30	70.0%	30.0%	80.0%	20.0%	90.0%	10.0%	100.0%	0.0%	35
31	68.0%	32.0%	78.0%	22.0%	88.0%	12.0%	98.0%	2.0%	34
32	66.0%	34.0%	76.0%	24.0%	86.0%	14.0%	96.0%	4.0%	33
33	64.0%	36.0%	74.0%	26.0%	84.0%	16.0%	94.0%	6.0%	32
34	62.0%	38.0%	72.0%	28.0%	82.0%	18.0%	92.0%	8.0%	31
35	60.0%	40.0%	70.0%	30.0%	80.0%	20.0%	90.0%	10.0%	30
36	58.0%	42.0%	68.0%	32.0%	78.0%	22.0%	88.0%	12.0%	29
37	56.0%	44.0%	66.0%	34.0%	76.0%	24.0%	86.0%	14.0%	28
38	54.0%	46.0%	64.0%	36.0%	74.0%	26.0%	84.0%	16.0%	27
39	52.0%	48.0%	62.0%	38.0%	72.0%	28.0%	82.0%	18.0%	26
40	50.0%	50.0%	60.0%	40.0%	70.0%	30.0%	80.0%	20.0%	25
41	48.0%	52.0%	58.0%	42.0%	68.0%	32.0%	78.0%	22.0%	24
42	46.0%	54.0%	56.0%	44.0%	66.0%	34.0%	76.0%	24.0%	23
43	44.0%	56.0%	54.0%	46.0%	64.0%	36.0%	74.0%	26.0%	22
44	42.0%	58.0%	52.0%	48.0%	62.0%	38.0%	72.0%	28.0%	21
45	40.0%	60.0%	50.0%	50.0%	60.0%	40.0%	70.0%	30.0%	20
46	38.0%	62.0%	48.0%	52.0%	58.0%	42.0%	68.0%	32.0%	19
47	36.0%	64.0%	46.0%	54.0%	56.0%	44.0%	66.0%	34.0%	18
48	34.0%	66.0%	44.0%	56.0%	54.0%	46.0%	64.0%	36.0%	17
49	32.0%	68.0%	42.0%	58.0%	52.0%	48.0%	62.0%	38.0%	16
50	30.0%	70.0%	40.0%	60.0%	50.0%	50.0%	60.0%	40.0%	15
51	28.0%	72.0%	38.0%	62.0%	48.0%	52.0%	58.0%	42.0%	14
52	26.0%	74.0%	36.0%	64.0%	46.0%	54.0%	56.0%	44.0%	13
53	24.0%	76.0%	34.0%	66.0%	44.0%	56.0%	54.0%	46.0%	12
54	22.0%	78.0%	32.0%	68.0%	42.0%	58.0%	52.0%	48.0%	11
55	20.0%	80.0%	30.0%	70.0%	40.0%	60.0%	50.0%	50.0%	10
56	18.0%	82.0%	28.0%	72.0%	38.0%	62.0%	48.0%	52.0%	9
57	16.0%	84.0%	26.0%	74.0%	36.0%	64.0%	46.0%	54.0%	8
58	14.0%	86.0%	24.0%	76.0%	34.0%	66.0%	44.0%	56.0%	7
59	12.0%	88.0%	22.0%	78.0%	32.0%	68.0%	42.0%	58.0%	6
60	10.0%	90.0%	20.0%	80.0%	30.0%	70.0%	40.0%	60.0%	5
61	8.0%	92.0%	18.0%	82.0%	28.0%	72.0%	38.0%	62.0%	4
62	6.0%	94.0%	16.0%	84.0%	26.0%	74.0%	36.0%	64.0%	3
63	4.0%	96.0%	14.0%	86.0%	24.0%	76.0%	34.0%	66.0%	2
64	2.0%	98.0%	12.0%	88.0%	22.0%	78.0%	32.0%	68.0%	1
65	0.0%	100.0%	10.0%	90.0%	20.0%	80.0%	30.0%	70.0%	0
66	0.0%	100.0%	10.0%	90.0%	20.0%	80.0%	30.0%	70.0%	-1
67	0.0%	100.0%	10.0%	90.0%	20.0%	80.0%	30.0%	70.0%	-2
68	0.0%	100.0%	10.0%	90.0%	20.0%	80.0%	30.0%	70.0%	-3
69	0.0%	100.0%	10.0%	90.0%	20.0%	80.0%	30.0%	70.0%	-4
70	0.0%	100.0%	10.0%	90.0%	20.0%	80.0%	30.0%	70.0%	-5

Table 22. 2 Funds for Life allocations for 2.0 × multiplier

Age	2.5 X Years to Retirement		2.5 X YTR + 10%		2.5 X YTR + 20%		2.5 X YTR + 30%		Years to Ret.
	2nd Fund	TDF	2nd Fund	TDF	2nd Fund	TDF	2nd Fund	TDF	
20	100.0%	0.0%	100.0%	0.0%	100.0%	0.0%	100.0%	0.0%	45
21	100.0%	0.0%	100.0%	0.0%	100.0%	0.0%	100.0%	0.0%	44
22	100.0%	0.0%	100.0%	0.0%	100.0%	0.0%	100.0%	0.0%	43
23	100.0%	0.0%	100.0%	0.0%	100.0%	0.0%	100.0%	0.0%	42
24	100.0%	0.0%	100.0%	0.0%	100.0%	0.0%	100.0%	0.0%	41
25	100.0%	0.0%	100.0%	0.0%	100.0%	0.0%	100.0%	0.0%	40
26	97.5%	2.5%	100.0%	0.0%	100.0%	0.0%	100.0%	0.0%	39
27	95.0%	5.0%	100.0%	0.0%	100.0%	0.0%	100.0%	0.0%	38
28	92.5%	7.5%	100.0%	0.0%	100.0%	0.0%	100.0%	0.0%	37
29	90.0%	10.0%	100.0%	0.0%	100.0%	0.0%	100.0%	0.0%	36
30	87.5%	12.5%	97.5%	2.5%	100.0%	0.0%	100.0%	0.0%	35
31	85.0%	15.0%	95.0%	5.0%	100.0%	0.0%	100.0%	0.0%	34
32	82.5%	17.5%	92.5%	7.5%	100.0%	0.0%	100.0%	0.0%	33
33	80.0%	20.0%	90.0%	10.0%	100.0%	0.0%	100.0%	0.0%	32
34	77.5%	22.5%	87.5%	12.5%	97.5%	2.5%	100.0%	0.0%	31
35	75.0%	25.0%	85.0%	15.0%	95.0%	5.0%	100.0%	0.0%	30
36	72.5%	27.5%	82.5%	17.5%	92.5%	7.5%	100.0%	0.0%	29
37	70.0%	30.0%	80.0%	20.0%	90.0%	10.0%	100.0%	0.0%	28
38	67.5%	32.5%	77.5%	22.5%	87.5%	12.5%	97.5%	2.5%	27
39	65.0%	35.0%	75.0%	25.0%	85.0%	15.0%	95.0%	5.0%	26
40	62.5%	37.5%	72.5%	27.5%	82.5%	17.5%	92.5%	7.5%	25
41	60.0%	40.0%	70.0%	30.0%	80.0%	20.0%	90.0%	10.0%	24
42	57.5%	42.5%	67.5%	32.5%	77.5%	22.5%	87.5%	12.5%	23
43	55.0%	45.0%	65.0%	35.0%	75.0%	25.0%	85.0%	15.0%	22
44	52.5%	47.5%	62.5%	37.5%	72.5%	27.5%	82.5%	17.5%	21
45	50.0%	50.0%	60.0%	40.0%	70.0%	30.0%	80.0%	20.0%	20
46	47.5%	52.5%	57.5%	42.5%	67.5%	32.5%	77.5%	22.5%	19
47	45.0%	55.0%	55.0%	45.0%	65.0%	35.0%	75.0%	25.0%	18
48	42.5%	57.5%	52.5%	47.5%	62.5%	37.5%	72.5%	27.5%	17
49	40.0%	60.0%	50.0%	50.0%	60.0%	40.0%	70.0%	30.0%	16
50	37.5%	62.5%	47.5%	52.5%	57.5%	42.5%	67.5%	32.5%	15
51	35.0%	65.0%	45.0%	55.0%	55.0%	45.0%	65.0%	35.0%	14
52	32.5%	67.5%	42.5%	57.5%	52.5%	47.5%	62.5%	37.5%	13
53	30.0%	70.0%	40.0%	60.0%	50.0%	50.0%	60.0%	40.0%	12
54	27.5%	72.5%	37.5%	62.5%	47.5%	52.5%	57.5%	42.5%	11
55	25.0%	75.0%	35.0%	65.0%	45.0%	55.0%	55.0%	45.0%	10
56	22.5%	77.5%	32.5%	67.5%	42.5%	57.5%	52.5%	47.5%	9
57	20.0%	80.0%	30.0%	70.0%	40.0%	60.0%	50.0%	50.0%	8
58	17.5%	82.5%	27.5%	72.5%	37.5%	62.5%	47.5%	52.5%	7
59	15.0%	85.0%	25.0%	75.0%	35.0%	65.0%	45.0%	55.0%	6
60	12.5%	87.5%	22.5%	77.5%	32.5%	67.5%	42.5%	57.5%	5
61	10.0%	90.0%	20.0%	80.0%	30.0%	70.0%	40.0%	60.0%	4
62	7.5%	92.5%	17.5%	82.5%	27.5%	72.5%	37.5%	62.5%	3
63	5.0%	95.0%	15.0%	85.0%	25.0%	75.0%	35.0%	65.0%	2
64	2.5%	97.5%	12.5%	87.5%	22.5%	77.5%	32.5%	67.5%	1
65	0.0%	100.0%	10.0%	90.0%	20.0%	80.0%	30.0%	70.0%	0
66	0.0%	100.0%	10.0%	90.0%	20.0%	80.0%	30.0%	70.0%	-1
67	0.0%	100.0%	10.0%	90.0%	20.0%	80.0%	30.0%	70.0%	-2
68	0.0%	100.0%	10.0%	90.0%	20.0%	80.0%	30.0%	70.0%	-3
69	0.0%	100.0%	10.0%	90.0%	20.0%	80.0%	30.0%	70.0%	-4
70	0.0%	100.0%	10.0%	90.0%	20.0%	80.0%	30.0%	70.0%	-5

Table 23. 2 Funds for Life allocations for 2.5 × multiplier

APPENDIX 12: 2 FUNDS FOR LIFE YEARLY ALLOCATION TABLES

Age	3 X Years to Retirement		3X YTR + 10%		3 X YTR + 20%		3 X YTR + 30%		Years to Ret.
	2nd Fund	TDF	2nd Fund	TDF	2nd Fund	TDF	2nd Fund	TDF	
20	100.0%	0.0%	100.0%	0.0%	100.0%	0.0%	100.0%	0.0%	45
21	100.0%	0.0%	100.0%	0.0%	100.0%	0.0%	100.0%	0.0%	44
22	100.0%	0.0%	100.0%	0.0%	100.0%	0.0%	100.0%	0.0%	43
23	100.0%	0.0%	100.0%	0.0%	100.0%	0.0%	100.0%	0.0%	42
24	100.0%	0.0%	100.0%	0.0%	100.0%	0.0%	100.0%	0.0%	41
25	100.0%	0.0%	100.0%	0.0%	100.0%	0.0%	100.0%	0.0%	40
26	100.0%	0.0%	100.0%	0.0%	100.0%	0.0%	100.0%	0.0%	39
27	100.0%	0.0%	100.0%	0.0%	100.0%	0.0%	100.0%	0.0%	38
28	100.0%	0.0%	100.0%	0.0%	100.0%	0.0%	100.0%	0.0%	37
29	100.0%	0.0%	100.0%	0.0%	100.0%	0.0%	100.0%	0.0%	36
30	100.0%	0.0%	100.0%	0.0%	100.0%	0.0%	100.0%	0.0%	35
31	100.0%	0.0%	100.0%	0.0%	100.0%	0.0%	100.0%	0.0%	34
32	99.0%	1.0%	100.0%	0.0%	100.0%	0.0%	100.0%	0.0%	33
33	96.0%	4.0%	100.0%	0.0%	100.0%	0.0%	100.0%	0.0%	32
34	93.0%	7.0%	100.0%	0.0%	100.0%	0.0%	100.0%	0.0%	31
35	90.0%	10.0%	100.0%	0.0%	100.0%	0.0%	100.0%	0.0%	30
36	87.0%	13.0%	97.0%	3.0%	100.0%	0.0%	100.0%	0.0%	29
37	84.0%	16.0%	94.0%	6.0%	100.0%	0.0%	100.0%	0.0%	28
38	81.0%	19.0%	91.0%	9.0%	100.0%	0.0%	100.0%	0.0%	27
39	78.0%	22.0%	88.0%	12.0%	98.0%	2.0%	100.0%	0.0%	26
40	75.0%	25.0%	85.0%	15.0%	95.0%	5.0%	100.0%	0.0%	25
41	72.0%	28.0%	82.0%	18.0%	92.0%	8.0%	100.0%	0.0%	24
42	69.0%	31.0%	79.0%	21.0%	89.0%	11.0%	99.0%	1.0%	23
43	66.0%	34.0%	76.0%	24.0%	86.0%	14.0%	96.0%	4.0%	22
44	63.0%	37.0%	73.0%	27.0%	83.0%	17.0%	93.0%	7.0%	21
45	60.0%	40.0%	70.0%	30.0%	80.0%	20.0%	90.0%	10.0%	20
46	57.0%	43.0%	67.0%	33.0%	77.0%	23.0%	87.0%	13.0%	19
47	54.0%	46.0%	64.0%	36.0%	74.0%	26.0%	84.0%	16.0%	18
48	51.0%	49.0%	61.0%	39.0%	71.0%	29.0%	81.0%	19.0%	17
49	48.0%	52.0%	58.0%	42.0%	68.0%	32.0%	78.0%	22.0%	16
50	45.0%	55.0%	55.0%	45.0%	65.0%	35.0%	75.0%	25.0%	15
51	42.0%	58.0%	52.0%	48.0%	62.0%	38.0%	72.0%	28.0%	14
52	39.0%	61.0%	49.0%	51.0%	59.0%	41.0%	69.0%	31.0%	13
53	36.0%	64.0%	46.0%	54.0%	56.0%	44.0%	66.0%	34.0%	12
54	33.0%	67.0%	43.0%	57.0%	53.0%	47.0%	63.0%	37.0%	11
55	30.0%	70.0%	40.0%	60.0%	50.0%	50.0%	60.0%	40.0%	10
56	27.0%	73.0%	37.0%	63.0%	47.0%	53.0%	57.0%	43.0%	9
57	24.0%	76.0%	34.0%	66.0%	44.0%	56.0%	54.0%	46.0%	8
58	21.0%	79.0%	31.0%	69.0%	41.0%	59.0%	51.0%	49.0%	7
59	18.0%	82.0%	28.0%	72.0%	38.0%	62.0%	48.0%	52.0%	6
60	15.0%	85.0%	25.0%	75.0%	35.0%	65.0%	45.0%	55.0%	5
61	12.0%	88.0%	22.0%	78.0%	32.0%	68.0%	42.0%	58.0%	4
62	9.0%	91.0%	19.0%	81.0%	29.0%	71.0%	39.0%	61.0%	3
63	6.0%	94.0%	16.0%	84.0%	26.0%	74.0%	36.0%	64.0%	2
64	3.0%	97.0%	13.0%	87.0%	23.0%	77.0%	33.0%	67.0%	1
65	0.0%	100.0%	10.0%	90.0%	20.0%	80.0%	30.0%	70.0%	0
66	0.0%	100.0%	10.0%	90.0%	20.0%	80.0%	30.0%	70.0%	-1
67	0.0%	100.0%	10.0%	90.0%	20.0%	80.0%	30.0%	70.0%	-2
68	0.0%	100.0%	10.0%	90.0%	20.0%	80.0%	30.0%	70.0%	-3
69	0.0%	100.0%	10.0%	90.0%	20.0%	80.0%	30.0%	70.0%	-4
70	0.0%	100.0%	10.0%	90.0%	20.0%	80.0%	30.0%	70.0%	-5

Table 24. 2 Funds for Life allocations for 3.0 × multiplier

List of Figures

Figure 1. Target-date fund and 2 Funds for Life strategies risk and reward

Figure 2. 2 Funds for Life strategy glide paths

Figure 3. Backtest of the Buffett strategy

Figure 4. Cashflow graph from Buffett strategy backtest

Figure 5. Allocation glide path from Buffett strategy backtest

Figure 6. Growth, CAGR, SWR, Survival Rate graph from Buffett strategy backtest

Figure 7. Drawdown graph from Buffett strategy backtest example

Figure 8. Number tables from Buffett strategy backtest example

Figure 9. Diversification charts from Buffett strategy backtest example

Figure 10. Backtest of Vanguard-like target-date fund

Figure 11. US total stocks and total bonds over one, five, and 15 years

Figure 12. Backtest of US Total Bond Market

Figure 13. Backtest of US Total Stock Market

Figure 14. Number of US ETF and mutual funds with >30% factor exposure to various factor combinations

Figure 15. Backtest of US small-cap value

Figure 16. Approximate relative size of US, Developed Ex-US International, and Emerging Markets (1900-2020)

Figure 17. Recent and expected returns by geography (source: RAFI, 1/16/2021)

Figure 18. Backtest of US Total Stock Market

Figure 19. Backtest of Worldwide Total Stock Market

Figure 20. Backtest of Emerging Markets

Figure 21. Risk and reward versus a mix of S&P 500 and intermediate-term US government bonds

Figure 22. Risk and reward from intermediate-term US government bonds to S&P 500 to US small-cap value

Figure 23. Risk and reward versus a mix of intermediate-term US government bonds, S&P 500, and US small-cap value

Figure 24. Relative growth of US small-cap value vs. the S&P 500 from 1928 through 2019

Figure 25. Risk and reward versus a mix of the US and ex-US Total Stock Market

Figure 26. Financial risk tolerance changes with age and circumstances.

Figure 27. Vanguard target retirement glide path

Figure 28. Worst drawdowns for lump-sum and monthly investing in Vanguard-like target-date fund (1970-2019)

Figure 29. Worldwide Total Stock Market drawdowns for lump-sum and monthly investments (1970-2019)

Figure 30. Backtest of Easy 2 Funds for Life strategy

Figure 31. Moderate 2 Funds for Life glide path

Figure 32. Backtest of Moderate 2 Funds for Life strategy

Figure 33. Easy, Moderate, and Aggressive 2 Funds for Life glide paths

Figure 34. Backtest of Aggressive 2 Funds for Life strategy

Figure 35. Backtest of Easy 2 Funds for Life strategy using a combination of US and international small-cap value

Figure 36. Backtest of Moderate 2 Funds for Life strategy using a combination of US and international small-cap value

Figure 37. Backtest of Aggressive 2 Funds for Life strategy using a combination of US and international small-cap value

Figure 38. Backtest of Easy 2 Funds for Life strategy using only international small-cap value for the second fund

Figure 39. Backtest of Moderate 2 Funds for Life strategy using only international small-cap value for the second fund

LIST OF FIGURES

Figure 40. Backtest of Aggressive 2 Funds for Life strategy using only international small-cap value for the second fund

Figure 41. Merriman Aggressive Target-Date Portfolio asset allocation

Figure 42. Comparison of Ultimate Buy-and-Hold, All-Value, and 3-Fund (US SCV, Int'l SCV, US IT Bonds) portfolios

Figure 43. Factor diversification pies from backtests of Ultimate Buy-and-Hold, All-Value, and 3-Fund portfolios

Figure 44. Backtest of 50% equities Ultimate Buy-and-Hold portfolio

Figure 45. Backtest of 37% equities 3-Fund (US & Int'l SCV, US IT Govt. Bonds) portfolio

Figure 46. Backtest of 70% equities Ultimate Buy-and-Hold portfolio

Figure 47. Backtest of 49% equities 3-Fund (US & Int'l SCV, US IT Govt. Bonds) portfolio

Figure 48. Backtest of 100% equities Ultimate Buy-and-Hold portfolio

Figure 49. Backtest of 65% equities 3-Fund (US & Int'l SCV, US IT Govt. Bonds) portfolio

Figure 50. Backtest of 50% equities Worldwide All-Value portfolio

Figure 51. Backtest of 41% equities 3-Fund (US & Int'l SCV, US IT Govt. Bonds) portfolio

Figure 52. Backtest of 70% equities Worldwide All-Value portfolio

Figure 53. Backtest of 56% equities 3-Fund (US & Int'l SCV, US IT Govt. Bonds) portfolio

Figure 54. Backtest of 100% equities Worldwide All-Value portfolio

Figure 55. Backtest of 77% equities 3-Fund (US & Int'l SCV, US IT Govt. Bonds) portfolio

Figure 56. Backtest of Merriman Aggressive Target-Date Glide Path

Figure 57. Backtest of Aggressive 2 Funds for Life strategy

Figure 58. Backtest of Aggressive 2 Funds for Life strategy using US and international small-cap value

Figure 59. Backtest of Buffett strategy with a surprise, early, age 55 retirement

Figure 60. Backtest of Vanguard-like target-date fund with a surprise, early, age 55 retirement

Figure 61. Backtest of Easy 2 Funds for Life strategy with a surprise, early, age 55 retirement

Figure 62. Backtest of Moderate 2 Funds for Life strategy with a surprise, early, age 55 retirement

Figure 63. Backtest of Aggressive 2 Funds for Life strategy with a surprise, early, age 55 retirement and only nudge rebalancing

Figure 64. Backtest of Aggressive 2 Funds for Life strategy with a surprise, early, age 55 retirement, one rebalance at 55, then nudge withdrawals thereafter

Figure 65. Inferred distributions of total real withdrawals and end balances for Vanguard-like target-date fund and Easy, Moderate, and Aggressive 2 Funds for Life strategies

Figure 66. Risk and reward versus a mix of intermediate-term US government bonds, S&P 500, and US small-cap-value using 1928-2019 historical returns

Figure 67. Alternative 2 Funds for Life strategies summary including safe withdrawal rates, total withdrawals, end balances, and maximum drawdowns at age 40, 65, and 95

Figure 68. Backtest for Vanguard-like target-date fund

Figure 69. Backtest for 10% minimum, 0 × YTR, Easy 2 Funds for Life strategy

Figure 70. Backtest for 20% minimum, 0 × YTR, 2 Funds for Life strategy

Figure 71. Backtest for 30% minimum, 0 × YTR, 2 Funds for Life strategy

Figure 72. Backtest for 0% minimum, 1.5 × YTR, Moderate 2 Funds for Life strategy

Figure 73. Backtest for 10% minimum, 1.5 × YTR, 2 Funds for Life strategy

LIST OF FIGURES

Figure 74. Backtest for 20% minimum, 1.5 × YTR, 2 Funds for Life strategy

Figure 75. Backtest for 30% minimum, 1.5 × YTR, 2 Funds for Life strategy

Figure 76. Backtest for 0% minimum, 2.0 × YTR, 2 Funds for Life strategy

Figure 77. Backtest for 10% minimum, 2.0 × YTR, 2 Funds for Life strategy

Figure 78. Backtest for 20% minimum, 2.0 × YTR, 2 Funds for Life strategy

Figure 79. Backtest for 30% minimum, 2.0 × YTR, 2 Funds for Life strategy

Figure 80. Backtest for 0% minimum, 2.5 × YTR, 2 Funds for Life strategy

Figure 81. Backtest for 10% minimum, 2.5 × YTR, 2 Funds for Life strategy

Figure 82. Backtest for 20% minimum, 2.5 × YTR, 2 Funds for Life strategy

Figure 83. Backtest for 30% minimum, 2.5 × YTR, 2 Funds for Life strategy

Figure 84. Backtest for 0% minimum, 3.0 × YTR, 2 Funds for Life strategy

Figure 85. Backtest for 10% minimum, 3.0 × YTR, 2 Funds for Life strategy

Figure 86. Backtest for 20% minimum, 3.0 × YTR, 2 Funds for Life strategy

Figure 87. Backtest for 30% minimum, 3.0 × YTR, 2 Funds for Life strategy

Figure 88. Backtest of Easy 2 Funds for Life strategy using US small-cap blend instead of US small-cap value

Figure 89. Backtest of Easy 2 Funds for Life strategy using US small-cap value

Figure 90. Backtest of Moderate 2 Funds for Life strategy using US small-cap blend instead of US small-cap value

Figure 91. Backtest of Moderate 2 Funds for Life strategy using US small-cap value

Figure 92. Backtest of Aggressive 2 Funds for Life strategy using US small-cap blend instead of US small-cap value

Figure 93. Backtest of Aggressive 2 Funds for Life strategy using US small-cap value

Figure 94. Backtest of Easy 2 Funds for Life strategy using US large-cap value instead of US small-cap value

Figure 95. Backtest of Easy 2 Funds for Life strategy using US small-cap value

Figure 96. Backtest of Moderate 2 Funds for Life strategy using US large-cap value instead of US small-cap value

Figure 97. Backtest of Moderate 2 Funds for Life strategy using US small-cap value

Figure 98. Backtest of Aggressive 2 Funds for Life strategy using US large-cap value instead of US small-cap value

Figure 99. Backtest of Aggressive 2 Funds for Life strategy using US small-cap value

Figure 100. Recommended 2021 Best-in-Class ETFs and alternatives

Figure 101. Overlap of target-date and small-cap value funds

Figure 102. Backtest of five years early Vanguard-like target-date fund

Figure 103. Backtest of on-time Vanguard-like target-date fund

Figure 104. Backtest of five years late Vanguard-like target-date fund

Figure 105. Backtest of five years early Aggressive 2 Funds for Life strategy

Figure 106. Backtest of on-time Aggressive 2 Funds for Life strategy

Figure 107. Backtest of five years late Aggressive 2 Funds for Life strategy

Figure 108. Backtest of Buffett strategy using 1970-2019 returns

Figure 109. Backtest of Buffett strategy using 1928-2019 returns

Figure 110. Backtest of Vanguard-like target-date fund using 1970-2019 returns

Figure 111. Backtest of Vanguard-like target-date fund using 1928-2019 returns

Figure 112. Backtest of Easy 2 Funds for Life strategy using 1970-2019 returns

Figure 113. Backtest of Easy 2 Funds for Life strategy using 1928-2019 returns

Figure 114. Backtest of Moderate 2 Funds for Life strategy using 1970-2019 returns

Figure 115. Backtest of Moderate 2 Funds for Life strategy using 1928-2019 returns

Figure 116. Backtest of Aggressive 2 Funds for Life strategy using 1970-2019 returns

LIST OF FIGURES

Figure 117. Backtest of Aggressive 2 Funds for Life strategy using 1928-2019 returns

Figure 118. Worst drawdowns for lump-sum, yearly, quarterly, and monthly contributions to a Vanguard-like target-date fund

Figure 119. Backtest of Easy 2 Funds for Life strategy with no rebalancing in accumulation and nudge rebalancing in retirement

Figure 120. Backtest of Easy 2 Funds for Life strategy with no rebalancing in accumulation and annual rebalancing in retirement

Figure 121. Backtest of Easy 2 Funds for Life strategy with annual rebalancing in accumulation and nudge rebalancing in retirement

Figure 122. Backtest of Easy 2 Funds for Life strategy with annual rebalancing in accumulation and annual rebalancing in retirement

Figure 123. Backtest of Aggressive 2 Funds for Life strategy with annual rebalancing in accumulation and nudge rebalancing in retirement

Figure 124. Backtest of Aggressive 2 Funds for Life strategy with annual rebalancing in accumulation and annual rebalancing in retirement

List of Tables

Table 1. Savings rates required so retirement withdrawals match preretirement spending

Table 2. Savings rates required so retirement withdrawals match preretirement spending less 33% for Social Security

Table 3. Morningstar style box method of dividing US stock market

Table 4. US Stock market style boxes with CAGRs and drawdowns (January 1972–February 2021)

Table 5. Example expense ratios and relative fund selection for US and international funds

Table 6. Return and risk measures for US and international funds

Table 7. Comparison of Buffett strategy, Vanguard-like target-date fund, and easy 2 Funds for Life strategies

Table 8. Comparison of Buffett strategy, Vanguard-like target-date fund, Easy 2 Funds for Life, and Moderate 2 Funds for Life strategies

Table 9. Comparison of Buffett strategy; Vanguard-like target-date fund; Easy, Moderate, and Aggressive 2 Funds for Life strategies

Table 10. Comparison of 2 Funds for Life strategies utilizing US small-cap value versus a combination of US and international small-cap value for the second fund

Table 11. Comparison of 2 Funds for Life strategies utilizing US small-cap value versus international small-cap value for the second fund

Table 12. Complex portfolio asset allocations

Table 13. Surprise early retirement comparison of Buffett strategy, Vanguard-like target-date fund, and 2 Funds for Life strategies with and without at-retirement rebalancing

Table 14. Comparison of 2 Funds for Life strategies using US small-cap blend instead of US small-cap value

Table 15. Comparison of 2 Funds for Life strategies using US large-cap value instead of US small-cap value

Table 16. Moderate 2 Funds for Life data table from the backtest

Table 17. Comparison of early, on time, and late target-date fund backtest results

Table 18. Comparison of 1970-2019 and 1928-2019 backtests of Buffett strategy; Vanguard-like target-date fund; Easy, Moderate, and Aggressive 2 Funds for Life strategies

Table 19. Backtest return sources, gaps, and expense-ratio assumptions

Table 20. Comparison of nudge withdrawals versus annual rebalancing for 2 Funds for Life strategies

Table 21. 2 Funds for Life allocations for 1.5 × multiplier

Table 22. 2 Funds for Life allocations for 2.0 × multiplier

Table 23. 2 Funds for Life allocations for 2.5 × multiplier

Table 24. 2 Funds for Life allocations for 3.0 × multiplier

Glossary

asset — Something useful or valuable. The things we invest in that are likely to provide future financial benefits and security, such as stocks and bonds, are assets.

backtesting — The process of looking at how an investing approach would have worked in the past by applying historical return sequences to a proposed asset allocation and set of cashflow assumptions.

Buffett Strategy — The simple investing approach Warren Buffett described as instructions for his wife's estate trustee in his 2013 letter to Berkshire Hathaway shareholders: "My advice to the trustee could not be more simple: Put 10% of the cash in short-term government bonds and 90% in a very low-cost S&P 500 index fund. (I suggest Vanguard's.)"

capitalization-weighted or cap-weighted — Refers to a method of investing in which the weight or percentage any single company represents in a portfolio fluctuates with its total market capitalization (outstanding shares times price). Most of the time, this means if you have 10 stocks in a portfolio and one of them doubles in price while the others stay the same, that stock will double its share of the portfolio.

cashflow rebalance nudges — A simple alternative to traditional rebalancing in which contributions or withdrawals are used to nudge allocations back in the direction they should go. For contributions, the entire contribution would go to the fund that is below its target allocation. For withdrawals, the entire withdrawal would come from the fund that is above its target allocation. (*See also* nudge rebalancing.)

circular bootstrapping — A method used in backtesting to expand the number of return sequences that can be tested by looping from the most recent available return to the oldest available return when necessary.

compound annual growth rate (CAGR) — This is the amount an investment would have to grow steadily every year, with profits reinvested at the end of each year, to produce a particular return. The CAGR provides a fair and meaningful way to compare real-world investments whose growth is not steady by calculating a steady equivalent growth rate.

dividends — A portion of a company's profits that are paid out to investors regularly. Investors in many stocks and most equity funds will receive periodic dividend distributions. The backtests in this book assume those dividends are reinvested. Most investors will be able to set that up to happen automatically in their brokerage accounts.

drawdown (DD) — The peak-to-trough decline of an investment or portfolio during a downturn. If an account with $10,000 drops to $9,000 before going back to $10,000, it is said to have had a 10% drawdown (the $1,000 drop was 10% of $10,000). Drawdowns help characterize the historical risk of different investing approaches.

equities — The same thing as stocks, which are partial ownership of a company.

exchange-traded fund (ETF) —Similar to a mutual fund (*see also* mutual fund) but can be purchased or sold on a stock exchange just like a regular stock. ETFs are often used to purchase a basket of stocks or bonds that follow an index, such as the S&P 500, or systematically defined market segments, such as small-cap value. They tend to be more tax-efficient than mutual funds but also have some disadvantages, such as the bid-ask-spread and only trading in whole shares at some brokerages.

ex-US — Used to describe funds that invest in a wide range of markets outside of the US. Typically, this includes international developed markets and emerging markets. Target-date funds often include an allocation to an ex-US fund.

expected returns — The most likely return an investor should expect to get if the future resembles the past. They are calculated by multiplying past returns by the likelihood of occurrence and summing the results.

fixed income — Another name for bonds, which are investments that pay investors fixed interest or dividend payments until their maturity date.

interest — Payment from a borrower or bank to a lender or depositor. Bonds and bond funds pay interest to their investors. The backtests in this book assume those payments are reinvested. Most investors will be able to set that up to happen automatically in their brokerage accounts.

median — The midpoint in a distribution. If we test 1,000 scenarios and half of the end balances are above $1M and half are below $1M, the median is $1M. The median is not calculated the same way as the average.

mutual fund – Similar to an ETF (*see also* exchange-traded funds) in that it provides a convenient way to purchase a basket of stocks or bonds. Mutual funds pool many investors' money to be managed by professional money managers who allocate funds across investments for the group's mutual benefit. They may or may not follow an index. Mutual funds trade after the stock market is closed at the value of the underlying assets in dollar amounts equated to a whole or fractional number of shares being traded. Mutual funds also have minimum purchase amounts, which may be a challenge for investors just starting to invest.

nominal returns — What we see in our bank account before realizing gains, paying taxes on those gains, paying additional investment fees, and subtracting the effects of inflation. In contrast, real returns adjust for the effects of inflation, making it easier to compare purchasing power at different points in time. (*See also* real returns.)

nudge rebalancing — A simple alternative to traditional rebalancing in which contributions or withdrawals are used to nudge allocations toward their desired value. For contributions, the entire contribution would go to the fund that is below its target allocation. For withdrawals, the entire withdrawal would come from the fund that is above its target allocation. (*See also* cashflow rebalance nudges.)

nudge withdrawals — A simple alternative to traditional rebalancing in which withdrawals are used to nudge allocations toward their desired value by taking the periodic withdrawals from whichever fund is above its target allocation.

portfolio — The name for a collection of financial investments such as stocks and bonds. Think of it as a recipe. When Warren Buffett recommends investors put 90% of their investments in the S&P 500 and 10% of their investments in short-term US government bonds, he's recommending a simple portfolio.

real returns — The returns we experience after adjusting for inflation. It's a way of looking at projected future results that reflects their purchasing power in today's dollars. Real returns are usually lower than nominal returns. Real returns accurately indicate purchasing power over time. (*See also* nominal returns.)

rebalancing — The process of selling some investments and buying others to bring the share of the overall portfolio back to its desired allocation percentages.

safe withdrawal rate (SWR) — The highest percentage of a portfolio that can be withdrawn annually, increasing with inflation over some duration, such as 20, 30, or 40 years, without running out of money in even the worst-case scenario of all those tested.

small-cap value (SCV) — Shorthand for small-capitalization value stocks. These are smaller companies that are out of favor. Consequently, their shares sell at relatively low prices compared to the value of the companies' assets, projected earnings, or some other metric. As a group, they have had higher long-term returns and volatility than the overall stock market.

Sortino ratio — A variation of the Sharpe ratio that differentiates harmful volatility from total overall volatility by using the asset's standard deviation of negative portfolio returns — downside deviation or risk — instead of the total standard

GLOSSARY

deviation of portfolio returns. The Sortino ratio considers that most investors are not concerned about volatility on the upside but do care if returns are negative.

target-date fund (TDF) — A fund built to adjust risk as it approaches a target retirement year. It reduces risk over time by decreasing the percentage it holds in stocks and increasing the percentage it holds in bonds.

treasury inflation-protected securities (TIPS) — A treasury bond issued by the US government and indexed to inflation. TIPS protect investors from a decline in the purchasing power of their money by adjusting prices so they maintain their real value.

Disclaimers

Everything in this book is provided for informational and entertainment purposes only and is not intended to substitute for professional financial advice. Nothing contained here implies a consulting or coaching relationship. Please consult a licensed financial or legal professional for advice on your own situation.

I'm sure there are mistakes within these pages. There's too much work here for there not to be. If I waited for it to be perfect, it would arrive in time for your heirs to learn how you should have invested. Despite the imperfections, I believe the broader conclusions drawn are correct and helpful. I welcome feedback to help correct any mistakes in future editions and updates of this book.

I also recognize I can't understand your life challenges any more than you can understand mine. Consequently, this book won't appeal to everyone. That's unfortunate because I believe the messages are just as valid for someone investing their first dollar as their millionth. Perhaps someone better equipped than me will adapt the message to a wider audience. I will be delighted if they do.

Printed in Poland
by Amazon Fulfillment
Poland Sp. z o.o., Wrocław